The
MOFFATT
NEW TESTAMENT COMMENTARY
Based on *The New Translation* by the
REV. PROFESSOR JAMES MOFFATT, D.D.
and under his Editorship

THE GOSPEL OF JOHN

THE
GOSPEL OF JOHN

BY

G. H. C. MACGREGOR
D.D., D.Litt.

HARPER AND BROTHERS PUBLISHERS
New York and London

EDITOR'S PREFACE

MOFFATT'S NEW TESTAMENT COMMENTARY

THE aim of this commentary is to bring out the religious meaning and message of the New Testament writings. To do this, it is needful to explain what they originally meant for the communities to which they were addressed in the first century, and this involves literary and historical criticism; otherwise, our reading becomes unintelligent. But the New Testament was the literature of the early church, written out of faith and for faith, and no study of it is intelligent unless this aim is kept in mind. It is literature written for a religious purpose. ' These are written that ye might believe that Jesus is the Christ, the Son of God.' This is the real object of the New Testament, that Christians might believe it better, in the light of contemporary life with its intellectual and moral problems. So with any commentary upon it. Everything ought to be subordinated to the aim of elucidating the religious content, of showing how the faith was held in such and such a way by the first Christians, and of making clear what that faith was and is.

The idea of the commentary arose from a repeated demand to have my New Testament translation explained; which accounts for the fact that this translation has been adopted as a convenient basis for the commentary. But the contributors have been left free to take their own way. If they interpret the text differently, they have been at liberty to say so. Only, as a translation is in itself a partial commentary, it has often saved space to print the commentary and start from it.

As everyman has not Greek, the commentary has been written, as far as possible, for the Greekless. But it is based upon a first-hand study of the Greek original, and readers may rest assured that it represents a close reproduction of the original writers' meaning, or at anyrate of what we consider that to have been. Our common aim has been to enable everyman to-day to sit where these first Christians sat, to feel the impetus and inspiration of the Christian faith as it dawned upon the minds of the communities in the first century, and thereby to realize more vividly how new and lasting is the message which prompted these New Testament writings to take shape as they did. Sometimes people inside as well as outside the church make mistakes about the New Testament. They think it means this or that, whereas its words frequently mean something very different from what traditional associations suggest. The saving thing is to let the New Testament speak for itself. This is our desire and plan in the present commentary, to place each writing or group of writings in its original setting and allow their words to come home thus to the imagination and conscience of everyman to-day.

The general form of the commentary is to provide a running comment on the text, instead of one broken up into separate verses. But within these limits, each contributor has been left free. Thus, to comment on a gospel requires a method which is not precisely the same as that necessitated by commenting on an epistle. Still, the variety of treatment ought not to interfere with the uniformity of aim and form. Our principle has been that nothing mattered, so long as the reader could understand what he was reading in the text of the New Testament.

JAMES MOFFATT.

PREFACE

SCHOLARSHIP in this country for long clung to the traditional view of the Fourth Gospel, and we still lack in English a satisfactory commentary on the whole text written from the standpoint of the more moderate among recent continental commentators. That the present volume will at all adequately fill up a very obvious blank I can hardly hope ; but it is offered as an attempt, however imperfect, to give the English reader in commentary form the results of the modern criticism of the Gospel so admirably set forth, e.g. in E. F. Scott's *The Fourth Gospel, its Purpose and Theology*.

The aim of the commentary is critical and exegetical rather than homiletic. Everything else has been subordinated to the attempt to elucidate the primary meaning of the words in their original setting. My aim, so far as possible, has been to allow the Gospel to interpret itself. Hence the large number of cross-references which I hope will not distract the more cursory reader, but will, I believe, repay the attention of the closer student. Throughout the earlier chapters, where the exposition is of necessity fuller, the text has been printed in blocks at the head of each section, the salient clauses being repeated in black type thoughout the exposition. In the later chapters it has been found possible simply to weave the text into the comments, so emphasizing it by the use of black type that text can be isolated from exposition at a glance. This plan has alike saved space and made it possible to read the book not as a catenation of snippets but as a continuous piece of prose.

Where one is conscious of having entered into the labours of so many scholars only general acknowledgment is possible. My indebtedness to E. F. Scott's masterly volume will appear on every page, and is far from exhausted by the numerous quotations I have ventured to make. Of modern commentaries I have found most helpful Bauer's revision of Holtzmann's volume in *Handcommentar zum Neuen Testament,* which is probably the most satisfactory commentary we possess. Loisy has proved most stimulating, if only because one is so often provoked to disagreement. Of the older commentators Westcott is still indispensable and Godet often wonderfully suggestive. In preparing the Introduction I have been much helped by Schmiedel's *Die Johanneischen Schriften,* and by Dr. B. H. Streeter, whose relevant section in *The Four Gospels* is quite admirable. My book appears too early to admit reference to the late Dr. Bernard's volume in the *International Critical Commentary,* which is understood to be in the press. One more tribute duty and affection alike demand—to my own revered teacher, Prof. H. A. A. Kennedy, of New College, Edinburgh, to whom for inspiration received at his feet and for encouragement in the years since one of his pupils is sincerely grateful.

It was with some hesitation that this commentary was undertaken five years ago at the request of the General Editor ; it has been carried through as a loved *Parergon* in the midst of a busy city ministry ; and with even greater diffidence it is now offered to ' everyman.' That he will agree with all my conclusions is not to be expected, especially as the English commentaries to which he has had access may not have prepared his mind for findings which for a generation have been the commonplace of the study. My prayer is that this book may enable him to understand better the meaning and message of Jesus Christ for the great age in which this Gospel was written, and thereby for the age in which he himself lives. Amid many engrossing critical problems I have tried to remember that author and readers alike can merit no sterner rebuke than the Master's own : " You search the Scriptures . . . but you refuse to come to me for life."

G. H. C. MACGREGOR.

St. John's and Renfield Church, Glasgow.
July, 1928.

viii

INTRODUCTION

No book in the New Testament has provoked conclusions more diverse than has the Fourth Gospel. ' The book,' it has been said,[1] ' is a Janus-like reality.' It presents now this face, now that ; it is full of contrasts, even of seeming contradictions, and this union of opposites has led to the most divergent views regarding its character and intention. Here we find inextricably interwoven reminiscence with reflection, history with its interpretation, narrative often intensely pictorial and dramatic with a profound philosophy of religion. This has been recognized by critics of all schools. Lightfoot [2] speaks of ' the accurate historical narrative of the facts, which forms the basis of the Gospel, and the theological teaching which is built as a superstructure upon this foundation.' Sanday [3] defines the Gospel as ' a blending of fact and of interpretation.' Drummond suggests that an Apostle may have ' portrayed the Master of his heart's devotion in colours drawn from half a century of vivid experience of his indwelling spirit, and blended together the actual and ideal in lines which are no longer separable.' Ernest Scott [5] sums up admirably when he says, ' The author, writing in a period of transition, is continually striving to find place within the same system for opposite types of thought and belief ' ; he has made his work a ' union of opposites,' and a ' blending of various tendencies.' Little wonder that, with a personality so elusive at the bar, the verdict of scholarship is still held in suspense. The problem is at least as many-sided as the solutions propounded for it.

[1] A. E. Garvie, *The Beloved Disciple*, p. xiii.
[2] *The Fourth Gospel, its Authorship*, p. 151.
[3] *Criticism of the Fourth Gospel*, p. 169.
[4] *Character and Authorship of the Fourth Gospel*, p. 397.
[5] *The Fourth Gospel*, pp. 10, 11.

INTRODUCTION

I. THE FOURTH GOSPEL AND THE SYNOPTICS

1. *The Evangelist's Knowledge of the Synoptics*

All criticism of the Fourth Gospel must begin with an attempt to relate the book to the Synoptic Gospels. And firstly, to what extent was ' John ' (the proper name is used throughout without prejudging the question of authorship) acquainted with the three earlier Gospels, and what use did he make of them ? Of late it has been generally assumed that he knew and used Mark ; but ' that he knew either of the others seems more than doubtful.' [1] Perhaps this statement should be so far modified as to say that the evidence, while supporting the conclusion that John did not use Matthew, favours the theory that he is dependent on Luke as well as on Mark. That John knew Mark intimately can hardly be questioned, and is sufficiently proved by a reproduction, which cannot be accidental, of a number of the out-of-the-way phrases of Mark. Compare, e.g., Jn. 6 : 7 with Mk. 6 : 37, Jn. 12 : 3 and 5 with Mk. 14 : 3 and 5, Jn. 14 : 31 with Mk. 14 : 42, Jn. 18 : 18 with Mk. 14 : 54, Jn. 18 : 39 with Mk. 15 : 9, Jn. 5 : 8–9 with Mk. 2 : 11–12. It may be noted also that where there is verbal variation between the Synoptics, John usually agrees with Mark as against Matthew and Luke. We are not, however, to suppose that John necessarily wrote with a copy of Mark open before him. ' The materials he uses have all been fused in the crucible of his creative imagination, and it is from the image in his mind's eye, far more vivid than the written page, that he paints his picture.' [2] Yet quite clearly John presupposes a knowledge of Mark on the part of his readers, and can therefore omit explanations which would otherwise be necessary (e.g. 3 : 24). ' The fact that this Gospel is written, so to speak, on the top of St. Mark, is the key to many difficulties.' [3]

That John was familiar with Luke's Gospel may be argued

Stanton, *The Gospels as Historical Documents*, p. 220.

[2] Streeter, *The Four Gospels*, p. 397.

[3] Charnwood, *According to St. John*, p. 89.

from the remarkable points of contact between the two Gospels in regard to the story of Martha and Mary. John assumes that his readers are acquainted with the story of the two sisters as told by Luke, and shows a peculiar interest in elaborating the balder Marcan narrative by a somewhat artificial cross-identification of persons and places as between Mark and Luke. It must suffice to refer the reader to the notes on 11 : 1 ff. and especially 12 : 2 ff., where John's version of the anointing is obviously the result of a conflation of Mark and Luke. There are also notable resemblances between the accounts of the Passion in Luke and John. Compare Jn. 19 : 1 with Lk. 23 : 22, where both Evangelists regard the scourging by Pilate as an attempt to induce the Jews to be content with something less than the death penalty ; Jn. 20 : 3 ff. with Lk. 24 : 24, to which John's story gives detail and precision ; Jn. 20 : 19 and 20 with Lk. 24 : 36 and 40 respectively (but in both these cases the parallel words in Luke are rejected by Hort). Literary dependence on Luke seems suggested by a comparison of Jn. 18 : 10 with Lk. 22 : 50, Jn. 19 : 41 with Lk. 23 : 53, Jn. 20 : 12 with Lk. 24 : 4 (two angels, not one as in Mark and Matthew), and especially Jn. 13 : 38 with Lk. 22 : 34, where John's wording is almost identical with Luke's just where the latter differs from Mark's (14 : 30). Finally, we find the most notable coincidence between John and Luke in the fact that both place the first Resurrection Appearance to the Disciples at Jerusalem, not (as do Mark and Matthew) in Galilee. (See also notes on 4 : 47, 6 : 3, 20 : 29.)

Between Matthew and John there are but few points of contact and none sufficiently striking to prove literary dependence ; Streeter [1] notes a number of minor agreements of Matthew and John against Mark, but denies that they have any significance. The evidence for John's use of Matthew is quite inconclusive, and the probability is that he had no knowledge of it, or else that knowing it he ignored it on account of its Judaistic and Apocalyptic outlook.

[1] *Op. cit.*, p. 410 ff.

2. *The Fourth Gospel compared with the Synoptics*

To pass from the Synoptic Gospels to that of John is to breathe a different atmosphere. The contrast is so sharp that the question forces itself upon us : If the Synoptic picture of Jesus is to be accepted as relatively trustworthy, what relation does this Fourth Gospel bear to the actual facts of our Lord's life ? True, the similarity of view-point, to which the first three Gospels owe the name ' Synoptic,' is by no means complete. Each is written from a different angle, and only relatively to John do they share the ' common view.' Yet taken together they present a sufficiently consistent picture ; and although ' the day is now over, or almost over, when the Fourth Gospel and the Synoptists could be played off against each other in a series of rigid antitheses,' [1] a summary of the main points of contrast must be attempted.

(*a*) *Chronology*.—Mark leads us to suppose that Jesus' ministry began only after the imprisonment of the Baptist (Mk. 1 : 14), while John quite definitely asserts that the two ministries overlapped (Jn. 3 : 23 ff.). The two narratives can be brought into harmony only by assuming that the first call of the inner circle to discipleship is dated back by John to a period prior to the opening of the Synoptic narrative—a suggestion which is to be rejected (see note, p. 46).

From the Synoptic narrative, though a definite period is never actually named, it would appear that Jesus' ministry covered only a single year, while John lengthens it to a period which includes at least three Passovers (2 : 13, 6 : 4, 11 : 55), and must therefore have lasted something over two years. But even the Synoptics contain hints that Jesus visited Jerusalem oftener than the condensed narrative of Mark might lead us to suppose, and if this be so John's chronology may well be nearer the truth. A two and a half years' ministry would agree better with the following three chronological data—that Christ was born under Herod, who died 4 B.C. (Matthew), that ' he was about thirty years old when he

---

[1] Moffatt, *Introd. to the Literature of the N.T.*, p. 540.

began to preach ' (Luke), and that he was crucified in A.D. 29 or 30 (according to patristic tradition and most modern reckonings). (See also note on 5 : 1.)

There is an important discrepancy concerning the day of Jesus' death. According to all four Gospels the Crucifixion took place on a Friday. But according to the Synoptics this was the 15th of the month Nisan, the first of the seven days of the festival and the day immediately following the celebration of the Passover meal (Mk. 14 : 12, 15 : 1, etc.), while according to John it was the 14th of Nisan, the day on the afternoon of which the Paschal lambs were slain, to be eaten the same evening after sunset, when the first day of the festival had begun ; for amongst the Jews the new day, in this case the 15th, began with sunset (Jn. 13 : 1, 29 ; 18 : 28, 19 : 14, 31, 42). From this divergence it follows that according to the Synoptists Jesus' supper with his disciples on his last evening was the regular Passover meal, while according to John the Last Supper took place on the evening before the Passover, and when the Jews were eating the Paschal lamb twenty-four hours later, ' Christ our Passover ' had already been slain. In this case John's date is almost certainly correct. There are hints even in the Synoptics that Jesus died before the Feast (e.g. Lk. 22 : 15, interpreted as meaning that the desire was not fulfilled) ; and indeed secular business such as the Arrest, the Trials, the buying of spices, not to speak of the Crucifixion itself, would have been impossible during the most sacred hours of the Festival. On the other hand it is argued that the Synoptists must themselves have been conscious of this difficulty, and would hardly have dated the events as they have if they had not been sure of their ground. There is also some force in the argument that, whereas the Synoptists have no motive for changing the correct date of the Crucifixion, it would be nothing more than characteristic of John were he to make the change for purely dogmatic motives, in order to emphasize Paul's saying that ' Christ our Passover is sacrificed for us ' (1 Cor. 5 : 7) by making it appear that Jesus died at the very time when the Paschal lambs were being slain. (See also notes on 1 : 29, 18 : 28,

xiii

19 : 29, 31.)   But the balance of evidence is strongly in favour of John's date.

(b) *The Scene of the Ministry*, according to the Synoptists, is laid almost entirely in Galilee, and, while they mention certain journeys outside Galilean territory (Mk. 7 : 24, 8 : 27, 10 : 1), they record no visit to Jerusalem until that which resulted in Jesus' death.   John, on the other hand, concentrates attention on a ministry in Judæa and in particular at Jerusalem, and when Jesus does appear in Galilee it is to stay there only for a brief interval (2 : 1 ff., 4 : 43 ff., 7 : 1 ff.). Doubtless the Synoptic and the Johannine representations are not mutually exclusive, especially if it can be argued that, with the transposition of chapter 5 to follow chapter 6, John has ' brought in the whole of his additional matter relating to a ministry in Jerusalem and Judaea partly before '—this, however, we have ventured to question above—' and partly after the limits of the Galilean ministry, as they are marked out in the Synoptic Gospels.' [1]   The discrepancy may be partly due to a difference of choice of matter natural enough if the Fourth Gospel incorporates the testimony of someone who had a special connexion with Jerusalem and records incidents which have come within his own experience.   The Synoptics do not explicitly deny a Judæan ministry, and indeed in such a passage as Jesus' lament over Jerusalem (Mt. 23 : 37), with its suggestion of repeated rejection after efforts often renewed, hint that our Lord may have frequently visited the capital before the fatal Passover.   Nevertheless allowance must be made for the idealistic tendency of our Evangelist, who desires to show that Jesus, so far from being an obscure teacher in such an outlying region as Galilee, taught and died at the headquarters of the national religion.

(c) In his *placing of certain incidents* and his analysis of the *determining factors* in the course of Jesus' ministry, John departs from the Synoptic tradition.   According to the Fourth Gospel the ' Cleansing of the Temple ' occurred at the beginning of the ministry, while the Synoptists evidently regard it as an act of provocation which finally precipitated

Stanton, op. cit., p. 229.

Jesus' death. That there were actually two 'cleansings' will hardly be maintained, and though it may be argued in favour of the Johannine placing that a protest against the desecration of the Temple would be called for on Christ's first public appearance, such an act whenever performed must inevitably have provoked arrest, and the balance of probability is against our Gospel. Once again John is influenced by dogmatic motives and by the desire to secure a suitable introductory incident to illustrate the theme, which is the key to the first section of the Gospel, that the new gospel of Christ is to supersede the old religion typified by the Temple. Having thus antedated the 'Temple-cleansing' John is under the necessity of substituting another incident as the event which precipitated the *dénouement*, and this he finds in the story of the raising of Lazarus, a miracle of which the Synoptists know nothing. That John is at variance with the earlier Gospels, even with regard to the event which provided the occasion for the arrest, is one of the greatest difficulties facing the harmonist.

(*d*) In his attitude to *miracle* John presents an interesting contrast to the Synoptists. As regards the type of miracle recorded it is noticeable that the cure of demoniacs, a class of miracle which not only, according to the Synoptists, was the most frequently performed, but also to the modern mind is the most credible, is entirely omitted. On the other hand 'nature miracles,' that is, miracles performed on inanimate objects, such as the turning of water into wine, the multiplication of the loaves, the walking on water—a type of miracle which presents peculiar difficulty—receive special emphasis. This is in line with John's tendency everywhere to heighten the miraculous. Those on whom the miracles are wrought have been ill for thirty-eight years, *born* blind, dead for no less than four days. Corresponding with this tendency is a new conception of Jesus' motive in performing miracles. According to the Synoptists it is because he is 'moved with compassion' (Mk. 1 : 41, 8 : 2), according to John Jesus' 'signs' are evidence of his divine power (and the more miraculous the more convincing the proof) and therefore 'display his glory ' (2 : 11). Whereas for the Synoptists faith is a condition of miracle (Mt. 13 : 58), John regards miracle as the supreme inducement to faith (14 : 11). Hence we find that according to the Synoptists Jesus, when asked for a ' sign ' as a prop to faith, refuses it (Mk. 8 : 12) ; whereas in Jn. 2 : 18–22, when met with the same request, he does not decline it, but points forward to his miraculous resurrection (the similar reference, which in Mt. 12 : 40 is added to the Marcan passage quoted above, seems due to a misconception of the true meaning of ' the sign of the prophet Jonas '), with the result in the sequel that when his disciples ' remembered ' they ' believed.' At the same time one admits that a twofold attitude towards the miraculous may be traced throughout the Gospel, for passages do occur in which faith based upon miracle is depreciated (e.g. 20 : 29). Wendt, for example, recognizes this when he distinguishes passages in which the term ' works ' is used of miracles from those in which ' signs ' is used, assigning the latter, in which the evidential value of miracle for faith is emphasized, to the ' evangelist ' as distinct from his original ' source.' In other words the Gospel, in so far as it may reflect the authentic tradition of a ' witness,' approximates to the Synoptic point of view regarding miracle ; and while the distinction which we have drawn in the main holds good, it is no doubt true that ' the difference of conception between the Synoptic and Johannine miracles may be greatly exaggerated ' ; and ' while it is true to say that in the Johannine miracles the motive of compassion recedes into the background,' nevertheless it is equally true that ' even in the Synoptic miracles something much greater than the compassionate sympathy of Jesus is hinted at.' [1]

(e) We turn now to Jesus' *discourses*, and again feel the sense of contrast. And first in respect of their form. The reader of the Synoptics will agree with Justin Martyr's verdict when, speaking of ' the very doctrine delivered by Christ himself,' he says : ' Short and pithy are his discourses ; no sophist was he ' (Apol. 1 : 14). The Johannine discourses impress one as discursive and dialectical, a limited number

---

[1] R. H. Strachan, *The Fourth Evangelist*, pp. 164, 166.

of great themes being repeated again and again on the most varied occasions. Yet, while this distinction is broadly true, our Gospel is not lacking in just such concise and axiomatic sayings as characterize Jesus' speech in the Synoptics.[1] No doubt to the casual reader they are almost lost in the Evangelist's elaboration of them, but a more careful study reveals them dotted here and there like gems in a cunningly wrought setting. In the Synoptics the most characteristic and fascinating of Jesus' discourses are the parables. But the Fourth Gospel does not contain a single true parable, the only passages which approach the parabolic form (e.g. ' the Vine,' 15 : 1–8 ; ' the Good Shepherd,' chap. 10) being rather ' allegories ' or figurative discourses.

The same contrast is presented in respect of the content of Jesus' teaching. In the Synoptics we find practical precepts adapted to concrete situations. Jesus deals with life's great moral problems, the relation of Man to God and to his fellows ; he speaks little of the mystery of his own Person and of his relation to the Father. His teaching deals almost exclusively with the question, What must one do to enter the Kingdom of God ? In the Fourth Gospel, on the other hand, we find set discourses, abstract rather than practical in character, abounding in enigmatic allusions and the elucidation of misunderstandings, which often in themselves are not a little artificial, and bearing constantly on such subjects as Christ's own divinity, his relation to the Father, or on mysteries of faith such as the indwelling of the Spirit or the efficacy of the sacraments. But nowhere is the contrast greater than in the demands which Jesus makes upon his followers. In the Synoptics indeed Jesus requires faith, but there ' faith ' is rather an act of moral ' trust.' In our Gospel his demand is for belief in the divinity of his own Person. ' What he asks of people is not, as in the Synoptics, moral conduct, but acceptance as true of his assurance that he has come from heaven.'[2]

But again one must beware of pressing too far the contrast

---

[1] Cf. Drummond, op. cit., p. 18 f., and p. xxiv below.
[2] Schmiedel, *The Johannine Writings*, p. 42.

with the Synoptics. There must have been a mystical as
well as a practical side to Jesus' teaching, and there are passages of a distinctly ' Johannine ' flavour even in the Synoptics. The most remarkable examples are Mt. 10 : 32 ff., and
in particular Mt. 11 : 25 ff. ; and if such conceptions have
found a place in the Synoptics at all, they cannot have been
merely passing thoughts, but must reflect a real element in
Jesus' teaching.

(*f*) But above all when one passes from the Synoptics to
John one is conscious of an alteration in the *portrait of Jesus*
himself. True, the earlier evangelists agree with John in
sketching the picture with a majesty above all human standards. Yet they have no hesitation in recording incidents
which suggest Jesus' common humanity. John, on the other
hand, often seems deliberately to suppress such traits. The
Synoptists record that Jesus was baptized by John like any
other seeker for the Kingdom ; our Evangelist tells only how
John witnessed the descent of the Holy Spirit on the chosen
Christ. In our Gospel we have no hint that Jesus was subject
to human temptation, nor that in an agony of human weakness
in the Garden he prayed that the cup of death might pass
from him. In fact such a prayer is implicitly denied (see
note on 12 : 27 f.). Similarly the cry of dereliction from the
Cross is omitted. From Mark (e.g. 1 : 35) we learn that Jesus
often sought a renewal of strength in prayer. But how John
thinks of Jesus' prayers is clear from 11 : 41 f., where at
Lazarus' grave it appears that Jesus did not need to pray
for his own sake, but only that he might confirm the bystanders' faith. To this may be added the emphasis placed
by John on Jesus' omniscience (cf. 1 : 42, 48 ; 2 : 24, 4 : 16,
6 : 61, 64 ; 5 : 6, 13 : 18, 16 : 19), and specially on his
inviolability and what has been termed his ' self-determination ' (7 : 30, 8 : 20, 59 ; 10 : 39, 12 : 36, 18 : 6, 19 : 11).
It is a postulate with John that Jesus can be compelled by
no external force, that he chooses his own time and at the
last ' lays down his life of his own accord ' (10 : 18, and see
notes on 2 : 4, 7 : 10, 11 : 6, 13 : 27, etc.). Such human
characteristics as do appear in the portrait of Jesus are

somewhat artificial (e.g. 11 : 35, where see note), or seem to have been deliberately introduced with the purpose of combating current ' docetic ' teaching, according to which Jesus was human only ' in semblance ' (cf. notes on 4 : 6, 6 : 20, 19 : 28, 34 ; 20 : 20).

(g) Finally we miss in the Fourth Gospel the sense of any *development* in Jesus' understanding of his own Person and Mission. The great turning-points, so clearly marked by the Synoptists, by which he passed to a fuller realization of his vocation—the Baptism, Temptation, the Confession of Peter after the rejection in Galilee, the Transfiguration, the Institution of the Supper—all are ignored, or so transformed and misplaced as to lose their real significance. Accordingly we find that, whereas in the Synoptics it is only comparatively late that even the inner circle recognize their Master as Messiah while from his hearers as a whole the secret is hidden until the final Passover, in this Gospel Jesus begins to publish his own personal claim from the first and is openly proclaimed as Messiah by the Baptist before ever he enters on his public ministry. Here at least there can be no doubt which is the truer representation ; John, writing long years after, has had his perspective foreshortened and has lost that sense of development which is still evident in the work of the earlier evangelists, whether or no they themselves were conscious of any such development.

Certain conclusions are inevitably suggested by such a comparison as the foregoing between the Synoptists and the Fourth Gospel. Admitting that when John alters details of the Synoptic story ' he is not flying in the face of a universal Church tradition embodied in three separate Gospels,' but is in fact differing from only one Gospel (Mark), on which the other two depend, and that not a Gospel ascribed to an Apostle, so that ' to speak . . . as though there were a three-to-one agreement against John is quite misleading,' when as a matter of fact ' the chronology of the Life of Christ is simply a question of Mark against John ' [1]; admitting again that sometimes a certain harmony between two apparently diver-

---

[1] Streeter, op. cit., pp. 418, 424.

gent accounts may be attained ; admitting finally that even
when we seem reduced to a categorical ' either—or ' there is
much to be said for the Johannine representation ; nevertheless the contrast presented by the two traditions remains
sufficiently striking, and we cannot but feel that the scale is
weighted in favour of the Synoptists, who write at an earlier
date and are not influenced, at any rate so consciously as is
John, by motives which are admittedly doctrinal and apologetic.   We are left with the impression that a writer who is
evidently primarily dependent on Mark, yet at times makes
so injudicious a use of his sources (as e.g. in the account of the
' anointing,' 12 : 1 ff.), and in the end gives us a Gospel
differing so signally from that of his predecessors, is hardly
likely to have been himself an Apostle.   Yet the free and
masterful way in which he deals with earlier material suggests
that he writes with a certain sense of independent authority.
At any rate the hypothesis that behind the Gospel lies some
such authority would considerably ease the critical difficulties
arising from a comparison with the Synoptics.

II. History or Didactic Drama ?

1. *How far is John a Biographer ?*

When estimating the value of the Fourth Gospel, we have
been too ready to criticize it for not conveying information
which it never professes to convey.   Admittedly the Evangelist's chief motive is not historical.   If he is a biographer at
all, then he is a biographer whose aim is not to convey facts,
but to impart spiritual truth ; a mere selection of incidents
has been made, and the selection has been dictated by the
desire not to communicate information, but to bestow upon
the reader ' life ' through faith : ' These signs are recorded so
that you may believe Jesus is the Christ, the Son of God, and
believing may have life through his name ' (20 : 31).   This,
one admits, is partially true also of the Synoptists.   They too
portray Jesus not merely as seen by the outward eye, but as
interpreted by the Spirit and appropriated by faith.   And
indeed all true history must involve a subjective as well as

an objective element. But in the Fourth Gospel 'the reflective element is less unconsciously and more creatively and artistically present.'[1] Even to-day there is much biography whose main end is not informative but didactic. In the introduction to a volume of biographical essays the author,[2] after quoting John Howe's summing-up of his own purpose in a funeral sermon, 'the little that I shall say of my subject shall be, not by way of history, but of character,' continues as follows : 'This admirably expresses my own motif in these lectures. . . . In the present case it does not at all come within my province to tell the external story of any of my worthies. I assume that the life itself is in each case less or more familiar to my readers. . . . My main design is from selected characteristics of their Life and Life-work to incite and quicken to higher and nobler service of the Master in our day and generation. This being so, I am perfectly at ease . . . in anticipation of being charged with "improving" Howe and Baxter, Rutherford and Henry, as the old divines called their reading of lessons from special events and circumstances. To draw such lessons and to drive them home into heart and conscience *is* my purpose and endeavour. . . . If anyone choose to fling stones at me as "didactic," "hortatory," "moralizing," and so on, so be it!' Truly the Fourth Evangelist might retort in exactly similar terms to some of his modern critics! He does not profess to give us an exhaustive survey of Jesus' life, but selects those incidents which have the richest didactic value. Thus we have seven typical miracles each chosen as a frontis-piece illustrating some great spiritual truth which is forthwith developed in a discourse by Jesus. The Gospel thus becomes a kind of 'historical sermon' which reminds us of the later Jewish homiletic method known as 'Haggadah' in which religious teaching is driven home by the all egorizing of sacred history. In choosing a 'Gospel' rather than a treatise or 'epistle' as the medium of his instruction, John shows himself conscious that the Christian life must always have

[1] Strachan, op. cit., p. 23.
[2] A. B. Grosart, *Representative Nonconformists.*

the sanction and quickening influence of a historical example.
For the living of that life nothing less will suffice than the
dynamic fact of the Incarnation of the ' Word ' of God in the
historical Jesus. Hence John chooses to impart Christian
doctrine not in the abstract but through the works and the
words of one who himself comes forward and says : ' A new
commandment *I* give unto you ' ; ' *I am* the Light of the
World, the Bread of Life, the Resurrection and the Life.'

The Gospel may be well described as a didactic meditation
on the *drama* of Christ's life. Indeed the author is essentially
dramatist rather than historian. ' The earthly life of Jesus
in this Gospel appears as a dramatic interlude in the life of
the Eternal Logos.' [1] The Gospel is a drama [2] in which the
protagonists are Jesus, the Word of God, and the evil powers
of darkness and unbelief. The Prologue is the Prelude ; the
dramatic climax is reached at the Passion, the moment when
Jesus' ' hour ' has come. Hence the material is chosen
primarily for its dramatic effectiveness, and many of the vivid
details, which have often been claimed as marks of an eye-
witness, may well be regarded rather as the creation of a vivid
dramatic imagination. The Gospel abounds in dramatic
moments—the declaration of Messiahship to the Samaritan
woman, the withdrawal of Judas into the outer darkness,
the meeting of Mary Magdalene with the Risen Master—while
' dramatic irony ' is apparent in Peter's boast that he will
lay down his life for Christ, in Caiaphas' unconscious prophecy
that Jesus should ' die for the nation, and not for the nation
only,' in the Pharisees' plaint that ' the whole world is gone
after him.'

Such a dramatic interpretation must provoke with new
urgency the question of the Gospel's actual historical value,
As will be seen below there is every reason for supposing the
existence of a substratum of authentic history ; but probably
criticism has been too much concerned to distinguish such a

---

[1] Strachan, op. cit., pp. 14, 15, 31.

[2] Hence the form of the analysis of the Gospel adopted below
(pp. 1–2), for which the writer expresses indebtedness to Von Soden,
The Books of the New Testament, p. 403 ff.

substratum, as if therein lay the Gospel's chief value. A living religion will always rest on something more than the necessary basis of historical credentials, and it is not the least of our Evangelist's merits that he appreciates the peril of tethering Christian faith and doctrine and practice too closely to the exact details of particular events in the earthly life of Jesus. On any estimation the religious value of this Gospel must always be greater than the historical. If it is history at all it is history written *sub specie aeternitatis* and under the impulse of a living religious experience. Hence to compare the Evangelist's work with a dramatist's is not to impugn its *religious* value, for in this case the drama expresses not merely the imaginary emotions and opinions of the figures which move across the pages, but the writer's own deepest convictions. ' Every scene he depicts . . . is the distilled essence of something that has been pondered upon and lived out in actual life until it has become of the very texture of his soul.' [1] And herein lies the chief value of the Gospel ; it is a transcript of the individual religious experience of a great Christian soul who is convinced that he also has known the Lord as truly and intimately as the first Apostles. ' This indeed is the abiding value of the Gospel, that it brings Jesus before us at once as a historical Person, and as the invisible Lord who is ever present with his people.' [2]

2. We revert to the *discourses* and ask whether we may seek in them authentic sayings of Jesus. Undoubtedly in reporting Jesus' teaching John reflects not the Jewish tradition, which sought to preserve, as nearly as possible in their original form, the epigrammatic dicta of ' wise men,' but rather the Greek method, which loved to put into the mouth of the speaker not the *ipsissima verba* spoken on a given occasion, but the sentiments which seemed to the writer to be proper to that occasion. John's practice indeed is not unlike that of Thucydides, who in a famous passage (I, 22) frankly admits that this is his method. But we have a better parallel still in Plato who, admitting that he owed his inspiration to the teaching of Socrates, never claims to reproduce

[1] Streeter, op. cit., p. 383. [2] E. F. Scott, op. cit., p. 359.

the *ipsissima verba* of his Master, but rather puts into the mouth of Socrates philosophical theories which, though in germ Socratic, are in their full development those of Plato himself. As in the Platonic Dialogues the speeches of Socrates owe not only style and language but also most of their matter to Plato himself, so in the case of the Fourth Gospel. In Jesus' discourses we have John's attempt to give his contemporaries a systematic summary of Christian teaching as he himself, under the inspiration of the Spirit of Jesus, conceived it, and his first readers, familiar with current Greek practice, would never suppose that Jesus' speeches were to be accepted as a verbatim report. Indeed so little careful is the author to distinguish between his own thoughts and those that he puts into the mouths of his characters, that it is sometimes impossible to tell where the speech which he is reporting ends and his own comment upon it begins. Note especially chapters 1 and 3. ' He seems nearly as careless to dissever what he himself says (in full persuasion that he expresses the mind of Christ) from what Christ actually said as the old prophets were in distinguishing " the word of the Lord " . . . and the testimony which they themselves thereupon proceeded to bear.' [1]

We do not of course question the probability that John has preserved many authentic sayings of Jesus which, it may be, provide the core round which a discourse is developed. We think of such sayings as : ' Unless a man be born from above, he cannot see the kingdom of God ' ; ' I am the bread of life ' ; ' If any man thirst, let him come unto me and drink ' ; ' I am the light of the world ' ; ' He that loves his life shall lose it ; and he that hates his life in this world shall keep it unto life eternal.' There is a striking saying of Ignatius (Eph. 15) that ' he that truly possesseth the word of Jesus is able to hearken unto his silence.' John, drawing upon his treasury of such authentic sayings as we have quoted, seeks as he meditates upon Jesus' word to fill in also ' his silences ' and so interpret to his age the mind of his Master. But he would claim that his interpretation has

[1] Charnwood, op. cit., p. 55.

come to him through direct inspiration from the risen Christ. For did he not believe in a Spirit who should ' draw upon what is Christ's and disclose it to his people ' (16 : 15 ; cf. 14 : 25 f., 15 : 26) ?

3. No understanding of the Gospel is possible without an appreciation of the part played by symbolism. What then for John is the *relation of fact to symbol* ? Let it be remembered initially that the symbolic or allegorical use of an incident does not necessarily imply that it is not ' true.' And if we ask with Pilate, What is ' truth ' ? we are reminded that the ' true ' and the historically accurate are not necessarily the same thing. Truth is sometimes better served, even by the historian, by the interpretation of the spirit of great events and the principles which inspired them, than by a meticulously accurate narrative of facts. Thus Baron F. Von Hügel writes in the *Encyclopædia Britannica* : ' The Fourth Gospel is the noblest instance of this kind of literature, of which the truth depends, not on the factual accuracy of the symbolizing experiences, but on the truth of the ideas and experiences thus symbolized.' Yet the truth of this dictum may be admitted without denying that there may be in the Gospel a basis of actual history. The probability is that John did not, at least consciously and deliberately, invent stories for the sake of their allegorical meaning, though he may well have modified and elaborated them, particularly in minor details (e.g. numbers, dates, names, etc.) with a symbolical purpose in view. That is, he selects out of a mass of traditional material such stories as when thus elaborated will best serve his purpose. Generally speaking, it is likely that he believed in his facts and recorded little that he did not suppose to be historical, even though his belief may not always have been justified. Yet it is not merely the bodily aspect of Jesus' story with which he presents us but its soul. To John facts and their symbolical meaning are related as flesh to spirit ; the former may be a necessary vehicle, but it is the latter which really counts : ' What gives life is the Spirit ; flesh is of no avail at all ' (6 : 63). It is in this sense that the oft-quoted words of Clement of Alexandria are to be under-

stood : ' Last of all John, perceiving that the bodily facts
had been set forth in the other Gospels, at the instance of his
disciples and with the inspiration of the Spirit composed a
spiritual Gospel.' [1] In the peculiar Philonic language current
in Alexandria the word ' bodily ' was used to denote the literal
sense of Scripture and of facts in general, while the ' spiritual '
signified their figurative or allegorical meaning. Clement
therefore means that it is the distinction of this Gospel to
present the soul of Christ's life-story rather than its body, and
to interpret the inward and eternal significance of the Christian revelation. And herein lies the peculiar value of our
Gospel considered as history. ' In history, as in religion,
it is the spirit that quickens, and unless we can penetrate the
spirit of great historical transactions, interpret the principles
out of which they spring, and throw ourselves with sympathetic
imagination into the passions which animated the great
human drama, we miss the only truth that is worth receiving.' [2]
As even one of our most advanced critics admits, John's
idealized history is ' genuine and true because reflecting the
heart's faith of a great Church in a great age.' [3]

III. Aims and Influences

The past quarter of a century has given us so many excellent
studies [4] of the purpose and environment of the Fourth Gospel
that no more is necessary here than the briefest sketch of the
Evangelist's aims and the influences which moulded his
thought. His aims may be classified as (1) interpretative,
(2) polemical.

1. The books of the New Testament all had their origin in
the practical needs of the early Church, and owe their vitality

[1] Eusebius, *Hist. Eccl.*, vi, 14.

[2] Drummond, op. cit., p. 29.

[3] B. W. Bacon, *The Fourth Gospel in Research and Debate*, p. 14.

[4] The reader is referred specially to the volumes by E. F. Scott and
R. H. Strachan already quoted, to Percy Gardner's *Ephesian Gospel*,
and, for a more conservative estimate, to Drummond's *Character and
Authorship of the Fourth Gospel*, and Lord Charnwood's *According to
St. John*. Schmiedel, *The Johannine Writings*, represents more radical
criticism.

to the fact that they sprang directly out of the life of that Church at various periods and in given circumstances. Our Gospel can be understood properly only as the Evangelist's attempt to *interpret* the Christian faith to the Church of his own day—a largely Gentile Church, with its headquarters at Ephesus, probably early in the first decade of the second century.

John seeks to interpret the Gospel of Jesus in the light of history during three-quarters of a century. By the time he wrote the last representatives of the Apostolic Age had passed or were passing away, the bonds with Judaism had been definitely broken, and a Church now largely Gentile had become the custodian of a religion which, severed from its historical origins, was unfolding itself into a far wider significance. If the Christian message was to live for a new age, it must be re-interpreted in new terms. To understand Christ it was necessary not only to know the actual facts of his life and teaching but also to take into account the great religious movement to which those facts had given the impulse. Hence almost unconsciously John alters the perspective of the earlier Gospels, and looking at Jesus' life across the intervening years reads into words and incidents the point of view of his own later age. A good example is 4 : 35-38, where see notes. John ' presents the facts of the divine life, not as men saw them at the time, but as they appeared long afterwards in the retrospect of an enlightened faith.' [1]

Again John interprets the Gospel in the light of personal religious experience. He seeks so to portray the Jesus of history as to emphasize the abiding power of the Christ of faith. As Ernest Scott well remarks, once Christianity was separated from its historical beginnings it was in danger ' either of evaporating as a philosophy or petrifying as a mechanical tradition,' and it is John's supreme service that by insisting that the inward fellowship of the Spirit was even closer than the outward one with the earthly Jesus, while at the same time giving the historical fact of Christ's incarnation its full value, ' he ensured for all time that the Christ of

[1] Scott, op. cit., p. 6.

inward experience should be no ideal abstraction, but the living Master who had once been manifest in the flesh.' [1]

Yet again John interprets the life of Jesus in the light of Paul's teaching. It is disputed whether John has to any great extent been directly influenced by Paul, or whether his theology should not rather be regarded as an independent and collateral development. Probably those are nearer the truth who hold that John owes a deep debt to his predecessor. It is true that the language of the Fourth Gospel differs from that of Paul, and that some of the Apostle's greatest conceptions appear to be insufficiently realized by the Evangelist. See for example notes in the commentary on faith (p. 80), sin (pp. 29, 218), the significance of Christ's death (pp. 28 f., 265). Yet, apart from special doctrines, John's whole outlook upon the Christian revelation is determined by Paul, for it was the latter, not John, who first conceived the glorified Christ of experience, rather than the human Jesus of history, to be the real object of faith. In minor details of doctrine also John and Paul touch at innumerable points—in the matter of the relation of faith to works (6 : 29), in the function assigned to Christ in creation (1 : 3 ; cf. Col. 1 : 16 f.), in the claim that believers are spiritually free (8 : 31 ff. ; cf. Gal. 4 : 21 ff., etc.), in the recognition that in Christ Jew and Gentile are one (4 : 21–24 ; Eph. 2 : 11 ff.). It was inevitable that the religious outlook of the Church at Ephesus, which had been a chief centre of Paul's activity, should be strongly coloured by Pauline doctrine. It was John's part to prevent that doctrine being ' sublimated into a philosophy ' by relating it to the historical facts of Jesus' life. ' The glory which Paul ascribes to the exalted Christ is thrown back by John on the actual life on earth. . . . The Lord who revealed himself to Paul in the experience of faith is to the evangelist one with Jesus Christ, who had lived and taught and suffered. Even then, while he still dwelt among us, " we beheld his glory as of the only-begotten of the Father." ' [2] So important a motive has this interpretation of the Pauline message been thought, that the ' Beloved Disciple ' is frequently regarded

[1] Idem, pp. 8–9. [2] Scott, op. cit., p. 51.

as an idealized Paul, while several critics have accepted the ingenious conjecture that under the figure of Nathaniel Paul is actually introduced into the Gospel.

Finally our Gospel sets out to interpret the Christian story and Christian experience to the new world of Hellenism by translating the Gospel into a form intelligible to Greek modes of thought. This must be discussed below in connexion with the doctrine of the Logos. Meanwhile suffice it to say that, whether or no the actual key to the understanding of the Gospel is to be found in 'a transmutation of Jewish and Christian ideas into their Greek equivalents,'[1] John's great achievement was to transplant the Gospel of Jesus into a new soil before its roots had time to wither.

2. There can be little doubt that certain definitely *polemical* aims can be traced in the Gospel. The controversial tone of Jesus' discourses as reported by John is intelligible only if they are related to the contemporary situation of the Church in John's own day, and treated as the Evangelist's attempt to repel attacks, to which Christianity was subject, in the early years of the second century, though on account of the narrative form in which John's work is cast this controversial interest is on the surface less obvious than in Paul's letters.

In the Gospel we see carried back into Jesus' own lifetime the Church's defence against contemporary Judaism which had set itself to combat Christianity by maligning the story of Jesus and ridiculing his claims. Hence John's eagerness to defend the career of Jesus from misrepresentation. So far from being an obscure missioner, Jesus taught at the head-quarters of the national religion (7 : 4, 18 : 20) ; though Judas' treachery might seem to hint that the Master could hold the loyalty not even of his closest intimates, the truth is that Jesus foreknew and for his own ends permitted the betrayal (6 : 64, 13 : 11) ; so far from Jesus dying as a malefactor, Pilate could find no fault in him (19 : 4) ; while the supreme ' offence of the Cross ' is overcome by John's characteristic teaching that it was self-determined and a step necessary to Christ's achievement of ' glory.' In a word just as ' the

[1] Manson, *The Incarnate Glory*, p. 37.

Jews,' irrespective of their different sects in Jesus' own day, appear in the Gospel as a kind of official opposition to Christ (see note on 1 : 19), so do the objections brought by them against Christ—' He makes himself equal to God '; ' Art thou greater than our Father Abraham ? '; ' Can this man give us his flesh to eat ? '—suggest the disputes between Jew and Christian of a later age, when Christian theology had been definitely formulated and Christianity and Judaism faced each other as rivals. In particular the Eucharistic discussion (6 : 32–59), which would be quite impossible in Jesus' own day before the sacrament was even instituted, becomes intelligible when related to a later Jewish attack upon Christian sacramental teaching.

It is possible that John has coloured his picture of the Baptist in the interest of his polemic against the Jews. Baldensperger indeed held that the Gospel was primarily intended as a polemic against a Jewish sect of Baptist disciples who exalted their Master above Christ. In support of this theory Acts 18 : 25, 19 : 3–4 are quoted as proving the existence of such a sect at Ephesus. Reference is also made in the Clementine Recognitions (1 : 54), which date perhaps from the early third century, to the fact that, ' Some even of the disciples of John, who seemed to be great ones, have separated themselves and proclaimed their own Master as Christ.' It is certainly significant that, on every mention of the Baptist, John pointedly emphasizes his subordination to Jesus (notes on 1 : 6, 19, 34 ; 3 : 13, 4 : 1), and it may well be that he wishes to counteract a contemporary Jewish movement which sought to buttress its opposition to the spread of Christianity by exalting the Baptist at the expense of Christ. Possibly the infection had spread even into the Church itself. But any such Baptist controversy cannot be more than a quite subordinate motive in John's mind, and may have to be eliminated altogether if, as appears to be the case, there is evidence that some at least of the Baptist passages are due to the hand of a Redactor.

There is little evidence that our Evangelist was influenced to any great extent by the contemporary Hellenistic ' Mystery

Religions.' Of these any lengthy discussion would here be out of place.[1] It will be enough to allude to two conceptions conspicuous in them which may be thought to have influenced John among other New Testament writers. First there is the conception of ' regeneration ' or ' new-birth,' whereby the initiate became partaker of a divine essence and was thereby ' reborn into eternity.' Each cult had its myth of the God who died and rose again, whether it be Osiris, Attis, or Dionysus—a myth which was dramatically enacted before the eyes of the assembled multitudes, and through a mystic sympathy with which the initiate himself was thought to obtain the guarantee of undying life. Secondly must be noted the sacramentalist tendencies of the Mystery Cults, which may be summarized thus : so far as the symbol was concerned, its virtue was thought to lie, not only in the spiritual reality it symbolized, but in the symbol itself as such ; so far as the worshipper was concerned the validity of the sacrament depended, not purely on spiritual receptiveness, but on the *ex opere operato* efficacy of the rite itself ; so far as the gift communicated was concerned, it was thought of, not as a purely spiritual bestowal, but as an impersonal semi-physical influence, for the communication of which, not grace and faith, but the symbol itself was the indispensable channel. Now it must be remembered that not even the use of much of the actual terminology of the Mysteries, as in the case of both Paul and John, necessarily involves the adoption of the ideas which it expresses. The Christian community at Ephesus, following upon the influx of heathen converts, must have been flooded with quasi-magical conceptions of religion drawn from the atmosphere of the Mysteries. Nor is it surprising to find our Evangelist using the language of the Mysteries, in chapter 3, when he speaks of the ' birth from above,' in chapter 6 as he develops his profound sacramental teaching. Like Paul, in his eagerness to find a common standing ground with those whom he would win for Christ, he sometimes uses categories which are theirs rather than his own, if indeed he does more than use imagery which is the

[1] See Angus, *The Mystery Religions and Christianity.*

common property of all mystics. And while adopting Mystery conceptions he infuses them with new meaning and new life. He speaks of ' regeneration,' but gives it a new ethical connotation, borrowed not from the Mysteries but from Paul ; the Spirit blows where it will and is confined to no material channel. It is only of Spirit that Spirit is born, and only by the power of the Spirit that regeneration is achieved. He accepts without question the ' real ' efficacy of the Sacraments. Yet he clearly desires to counteract the prevalent tendency towards a materialistic view of them, and all the emphasis is on their spiritual aspect : ' What gives life is the Spirit : flesh is of no avail at all ' (6 : 63).

There remains for consideration the Evangelist's attitude towards certain internal controversies of the Church and in particular towards ' Gnosticism,' the battle of which with the orthodox faith had already begun at the time of writing. The Gnostic heretics of the second century were men who attempted to interpret the figure and message of Christ in such a way that they would fit into a preconceived Hellenistic theology, every Gnostic system being ' an attempt to blend Christianity with the theosophical speculations of the age.' [1] Fundamental is the idea of a dualism running through the whole universe. God is by nature good and pure : the material creation evil and tainted. Therefore by no possibility can a world essentially evil be the creation of the supreme deity, nor can there be any direct contact between God and the material world. Hence the conception of subordinate divine beings, intermediate agencies, æons, emanations of the Deity, which bridge the gap between God and the world. These were thought of as the ' archons ' or rulers of a huge system of concentric spheres over-arching the earth, and were originally identified with the heavenly bodies themselves, whose movements were supposed to sway human destinies, and provided the astrologer with his stock-in-trade. A similar dualism was thought to exist in the nature of man, whose soul and body are as alien one to the other as are God and the world. The soul is a spark emanating from God Himself, while the body

---

[1] Foakes-Jackson, *Hist. of the Christian Church*, p. 122.

but part of the impure matter of which all created things consist. From such a prison there is no escape for the soul save in a ' gnosis ' or knowledge of its divine nature. That is, man's salvation is to be wrought out, not by moral effort, but by the communication of a certain esoteric ' knowledge ' which will enable the possessor to propitiate the intermediate powers, often malignant, and so open the way to God. Thus, as Dobschütz has well put it, ' Gnosticism is, in the first place, intellectualism ; one-sided over-valuation of knowledge at the expense of moral activity.' Finally, holding this dualistic conception of the universe, Gnostic thinkers within the Church naturally scouted the idea that the Logos, the highest emanation of the Father, could in any true sense take upon himself a material body. Hence the denial of the reality of the Incarnation, and the refusal to admit the true humanity and real suffering of Jesus ; in a word what is known as ' Docetism.'

We have within the New Testament clear indications of the spread of such more or less developed Gnostic tendencies. In particular may be noted the heresy which Paul attacks in his letter to the Colossians. As regards the Fourth Gospel's relation to Gnosticism two extreme positions have been taken up. It has by some been definitely claimed as a product of Gnostic Christianity, and was indeed referred, in antiquity, to the Gnostic Cerinthus as its author ; by others it has been as definitely regarded as a polemic against the rising heresy. The truth is midway between the extremes. Tinged with Gnostic influences John certainly is. He shares with the Gnostics a certain dualism in his conception of both man and the world (note on 1 : 5, 1 : 10, 15 : 18), and a certain intellectualism in his conception of faith (note on 3 : 15) and in his insistence upon the necessity of ' knowing' God (note on 8 : 19, 6 : 69, 17 : 3). There is a dualism which envisages a deep division set between light and darkness (1 : 5), the children of God (1 : 13) and those of the devil (8 : 44), spirit and flesh (3 : 6), the Church and the world (17 : 16). On the other hand this dualism is balanced by a glorious universalism (3 : 16, etc.) which enabled Johannine Christianity to win the world as Gnosticism, with its Gospel for the privileged few, could

c

never have won it. Again there are certain terms and expressions (e.g. ' gnosis,' ' pistis,' ' sophia ') which John significantly avoids except in verbal form, apparently because of their Gnostic colouring. The hierarchy of spiritual intermediaries entirely disappears. There is no trace in the Gospel of the Gnostics' contempt of the Old Testament, whose God, they held, was but a lower divinity and creator of the evil material universe. Above all John combats Gnostic "Docetism ' by insisting emphatically on the reality of the Incarnation, true humanity, sufferings and death of Christ (1 : 14, 4 : 6, 6 : 20, 19 : 28, 34).

We conclude then that, though in some degree sympathetic towards Gnostic philosophy, John with studied insistence repudiates its more glaring errors. Possibly he may at one time have been a more advanced Gnostic, and in the Gospel we see him moving away from Gnosticism while still feeling its attraction. Or alternatively we may suppose that, without ever being in the true sense a Gnostic, John may have reached by his own individual thinking views which seem akin to Gnosticism, but were in truth simply part of the common culture of his day, and were only later specially identified with one prominent school. In any case ' He did a great service to his age by showing that one could be a thinker, appreciate knowledge, stand in the midst of a stream of thoroughly intellectual movements, and yet remain a faithful son of the Church.' [1]

IV. THE DOCTRINE OF THE LOGOS

John's interpretation in terms of Greek philosophic mysticism of the Hebrew conception of a Personal God, illuminated anew by the Christian revelation and the religious experience of the Early Church, is summarized in the Prologue of his Gospel, which is cast in the form of a hymn, whose keynote is the ' Logos ' or ' Word.' ' The author has so uttered this thought at the outset that to the simple or quite-awake reader it is present right through to the end. It is somewhat as in

---

[1] Schmiedel, *The Johannine Writings*, p. 236.

a certain movement of Beethoven—one single note is kept vibrating . . . from start to finish.' [1]   There has been much discussion as to whether John's conception of the Logos owes more to Jewish or Alexandrian influences—a singularly futile dispute since John must certainly have been indebted to both ; if he was able adequately to present the Gospel to a heterogeneous Church, it was just because in the forefront of his Gospel so many converging streams of thought are gathered into one clear pool in which is reflected the face of Jesus Christ.

In nearly all religions is found the idea of some intermediary vehicle whereby God is to reveal Himself to man.   In the Old Testament, and particularly in the prophetic writings, the idea of the ' Word of the Lord ' as such a vehicle is of frequent occurrence ; in poetical passages that ' Word ' is sometimes all but personified.   The process is carried farther in the popular Aramaic paraphrases of the Old Testament known as Targums, in which reverence forbids the assumption of direct contact between God and the world, and the ' Memra,' or Word of God, is supplied as the vehicle of intermediate action in God's dealings with men.   Thus Gen. 3 : 8 in the Targum reads, ' They heard the voice of the Memra of the Lord God walking in the Garden.'   The parallelism of the first verses of the Prologue with the opening verses of Genesis seems to prove that John is moulding his thought of the creative Logos upon this Old Testament conception of the Word as the vehicle of Divine activity.

A similar stream of thought may be traced in Greek philosophy.   But the Greek expression for ' word ' (logos) means at the same time ' reason,' and from Greek philosophy comes the idea that not only the individual man but also the world possesses a ' reason '—the reasonable order which rules in the world and holds it together (cf. Paul's thought of Christ in Col. 1 : 17 : ' All things have been created by him and for him ; he is prior to all, and all *coheres in him* ').   In this sense Heraclitus (*c.* 500–450 B.C.) introduced the term ' logos ' into Greek philosophy, and the Stoics (from *c.* 300 B.C.) adopted this idea that the ' logos ' is the reasonable order

[1] Charnwood, op. cit. , p. 54.

that rules the world ; in particular we have the notion of a plurality of ' logoi,' corresponding with the plurality of ' ideas ' in Plato, of which the highest represents the deity, and of the ' spermatikos logos ' as the agent of the deity in creation. Parallel with this conception is the idea, of which there are traces in the Old Testament, of the ' Wisdom ' of God, as a second divine being distinguished from God Himself, who is represented as assisting God at the creation—a figurative way of saying that at the creation God made use of His Wisdom (cf. Job 28 : 12 ff. ; Prov. 8 : 22 ff. ; Wisdom of Solomon 7 : 22 ff.).

But it was Philo, the famous Jewish thinker of Alexandria (*c.* 20 B.C.–*c.* A.D. 50), who combined these Greek and Hebrew conceptions and brought the idea of the Logos to its fullest development. He took over the main Stoic conception, but so identified it with Plato's idea of the ' Good ' and the Hebrew thought of the ' Wisdom ' of God, that instead of being merely immanent in creation the Logos for him became endowed with an independent existence. In the Philonic ' Logos ' the Greek idea of immanent reason is combined with the Hebrew idea of divine creative-energy and self-revelation. Yet Philo's Jewish faith forbade the identification of the Logos with the Deity Himself, and it therefore sometimes appears as a kind of ' second God ' independent of but subordinate to the God of the Old Testament, though Philo's monotheism makes it unlikely that this assertion of the existence of a second divine agent is intended in anything more than a figurative sense. There is in fact an inevitable clash between the primary Greek conception and the demands of Hebrew monotheism, an antinomy which is never wholly reconciled.

It must be admitted that ' the underlying intention of the usage in Philo and the Targums is absolutely different. Philo is working out a philosophical system designed to effect a synthesis between . . . the religious tradition of the Hebrews and Greek Neoplatonism. The Targums are popular renderings of the Old Testament lessons intended for congregations . . . who were sufficiently advanced to find difficulty in the

more startlingly anthropomorphic expressions of the Old
Testament.' Phrases such as the ' Word of the Lord '
(Memra) ' are merely reverential paraphrases.' ' To Philo,
on the other hand, the Logos is the name of a Divine Principle
conceived of, along the lines of Greek philosophical thinking,
as a connecting link between Transcendent Deity and the
material universe.' [1] Now John was no doubt impregnated
with Old Testament thought ; he may well have been influenced by the Targumic idea of the Memra (though it is
uncertain whether that usage was earlier than his time) ; but
in so far as the Prologue is quite clearly a philosophically conceived attempt to build a bridge between Greek and Hebrew
modes of thought, John must be pronounced indebted for his
Logos-doctrine to Philo, who was the first to attempt such
a synthesis by popularizing the term ' Logos.' Through
Alexandrian usage the ' Logos' had become a current philosophical term, much as is ' evolution ' or ' élan vital ' in our
own day ; John seized upon it as an invaluable category for
the interpretation of the Gospel ; and to that extent he is
indebted to Philo, even though he may have read the works
of the great Alexandrian no more closely than many who use
their categories have read Darwin or Bergson. But one
supreme distinction between John's thought and Philo's must
be noted. Even admitting that sometimes Philo ascribes a
real personality to the Logos ' he is thinking all the while of
the divine reason and activity, which he personifies as the
intermediate agent between God and the world. John, on
the other hand, starts from an actual knowledge of the earthly
life of Jesus, and the conception of the Logos is always blended
in his mind with the impression left on him by the Person.' [2]
John is primarily concerned not with the Word as a philosophical principle but with the Word made flesh and manifested in human history in the whole life of Jesus Christ.

It is for this reason that the theory—backed though it is
by so great a name as Harnack's—according to which the
Prologue is a mere introduction, added it may be as an afterthought, falls to the ground. As we have already noted, the

[1] Streeter, op. cit., p. 375.   [2] Scott, op. cit., p. 62.

thought of Jesus as the revelation of the Logos in history is the key-note which vibrates throughout the entire Gospel. The Logos-doctrine is everywhere presupposed in the body of the Gospel, though the actual use of the term ceases with the Prologue. It is this that explains the insistence on the omniscience and omnipotence of Jesus, his inviolability, the minimising of the purely human elements in his personality, his continual reference to his own Person as the source of life, and in particular such claims to pre-existence as we have in 1 : 30, 17 : 5, 8 : 58. Finally, though the term ' Logos ' is never used of Christ in the body of the Gospel, its content reappears under the categories of ' Truth,' ' Light,' and ' Life.'

The word ' truth ' is used to describe the Logos in his *reality*. The conception runs back to Plato's doctrine of ' ideas,' the fixed forms which are regarded as the original patterns of which all particular things in the material world are only copies, the highest idea, the Idea of the Good, representing God. Thus for John ' truth,' the supreme reality, becomes an equivalent for the divine nature. God is ' the only real ' (17 : 3), and all other things are ' true ' or ' real ' only in so far as they reflect God's thought and purpose. Thus Christ, being the Logos, whose supreme mission is to be the medium of the divine revelation, is in his own Person ' the truth,' and the only means whereby men can lay hold of the eternal reality.

Closely akin to ' truth ' is the idea of ' light,' under which category John expresses the thought of the Logos as the source of divine revelation. Indeed ' light ' for John is broadly speaking identical with ' truth,' with the further implication that the higher reality is ever seeking to manifest itself. As essentially one with that higher reality Christ the Logos is ' the truth '; as one, who in his own Person reveals that reality, he is ' the light.' Yet no one definition can exhaust the content of this characteristic Johannine word. ' The term is chosen because of its very largeness and vagueness. Light is the immemorial symbol of all that is divine and holy ; it suggests gladness, security, quickening, illumination. . . . Taken generally, however, light is the equivalent,

in the language of the imagination, of what is abstractly called
" the truth." '[1]

Finally, John sums up the spiritual gift communicated
through Christ the Logos under the category of "life.' Sometimes the expression used is ' eternal life,' but the epithet
does not postpone the promise to the future, for John insists
that through Christ ' life ' is bestowed here and now, but rather
suggests the origin of such life in the higher ' eternal ' world.
John gives us no exact definition of what he means by ' life,'
for 17 : 3 defines not ' life ' itself but the means of its communication, and ' life ' is something greater than the knowledge of
God through Christ by which it is conditioned and mediated.
John assumes that in God, the supreme ' reality,' and in the
Logos, who is the ' light ' revealing Him, there exists a ' life '
different in kind from mere physical life, which is the ' real '
or ' eternal ' life (cf. 1 : 4, 5 : 26). It has been held indeed
that in some passages John appears to regard this ' life ' as
an almost ' semi-physical ' bestowment, particularly in the
Eucharistic discourse in the sixth chapter (6 : 51–59). Men
to possess true life must become incorporate with Christ and
absorb his divine substance into their own nature. But this
is just an instance of how the Evangelist may use the current
language of the ' Mysteries ' without in any way consciously
committing himself to their semi-magical conceptions. Such
teaching would be utterly out of harmony with the general
trend of his thought. It may be that, in accordance with
the Logos hypothesis, the true life is regarded as a higher
kind of being, almost as a substance which can be transferred
from person to person. But for John the divine life is pre-
eminently the life of Jesus ; and the gift of Jesus to men is
just the secret of his own moral and spiritual personality.
' The words that I speak unto you,' says Jesus, ' they are
spirit, and they are *life* ' (6 : 63).

V. LITERARY STRUCTURE

Whether or no the Gospel is a literary unity, the integral
work of a single author, has been keenly debated. While

[1] Scott, op. cit., p. 254.

the famous judgment of Strauss is still staunchly upheld, that the Gospel can be divided no more than the seamless coat of our Lord, others would suggest that, broadly true though the comparison may be, ' the seamless coat had also a warp and woof and a tasselled fringe,' [1] that the Gospel is full of gaps and seams, textual dislocations and logical inconsistencies, which can only be explained on the theory either of a combination of several documents, or of a later editorial revision. According as they adopt the first or second theory the upholders of the composite nature of the Gospel may be divided into two groups—' partitionists' and ' revisionists.' The former will distinguish between an original source or sources and the later complete work into which they have been incorporated ; the latter will explain discrepancies and dislocations by arguing that a later Redactor has ' recast the Gospel for purposes which originally it was not intended to serve.' [2]

It must be confessed that the various partition theories have been generally discredited. They are vitiated to begin with by the desire to rescue some preferred element, e.g. an original Johannine *Grundschrift*, at the expense of the rest of the Gospel ; the principles of any such analysis must always be too subjective to command assent ; and indeed the whole process is based on a false analogy with the methods of Pentateuchal criticism. One feels that every attempt to analyse the Gospel in detail, giving this verse to one hand and that verse to another, is foredoomed to failure—whether the aim be to distinguish theology thrust into older history, or history superimposed upon an earlier doctrinal dissertation. Whether it be Wendt separating from the Gospel an original source composed of ' Logia ' of Jesus, or Wellhausen with his ' foundation-document ' resembling a Marcan outline, the process savours too much of ' scissors and paste.' As Streeter [3] caustically remarks : ' If the sources have undergone anything like the amount of amplification, excision, rearrangement and

---

[1] Bacon, *Introd. to the N.T.*, p. 268.
[2] Moffatt, *Introd. to the N.T.*, p. 551.
[3] Streeter, op. cit., p. 377.

adaptation which the theory postulates, then the critic's pretence that he can unravel the process is grotesque. As well hope to start with a string of sausages and reconstruct the pig.'

The truth is that the Gospel impresses us, as few books do, by its unity. Even Wellhausen [1] admits this : ' In spite of its different strata it can be historically regarded as essentially a unity.' Every page bears the stamp of the genius and experience of one unmistakable and tremendous personality, whose individuality is so marked that it never permits him to hide himself, as Shakespeare does, for example, behind the characters he creates. If there be diverse elements in the Gospel, then they have been fused together and recreated in the mind of an original thinker. ' A poet of strong powers of thought and marked individuality, who has undertaken to raise an entirely new song, is here.' [2]

Detailed analysis of the Gospel into several supposed strata is therefore ruled out ; but not necessarily the general hypothesis that an earlier hand than the Evangelist's (possibly even an earlier written source) has played a part in the Gospel's growth. No doubt the author has so far assimilated the earlier material and stamped it with his own hall-mark that the separation of the two strata is no longer possible. But it may still be argued that as he wrote he had the earlier tradition at his disposal as a source distinct both from the Synoptics and his own recollections, probably actually as a written document. It appears to the present writer that the special characteristics of the Gospel are best explained by the supposition that the Evangelist, not himself an eye-witness of the historical Jesus (or possibly a witness only during his closing days), but rather one whose concern was to interpret to his own age the significance of Jesus in men's experience, had before him the written memoirs of an actual eye-witness, which he incorporated in his own work, leaving upon the whole the unmistakable stamp of his own individuality, yet retaining something of the vivid touch of the earlier narrative,

[1] *Das Evangelium Johannis*, p. 119.
[2] Schwartz, quoted by Stanton, op. cit., p. 41.

whereby he adds life and vigour and colour to his own master-piece. The material of the Gospel did not spring into being in a day. It passed through a formative period before it finally became crystallized, a single gem with many facets, in the mind of that ' poet of strong powers of thought ' who gave it to the world. During that period the memoirs of an eye-witness may well have played an important part as a nucleus around which would gather the tradition and teaching which ultimately took form in our Gospel. One is therefore disposed to assume some sort of mediate authorship, i.e. that a later writer, relying in part for his facts upon memories of a witness, transmitted orally or more probably in writing, has given us the Gospel in its present form. Features which give colour to such a supposition may be briefly summarized :

(*a*) The combination of dependence and freedom already noted in the Gospel's relation to the Synoptists (see p. xx).

(*b*) The Gospel, while in general a mirror of the Evangelist's own time, frequently reflects the view-point of an earlier day. (See e.g. note on 5 : 2.) The controversies about the Sabbath in chapters 5 and 7 are true to the historical circumstances of Jesus' own time, though they are merged into discussions, which can have had reality only to the Evangelist's contemporaries, about the Person of Jesus himself.

(*c*) There is sometimes a similar diversity of standpoint in regard to doctrine. Some passages seem to reveal the out-cropping of an older doctrinal stratum, ' concessions ' to an earlier point of view, ' isolated ideas which cannot be reconciled with the characteristic Johannine thought,' but ' can only be regarded as fragments of earlier doctrine that have simply been taken over without any, or with a very imperfect, attempt at assimilation.' [1] Note, e.g., diversity of teaching with regard to the conceptions of Resurrection, Judgment, the Ascension, the Parousia, and see note, p. 29.

(*d*) Passages occur which are apparently ' conglomerates.' Good examples are 4 : 35–38 and 10 : 1–16. Two or more extracts, through which it is difficult to trace a single sequence of thought, have been placed together in a single paragraph

[1] Scott, op. cit., p. 9.

as dealing with similar topics ; a reasonable theory would be that a collection of passages dealing with kindred subjects has been made from an earlier source, which, in the examples quoted, is clearly not the Synoptics, though echoes there may be of Synoptic imagery.

(*e*) Very suggestive, finally, is the extraordinary vividness of much of the detail combined with a strange lack of sustained interest in history as such. Just as we are looking for the climax of some dramatic scene the narrative drifts over into a doctrinal meditation. The author introduces his characters, rivets attention upon them, only to allow them to ' evaporate from the stage.' See e.g. the scene with Nicodemus, and the interview with the Greeks. It is noticeable too that some of the most realistic touches occur in scenes which quickly resolve themselves into discourses which can hardly be historically accurate reports ; e.g. the conversation with the Samaritan woman. In short, while there are many touches of detail which are convincingly life-like, the general setting of most of the scenes is unconvincing. It is in the relatively unimportant detail, not in its larger outlook, that the Gospel manifests its interest in history, which would seem to suggest that we must look for an eye-witness, if anywhere, in the compiler of memoirs which have been incorporated, rather than in the author of the Gospel as a whole.

If such an earlier source indeed lies behind the Gospel, why have we no clearer traces of it ? Eusebius, in a well-known passage (3 : 24) writes : ' Nevertheless, of all the disciples of the Lord, only Matthew and John have left us written memoirs. . . . Matthew, having previously preached to the Hebrews, when he was about to go to other peoples, committed to writing the Gospel that bears his name in his native tongue ; . . . John, having spent all his time in oral preaching, at last came also to write.' Now, scholarship is agreed that if we owe anything to Matthew's own hand, it is not ' the Gospel that bears his name,' but the hypothetical collection of Logia which we know as ' Q.' May not the facts be similar in the case of the Fourth Gospel, into which may have been merged an earlier source, which itself has

vanished as completely as Matthew's Logia ?   In all ancient
literature it is notorious that once a lesser work has been
incorporated into and superseded by a greater one, which has
itself become authoritative, the earlier work soon ceases to
circulate separately.

There are also unmistakable signs in the Gospel of revision
by a later Redactor.   Parenthetic comments occur which so
clearly misunderstand the real point of the context as to prove
that they are due to a later hand.   (See notes on 2 : 21, 6 : 46,
8 : 27, 12 : 16, 18 : 9.)   'A writer may be negligent and
maladroit, and once in a way even a little forgetful, but he
must know what he himself means and cannot lose forthwith
all idea of what he has himself said.'[1]   To the Redactor, too,
is probably due the dislocation of the original order of the
text which we shall have frequent cause to suspect, and the
abrupt insertion of certain brief passages which seem to mar
the artistry of the Evangelist's original scheme.   Most of the
traces of redactional interference seem to be due to the
throwing back into the body of the Gospel of the view-point
of the Appendix (chap. 21), which will demand special
discussion later.

As to the Gospel's structure we conclude then that an
earlier source may have been incorporated, but has been so
far assimilated as to be no longer separable.   Certain redactional passages, which have not received the unifying stamp
of the Evangelist's own mind, will be more easily isolated.

VI. THE 'BELOVED DISCIPLE' AND THE AUTHORSHIP OF THE GOSPEL

1. If we assume that the historical background of the
Gospel has been filled in from details drawn from the memoirs
of an eye-witness, we naturally find this witness in 'the
disciple whom Jesus loved.'   But who is he whose identity
is veiled by this beautiful title ?

(a) At one extreme is the traditional view that the Beloved
Disciple is John the son of Zebedee.   The possibility of this

[1] Wellhausen, *Ev. Joh.*, p. 4.

may be admitted—at any rate if we are content to accept John merely as Witness and not as Evangelist—but there are powerful arguments against it. What we know of the temperament of the son of Zebedee reflects little either of the nature we would look for in one deemed worthy of such peculiar intimacy with Jesus, nor of the spirit of the Gospel to which tradition has attached his name. Ambitious quarrels about precedence in the Kingdom, passionate eagerness to call down fire upon the inhospitable Samaritans—these are the memories which the Synoptics leave us of John, a ' Son of Thunder ' rather than ' the Apostle of Love.' And if it be argued that the grace of God may have transformed the fiery zealot into the tender intimate of Christ, the reply is that the title ' Beloved Disciple ' has reference not to the Apostle's old age, but to the days of his ' thundering.' Add to this the fact that the historical and doctrinal affinities of the Fourth Gospel make it extremely unlikely that the son of Zebedee had any connexion with it. Is it probable that John, whom the Synoptists represent as the close companion of Peter, can be the source of a stream of tradition so divergent from the Synoptic stream, which Mark is said to have derived from Peter ? Finally, as the curtain falls upon John's appearances on the New Testament stage, we find him belonging to the Judaic party in the Church, while the Gospel, even those parts which it is most natural to trace back to the Witness, has a clear anti-Judaic bias.

(b) At the other extreme is the theory that the Beloved Disciple is an ideal figure, whether it be John the Apostle who is idealized, or whether ' Paul, and whosoever has had Paul's experience . . . is the Disciple whom Jesus loved,' but in any case a purely symbolic character, ' that ideal disciple whom Jesus would choose and who reads his soul aright.' [1] It is unnecessary to discuss this theory, which is admirably dealt with by Dr. Stanton.[2] Suffice it to say that if the Evangelist introduced the figure as a device to illustrate the ideal attitude of the believer to Christ and his Gospel, his readers would certainly never guess his purpose, nor are

[1] Bacon, op. cit., pp. 326, 320.   [2] Stanton, op. cit., p. 134 ff.

his allusions either numerous or pointed enough to create any well-defined impression of the ideal which he means to portray.

(c) The middle course is probably the safest, and, admitting that in any case the figure has to some extent been idealized, a more attractive theory is that which finds the Beloved Disciple in a young Jerusalemite of good family, possibly with priestly connexions, not one of the Twelve, but a ' supernumerary,' whom Jesus admitted to peculiar intimacy during the closing period of his ministry. This theory was first put forward by Delff, was cautiously commended by Sanday, and appears to be finding increasing support. The evidence has been so exhaustively examined, particularly by Dr. Garvie in his ' Beloved Disciple,' that here only the briefest summary is necessary. The external evidence agrees well enough with this theory, while Sanday is certainly justified in his statement that ' if we confine ourselves to the indications contained in the Gospel itself, it would not follow with any stringency that the eye-witness of the events was the Apostle John, the son of Zebedee.' [1] Dr. Garvie would trace the Beloved Disciple in the anonymous follower of 1 : 35 ; but the words of 13 : 23 (the Last Supper scene) read like the first introduction of a character not previously mentioned, the other definite references being 18 : 15 (but the identification here is doubtful ; see below, p. xlviii), 19 : 26, 20 : 2, 21 : 7, 20 ff. If this surmise be correct, then presumably the Beloved Disciple was in intimate fellowship with Jesus only during the closing days, though he may well have been a constant witness and hearer, while as yet perhaps an unconfessed disciple, whenever our Lord was in Jerusalem. Here surely we have the most natural explanation of the focusing of interest on scenes and discourses at or near Jerusalem and on Passion Week in particular, and the comparative neglect of the Galilean episodes. Dr. Garvie suggests that the Beloved Disciple may have been the householder who provided the Upper Room, and this fits in admirably with much of the evidence (Garvie, p. 144 f.) and possibly would help to explain his desire for anonymity (p. 203 f.).

[1] Sanday, *Criticism of the Fourth Gospel*, p. 97.

2. But though we may accept this picture of the Beloved Disciple as a Witness, it does not follow that he was also the author of the Gospel. To begin with, it is more likely that the predicate ' whom Jesus loved ' was used of the disciple by another. That he should so distinguish himself would be, to say the least, an affectation ; but it would be natural enough for a devoted follower so to speak of his idealized teacher. The tradition that the Witness is also the Evangelist rests on 21 : 24, which, as even Westcott admits, cannot be from the hand of the original author, and represents a later, and probably erroneous, identification. Apart from this verse there is really nothing to suggest that the Beloved Disciple is the author. And even 21 : 24 is hesitating. In any case it is on the ' witness ' rather than on the ' writing ' that the emphasis is laid. ' The words " and wrote these things " seem to be added to " beareth witness concerning these things," as a kind of afterthought. Most prominence at all events is given to his having borne witness. From the position and form of this reference to writing, it is not unfair to infer that there may have been some uncertainty in the mind of the framer of the statement as to the extent to which it was to be attributed to the same disciple.' [1] Even the Redactor, though sure that the Beloved Disciple is the Witness, is not quite so sure that he is the actual author of the Gospel.

Other passages quoted as proof that the Evangelist was himself an eye-witness may be otherwise explained. The words (1 : 14) ' we have seen his glory ' do not necessarily imply more than spiritual perception, and even if, as is perhaps more likely, physical sight is also implied, the words might be taken not as the personal testimony of the author, but merely as the general witness of the Christian community, which once long ago had seen and known the Word made flesh. Still more weight has been laid on 19 : 35 (' he who saw it has borne witness ; his witness is true ; God knows he is telling the truth ') where, it is argued, the Evangelist is definitely bearing testimony to his own authorship, and

---

[1] Stanton, op. cit., p. 134.

asserting that he himself was a witness of the events. But see note *in loco* ; the verse should almost certainly be assigned to the Redactor, and is an example of how the point of view of the Appendix is thrown back into the body of the Gospel in order deliberately to identify the author with the disciple whom Jesus loved—one of the chief aims of the Redactor (see below, p. 368). ' Whoever heard of a writer employing such ambiguities (as 19 : 35) to make the simple statement, " I myself saw this " ? ' [1] The truth is that the Gospel's so-called ' self-testimony raises more riddles than it solves.' [2]

We conclude then that the Evangelist was not himself the Beloved Disciple-Witness, but rather a younger contemporary and admiring follower of the latter, standing in much the same kind of relation to him as did Mark, the author of another of our Gospels, to Peter. It is not even necessary to suppose that he had seen a great deal of the Beloved Disciple. ' A brief and, as it seemed in the halo of later recollection, a wonderful connexion—perhaps also a few never-to-be-forgotten words of Christ derived from his lips— would make the attitude towards the Beloved Disciple expressed in the Gospel psychologically explicable.' [3]

An interesting suggestion has recently been made [4] that the Evangelist, as distinct from the Beloved Disciple, actually appears in the Gospel at 18 : 15 under the guise of the anonymous disciple who was ' an acquaintance of the High Priest.' It would then follow that he was probably a young man of aristocratic connexions and of priestly family ; other interesting implications suggested by this theory are meanwhile reserved (see p. lxiv).

VII. THE RELATION OF THE APPENDIX TO THE QUESTION OF AUTHORSHIP

We have already seen cause to suppose that the Gospel has undergone revision at the hands of a later Redactor, to

[1] Bacon, op. cit., p. 192.
[2] Jackson, *The Problem of the Fourth Gospel*, p. 39.
[3] Streeter, *The Four Gospels*, p. 433.   [4] Strachan, op. cit., p. 49.

whom the final chapter and certain kindred sections in the body of the Gospel are to be assigned. The aim of the Appendix and its relation to the Gospel are fully discussed in an introductory note to chapter 21. The purpose of the Redactor's revision so far as it affects the question of authorship expresses itself in an attempt to establish for the Gospel a guarantee of Apostolic authorship. This he endeavours to secure—

(a) By the identification of the Evangelist with the Beloved Disciple-Witness, which is definitely suggested in 19 : 35 and 21 : 24, and which once so suggested would be likely quickly to gain acceptance. As time passed there would naturally be a disposition to magnify the Beloved Disciple's connexion with the book, and, assuming the Evangelist to have been a disciple of the Witness, it is likely enough that one who had been a teacher of the actual author and whose testimony was embodied in his work, would become in the estimate of the Church transformed into the author. This tendency is deliberately encouraged by the Redactor.

(b) The Apostolic guarantee is clinched by the further identification of the Beloved Disciple with John the son of Zebedee. At 21 : 2, by introducing by name 'the sons of Zebedee' for the first time, the Redactor cautiously suggests, by a process of elimination, that the Beloved Disciple is to be identified with one of them. It may even be argued with some show of reason [1] that the absence throughout the Gospel of any mention of John, the son of Zebedee, by name, and the presence of certain awkward anonymous expressions which apparently refer to him, is due to the deliberate cancellation by the Redactor, in the interest of his theory that the Beloved Disciple is John, of all independent references to John by name. In other words, the use of anonymous expressions in situations where the reader would instinctively supply the name of John, as for example at the call of the disciples at 1 : 35 ff., would lead the reader to assume that the reference was to the great anonymous Beloved Disciple—and this was deliberately intended by the Redactor. If it be objected

[1] Bacon, op. cit., p. 138 ff.

that this is an incredibly vague way to assert that the Beloved Disciple is the son of Zebedee, the reply is that the Redactor's aim is not so much to prove the identification as to secure that nothing in the Gospel will cause perplexity to those who have already accepted a gradually hardening tradition. Here, too, the Redactor is but adding momentum to a tendency already well under way. By the time the Gospel was published the Beloved Disciple would have become a very indefinite figure, his personality having become merged in that of his disciple the Evangelist. If, as will now be argued, the latter is to be identified with John the Elder of Ephesus, then once the view gained ground that the latter was indeed the Beloved Disciple, it was almost inevitable that the Anonymous Witness should in turn also be identified with the Apostle who bore the same name ' John.'

VIII. JOHN, THE ELDER OF EPHESUS, AND THE EXTERNAL EVIDENCE

Tradition is practically unanimous that the Fourth Gospel had its origin at Ephesus, and that its author was that ' John ' who figured there as a leader in the Church during the closing years of the first century, and was early identified with the Apostle John, the son of Zebedee. ' The Christian writers who look upon him (the son of Zebedee) as the author do not say that the Apostle composed it, no matter where he lived, but they say, " the John who was head of the Church of Asia Minor wrote it," so that the Apostle may be held to be the author of the Gospel only if we can think of him as living in Ephesus.' [1] Does the external evidence prove the residence of the son of Zebedee in Ephesus, or does it rather point us to another ' John ' with whom he has been confused ?

Our critical study of the evidence afforded by the Gospel itself has pointed to the conclusion that the author is one who does not himself claim to be an Apostle and yet writes with the authority of one who is familiar with first-hand tradition and possibly has some personal connexion with Jesus' immediate

[1] Schmiedel, *The Johannine Writings*, p. 179.

disciples. Such a figure appears in the person of ' John the Elder,' and the theory that the Evangelist is to be found in this John, who is distinct both from the Apostle John and the Beloved Disciple, seems to the present writer best to meet the facts.

' The Elder ' appears in the New Testament as the writer of the Second and Third Epistles which have been traditionally ascribed to ' John,' and Dr. Charles, in his Commentary on *Revelation*,[1] gives an analysis of the language of the Gospel and Epistles of ' John ' which confirms the impression made even on a casual reader that, not only the First Epistle, but also the Second and the Third are by the same writer as the Gospel. That ' John the Elder ' is a person quite distinct from the Apostle of the same name seems clearly proved by the famous passage of Papias (written probably *c.* 140–150) quoted by Eusebius (*Hist. Eccl.* iii, 39) : ' And again on any occasion when a person came who had been a follower of the Elders, I would inquire about the discourses of the Elders—what was said by Andrew, or by Peter, or by Philip, or by Thomas or James, or by John or Matthew or any other of the Lord's disciples, and what Aristion and the Elder John, the disciples of the Lord, say.' As Eusebius himself proceeds to point out, the name ' John ' is twice mentioned, and the second John, coupled with Aristion under the designation ' Elder,' can hardly be the same person as the first John, who is classed with six other Apostles. True both are called ' disciples of the Lord ' ; but with the end of the first century and the passing of those who had known Jesus in the flesh the title ' disciple ' was used to include others besides those who could claim a personal acquaintance with the Master. Moreover, the change of tense from ' said ' to ' say ' suggests that the second John was still alive when Papias gathered his information, while the first John and those classed with him were dead. ' So that,' concludes Eusebius, ' Papias hereby makes it quite evident that their statement is true who say that there were two persons of that name in Asia, and that there are two tombs in Ephesus, each of which even now is called

[1] p. xxxiv ff.

the tomb of John.' In confirmation of the theory that there were two Johns it is interesting to note that the ' Apostolic Constitutions,' a fourth-century document based on older materials, names as contemporary Bishops of Ephesus ' Timothy ordained by Paul, and John ordained by John.' This would suggest that before A.D. 100 (up to which date the list of Bishops is compiled) a second John, ordained by the Apostle of the same name, had already attained prominence in Asia ; if the ordination of the second John by the first implies, as in the case of Paul and Timothy, a close relationship, the subsequent confusion of the two will become the more credible.

The theory that the ' John ' who was leader of the Ephesian Church and author of the Fourth Gospel was not the Apostle but ' the Elder ' accords well with the following lines of evidence :

1. The evidence for the early death as a martyr of John the Apostle. This may be briefly summarized :

(a) The prophecy of Jesus in Mk 10 : 35 ff., which would certainly gain point if, at the time when Mark wrote, the prophecy had been fulfilled.

(b) According to the ' De Boor fragment ' of Philip of Side, a Church historian of the fifth century, and the Chronicle of George Hamartolus, a tenth-century chronographer, Papias, in his second book, recorded that ' John the Divine and James his brother were killed by the Jews.'

(c) The Syriac Martyrology, dated A.D. 411 and drawn up at Edessa, commemorates the martyrdom of ' John and James the Apostles ' on December 28th. This, if a fact, must have happened before A.D. 70.

(d) Certain minor pieces of evidence contained in allusions by various early Christian writers, including Heracleon, Clement of Alexandria and Chrysostom, are summarized by Dr. Charles.[1]

Each of these pieces of evidence is disputed and alone would be inconclusive ; but the cumulative effect is considerable, and there is an increasing readiness to accept the

[1] *Revelation,* vol. i, p. xlv ff.

probability of John the Apostle's early death. ' The wonder is that any evidence at all should survive of a tradition apologetically so inconvenient.' [1]

2. The hesitation of our authorities as to John the Apostle's residence in Asia :

(a) The book of Acts is silent on the subject, while in Acts 20 : 29 Paul, in taking leave of his Ephesian friends, warns them of the ' fierce wolves which will get in among you ' —words which the writer would hardly have put into Paul's mouth had he supposed that the most prominent of Paul's successors in Ephesus was the Apostle John.

(b) Ignatius of Antioch, in his letter to the Ephesian Church written on his way to martyrdom (c. 110–117), claims that the Church is an Apostolic foundation on account of Paul's affection for it, but is silent about any residence of John in the city ; yet had he known of it, what stronger claim for the community's Apostolic dignity could he have adduced ? ' The tradition of Asia Minor,' writes von Dobschütz, ' knows but one John only ' (in spite of the passage from Eusebius quoted above) ' who accordingly must be either the Apostle or the Elder.' The silence of Ignatius strongly suggests that the only John resident in Asia was the Elder.

3. The Apologetic tone of many of the early references to the Gospel, which suggests that the claim to Apostolic authorship was challenged from the first.

(a) The fact that such a guarantee of authorship as Jn 21 : 24 was required at the time the Gospel was published hints that at the beginning of the second century there was already a divergence of opinion.

(b) The strange argument of Irenæus (c. 185) whereby he endeavours to prove a priori, by the analogy of the four winds, the eternal necessity of four Gospels, and that ' all those are vain, unlearned and also audacious, who represent the aspects of the Gospel as being either more in number than four or fewer,' can only be explained by the existence of a considerable party who rejected the authority of the Fourth Gospel.

[1] Streeter, op. cit., p. 435.

(c) Hippolytus, the Roman theologian (c. 190–235), wrote a *Defence of the Gospel and Apocalypse of John.* But no one defends what nobody attacks. And the defence becomes all the more significant when we discover that the attack on the Apocalypse at least, and therefore perhaps also that on the Gospel, was being made not by heretics outside the Church, but by the presbyter Gaius. 'The opposition to the Gospel can be definitely localized in orthodox circles in Rome.' [1]

(d) The reference to the Gospel in the Muratorian Fragment on the Canon is strongly apologetic. The document may be held to reflect the official view of Rome about A.D. 200. Whereas Luke is dealt with in seven lines, no less than twenty-five are given to John. The writer insists that neither Mark nor Luke claims to be an eye-witness, but he expressly defends John's claim : 'It was revealed to Andrew, one of the Apostles, that John was to write all things in his own name, and they were all to certify. And, therefore, though various elements are taught in the several books of the Gospel, yet it makes no difference to the faith of believers, since by one guiding Spirit all things are declared in all of them. . . . For so he declares himself (in the opening words of the First Epistle) not an eye-witness and a hearer only, but a witness of all the marvels of the Lord in order.' This reads like a defence of the Gospel against the charge that it could not be Apostolic on account of its divergencies, particularly as regards order, from the Synoptics : if there be a divergence, John is to be preferred, as he was a witness and the others were not.

4. The lateness of the evidence for the full recognition of the Gospel as Apostolic compared with the earliness of the evidence for its use. Significance lies in the fact that in certain quarters it was not the antiquity, but the apostolicity, of the Gospel which was held in question. Would there have been this hesitation if all the world knew beyond doubt that round about the year 100 the Apostle John was still alive at Ephesus ? Thus :

[1] Streeter, op. cit., p. 438.

(*a*) About A.D. 175 there existed at Rome a small sect nicknamed by their opponents ' the Alogi ' (a pun, for the Greek might be translated both ' Anti-Logosites ' and ' Unreasonable folk ') who rejected the Gospel, and actually ascribed it to the Gnostic Cerinthus. The existence of such a sect, while testifying to the wide use of the Gospel, shows that its authority was not yet universally accepted. In other respects the Alogi seem to have been conservative rather than heretic, and perhaps numbered among themselves that Gaius against whom Hippolytus directed his *Defence*.

(*b*) Justin Martyr (died *c*. A.D. 165 as a martyr at Rome) almost certainly knew and used the Gospel, for he refers in his *First Apology* to the ' Memoirs of the Apostles which are called Gospels,' which may be assumed with some probability to be the Gospels of Matthew and John, and in the *Dialogue with Trypho* to ' Memoirs which were composed by the Apostles and their followers '—presumably Matthew and John on the one hand, and Mark and Luke on the other. But whereas Justin quotes the Synoptics over one hundred times, he quotes John only thrice. Frequently inappropriate texts are quoted from the Synoptics in support of an argument, while sayings recorded in the Fourth Gospel, which if quoted would have been conclusive, are ignored. Are we to conclude that Justin himself doubted the Apostolicity of the Gospel, or at any rate felt that in the eyes of the Church as a whole it had not yet the authority of the earlier Gospels ? ' In fact Justin acts like a modern apologetic writer trying to establish the pre-existence of Christ, but, in deference to critical objections, attempting to do so without reference to the Fourth Gospel." [1]

(*c*) A similar conclusion is suggested by a study of the Epistles of Ignatius of Antioch (*c*. 115), whose testimony to the Gospel is thus summed up by Dr. Streeter [2] : ' His whole outlook and his theology have been profoundly influenced by the study of this Gospel ; but his use of it suggests that it is not yet recognized in his own Church as on the same level of authority as Matthew.'

[1] Streeter, op. cit., p. 441.　　[2] Idem, p. 455.

(*d*) Similarly, though the influence of the Fourth Gospel may with some probability be traced in the *Didaché* (dated by Harnack between 130 and 160 ; by others even earlier), the Epistle of Barnabas (variously dated between 70 and 140, the later date more probable), the Second Epistle of Clement (*c.* 120–150), the Shepherd of Hermas (*c.* 130–140), the Epistle to Diognetus (date and locality uncertain), it is only when we come down the years as far as Theophilus of Antioch (*c.* 180) that the Gospel is unequivocally quoted as inspired scripture and expressly ascribed to the Apostle John.

To sum up, though the influence of the Gospel is evident quite early in the second century, and apparent quotations are found thus early in contemporary writings, but *without authentication of authorship*, it is not till *c.* 180 that the Gospel is quoted as definitely Apostolic. Would this be so if the author were indeed the Apostle John or even that ' Disciple,' distinct from the son of Zebedee, ' whom Jesus loved ' ?

5. The significant use, with reference to the ' John ' who lived in Ephesus and wrote the Gospel, of the title ' disciple ' rather than ' apostle.' This would suit the Elder, especially if he had already become identified with the Beloved Disciple, better than the Apostle John.

Even Irenaeus, though he speaks of John some sixteen times as ' the disciple of the Lord,' only twice, and that merely by implication, allows him the title Apostle. Is this unconscious evidence that the ' John,' of whom Irenaeus claimed to have heard Polycarp and the Elders speak (see below, p. lvii), was not the Apostle but the Elder ? In the evidence of Polycrates too (p. lx) there is a significant absence of the decisive title Apostle. The same thing is true of the Monarchian Prologue to the Gospel (probably to be dated during the first third of the third century) which, while it refers to John as ' Evangelist ' and ' Disciple,' never expressly designates him as the ' Apostle John.'

6. Even such evidence as is usually claimed most strongly to confirm the residence of John the son of Zebedee in Asia and the Apostolic authorship of the Gospel may be otherwise

<u>interpreted</u>. It is admitted, of course, that once tradition had hardened, belief in the Apostolic authorship became universal. Among the great names, Origen (A.D. 185–254), Clement of Alexandria (died *c.* 200), Eusebius (Bishop of Caesarea, A.D. 314–340), though the latter emphasizes the existence of a second ' John,' have no doubt that he who ruled the Asian Church and wrote the Fourth Gospel was John the Apostle, the disciple whom Jesus loved. But stress has been laid specially on the evidence of three witnesses :

(*a*) Irenaeus (Bishop of Lyons, died *c.* 200), in a series of references to the residence in Asia of a John whom he regularly styles ' the disciple of the Lord,' states that ' John, the disciple of the Lord, who also leaned upon his breast, published a Gospel during his residence at Ephesus in Asia ' (Eusebius, *H.E.*, v, 8), that the Gospel in question began ' In the beginning was the Word, etc.,' and that ' all the elders, they of Asia who had conferred with John the disciple of the Lord, bear witness that their tradition had been delivered to them by John, for he remained on with them until the days of Trajan ' (*ibid.*, iii, 23). But the most important evidence is contained in the letter written by Irenaeus to his old friend Florinus, then resident in Rome (*c.* 190) : ' For I saw thee, when I was still a boy, in lower Asia in company with Polycarp, while thou wast faring prosperously in the royal court, and endeavouring to stand well with him. For I distinctly remember the incidents of that time better than events of recent occurrence . . . so that I can describe the very place in which the blessed Polycarp used to sit when he discoursed, and his goings out and his comings in, and his manner of life, and his personal appearance, and the discourses which he held before the people, and how he would describe his intercourse with John and with the rest who had seen the Lord, and how he would relate their words ' (Eusebius, *H.E.*, v, 20). This would be conclusive evidence of the residence of the Apostle John in Asia, had we not already seen that Papias, also according to Irenaeus a friend of Polycarp, witnesses to the existence in Asia of another ' John ' who was commonly styled a ' disciple of the Lord.' Is it possible that Irenaeus is mistaken when he identifies the ' John,' of whom Polycarp spoke, with the Apostle ? In general we have little reason to trust Irenaeus' critical judgment ; witness his extraordinary *a priori* argument for the eternal necessity of a fourfold Gospel. In the passage in question he is evidently making the most of his connexion with Polycarp ; it is not likely that he was himself long resident in Asia, or was anything more than a youthful and casual hearer of Polycarp at Smyrna. That his knowledge of Polycarp was slight is evident from his statement that Polycarp ' received his appointment in Asia from Apostles as Bishop in the Church of Smyrna' (*Adv. Haer.*, iii, 3, 4), whereas according to the Eastern tradition (e.g. in the Life of Polycarp ascribed to Pionius) he was merely ordained deacon and nominated as his successor by one Bucolus, Bishop of Smyrna, and not even Bucolus was the first Bishop. If then Irenaeus' connexion with Polycarp was but slight, he may well have been guilty of a misunderstanding. Possibly Polycarp, like his contemporary Papias, was in the habit of alluding to John the Elder as the ' disciple of the Lord,' and Irenaeus, at the time a mere lad, may simply have assumed that John the Apostle was meant. In any case it is not a little significant that Irenaeus regularly styles ' John ' a ' disciple of the Lord ' ; the decisive title ' Apostle ' is absent from his testimony, though he habitually uses it of Paul. Indeed, Dr. Burney, on the basis of this fact, has seriously questioned whether Irenaeus ever made the mistake, usually attributed to him, of identifying the John of his informants with the Apostle. ' We conclude,' he says, ' without hesitation that by " John the disciple of the Lord " Irenaeus means John the presbyter. . . . It is Eusebius who, jumping to the conclusion that John the Apostle must be the Evangelist, attaches to Irenaeus the charge of misconstruing Papias's evidence which has stuck to him ever since. In reality Irenaeus appears to be an impeccable witness as to the early Asian tradition in regard to John ; and he completes our evidence that John the Evangelist and disciple of the Lord, who survived to old age at Ephesus, was not the son of Zebedee, but the Presby-

ter." [1] Burney's argument is very attractive, though it may
not carry complete conviction.

(*b*) The evidence of Papias which, according to Burney,
Irenaeus has been falsely charged of misconstruing, is con-
tained in the famous passage already quoted (p. li). Irenaeus
(*Adv. Haer.*, v, 33, 4 ; Eusebius, *H.E.*, iii, 39) states that
Papias, ' a companion of Polycarp,' and Bishop of Hierapolis
in Asia Minor, was ' a hearer of John '—meaning apparently
the Apostle. For this Eusebius takes him to task, quoting
Papias himself to prove that the ' John ' in question is not
the Apostle but the Elder. Supposing (*pace* Burney) that
Irenaeus does indeed mean the Apostle, it seems probable that
Eusebius is right and Irenaeus is again guilty of confusing the
two Johns. Once assume that, as a young man, Irenaeus
misunderstood Polycarp's references to ' John,' and it is easy
to see that, when later he came to read Papias, he would take
it for granted that the latter was referring to the same John
as his contemporary and friend Polycarp. ' Hence any
reference to John which Irenaeus found in Papias that was
in the slightest degree ambiguous he would invariably interpret
on the assumption that Papias, like Polycarp, when speaking
of the personality or the writings of John, the disciple of the
Lord, in Asia, could only mean the Apostle and author of the
Gospel. Besides Irenaeus, we know, accepted 2 John as
the work of the disciple of the Lord, who wrote the Gospel,
whom he identified with the Apostle. The author of 2
John styles himself " the Elder." By Irenaeus, then, " the
Elder " would naturally be taken as an alternative title of
the Apostle.' [2]

The passage from Papias which we are considering ends
with the words : ' I did not think that I could get so much
profit from the contents of books as from the utterances of a
living and abiding voice.' Would not this agree better with
the view that Papias himself considered the Gospel to be the
work, not of the Apostle, but of the Elder ? If he really
possessed a written record, which he was convinced to be from

[1] C. F. Burney, *The Aramaic Origin of the Fourth Gospel*, p. 141.
[2] Streeter, *The Four Gospels*, pp. 447–8.

the hand of the Apostle John himself, how could he suppose that any second-hand oral tradition was to be preferred as evidence for ' what was said by . . . John or Matthew or any other of the Lord's disciples ? '

Finally, though Eusebius tells us that Papias used ' testimonies,' or proof-texts, from the First Epistle of John, he is silent about any use by Papias of the Fourth Gospel. But suppose that Papias knew the Gospel to be by the Elder, and when he quoted it did so under such a title as, e.g., the ' Memoirs of the Elder,' it would never occur to Eusebius, by whose time the Apostolic authorship had long ceased to be questioned, that such a work was to be identified with our Fourth Gospel. The ' Silence of Eusebius,' on which theme volumes have been written, would thus be explained.

(c) Polycrates, Bishop of Ephesus, in a letter to Victor of Rome, written A.D. 195, says : ' Moreover John, who was both a martyr and a teacher, who leaned upon the bosom of the Lord, and became a priest wearing the sacerdotal plate—he fell asleep at Ephesus.' The interesting point here is the reference to the priestly connexions of John of Ephesus, which would fit in well with the allusion in Jn. 18 : 15, whether the ' disciple who was an acquaintance of the high-priest ' be identified, as we have suggested, with the Evangelist himself, or with his teacher, the Beloved Disciple, from whom, by the time of Polycrates, the Evangelist would no longer be distinguished. It is generally assumed, probably rightly, that Polycrates, like Irenaeus and Papias whom he may have read, confused the two Johns and understood the John, to whom he alludes in the passage quoted, to be the Apostle. And, if he had any doubt in the matter, there would be every temptation to make the assumption. For Polycrates here is hardly an unbiased witness. The whole purpose of his letter to Victor is to defend the Churches of Asia, which had just been excommunicated by Rome for declining to conform to the Roman practice in regard to the keeping of Easter. He is concerned to prove that in Asia as well as in Rome ' great lights have fallen asleep,' and he claims for Asia the graves of Philip and his daughters, John, Polycarp, and other lesser lights. And what better defence than to hint that Ephesus, too, no less than Rome, had her Apostle ? ' Tradition always errs on the patriotic side, and in much less time (than that which had elapsed between John's death and Polycrates' letter) would have contrived to identify John of Asia with the only Apostle who could compare with Peter in prestige." [1] Yet it is significant that, while Polycrates definitely calls Philip an Apostle, John has no such title here given him ; also Polycrates gives him a curiously lowly place in his list of the ' lights of Asia.' Philip stands first, then his daughters, then John. Does Polycrates unconsciously preserve a traditional order of precedence dating from a time when ' John ' was not yet regarded as an Apostle, and was therefore inferior in dignity to Philip ?

From the foregoing study of the external evidence it is easy to understand how within one hundred years John the Elder and Evangelist of Asia would almost inevitably come to be identified with the Apostle of the same name. The Redactor himself did much to set the tendency under way, and the naïve desire to secure Apostolic authority for the Asian tradition would hasten it. Indeed, there is a strong suspicion that a similar confusion has taken place between Philip the Apostle and Philip the Evangelist. At any rate it is a curious coincidence that the Evangelist of Acts 21 : 8 and the ' Apostle ' of Polycrates' letter to Victor should both have had daughters who were prophetesses. The ease with which such confusion would take place is also shown by the fact that John the Seer, who (as was remarked as early as Dionysius of Alexandria, 248–265) must have been quite a different person from our Evangelist, was also identified with the Apostle by Justin Martyr. If John the Elder and writer of the Gospel also lived in Asia tradition would almost certainly fail to distinguish these two Asian Johns from one another and from the Apostle of the same name. ' However diverse in character, language and doctrinal standpoint, the four anonymous writings of the Ephesian Canon (the three Epistles and the Gospel) would inevitably come to be

[1] Streeter, op. cit., p. 454.

attributed to the same apostolic hand as the pseudepigraphic fifth, the Revelation.'[1]

IX. THE DATE OF THE GOSPEL

In attempting to determine the approximate date of the Gospel's composition we may fix two extreme limits.

The *terminus a quo* is the date of the latest of the Synoptics to which John has been shown to be indebted, in this case Luke, which may be dated *c.* 80, or, if it be held proved that Luke used Josephus, *c.* 95.

As for the *terminus ad quem*, by no possibility can it be pushed back later than say *c.* 180, by which time, e.g., Irenaeus regarded all four Gospels as Holy Scripture. As we have seen, references to the Gospel, but without authentication of its Apostolic origin, may be traced with various degrees of probability in earlier writings. A cautious conclusion would be that, although 'the first reliable traces of the existence of the Fourth Gospel are found in the *Apology* of Justin Martyr,'[2] yet its use by *c.* 135 by Basilides (*flor.* 117–138) and the Valentinian Gnostics seems so probable that the *terminus ad quem* may be safely brought forward at least to that date. There is a certain amount of evidence, inconclusive in detail but in its cumulative effect impressive, that the Gospel was known considerably earlier. If it be held proved that John the Elder is the author, the date of composition can hardly be later than 100–110. If Papias' description of 'John' as a 'disciple of the Lord' and Polycarp's as one 'who had seen the Lord' are to be taken literally, it will be almost necessary to bring the date forward to the previous decade ; this would certainly be the case if we identify the anonymous disciple of 18 : 15 with the Evangelist. But even so, a date earlier than 95 is not necessary. Both Gospel and First Epistle leave the impression that they are the work of an old man. The Gospel is clearly the fruit of a lifetime of Christian experience, meditation and communion, while a writer who in one paragraph can address his readers

[1] B. W. Bacon, *Jesus and Paul*, p. 200.
[2] Heitmüller, *Die Schriften des Neuen Testamentes*, ii, p. 709

as both 'fathers' and 'little children' (1 Jn. 3 : 13 and 18), is likely to have been a man of venerable age. Perhaps A.D. 95–105 is the likeliest decade in which to date the Gospel.

X. Conclusion

We conclude then that three persons have played their part in reducing our Gospel to its present form, of whom the second is the author in the true sense of the word, who has stamped upon the book the marks of his genius and welded it into an organic whole.

(1) Behind the Gospel stands the figure of the Witness, the 'Disciple whom Jesus loved,' a young Jerusalemite disciple, outside the number of the Twelve, but admitted to the inner circle during the closing days. In his memoirs, if indeed he ever wrote such, he probably recorded mainly what he himself had seen and heard, though he may well have also questioned the Eleven, and of the information thus gained some might point ultimately to, amongst others, John, the son of Zebedee, who on that assumption might, as Harnack says, 'stand in some way or other behind the Fourth Gospel.' More than this we cannot claim for John the Apostle. The Witness must remain shrouded in his self-chosen anonymity unless we care to venture into the perilous realm of conjecture. Perhaps the most plausible suggestion is Dr. Swete's, which identifies the Beloved Disciple with the ' Rich Young Ruler.' The latter is introduced by the Synoptists towards the close of the ministry, just as is the Beloved Disciple in our Gospel ; he questions Jesus about ' eternal life,' a theme which dominates the Fourth Gospel ; and finally we are told that ' Jesus beholding him loved him.' He may have repented of his ' great refusal ' and thrown in his lot with Jesus, and after the tragedy of the Crucifixion the old hesitation and diffidence may have reasserted itself in his desire to remain anonymous. The same qualities appear in Nicodemus, that other ' ruler ' who ' came to Jesus by night,' who, it has been suggested, is the Fourth Gospel parallel to the Young Ruler. Can it be that the Witness had once been among those men-

tioned with reproach in 12 : 42 f. ? But, to use a phrase of Sanday, all such conjecture must, however interesting, remain nothing more than ' pious speculation.'

(2) The Evangelist himself, afterwards John the Elder of Ephesus, we conceive to have been a younger contemporary and disciple of the Witness. If he appears in the Gospel as the anonymous disciple of 18 : 15, we may assume that he had priestly connexions, from which it would follow that he may originally have been a Sadducee.[1] Such a supposition might help to explain the absence of the name ' Sadducee ' from the Gospel (perhaps because John regarded it as a nickname), the complete ignoring of the demon-world, and the conception of the resurrection appearances held by the Evangelist, who certainly does not unduly stress their bodily aspect : for, says Luke, ' the Sadducees say there is no resurrection, neither angel nor spirit ' (Acts 23 : 8). If 18 : 15 be taken to refer not to the Beloved Disciple, but to the Evangelist, Polycarp may still be right in classing John among those who had ' seen the Lord.' Jn. 1 : 14 and the opening verses of the First Epistle suggest that the Evangelist, though perhaps a mere boy at the time, may himself have seen and heard Jesus in the flesh. Though not old enough to have been a personal follower, Jesus may have had a place in his childhood's memories, so that he felt himself to belong to the generation (' we,' 1 : 14) to which the great revelation had been made.

Whoever he was, the Evangelist was almost certainly a Jew, and in all probability, at least by birth and early training, a Jew of Palestine. He appears to have a first-hand knowledge of the topography of Palestine, and especially of Jerusalem, and also to be acquainted with Rabbinic tradition and the usages of the Temple system, though it may be argued that such knowledge might be acquired by a pilgrim to Jerusalem. Again, steeped though he is in Greek culture, the cast both of his thought and his language is essentially Hebraic. Though free from the grammatical mistakes which betray the Hebraic origin of the Apocalypse, John's Greek style, with its limited

[1] Cf. Strachan, *The Fourth Evangelist*, p. 158 ff.

vocabulary, paratactic clauses, and poetic parallelisms, betrays a Jewish mind not yet complete master of the full resources of the Greek language. Indeed, on the strength of this linguistic evidence Dr. Burney [1] concludes that the Gospel as we now have it is a translation of an Aramaic original. Specially interesting are his examples of passages, difficult and obscure in the Greek, which become perfectly intelligible on the assumption of mistranslation of the Aramaic original : e.g. 7 : 37–8, 8 : 56, 10 : 29. Only a Semitic expert is qualified to judge whether or no Burney has proved his case, but at least he has made it clear that the Evangelist was a man whose thoughts naturally expressed themselves in Aramaic idiom. The Gospel's close, sometimes even verbal, dependence upon the Greek Gospel of Mark would seem to weigh against the theory that it was actually written in Aramaic. Curiously the phenomena, on which Burney bases his argument, occur much more frequently in the discourses than in the narrative portions of the Gospel, which suggests that the discourses alone may have been translated from an original Aramaic draft. Would this imply that they embody a larger proportion of authentic sayings of Jesus, originally spoken in Aramaic, than is usually granted ? Dr. Burney's researches have at least shown that more prominence, than has of late been allowed, must be given to the Jewish basis of much that is distinctive in our Evangelist's thought.

Removing later in life from Jerusalem to Asia Minor the Evangelist would come into touch with the Alexandrine modes of thought which have left so clear an influence on his Gospel. Eventually we are to suppose that he settled in Ephesus (though Burney, in order to secure the necessary Aramaic-speaking readers, suggests that the Gospel may have been written at Antioch in Syria, where John is presumed to have resided for a time before his final settlement at Ephesus), where in his old age he wrote the Gospel for the benefit of the largely Hellenistic Church of which he had become the leader. The relation of the First Epistle to the Gospel has been much disputed, but any discussion of the

[1] C. F. Burney, *The Aramaic Origin of the Fourth Gospel*, 1922.

B

problem is outwith the scope of the present volume. If, as we have seen reason to conclude, the Epistle is from the same hand as the Gospel, we may suppose that its purpose was to commend to the Churches of Asia the general standpoint and teaching of the Gospel, and to conciliate such conservative opinion, as might look askance at this new-fangled ' spiritual Gospel,' by insisting, as does the Epistle from its very first words, that ' for all his sympathy with the philosophic intellectuals, the author will have nothing to do with any kind of Gnostic ' docetism ' which makes the humanity of Christ unreal.' [1]

(3) Before it reached its final form the Gospel was revised by a later Redactor. The occasion of this revision may have been the death of John of Ephesus. Certainly the latter was dead by the time the Appendix was added, for 21 : 20–24 is obviously intended to correct some current misconception of a traditional saying of Jesus about the Beloved Disciple, which the latter's death, or rather the death of the person who had come to be identified with him, had made a stumbling-block to faith. Whether or no the Gospel had been published earlier without the Appendix must remain uncertain. But with the death of the great leader of the Ephesian Church the need would be felt of a permanent record of his teaching, and it may be that the Gospel, which hitherto had been reserved for the instruction of an inner group of advanced disciples, was now revised for publication to a wider circle. This revision was undertaken by the Redactor, who evidently felt himself free to rearrange the order of the sections, and also, it may be, to interpolate a certain amount of new material and to emphasize certain polemical topics (e.g. the question of the ' Baptist Sect ') which had become of greater urgency since the time when the Evangelist first wrote his Gospel. If it be held proved that the Gospel was originally written in Aramaic, an attractive theory would be that it was the Redactor who translated it into Greek. Such a theory has the great advantage that it provides a more definite occasion not only for the interpolation of new material, but also for

[1] Streeter, op. cit., p. 470.

the disturbance of what appears to have been the original order of the text. This cannot always be put down to accident, nor is it quite easy to understand why a chance ' editor ' should have set himself to rearrange and to insert additions into a Gospel already in circulation in much the same form as that in which now we have it. But if at some point it was necessary for the Gospel to be translated and adapted for the use of a new and wider circle of readers, we may well suppose that the translator might take the opportunity of making what additions he felt to be necessary : and, as will be noted in the commentary, the most obvious cases of disarrangement of the text occur just at the points where interpolation is suspected.[1]

Finally, be it said that to hold the Redactor responsible for encouraging the tendency to identify the Evangelist with the Beloved Disciple and the latter with John the son of Zebedee (both parts of which double identification we hold to be incorrect) is not, as Sanday alleges, ' wantonly to accuse him of untruth ' and thereby to ' libel the dead.' To write, or to publish another's work, under a pseudonym was a recognized literary device of the age, and no blame whatever attached to those who did so. Witness the second-century writer who published the story of Paul and Thecla under the name of the Apostle Paul, and when reproached for doing so merely replied that he did it out of love for Paul. Tertullian, who records the incident, imputes no blame to him, but merely ridicules him, ' as if his work could do anything to increase the fame of Paul ! ' Ancient literary ethics were not ours, and we must refrain from reading back modern standards into a remote past.

Have we not been apt to overestimate the importance of the question of our Gospel's authorship ? Is the Gospel any the less precious if John the son of Zebedee had no part in its composition ? One recalls the oft-quoted words of Thiersch : ' If there were a great picture which tradition had affirmed to be painted by Raphael, and it was proved not to have been painted by Raphael, but by some otherwise unknown artist,

[1] See an article in *The Expositor*, November 1923, p. 370 ff.

the world would have not one great painting the less, but one great painter the more.' Whoever wrote it, the Fourth Gospel will always be the Holy of Holies of Christian literature. Whoever Witness, Evangelist, Redactor may have been, to all three the world owes its gratitude for the book which is, as Luther puts it, the 'chiefest of the Gospels, unique, tender, and true.'

THE GOSPEL OF JOHN

ANALYSIS

PRELUDE. CHAPTER I

1. Prologue : The Incarnation of the Logos (1–18).
2. Historical Introduction : The Old Master and the New (19-51).

ACT I. THE NEW GOSPEL AND THE OLD

1. The Relation of the New to the Old.
   Illustrations :
   - (i) Water turned into Wine. (2 : 1–11.)
   - (ii) Cleansing of the Temple. (2 : 12–22.)

   Themes :
   - (i) The New Birth—in relation to Pharisaism. (2 : 23–3 : 13 ; 3 : 31–36.)
   - (ii) The New Master—in relation to the Baptist. (3 : 22–30.)
   - (iii) The New Worship—in relation to the Samaritans. (4 : 1–42.)

2. The Appropriation of the New Gospel.
   Illustrations :
   - (i) The Officer's Son healed : Christ restores Life. (4 : 43–54.)
   - (ii) The 5,000 fed : Christ sustains Life. (6 : 1–15.)
   - (iii) Christ walks on the Water : The ever-present Saviour. (6 : 16–21.)

   Theme :
   The partaking of Christ the Bread of Life. (6 : 22–71.)

3. The Result of the New Gospel.
   Illustration :
   The Lame Man healed on the Sabbath. (5 : 1–16.)
   Theme :
   Religion not restrain but Life. (5 : 17–47 ; 7 : 15–24 ; 8 : 12–20.)

[handwritten note in margin: not right]

ACT II. THE CONFLICT OF THE NEW GOSPEL WITH THE OLD

1. The Divine Origin of the Christ.
    Illustration :
        Jesus and his Brothers. (7 : 1–14, 25–27.)
    Theme :
        Christ's Divine Commission. (7 : 28–8 : 11 ; 8 : 21–59.)
2. The Divine Nature of the Christ.
    Illustration :
        The Blind Man healed. (9 : 1–38.)
    Theme :
        Christ the Light, the Good Shepherd, the Door. (9 : 39–10 : 42.)
3. The Divine Work of the Christ—the Gift of Life and the Awaking of Faith.
    Illustration :
        The Raising of Lazarus. (11 : 1–57.)
    Themes :
        (i) The Homage of a Disciple. (12 : 1–8.)
        (ii) The Homage of the Jews. (12 : 9–19.)
        (iii) The Homage of the Gentile World. (12 : 20–36.)
    Conclusion :
        The Struggle of Faith with Unbelief. (12 : 37–50.)

ACT III. THE ENJOYMENT OF THE NEW GOSPEL : CHRIST'S COMMUNION WITH HIS OWN
    Illustrations :
        (i) The Washing of the Disciples' Feet. (13 : 1–38.)
        (ii) The Allegory of the Vine. (15 : 1–17.)
    Themes :
        (i) The Time of Separation. (15 : 18–16 : 33.)
        (ii) The Promised Communion. (14 : 1–31.)
        (iii) The Prayer of Consecration. (17 : 1–26.)

FINALE

1. The Arrest and Trial. (18 : 1–19 : 16.)
2. The Crucifixion of Christ. (19 : 17–42.)
3. The Resurrection of Christ. (20 : 1–31.)

EPILOGUE

The Appendix. (21 : 1–25.)

THE GOSPEL OF JOHN

PRELUDE

Section I. Prologue: The Incarnation of the Logos (1 : 1–18)

The first eighteen verses form an introductory preface to the
Gospel. This 'Prologue' is poetical in structure, and is
virtually a Hymn to the Logos, consisting of a scheme of
distiches and tristiches, each showing a more or less complete
and characteristically Hebraic parallelism within itself, with
the addition of two prose parentheses at verses 6–8 and 15.
Though the Prologue cannot be fully understood except in the
light of the Gospel itself, it may be regarded as a summary in
the sense that it adumbrates the three cardinal ideas of the
Gospel: (1) Jesus Christ in his Person is the Revelation of
God (vers. 1 and 14); (2) the peculiar work of Jesus was
to impart life (ver. 4); (3) this life is communicated through
union with Christ (vers. 12–13).

St. John, says Chrysostom, 'made ready his soul as some
well-fashioned and jewelled lyre with strings of gold, and
yielded it for the utterance of something great and sublime
to the spirit,' and here we have the prelude to his symphony.

The Logos existed in the very beginning,	1
the Logos was with God,	
the Logos was divine.	
He was with God in the very beginning:	2
through him all existence came into being,	3
no existence came into being apart from him.	
In him life lay,	4
and this life was the Light for men :	
amid the darkness the Light shone,	5
but the darkness did not master it.	

3

The first sentence strikes the keynote which rings through
1 the whole Gospel: **The Logos existed in the very beginning.**
The appearance on earth of the Incarnate Logos is the first
act of a New Creation to be compared and contrasted with
the first creation of the universe. (Paul voices the same idea
in 2 Cor. 4: 6.) Here, as in Gen. 1 : 1, **the beginning** is
the initial moment of the world's creation, but the word
existed implies the *eternal* pre-existence of the Logos in the
sense of Prov. 8: 23 (of Wisdom): ' I was set up from everlasting, from the beginning, or ever the earth was.' (Cf.
17: 5 and 1 Jn. 1: 1, Rev. 3: 14.) The term **Logos**, though in
the N.T. used absolutely only here and at 14, is introduced
without any explanation as one of those semi-popular scientific
terms current at the time which all would understand. (See
Introduction, p. xxxiv ff.)

The Logos was with God : ' towards God,' ' not absorbed
in Him, but standing over against Him as a distinct person '
(E. F. Scott). The word **with** (in the Greek), while emphasizing the communion of the Logos with God, yet safeguards the idea of his individual personality: it expresses
nearness combined with the sense of *movement towards* God,
and so indicates an active relationship. The Logos and God
do not simply exist side by side, but are on terms of living
intercourse, and such fellowship implies separate personality.
The Logos, as Chrysostom says, is ' not in God but with God, as
person with person, eternally.' This distinction of persons, so
strongly emphasized by the second proposition of verse 1,
though still implied, is resolved into a community of essence in
the third proposition, **the Logos was divine.** John does not say
' the Logos was *God* ' ; still less does he imply merely that the
Logos possessed certain divine *qualities*. He means that the
Logos was partaker of the divine *essence*. In what sense
Christ can thus be ' God ' and yet not the whole Godhead but
a Person distinct from God, is just the problem which the
doctrine of the Trinity seeks to solve.

2–3 After summing up in a single sentence the three propositions
of verse 1, John dwells upon the part played by the Logos in
the World's Creation. **Through him all existence came**

into being : the last three words imply a subtle contrast with the eternal being of the Logos (cf. 8 : 58, ' I have existed before Abraham was born ') ; **through** implies that the Logos is not the Source of Creation but the *agent* of God, who is Himself the Source, a distinction which Paul also makes in 1 Cor. 8 : 6, ' There is one God the Father *from* whom all comes . . . one Lord Jesus Christ *by* whom all exists.' The repetition of the same truth in a negative form is an example of the poetic parallelism which we have remarked in the Prologue, but it is characteristic even of John's prose (cf. 3 : 16, 1 Jn. 1 : 5, 5 : 12). In the words no existence . . . apart from him John disowns the multitude of intermediate spiritual beings who, according to the Gnostics, mediated the creative activity of the supreme God—' the angelic Rulers and Powers ' of Col. 2 : 15 (see Introduction, p. xxxii).

In John's conception of the creative activity of ' the Word ' we have an echo both of the Stoic doctrine of the ' Spermatikos ' or ' generative ' Logos, and also of the formula of creation in Gen. 1 ' and God *said*.' ' John gathers up all these sayings of God into a single *saying*, living and endowed with activity and intelligence, from which all divine orders emanate ' (Godet). God's instrument of creation was the Word of power in which He uttered Himself.

Westcott and others join the last words in the Greek of verse 3 (A.V. ' that was made ') with verse 4, and translate, ' Without him was not anything made. *That which hath been made* was life in him,' i.e. ' creation has not '' life in itself '' (5 : 26), but it had and has life in the Word ' (Westcott). But the natural expression would then be not ' was life,' but ' had life ' ; this punctuation, which has the support of the earliest ' Fathers ' (the usual punctuation being ' little if at all earlier than the Fourth Century '—W. H.), was possibly suggested by the apparent tautology of verse 3 as usually punctuated.

If it be retained as the earlier and more difficult and therefore undoubtedly the preferable reading, an interpretation other than Westcott's seems necessary. Loisy takes ' that which was made ' as a ' nominative absolute,' picked up with a

5

change of case in the following clause (for which construction cf. 1 : 12, 15 : 2, 17 : 2, 24), and gives the meaning ' as for that which was made (i.e. the created world), in it there was life ' (ce qui etait devenu, en lui—en cela, dans le monde—fut vie). ' In it ' then refers not to the Logos but to creation : through the activity of the Logos the life-principle first appeared in the world. With one slight modification this seems a perfectly acceptable interpretation : take ' life ' not as subject, but as predicate (the Greek has no definite article) and supply ' the Logos ' as the subject : ' as for creation, in it the Logos was the principle of life, and this life (this time with the article) was the light of men.'

4 Whatever rendering be adopted the central thought remains that in him life lay. If we accept the punctuation in the text there is a gradation from the ' through him ' of verse 3 to the in him of verse 4. Creation, which came into being through the Word, now finds the spring of its life *in* him : ' having been the root of the tree the Logos was also its sap ' (Godet). (For the significance in the Gospel of the term ' life ' see Introduction, p. xxxix.) The meaning here is more comprehensive than usual, and can hardly be restricted to any particular form of life : from the Creative Logos springs life in its most perfect development for every form of existence according to its measure (cf. Acts 17 : 28, ' in him we live and move and exist '). The reference is still to the pre-incarnate Logos, and the force of the imperfect tense lay is to suggest the ideal possibility rather than the realized enjoyment of ' life.' The Word alone had power to give life ; but it was only by the manifestation of the Word and his acceptance by men that the power could be released and the ideal realized in experience.

This life was the Light for men : could men but have appropriated this life, they would have been partakers of the *light*—another important Johannine term (for which see Introduction, p. xxxviii). That life, which for all things else was but the fountain of existence, for man, as a rational and moral being, contained the promise of *light*, a term chosen perhaps just because of its largeness and vagueness and almost

impossible to sum up in one definition, but referring generally to
the divine *truth* (for which see Introduction, p. **xxxviii**), which
illuminates both reason and conscience. In the case of man
the ideal life manifests itself specially in the *knowledge of moral
good*, a gift accessible only to the possessor of both reason and
conscience, the two faculties which distinguish man from the
rest of creation. As beauty is the normal accompaniment of
life in a flower, so should *light* be the normal accompaniment
of life in man. For this connexion of life and light we may
compare Ps. 36 : 9, 'With Thee is the fountain of life : in Thy
light shall we see light.'

But though **amid the darkness the Light shone, the darkness** 5
did not master it. The divine truth was seeking to reveal itself even before the Incarnation—for the reference in **shone**
is not yet to the appearance of the Logos in Christ. In no age
did God leave Himself without the witness of 'the Light':
in the very heart of humanity given over to moral and
spiritual *darkness* the *light* was shining had men but the
spiritual insight to 'comprehend it' (A.V.). In this opposition of light and darkness (cf. 8 : 12, 1 Jn. 1 : 5-7) there is
perhaps an echo of the Gnostic antithesis of two worlds,
the lower and the higher, the earthly and the heavenly, the
world of light and the world of darkness (see note, p. xxxii).
But John is concerned not with a metaphysical or cosmic
but rather with a moral antithesis, and he can hardly be
accused of the physical dualism with which the Gnostics
were tainted. The Prologue, like the Gospel, contemplates
the conflict not of a dualistic universe but of faith with
unbelief.

The darkness did not *master* **it**: the word in Greek, as
indeed in English, has two senses: either (*a*) to 'grasp,'
'comprehend' (of mental grip: so we speak of 'mastering a
problem') ; or (*b*) to 'overcome,' 'subdue.' The Greek inter-
preters, Origen, Chrysostom, etc., take the word in the latter
sense, e.g., Theophylact says, 'The darkness pursued the
light, but found it invincible.' The word occurs in just this
sense in 12 : 35, 'Walk while you have the light, that the
darkness may not *overtake* you' (cf. 1 Thess. 5 : 4). The clause

7

would then mean that the surrounding darkness could not *subdue* the light. ' The whole phrase is indeed a startling paradox. The light does not banish the darkness ; the darkness does not overpower the light. Light and darkness co-exist in the world side by side '(Westcott). But the first (*a*) interpretation gives the word its radical meaning, which is to ' seize ' or ' take possession of ' (cf. Rom. 9 : 30, ' attained righteousness ' ; 1 Cor. 9 : 24, ' gains the prize ' ; Phil. 3 : 12, ' I press forward to *appropriate* it '). By Plato the word is used of mental comprehension, as here in the A.V. rendering. According to this interpretation the reference is to the failure of men in their moral darkness to appreciate and *appropriate* the light, a meaning which, in view of verses 9–11 (which in the original draft of the Gospel perhaps followed immediately after verse 5, see below), seems most in harmony with the context. Dr. Burney, apparently preferring the sense of (*b*), but recognizing that (*a*) is the natural meaning of the Greek word, explains the difficulty by the suggestion that, when the Gospel was translated into Greek, one Aramaic word meaning ' to darken ' was confused with and translated as another almost identical word meaning ' to receive,' the sense of the original Aramaic being ' the Light shone in the darkness and the darkness did not obscure it.'

6 A man appeared, sent by God, whose name was John : he
7   came for the purpose of witnessing, to bear testimony to the Light, so that all men might believe by means of him.
8   He was not the Light ; it was to bear testimony to the
9   Light that he appeared. The real Light, which enlightens every man, was coming then into the world :
10   he entered the world—
     the world which existed through him—
     yet the world did not recognize him ;
11   he came to what was his own,
     yet his own folk did not welcome him.
12 On those who have accepted him, however, he has conferred the right of being children of God, that is, on those who
13   believe in his Name, who owe this birth of theirs to God,

not to human blood, nor to any impulse of the flesh or
of man.

The anticipation in verses 6–8 of John's witness, to which 6
we recur at verse 19, seems very abruptly introduced into the
Prologue. Verses 6–8 interrupt the exposition of the Logos
doctrine, and verse 9 would very fittingly follow immediately
after verse 5 ; nor is there any place for these verses in the
rhythmical scheme into which the Hymn to the Logos falls.
The whole passage 1–18 is so carefully composed that we can
hardly believe that the original author is responsible for the
violent interruption caused by these verses, which should probably be assigned to the Redactor (see p. xliv). The motive
for the addition is in the first place the Redactor's desire
to assert the superiority of Jesus to John, which we have
noted as one of the polemical aims of the Gospel (see p. xxx).
The introduction of John at this point also serves to connect
the theological doctrine of the Logos with the historical
narrative in such a way that the Gospel is brought more into
line with the Synoptic tradition—another characteristic aim
of the Redactor. 'Dans la tradition synoptique le baptême
du Christ apparût comme la consécration de son rôle mes-
sianique ; . . . de là vient que la définition même de l'incarnation du Logos se trouve maintenant comme enchassée dans le
paragraph consacré au Baptiste ; . . . mais la combinaison
appartient au rédacteur qui a surchargé le prologue '(Loisy).

A man appeared, sent by God—the words **man, appeared**
imply a subtle contrast (but is it intentional ?) with the
eternal *existence* of the *divine* Logos, while in **sent** we have
a reference to Mal. 3 : 1, another echo of the Synoptics (Mk.
1 : 2, etc. ; cf. also Jn. 3 : 28)—**whose name was John.** It
has been noted that our author alone among the Evangelists
omits the epithet ' Baptist,' by which tradition distinguished
the Prophet from John the Apostle, from which omission it has
been rather gratuitously deduced not only that ' the author
of our Gospel must have known the forerunner otherwise
than by tradition ' (Godet), but even that he is ' himself
the other John of the Gospel history,' and that therefore ' it is

perfectly natural that he should think of the Baptist, apart from himself, as John only' (Westcott). As no other John is mentioned by name in the Gospel the distinguishing epithet is unnecessary. Moreover, our Evangelist, in contrast to his predecessors, ignores the fact that Jesus was *baptized* by John

7 (see p. 33). **He came for the purpose of witnessing,** one of the fundamental ideas of the Gospel, for indeed 'the whole of the Gospel is a citing of witnesses' (Dods). The first of this 'cloud of witnesses' is John, who came **to bear testimony to the Light** both by fanning, by means of his call to repentance, the light of conscience wherein the Logos was already immanent in men's hearts (cf. 4 *b*), but chiefly by pointing them to him who was himself the Logos incarnate. Here, as throughout the Gospel, the end of all witnessing is that **all men might believe by means of him,** that is, believe in Christ through John, not believe in God through Christ ; the point in question is the support lent to faith not by Christ but by John. For the significance of the term **believe** in the Gospel compare 3 : 15. While from one point of view the life-giving power of Christ is self-evident (5 : 34), yet if **all men** are to believe, there must be many who 'believe though they have never seen' (20 : 29), and whose faith must be supported by the witness of others.

8 *He* **was not the Light :** the emphasis is not on the verbal idea but on the subject : 'it was not *John* who was the Light, but another' ; it was merely **to bear testimony to the Light that he appeared** (the last word being added to supply an awkward ellipse in the Greek). Though the same contrast between Christ and John appears also in the Synoptics (Mt. 3 : 11-12, etc.), the absolute superiority of Jesus would hardly be so emphasized and reiterated throughout the Gospel (1 : 15, 3 : 28-30, 5 : 36, 10 : 41) were it not being denied in certain quarters. Our Gospel insists that John is not the light, but merely a lamp that burns and shines with a borrowed

9 glow (5 : 35), in contrast to the Logos who is **the** *real* **Light.** 'True' or 'real' in our Gospel (cf. 6 : 32, 15 : 1, 17 : 3, etc.) signifies not so much the true in opposition to the false as the ideal and perfect *pattern* in contrast to the imperfect or sym-

bolical imitation. There is here an obvious kinship of thought
with the Platonic theory of 'ideas,' but, as Loisy rightly
remarks, 'It does not follow (from this trace of Hellenism)
that the spiritual world is the " world of ideas " (Heitmüller) :
it is the world of divine and heavenly *realities*.' John is
preparing the way for his claim that in Christ we have the
absolute revelation of God, a message which may be capable of
new and larger interpretation (cf. 16 : 14, 'He—the Spirit—
will draw upon what is mine and disclose it to you '), but will
always be the same message revealed through him perfectly
and therefore once for all. The forerunners of Christ, even
John, the greatest of them, were only reflections of the light
which was directly manifest in him, who is accordingly the
only *genuine* light which enlightens every man (cf. ver. 4)—
the words on which the Quakers found their doctrine that to
every man God gives a sufficiency of inward light and grace :
every conscience in some degree is illuminated by the immanent Light, which from the beginning of time, and now
particularly in the days of the Baptist, **was coming into the
world.** The last words should almost certainly be connected
with ' the real Light,' and not with ' every man,' as understood by most ancient commentators and some modern, who
translate with the A.V. ' (the Logos) was the true light, which
lighteth every man that cometh (or " as he is coming ")
into the world,' implying that the inner light is a man's birth-
gift bestowed in largest measure at the moment when he enters
life, an idea which, ' in spite of Wordsworth's greatest Ode, is
hardly true ' (Westcott). In support of this reading it may
be noted that there seems to have been a common Rabbinic
phrase, ' all comers into the world ' (e.g. see a striking parallel
to our passage from the Midrash Rabba on Leviticus, par.
31,6 : ' Thou givest light to those that are above and to those
that are below, and to *all comers into the world* '). But here
' coming into the world ' seems to demand the same reference
as ' entered the world ' in the following verse, and indeed in
our Gospel the phrase is applied almost technically to the
appearing of Christ (3 : 19, 6 : 14, 12 : 46, 18 : 37). Here
the words are not explanatory of the relative clause—' which

lighteth every man by coming into the world' (Godet)—
but contain in themselves the main verbal idea of the sentence, 'was' and 'coming,' though widely separated in the
Greek, being linked together as a periphrastic imperfect (cf.
11 : 1, 18 : 18, etc.), possibly with the intention of 'describing
a coming which was progressive, slowly accomplished,
combined with a permanent being' (Westcott). This gradual
self-manifestation of the immanent Logos reached its consum-
10 mation when **he entered the world**. Those who delight in
meticulous analysis may find a gradation in the three phrases,
'entered the world,' 'came to what was his own' (11), 'tarried
among us' (14), understanding the first of the vague 'manifestation of the Light as immanent' (Westcott), the second
of the more definite O.T. revelation, and the third, and this
only, of the appearance of the Word incarnate in Christ.
Though not excluding altogether the wider reference, we may
assume that from 10 onwards John has chiefly in view the
personal revelation of the Logos in Christ. The gradation
is not so much one of time as of emphasis : the Logos 'was
on his way to the world,' 'he arrived,' 'he came to his own
folk,' 'he actually made himself one with them.' **The world**
should no doubt be understood here in its primary sense of
the sum total of the results of the creative activity of the
Logos, **the world which existed through him**. The Logos
filled the world 'as the Spirit of an artist fills his work' (Godet),
and **yet the world did not recognize him** (cf. 1 Cor. 1 : 21).
Here is the first hint of that tragic opposition of the world to
the Christian community which is everywhere presupposed in
the Gospel, and is doubtless due to the historical conditions
under which it was written (cf. 7 : 7, 15 : 18, 16 : 20, 17 : 14,
etc., 1 Jn. 2 : 15–17, 5 : 19). Though there are frequent
traces of the Synoptic conception of God's universal love
for all the world (1 : 29, 3 : 16, 4 : 42, 6 : 33, 8 : 12, 12 : 47,
etc.), John in general conceives the work of Christ to be to
draw to himself certain disciples out of the unbelieving mass
and to consecrate them as a people apart, within the world
and yet 'his own' and no part of it (13 : 1, 14 : 19, 22 ; 17 : 9,
etc.), just as Yahweh chose Israel as His 'peculiar people.'

Here is the significance of the next verse, he came to what 11 was his own, or to his *own home* (cf. 19 : 27, 16 : 32), a phrase no doubt applicable to the world in general, thought of as the property of the Logos who created it, but more probably referring to a smaller circle within the larger one (13 : 1—' his own which were in the world '), that is, to the land and people of Israel, who in a special sense were God's ' peculiar treasure ' (Exod. 19 : 5, Deut. 7 : 6-7). Yet his own folk did not welcome him, gave him no reception, the word used of welcoming a traveller to his rightful home, as in 14 : 3—' I will come back and *take you* to be with me.'

The Logos finds his own home shut against him, and yet 12 there is a minority of *individuals*, so few as almost to be a countable number (the force of the Greek pronoun), who have accepted him, and on these he has conferred the right of being children of God.   The man who ' accepts ' (not so strong a word as ' welcome ' above, but implying the desire to take something which is within reach : cf. 13 : 20) the Logos receives a legitimate title or warrant, a faculty not inherent (as maintained by the Gnostic doctrine of the higher nature) but bestowed (Gk. *exousia*—not *dynamis*), in virtue of which he may *become* (A.V.) a *child* of God.   The gift in view is not yet sonship but rather the title to sonship, which becomes a reality through the ' new birth.'   There is an interesting parallel from Philo (*Conf. ling.* 28, quoted by E. F. Scott, *The Fourth Gospel*, p. 153) :   ' They who have real knowledge of the one Creator and Father of all things are rightly addressed as the sons of the one God.   And even if we are *not yet* fit to be called the sons of God, still we may deserve to be called the children of His eternal image, of His most sacred Logos.' When speaking of man's relation to God John regularly uses ' child,' not ' son ' as does Paul, the reason being that Paul's view of sonship is governed by the legal idea of ' adoption,' which carries with it a new standing as ' son ' in God's sight (cf. Rom. 8 : 15, Gal. 4 : 5, Eph. 1 : 5), whereas John's view is wholly mystical, and is focused on the begetting of the ' child ' by the direct communication of God's life : ' son ' implies the

C   13

dignity of heirship, 'child' a community of nature. We perhaps have here an echo of the language of the Greek Mystery-Religions, which employed the word here translated 'right' (*exousia*) to express the 'power' bestowed upon the 'reborn' man to become as God Himself. But John's interest is not in pagan mysticism but in Christian experience : he knew, as we all do, that what prevents a man from being a 'child of God' is not a disability of nature, but an inability of will which makes it impossible for him to *believe* that God is a Father. He therefore defines the new power which comes with the acceptance of the Logos by describing its possessors as **those who believe in his Name,** that is, acknowledge him to be all that he professes to be (*name* implying the sum of the qualities which belong to its bearer), for it is only through *faith* that they can claim their right to sonship (1 Jn. 5 : 1, and for the part which must be played by the believer in the realization of sonship, cf. 2 Pet. 1 : 3 ff., 10 ; Phil. 2 : 12–13). In this verse John substitutes for Jewish nationalism the great Christian idea of individualism in matters of faith, while in his conception of a minority who have welcomed the light we have a parallel both with the Synoptic idea that ' many are called and few chosen,' and also with the Pauline doctrine of a divine election : ' only while Paul insists on the direct agency of God in choosing or rejecting, John makes use of the idea of predisposition on the part of men themselves ' (Scott, op. cit., p. 278).

13   This believing minority is now further described as those **who owe this birth of theirs to God, not to human blood, nor to any impulse of the flesh or of man**—the negative clauses bearing no particular significance in themselves, but emphasizing by way of contrast the true source of life, which is neither ordinary physical generation, nor sexual instinct, nor human purpose, but God Himself (cf. Rom. 8 : 4 ff., Gal. 5 : 16 ff.). Unless the relative clause be taken rather unnaturally not with the preceding words ' those who believe ' but by a construction *ad sensum* with ' children of God,' as descriptive of divine sonship in the ideal, the past tense of the verb (A.V. ' were born ') would appear to imply that

regeneration, instead of being the *result* of the right bestowed by the Logos on believers, is anterior to faith, and due to an inherent spirituality of nature. This would be a Gnostic but hardly a Johannine conception. Perhaps this is to insist too rigorously on strict grammar ; but the difficulty would be overcome and the sense greatly improved were it possible to adopt the Latin variant, according to which the relative sentence is a definition of the source of the life not of believers but of the *Logos*, who being born of God was thus able to give to those who received him power to become the children of God (cf. a somewhat similar thought in 6 : 57). Dr. Burney (*Aramaic Origin*, p. 34) shows that assuming an Aramaic original the difference between the two readings involves solely the insertion or omission of a single letter. He would render ' he has given them power to become sons of God *in as much as he was born*. . . .' But even if this reading be accepted it is hardly true to say with Burney that ' the writer is drawing out the mystical import of the Virgin Birth,' for the words in question would exclude the idea of human mother no less than of human father (cf. Heb. 7 : 3). The thought of the Virgin birth is outside John's perspective altogether ; indeed, he would seem to replace that doctrine by the doctrine of the incarnation of the Logos, who even before his birth in time was the eternal Son of God, and became man by his own voluntary act. Hence the transition to the next verse.

So the Logos became flesh and tarried among us ; we have 14 seen his glory—glory such as an only son enjoys from his father—seen it to be full of grace and reality. (John 15 testified to him with the cry, ' This was he of whom I said, my successor has taken precedence of me, for he preceded me.') For we have all been receiving grace after grace 16 from his fulness ; while the Law was given through 17 Moses, grace and reality are ours through Jesus Christ. Nobody has ever seen God, but God has been unfolded by 18 the divine One, the only Son, who lies upon the Father's breast.

14 So the Logos became flesh and tarried among us—the most amazing of all paradoxes, the effect of which is heightened by the implied contrast with verse 1: he who '*existed* in the very beginning' '*became*'; he who 'was *divine*' 'became *flesh*'; he who 'was *with God*' 'tarried *among us*.' Flesh or 'flesh and blood,' though no doubt descriptive of humanity from the side of its weakness and mortality, is the regular Jewish term for a human 'personality' in its totality, and does not exclude the idea of 'soul' and 'spirit.' The meaning is that the Logos became a *real human person*. True, at the Incarnation the Logos became not 'a man' but 'man,' 'flesh.' He did not then acquire personality, for he already possessed it, but he identified his pre-existent personality with real human nature. John thus combats prevalent 'Docetic' ideas concerning the person of Christ, which held that he was man only in appearance (cf. 1 Jn. 4: 1-3, 2 Jn. 7). The Logos became a real man and a whole man, and that without ceasing to be himself. Beyond noting that as compared with Paul's letters the emphasis is removed in our Gospel from Christ's death to his coming in the flesh we need not concern ourselves here with the mass of theological speculation which has grown up around these words. By the vague word **became** John commits himself tc no precise theory of the incarnation. His purpose was not to reason out the 'how' and the 'why' of the union of the Logos-nature with human nature, but to impress it upon his readers as a fact already realized in his own experience, by the knowledge of which they too 'might have life.' The difficulty begins when one attempts to define in terms of metaphysics a conviction based on actual religious experience. But John does not trouble himself about such questions: 'The Logos doctrine as John accepted it was only an attempt, and necessarily a vain attempt, to define by reason a truth which he had apprehended by faith' (Scott, *The Fourth Gospel*, p. 163).

The words **the Logos became** flesh mark the transition to the subject of the Gospel proper, which is not metaphysics but 'spiritualized' history, not the Logos but Jesus Christ. Hence **the Logos** is never again expressly mentioned. Yet

John did Christianity a great service by thus bringing the historical faith into relation with contemporary philosophic thought and holding the balance between the two. By his emphasis on inward religious experience he saved Christianity from the danger of either dissolving into philosophical allegory or degenerating into mere historical reminiscence. The antithesis between the 'eternal' and the historical is once for all resolved in the Logos who became flesh and **tarried among us,** or (to give the Greek word its original force, though in late Greek it meant simply 'to dwell') '*tabernacled* among us,' as Yahweh tabernacled among His people in the Wilderness (2 Sam. 7: 6, etc.). The Logos, like Yahweh, was 'himself a pilgrim among his pilgrim people' (Godet), perhaps with the notion of a transient sojourn, as suggested by the idea both of a tent and of the shortness of human life in the flesh (2 Cor. 5: 1; 2 Pet. 1: 13). In the form of the Greek word there is probably an allusion to the 'Shekinah' or 'divine presence,' the word used in the Targums, or Rabbinic expositions of the O.T., to denote God as manifesting Himself in human life—it being thought irreverent to bring God Himself into too close touch with humanity. (Cf. Gen. 28: 16, where Jacob's words, 'God is in this place,' are interpreted by the Targumist 'the glory of the Shekinah of Yahweh is in this place.') The same reference should probably be traced in Rev. 21: 3. It is obvious that the writer's affinities are far more with Jewish than with Hellenistic thought; thus when he adds **we have seen his** *glory* there is almost certainly a reference to the second term used in the Targums to describe God's self-manifestation, the 'Yekara' or 'glory' of the Lord (Hebrew 'kabhodh.' Cf. Exod. 3: 6, 'he was afraid to look upon God,' which is interpreted by the Targumist 'he was afraid to look upon the manifestation of the Yekara of the Lord'). This lends probability to the view that for his Logos conception John is largely indebted to the idea of the 'Memra' or 'Word' of God—the third Targumic term used of God's self-manifestation—as well as to contemporary Hellenistic thought. As the glory of Yahweh filled His Tabernacle (Exod. 40: 34, etc.), so, says John, did the divine glory manifest itself in the person of Christ **among us** men, and **we have seen** it. This clause is held to prove that the writer was an actual eye-witness of Jesus. No special force can be claimed for the word translated ' seen,' for though it originally implied a prolonged intense gaze it came later to mean simply ' see.' If the aorist tense seems to be too definite to imply a mere generalization—' we ' referring to Christians in general and ' have seen ' ' not to physical sight but to the penetrating vision of enlightened faith ' (Loisy)— then we may perhaps assume that the writer, though not necessarily a personal follower of Jesus, had as a child come into personal contact with him, and so felt himself to belong to the generation (' we ') to which the divine revelation had been made in a form perceptible to the senses (cf. 1 Jn. 1 : 1–3). Yet the idea of spiritual contemplation is certainly not excluded : ' This beholding John treasured as the wealth and joy of his life ' (Dods). The glory of Christ was *unique—* **glory such as an** *only son* (cf. 3 : 16, 1 Jn. 4 : 9) **enjoys from his father**—for it is the reflection of a sonship which is quite unique, to which ' the right of being children of God,' possessed by the rest of mankind, presents no parallel. The term **only-son** (Gk. *monogenes*) had already been applied by Philo to the Logos, and so provided John with a speculative basis for the doctrine of Christ's sonship, and affords a link between the Prologue and the Gospel proper. But the translation ' only-*begotten* ' tends to obscure the sense, for the emphasis is not upon the generation from the Father— as is usually the case when Philo applies the term to the Logos—though of course the idea of oneness of essence is implied, but to the uniqueness of the ethical relationship existing between father and son—a good illustration of the difference in outlook of the two writers : Philo uses the word as a technical term of philosophy, John to express the unique relationship of an only son who is united to his father by a bond of mutual love supreme and unique (cf. 17 : 23, 24, 26 ; and for use of word to denote an ' only child ' Lk. 7 : 12, Heb. 11 : 17). The unique Sonship of Christ is one of the central themes of the Gospel, which, as contrasted with the Synoptics, regards the confession of Christ's sonship not as faith's climax (Mt. 16 : 16) but as its starting-point, almost its presupposition. To describe Christ as the ' only Son ' of God is simply to acknowledge the divine character of his nature and teaching. Hence the reference to his **glory,** which implies his divine majesty and power ; this John no doubt considered to be manifested in a special degree in Christ's miracles (2 : 11), but he here acknowledges that it consists primarily in his unique filial consciousness, ' the inward certainty of his exceptional relation to the Father and the moral splendour which the certainty of such a bond spread over his whole person ' (Godet). In other words, Christ's ' glory ' is primarily not metaphysical but ethical and spiritual, and John therefore further defines it by saying that it is **full of grace and reality** ('full' is to be taken not as a nominative referring back to the Logos, but as an indeclinable form in agreement with the accusative 'glory'). The two supreme qualities having their source in the Logos, which are defined metaphysically as ' life ' and ' light,' when viewed from the ethical standpoint become **grace** and **reality** respectively. The phrase ' mercy and truth ' is frequent in the O.T. (cf. Ps. 25 : 10, Exod. 34 : 6, etc.), but for ' mercy ' John substitutes ' grace,' thus emphasizing the truth that God does not merely spare men out of compassion, but that in Christ he actively loves and blesses them (3 : 16). Just because the glory of Christ is revealed above all in his grace we find that the word ' glory ' is frequently used in our Gospel with special reference to the Cross, which is the supreme symbol of his grace. Note specially 13 : 31, ' now— immediately after Judas goes out to betray him—is the Son of man glorified,' and see notes on 7 : 39 and 11 : 4. (For the force of ' reality ' see note on ' real ' (ver. 9) and on 17 below, and Introduction, p. xxxviii.)

The testimony of the Baptist, suddenly reintroduced at verse 15, interrupts most awkwardly the clear connexion between 14 and 16, and seems a rather superfluous anticipation of 27 and 30. Moreover, the text is doubtful, and it is not clear to what occasion the Baptist refers in the words 'This was he of whom I said.' The verse is almost certainly interpolated by the

Redactor with the purpose of setting once again in the fore-front of the Gospel the truth of Christ's eternal existence and his consequent superiority to John. We may postpone consideration of John's testimony till verses 27 and 30.

16 When 15 is omitted the next words continue the thought of 14, 16 developing the idea of 'grace,' 17 and 18 that of 'reality.' We know Christ's glory to be full of grace and reality for—as a fact of experience—**we have all been receiving grace after grace from his fulness.** By the addition of the word **all** John extends the scope of his words to include not only the witnesses of 14 but all Christians who ' believe even though they have never seen.' **Fulness** picks up the thought of ' full ' in 14, and in both there is probably an implied denial of the Gnostic doctrine that the Logos-Spirit merely descended temporarily, out of the divine ' fulness,' upon the man Jesus. John like Paul insists that the ' fulness ' is his—Christ's—own, that ' it is in Christ that the entire Fulness of deity has settled bodily ' (Col. 2 : 9 and cf. Col. 1 : 19, Eph. 1 : 23, 3 : 19, 4 : 13). The totality of the divine attributes is summed up in Christ, and from him, as from a spring of divine life, Christians are daily receiving **grace after grace.** The literal meaning is ' grace in exchange for grace,' implying not merely that one grace is heaped upon another, but that every grace appropriated and used is made good by the gift of more grace to take its place. There is an interesting parallel in Philo (*Post. Cain.* 43) : it is not God's will that men should be sated with one grace, for He gives them ' a second grace in exchange for the first and a third in exchange for the second and ever new graces in exchange for old.' As one wave follows another from the depths of the ocean, so there flows from Christ's fulness ' wave upon wave of grace.' And it is from Christ's fulness alone that it flows ; for, though it is true that

17 **the Law was given through Moses,** yet **grace and reality are ours,** not through Moses or any other religious leader, however great, but only **through Jesus Christ.** Here we have at last the express identification of the eternal Logos with Jesus, who is here mentioned by name for the first time. John contrasts the Gospel of Jesus with the Law of Moses.

The Law was given ' as an addition to the essential scheme of salvation ' as though ' designed to meet special circumstances ': the Gospel is ours, ' came,' ' according to the due course of the divine plan ' as something which ' satisfies man's essential nature' (quotations from Westcott). The Law demanded obedience from men: the Gospel revealed the *grace* of God to men. The Law spoke only through symbols, and gave men but ' a mere shadow of the bliss that is to be ' (Heb. 10: 1, Col. 2: 17): in Christ we have not symbol but substance, not the shadow of bliss but its *reality*. According to John this ' reality,' this ' eternal life,' which is the supreme reward of faith, is identical with the knowledge or vision of God (17: 3), and it can be bestowed only by Christ, because nobody has ever seen God (a favourite Johannine thought ; 18 cf. 5: 37, 6: 46, 1 Jn. 4: 12, 20) with the vision of sense, not even Moses, who prayed to be granted that vision (Exod. 33: 18 ff.) ; but God has been unfolded by the divine One, the only Son, who lies upon the Father's breast, a position symbolical of the tenderest possible relationship (cf. 13: 23, Num. 11: 12, Deut. 13: 6), which John assigns to Christ not merely in virtue of his Ascension (an incident for which John has no place in his scheme of thought, see p. 359 f.), but in virtue of that glory which he had ' before the foundation of the world ' (17: 5). The correct reading is almost certainly not, as in A.V., ' the only-begotten Son,' but ' God only begotten,' referring of course to Christ. There is little difference in the meaning except that the latter reading emphasizes more strikingly the unique divinity of Christ's Person by combining in one phrase the two great predicates which have already been applied to the Logos—his divine nature (ver. 1) and his unique Sonship (ver. 14). In any case some such periphrasis as that in our translation is necessary to bring out the full meaning. The word here translated **unfolded** is used of ' interpreting' dreams (Gen. 41: 8, etc.), and tne substantive form, ' interpreter ' or ' exegete,' was the name given in the language of the Greek Mysteries to the priest who initiated the worshippers into those rites through which they hoped to ' see God ' and thereby be ' reborn and become themselves immortal and divine. In Christ alone, says John, do we find the real interpretation, the true ' exegesis ' of God. Thus the Prologue ends : henceforth we quit speculation for the sure ground of history, for John realized that ' the knowledge of God cannot be the result of a philosophical investigation ' (Godet) ; our theme is therefore no longer the Logos but Jesus Christ.

SECTION II. HISTORICAL INTRODUCTION : THE OLD MASTER AND THE NEW (1 : 19–51)

The attitude of our writer to the Baptist has already been noted (p. xxx). The witness to Christ by his ' Forerunner,' already anticipated in the Prologue (6–8, 15), is now resumed in greater detail with the customary emphasis upon John's subordination to Jesus.

19 Now here is John's testimony. When the Jews of Jerusalem despatched priests and Levites to ask him, ' Who are you ? '
20 he frankly confessed—he did not deny it, he frankly
21 confessed, ' I am not the Christ.' They asked him, ' Then what are you ? Elijah ? ' He said, ' I am not.'
22 ' Are you the Prophet ? ' ' No,' he answered. ' Then who are you ? ' they said ; ' tell us, so that we can give some answer to those who sent us. What have you to
23 say for yourself ? ' He said, ' I am
the voice of one who cries in the desert,
" level the way for the Lord "—
24 as the prophet Isaiah said.' Now it was some of the
25 Pharisees who had been sent to him ; so they asked him, saying, ' Then why are you baptizing people, if you are
26 neither the Christ nor Elijah nor the Prophet ? ' ' I am baptizing with water,' John replied, ' but my successor is
27 among you, One whom you do not recognize, and I am
28 not fit to untie the string of his sandal.' This took place at Bethany on the opposite side of the Jordan, where John was baptizing.

The Jews in our Gospel are regarded as the ' official opposition ' to Jesus and his party, a point of view which reflects conditions at the time of the Gospel's composition, when Judaism and Christianity were confronting each other as rivals : note especially the conflict between Jesus and ' the Jews ' in chapter 6, which centres on questions in dispute, not in Jesus' own day but at the end of the first century, when the Supper was one of the objects of the Jewish attack on Christianity. The term ' Jews,' which originally denoted the inhabitants of Judaea, had since the Exile come to be applied to all Israelites, including, e.g., the Galileans (6 : 52), and here has a distinctly official flavour signifying the ' entire theocratic community as summed up in its official heads and as historically fixed in an attitude of hostility to Christ ' (Whitelaw). The nation in its religious capacity was officially represented by the Sanhedrim, here vaguely called the Jews of Jerusalem, one of whose functions was to test the claims of ' prophets.' Hence the deputation sent to question John. We may compare Mk. 11 : 27, where the Sanhedrim claims the same authority to test Jesus' claims ; but whereas Mark accurately describes the members of the Sanhedrim as ' chief priests and scribes and elders,' John, ' who has no thought of the Sanhedrim as it was constituted in reality ' (Loisy), more loosely calls the delegates ' priests and Levites,' that is, the two classes representative of the religious side of the nation, ' the higher and lower order of Temple Officials ' (Holtzmann).

In exercise of their authority as guardians of the people's 20 religion the deputation demand of John ' Who are you ? what notable personage do you claim to be ? ' John in reply energetically denies his identity with any of the religious leaders of popular expectation. *He* is not the Christ or the Messiah (the pronoun is emphatic), a denial the force of which lies not so much in the negation as in the implication that someone else *is* the Christ. He is not Elijah, whose personal return 21 would, according to current expectation, herald the appearance of the Messiah (Mal. 4 : 5). In contrast to our Gospel the Synoptics persistently identify John with Elijah, and that upon the authority of Jesus himself (Mt. 11 : 14, 17 : 12, Mk. 9 : 11-13, and compare Mk. 1 : 6 with 2 Kings 1 : 8). But it was in a spiritual sense that Jesus accepted John as Elijah (cf. Lk. 1: 17, ' He will go in front of him *with the spirit and power* of Elijah '), whereas the Jews looked for a personal return of Elijah in the flesh. Neither is John **the Prophet**; that is, ' the prophet like unto Moses ' of Deut. 18: 15, another of the leaders who, according to current expectation, would usher in the Messianic age. It seems that the Jews distinguished him from the Messiah (7: 40, 41 ; but are they identified in 6: 14 ?) ; Christian tradition, on the other hand, came to identify them (Acts 3: 22, 7: 37), Christ being regarded as a second and a higher Moses, whose Gospel had supplanted the Mosaic Law. In the Synoptics, instead of this definite allusion to ' *the* Prophet ' we have the vaguer phrase (used of Christ) ' one of the prophets ' (Mk. 8: 28), and a possible identification of Jeremiah with ' *the* Prophet ' (Mt. 16: 14).

22-23 When the deputation, loath to return with their mission unaccomplished, insist on an answer, John, unwilling to claim for himself any personality worthy of investigation (for this modesty cf. 3: 25-30 ; Westcott aptly quotes, ' Thou art to me No bird, but an invisible thing, A voice, a mystery '), replies that he is merely the voice of one who cries . . . The quotation from Is. 40: 3 (based on the Synoptic form rather than on the text of the LXX), which in the Synoptics (Mk. 1: 2-3 and par.) is applied to John, is by our Evangelist put into John's own lips, and conveys an obvious hint as to the significance of his mission. Just as a special road must be levelled when a king desires to cross a desert—a fruitless waste symbolical of the spiritual condition of the world to which Christ came—so is John to prepare the way for the Messiah. Though our Evangelist omits all reference to John's ethical message of repentance, yet it is implied here, for the recognized preparation for the Messiah was repentance : ' If Israel repent but for one day the Messiah will come.'

24 Though the priestly party, from whom the deputation was drawn (19), was for the most part Sadducean, the Evangelist, possibly to explain the reason for this very subtle and minute interrogation, adds that on this occasion John's questioners were either Pharisees themselves (so our translation : **those**

sent were of the Pharisees), or at least had been primed by
the Pharisees (if we translate with other scholars: ' (they)
were sent from the Pharisees '), and were therefore particularly
interested in questions of ritual such as baptism (4 : 1). This
is more natural than to suppose that the reference is to a
second and separate deputation. Our Evangelist (7 : 32)
gives the composition of the Sanhedrim as ' high-priests
(Sadducean) and Pharisees,' the latter of whom he regards
rather unhistorically not as a popular party scattered
throughout the whole country, but as a competent religious
authority with its headquarters at Jerusalem. It was this
section of the Sanhedrim which stood behind the deputation.
The Evangelist undoubtedly stage-manages the whole scene
in order to lead up to his reference to the ' Baptism by the
Spirit,' which is its chief motive.

The rite of Baptism had a Messianic significance, for it was 25
expected that a general purification of the people would take
place before the coming of the Messiah (Ezek. 36 : 25,
Zech. 13 : 1, Is. 52 : 15). If John denies his identity with
any of the expected Messianic figures, *why then does he
baptize ?* The connexion between answer and question is
not very clear, perhaps because, as Heracleon says, ' John 26
frames his answer to the Pharisees' deputation to fit not their
question but his own desire,' i.e. to lead up to his testimony
to Christ: ' It is true that I am baptizing, and from that
fact you rightly conclude that I have some connexion with
the Messiah ; but my baptism is not the true Messianic purification : it is but symbolical, with water, but the symbol
will soon give place to the reality (the " baptism with the Holy
Spirit " of 33), for my successor is—or stands—among you,
One whom you do not recognize ' (a variant reading adds the 27
words ' who has taken precedence of me,' possibly an interpolation from 30, q.v.). The words may be taken either
literally as implying that Jesus is present in person though
unrecognized among John's hearers (the emphatic word
' stands ' favours this), or more probably in the general sense
(cf. 10) that the Christ they are looking for is already dwelling
all unknown to them upon the earth. Justin (Trypho 8 : 49)

25

alludes to the Jewish tradition of a hidden Messiah who was to be revealed by Elijah. John, so far from seeking to rival that Messiah, holds himself unworthy to perform for him even the most servile task (Mk. I : 7), and one generally considered below the dignity of a disciple : ' Every service which a servant will perform for his master, a disciple will do for his Rabbi, except loosing his sandal thong ' (Talmud).

28   Our Evangelist characteristically (see p. xliii) has no further interest in the result of the deputation, a historical incident introduced simply for the sake of the testimony to which it has led. He now seeks to lend this testimony an air of greater authority by the precision with which he fixes the locality. The name **Bethany** is to be preferred to ' Bethabara ' (A.V.), both on textual grounds and also because the addition **beyond Jordan** is obviously meant to distinguish it from the better-known village of the same name near Jerusalem. The substitution of ' Bethabara ' is probably due to Origen, who himself states that all the old MSS. read ' Bethany,' but that he could find no place of that name on the banks of Jordan, while a place was pointed out to him called ' Bethabara.' But where was this Bethany ? Furrer identifies it with a place now in ruins called Betâne, and possibly the same as Betonim (Josh. 13 : 26). But this place is some way from Jordan, which would be at variance with the Synoptics. Conder thought the Evangelist referred to the province of Batanea, the ancient Bashan, over into which the ford ' Abara ' leads, but an allusion to so wide an area seems pointless. ' Bethany ' may mean ' house of the ferry-boat,' in which case the site may be identical with that of ' Bethabara ' which has the same meaning. The only argument in favour of the latter reading is the rather too ingenious one (Loisy) that ' Bethany ' might possibly have been substituted for an original ' Bethabara ' on the strength of 10 : 40 and 11 : 1, where the name ' Bethany ' occurs immediately after a reference to ' the place where John baptized.' The locality is quite uncertain, but whatever its name it was probably an obscure village in Peraea, not to be confused with the Bethany on the Mount of Olives.

Next day he observed Jesus coming towards him and exclaimed, 29
'Look, there is the lamb of God, who is to remove the
sin of the world! That is he of whom I said, " The man 30
who is to succeed me has taken precedence of me, for he
preceded me." I myself did not recognize him ; I only 31
came to baptize with water, in order that he might be
disclosed to Israel.' And John bore this testimony also : 32
'I saw the Spirit descend like a dove from heaven and
rest on him. I myself did not recognize him, but He who 33
sent me to baptize with water told me, " He on whom
you see the Spirit descending and resting, that is he who
baptizes with the holy Spirit." Now I did see it, and I 34
testify that he is the Son of God.'

This narrative is the Evangelist's substitute for the Synoptic 29
account of Jesus' baptism. **The next day** (for these precise
notes of time cf. 35, 43, 2 : 1, etc.) **John observed Jesus coming
towards him.** The question whence and why Jesus came
is quite irrelevant. 'Christ was probably coming directly
from the Temptation' (Westcott) ; but such artificial attempts
to harmonize our Gospel with the Synoptics are to a degree
'musty' (Holtzmann). The meeting of John with Jesus,
which in the Synoptics (Mk. 1 : 9) has for its object Jesus'
baptism, has here an entirely different significance. So far
as our Evangelist has any interest at all in the baptism, he
appears to regard it as already past (see below, 1 : 32). Jesus
is brought upon the scene at this point simply to furnish John
with another occasion to bear witness to him : this he does
in the words, '**Look, there is the lamb of God** . . .' The definite
article would seem to imply that this was a recognized Messianic
title (cf. ' *the* prophet ') ; but it is likely that the Evangelist
is throwing back into John's words a title which, as applied
to Christ, had in his own day become stereotyped (1 Pet. 1 : 19,
Rev. 5 : 6, 12). The title does far more than merely designate
Jesus as ' one whose confidence had never been disturbed,
whose steadfast peace no agitations of life had ever ruffled '
(Seeley). It seems to be jointly derived from the sacrificial
ritual and from the ' Servant ' passage in Is. 53, and therefore

includes the threefold idea of patient submission, vicarious suffering and redemption from sin. The last of these conceptions in particular is implied in the almost certain allusion to the Paschal Lamb with which our Gospel throughout appears to identify Jesus (see 19: 29, 31, and Introduction, p. xiii; cf. also 1 Cor. 5: 7).

Christ is the lamb *of God*, not merely as the lamb provided by God (Gen. 22: 8), or offered to God, though both these ideas may be present, but rather as being the 'only Son' of God (18, and cf. Is. 53: 11, '*my* righteous servant'); it is as such that he is to remove the sin of the world. The thought of *redemption* inherent in the conception of the Paschal Lamb, rather than of vicarious suffering drawn from Is. 53, seems to be carried out by the word remove (*airein*), which in LXX and N.T. Greek regularly means not to 'take upon oneself' (the 'bearing' of sin in Isaiah is translated in the LXX by *pherein* or *lambanein*), but to 'take out of the way' (cf. 20: 1 and esp. 1 Jn. 3: 5). But the latter thought, while enriching the former, also includes it, for a lamb can only 'remove' sin by vicariously 'bearing' it, and this Christ did (Mt. 8: 17) for the sin of the world—a thought grandly universalistic (cf. 3: 16, 1 Jn. 2: 2) to which it is often objected that the Baptist, with his narrowly patriotic outlook, could hardly have attained. Moreover, apart altogether from the discrepancy with the Synoptic account, is it possible that thus early the Baptist could have appreciated and proclaimed the redemptive efficacy of Christ's death, a faith which only came home to the disciples themselves after the Resurrection (Lk. 24: 21, 26) and of which we have the earliest expression in 1 Cor. 15: 3? We have here a good example of the 'interpretative function' of our Evangelist, who is putting his own thoughts into the Baptist's words, and presenting under the guise of history the truths of his own spiritual experience. Yet it should be remembered that even the Synoptics hint that the Baptist did not limit the work of the Messiah to his own people (Mt. 3:9): he may have been influenced by the universalistic outlook of passages such as Gen. 22: 18, Is.

19 : 23-25, 52 : 15, while, as even Strauss admits, 'a penetrating mind like that of the Baptist might, even before the
death of Jesus, gather from the O.T. phrases and types
the notion of a suffering Messiah, and his obscure hints
on the subject might not be comprehended by his disciples
and contemporaries.' It must be remembered also that the
Baptist may have known something of the mind of Jesus
himself, to whom he was related, and whose meditations on the
meaning of Messiah's mission he may have shared. Nevertheless one cannot escape the conviction that we have here
not literal history, but its interpretation. Indeed, even the
' interpretation ' is not strictly true to the thought of the
Gospel as a whole, a fact which lends some colour to the
suspicion that the Redactor's hand may be traced in the
' Baptist ' sections (see p. xxx). According to our Evangelist
the work of Christ is rather to bestow life than to remove sin,
the problem of which, so central in the mind of Paul, to him
is of quite subordinate interest. Thus in this great saying
of the Baptist, ' it is fairly certain that we have nothing but
a vague concession to earlier doctrine ' (Scott, *The Fourth
Gospel*, p. 219). The writer who ' found the expression already
coined ' (Holtzmann) may have taken it over from current
doctrine without fully appreciating all its implications. (For
similar ' concessions ' cf. 1 : 43, 4 : 41, 6 : 63, 14 : 3, 20 : 17.)

In the approaching Christ John now discovers to the people 30
him of whom he had previously hinted : **That is he of whom
I said, ' The man who is to succeed me** (in point of time) **has
taken precedence of me** (in dignity : ' mightier,' Mk. 1 : 7),
for he preceded me ' (in eternity, in virtue of his pre-existence,
ver. 2). The allusion contained in **of whom I said,** if not to
a previous unrecorded testimony, may be to 27, at any rate
if it be possible to retain the longer reading in that verse,
q.v. ; ver. 15 we have held to be an interpolation anticipating
this verse. But it is exceedingly probable that both verses,
as well as the longer reading in 27, may be redactional additions due to the desire to emphasize Christ's pre-existence
and his consequent superiority to John, in which case it is
the interpolator, not the Baptist, who is in reality harking

back to words which he has previously put into the Baptist's mouth.

31 'I myself did not recognize him' (possibly with an allusion to 26, 'you do not recognize'), that is as Messiah, though probably the two were acquainted as friends (Mt. 3 : 14). According to our Evangelist the chief significance of the vision about to be related is to be found not, as the Synoptists imply, in the divine recognition vouchsafed to *Jesus* and the consequent heightening of his own divine self-consciousness, but in the revelation of his Messiahship, hitherto unrecognized, to *John*. Hence it is John who sees the vision, not Jesus, as in the Synoptics (Mk. 1 : 10–11, Mt. 3 : 16–17). The sole object of John's mission is that he may discover to the people 'the hidden Messiah'; the call to baptize had come to him from God simply that thereby there might be provided the occasion for the manifestation of that Messiah by means of a prearranged vision; John now **bears testimony** that Jesus must be Messiah, for in his case alone the promised

32 vision had been granted: '**I saw the Spirit descend like a dove from heaven and rest on him.**' The reference to the descent of the Spirit on Jesus, borrowed from the Synoptic account of the baptism, proves that our Evangelist thinks of the baptism as already past. The Spirit was a recognized Messianic endowment (Is. 11 : 2, 42 : 1, 61 : 1). The figure of the *dove* may be borrowed from the thought of Gen. 1 : 2, which the Talmud explains: 'The Spirit of God was borne over the waters as a dove which broods over her young' similarly Noah's dove is a symbol of a new creation. But in what sense did the Baptist 'see' the Spirit '**descend like a dove**'? The word implies a steady contemplative gaze, and is probably used here of inward vision. It is the manner of the Spirit's descent, gentle and peaceful (in contrast to the expected warrior Messiah), not his bodily appearance, which is compared with a dove, and the language need not imply that an actual dove was visible, though Luke (3 : 22), from his usual materialistic standpoint—so characteristic of the Physician—describes the vision as an objective fact apparent to all. But such visions are granted only to the spiritually

receptive (cf. 12 : 29). It was not the descent of the dove
(omitted altogether from the corresponding words in 33)
that was the sign to John of Jesus' Messiahship, but his possession of the Spirit. This is brought out by the addition
of the word **resting** ; for Christ, as distinguished from the
prophets and heroes of old on whom the gift came inter-
mittently (2 Kings 3 : 15), the Spirit was a permanent endowment : ' God gives him the Spirit in no sparing measure '
(3 : 34). That Jesus thus possessed the Spirit was abundantly
evident to John—' as plain as if he had seen the Spirit in
visible shape alighting upon him' (Dods). The Baptist there- 33
fore recognized that in Jesus, ' whom I myself did not recognize ' (as Messiah), there had been revealed to him One who,
in virtue of his own possession of the holy Spirit, was able to
baptize not merely with water, but **with the holy Spirit.** For
the pouring out of the holy Spirit as a Messianic phenomenon
parallel with the Messianic ' sprinkling ' (Ezek. 36 : 25), of
which the ' baptism with water ' is symbolic, we may compare Joel 2 : 28. But what is meant by the ' baptism with
the holy Spirit ' ? It implies the *positive* bestowal of new life
as contrasted with the *negative* cleansing from past sin implied
by water-baptism. In our Gospel John is typical of the old
order, Christ of the new—and, as opposed to Judaism, the
characteristically Christian graces are all positive. Luke
(3 : 16) brings this out by the addition, ' he will baptize you
with the holy Spirit *and fire*,' in which connexion the author
of *Ecce Homo* writes, ' Baptism means cleansing and fire
means warmth. How can warmth cleanse ? The answer is
that moral warmth does cleanse. No heart is pure that is
not passionate ; no virtue is safe that is not enthusiastic.
And such an enthusiastic virtue Christ was to introduce.'
Similarly R. L. Stevenson (aptly quoted by Strachan), ' We
are not damned for doing wrong, but for not doing right ;
Christ would never hear of negative morality ; " thou shalt "
was ever his word, with which he superseded " thou shalt
not." '

On the strength of the vision (' now I did **see it** ') John is 34
able to testify that Jesus ' **is the Son of God** '—a Messianic title

the stages in the development of which may be traced in the
O.T. thus: 2 Sam. 7: 14, Ps. 2: 7, Dan. 3: 25. This great
declaration, which in the Synoptic account comes from God
Himself (Mt. 3: 17, in third person, addressed to the bystanders;
Mk. 1: 11, Lk. 3: 22, in second person, addressed to Jesus),
our Evangelist puts in the mouth of John. The perfect tense
'I have testified' may refer either to John's witness in
general, or more particularly to verse 29, in which case
'Son of God' is equivalent to 'lamb of God,' each being a
designation of the Messiah. Some early authorities read
'the chosen one of God,' another Messianic title (Is. 42: 1),
but the Synoptic parallels make the former reading more
probable. (For the full content of the phrase 'Son of God,'
see ver. 14 and again ver. 49.) If here the title seems to be
used merely as an equivalent for 'Messiah,' it is not that the
phrase here lacks its full Johannine content, but rather that
our Evangelist throughout interprets the Messiahship in a far
higher sense than do the Synoptists. The narrow national
conception is so completely absent that 'throughout the
Gospel the Messianic title denotes nothing more definite than
the higher nature and dignity of Jesus as the Son of God. It
is still retained in accordance with the consecrated tradition,
but its meaning is entirely merged in that of the other title.
"The Christ" and "the Son of God" are again and again
co-ordinated as simply equivalent terms (11: 27, 20: 31,
1: 49)' (Scott, *The Fourth Gospel*, p. 183).

What of the relation of this whole section to the first three
Gospels? Like the Synoptists our Evangelist finds in John's
testimony to Jesus a starting-point for his Gospel history.
Moreover, the section appears to be largely built up of Synoptic
material. Verses 23–28 are clearly based on Mk. 1: 2–8,
verses 29–34 on Mk. 1: 9–11. The visit of the deputation
may have been suggested by the similar investigation into
Jesus' authority, and the conversation which follows may be
a purely literary compilation based partly on Herod's speculation about Jesus (Mk. 6: 14–16) and partly on the questions
leading up to Peter's confession (Mk. 8: 27 f.). On the other
hand, it is hardly probable that the Evangelist would have thus

boldly related to the Baptist material used by the Synoptists
in relation to Christ. It must be remembered that such
questions, reflecting as they do current Messianic expectations,
would be frequently asked, and it is just possible that we
have incorporated here actual reminiscences of 'the Witness,'
though no doubt they have been considerably idealized by
the reflections of the Evangelist upon them. In favour of the
substantial independence of the narrative is the fact that
in one or two points it runs counter to the Synoptic tradition :
the Baptist denies that he is Elijah, whereas the Synoptics
repeatedly insist on the identification ; our Gospel again
alludes to '*the* Prophet,' and distinguishes him from the
Messiah, whereas the Synoptic phrase is ' one of the prophets,'
and traditional Christian doctrine identified 'the prophet'
with the Messiah. Any fair comparison between the Synoptic
and Johannine accounts of the Baptist must begin with the
observation that, while the Synoptic account leads up to and
virtually ends with the baptism of Jesus, the Fourth Gospel
regards the Baptist's testimony as subsequent to the baptism,
which, though no doubt taken for granted as a recognized
tenet of the Christian faith (Acts 1 : 22), is tacitly ignored—
even the traditional title ' the Baptist ' being dropped. Our
Evangelist introduces John simply for the sake of his testimony to Jesus, and omits all reference both to his work as a
preacher of repentance and to the baptism of Jesus which
crowned it. His reserve concerning the baptism may be
partly due to the desire to take the wind out of the sails of
the ' Baptist-party ' who, on the strength of Jesus' baptism
by John, would claim that their Master, far from being inferior
to Christ, was in reality his patron. But it is of more importance to note that the Johannine theology has little room for
the baptism and its accompanying bestowal of the holy Spirit,
or at any rate for the interpretation which the Synoptists
put upon these events. The Incarnate Logos needs no further
attestation of his Sonship. The baptism is therefore omitted
altogether, while the descent of the Spirit, though retained
out of respect for tradition, is narrated not as a divine acknowledgment of Jesus but as a divine guarantee to John, and

as the occasion of the latter's testimony to Jesus' Messiahship. 'The descent of the Spirit is nothing more than the sign by which John recognizes the Incarnate Logos' (Loisy). We thus have here another concession (cf. 29) to earlier doctrine, the Synoptic tradition being adapted to the Johannine theology of the incarnation. Yet it would be a mistake to assume that there is no place in the thought of our Evangelist for the bestowal of the Spirit upon Jesus. The Spirit is always clearly distinguished from the Logos, and therefore may be bestowed even upon One in whom the Logos has already become incarnate. Christ may, as the Logos, 'come from above and testify to what he has seen and heard' there (3 : 31–32) ; but if his testimony has authority as 'the words of God,' it is because 'God gives him the Spirit in no small measure' (3 : 34).

THE OLD MASTER AND THE NEW (1 : 35–51)

35 Next day again John was standing with two of his disciples ;
36 he gazed at Jesus as he walked about, and said, ' Look,
37 there is the lamb of God ! ' The two disciples heard
38 what he said and went after Jesus. Now Jesus turned, and when he observed them coming after him, he asked them, ' What do you want ? ' They replied, ' Rabbi ' (which may be translated, ' teacher '), ' where are you
39 staying ? ' He said to them, ' Come and see.' So they went and saw where he stayed, and stayed with him the rest
40 of that day—it was then about four in the afternoon. One of the two men who heard what John said and went after
41 Jesus was Andrew, the brother of Peter. In the morning he met his brother Simon and told him, ' We have found the messiah ' (which may be translated, ' Christ ').
42 He took him to Jesus ; Jesus gazed at him and said, ' You are Simon, the son of John ? Your name is to be Cephas ' (meaning ' Peter ' or ' rock ').

35 The witness of John, dealt with in the last paragraph, is now repeated, this time in the presence of two of the Baptist's disciples ; the calling of the first disciples is thus brought back

into a quite definite relation to John's testimony to Christ
as Messiah. The Baptist calls the attention of his disciples
to Jesus as he walked about, by repeating in shorter form
the tribute of verse 29: ' Look, there is the lamb of God ! ' 36
Again, it is superfluous to enquire concerning the where and
whence of Jesus' ' walking.' The scene is staged in order to
throw into relief the transference of the disciples' loyalty
from the Old Master to the New. John does not definitely bid
his disciples follow Jesus, for his words are to be understood
as addressed to a wider circle ; but by repeating in their hearing
his testimony of the previous day he hints that here is the
Master greater than himself, for whose coming he has prepared
them. The disciples took the hint, and of their own free
will went after Jesus. The phrase is used in a double sense, 37
implying not merely that they followed in Jesus' tracks, but
that ultimately they became his disciples, an almost technical
use of the word ' follow,' both in this Gospel and the Synoptics.
(Mk. 1 : 18, 2 : 14, etc.)

The difference of outlook between our Gospel and the
Synoptics is well illustrated by the fact that while the latter
(Mt. 11 : 2-6) represent the Baptist as sending two disciples
to demand of Jesus whether he is the Christ, according to
our Evangelist it is to the Baptist's own testimony that
Jesus owes his first disciples. Observing the two follow- 38
ing him Jesus turned round, no doubt desiring to encourage
their first timid advances. This thought of the ' divine
initiative ' is constantly emphasized in the Gospel (1 : 48,
and especially 15 : 16, ' You have not chosen me, it is I who
have chosen you '). From the would-be disciples' answer,
' Rabbi ' (which may be translated, ' teacher '), it has been
inferred that they did not trust the Baptist's witness to
Jesus as Messiah, and therefore refrained from addressing him
by any higher title than ' teacher ' ; but in 49 the same mode
of address is combined with the Messianic titles. ' Rabbi ' was
a title which seems to have come recently into vogue, and
means ' my greatness ' (compare ' His Majesty,' ' Monsignor,'
etc.), and the use here of the title ' teacher ' perhaps implies
a hint that the speakers are ready to be disciples. Whatever

expectations the two may have cherished concerning Jesus, the immediate impression he created was that of a wandering ' teacher,' and therefore they ask ' where are you staying ? ' evidently in the hope that an invitation to Jesus' lodging will provide an opportunity for a more intimate conversation than is possible in the open air. Jesus at once responds with
39 the invitation to ' come and see,' and the unforgettable moment which marks the disciples' first interview with their Master is precisely fixed as about four in the afternoon, that is, just the time when men would leave their work. This is the only interpretation of ' the tenth hour ' admissible in the N.T., though Westcott argues for 10 a.m., in order—surely quite needlessly—to allow more time for the talk. Though the Romans probably calculated their civil day, by which leases, etc., were dated, from midnight to midnight, throughout the whole Graeco-Roman world the hours of each day were reckoned from sunrise to sunset. This method of reckoning suits perfectly the other references in the Gospel (4 : 6, 52 ; 19 : 14).

From the precise fixing of the hour it has been inferred that the writer must have been present in the person of the unnamed disciple of 40, a possibility which, in view of our hypothesis that the memoirs of a witness may lie behind the narrative, cannot be altogether ruled out. But it is unlikely that ' the Witness ' was so early a member of Jesus' company, and if any particular significance is to be attached to ' the tenth hour ' it is probably symbolical ; thus in 11 : 9 the twelve hours of the day perhaps represent the duration of the universe, ' the last hour ' (1 Jn. 2 : 18) would be the Evangelist's own day, while ' the tenth hour,' the number of perfection, would mark the beginning of the Christian era. It is interesting to compare this incident with that narrated in Lk. 24 : 13–35. In each case two disciples spend the evening hours with Jesus (Lk. 24 : 29), one of them is unnamed (18), and the outcome is that the Master's true nature is revealed to them (31).
40 Andrew is defined as the brother of Peter, who by the time the Gospel was written had completely overshadowed him.

The second of the two disciples, here unnamed, has been universally held by tradition to be the Evangelist himself in the
person of John the son of Zebedee. This has been inferred
from the reading of the A.V., ' He (i.e. Andrew) *first* findeth his 41
own brother,' which was supposed to imply that John *afterwards* found *his* brother James, the tally of the first four
disciples according to the Synoptics thus being completed.
It must be confessed that such an exegesis could hardly have
occurred except to one already biased in favour of the
traditional theory of authorship. If the expression ' first '
is to be retained at all, the suggestion probably is that this is
the first instance of that providential ' finding ' which is
repeated at 43 and 45. But a better reading is, as in our
text, **in the morning he met his brother Simon.** The phrase,
' *His own brother* ' (A.V. and R.V.), does not necessarily imply
the corresponding thought of *someone else's* brother, for at
this period the Greek word (' idios ') probably meant little more
than ' *his.*' Dr. Garvie (*The Beloved Disciple*, p. 80) in the
unnamed disciple also traces ' the Witness,' whom however he
identifies not with John but with the ' Beloved Disciple' who,
he considers, is not one of the Twelve (Introduction, p. xlvi).
But it is surely improbable that the writer should have merely
implied his own presence in a manner so impossibly vague that
the allusion would never be recognized save by those already
on the lookout for it in the interests of a particular theory of
authorship. If it be insisted that the mention of **one of the
two men** (40) demands a reference, if not explicit then implied,
to the second of the two, then the most natural explanation
is to suppose that in the original Gospel John was mentioned
by name as the second of the two disciples, that he also was
described as having found his brother, and that the whole
clause was subsequently cut out by the Redactor in the
interests of his identification of the Gospel's anonymous disciple
with the son of Zebedee (Introduction, p. xlix, and Bacon,
The Fourth Gospel in Research and Debate, pp. 202-3).

The impression made by Jesus during the evening's intercourse is illustrated by Andrew's words to his brother, **'We
have found the Messiah,'** upon the lips of a Jew ' the most

comprehensive of all Eurekas' (Dods). The discovery, so slowly worked out in the Synoptics, is here reached with a leap in the first moments of enthusiastic discipleship. The Baptist's circle has hitherto been on the tiptoe of expectation for 'the hope of Israel': in Jesus they have found him. The Hebrew form Messiah' is used only here and at 4 : 25 in the N.T., and is therefore for the benefit of Hellenist readers translated ' Christ.'

42 When Peter is introduced Jesus **gazed at him** : the word (cf. 36) suggests a glance which reads the heart, a super-natural power ascribed to Jesus in the Gospel (2 : 25). With what our author probably regards as divine prescience rather than a natural psychological insight Jesus recognizes at first sight that here is a man whose character is likely to prove hard and firm, and he therefore greets him with the words, **'You are Simon, the son of John ? Your name is to be Cephas '** **(meaning ' Peter ' or ' Rock ')**. The future tense of the last clause is perhaps meant to imply a miraculous forecasting of the later incident (Mt. 16 : 18), where Jesus says ' Peter *is* your name.' There is probably an echo of the latter passage in the half-ceremonious ' thou art Simon ' (Mt. 16 : 18 : ' thou art Peter,' which in this context is natural enough as picking up Peter's previous words, ' thou art the Christ,' in 16). Mark (3 : 16) more naturally dates the renaming of Simon after a longer period of acquaintanceship, and on the whole it is more probable that our Evangelist has antedated the scene than that we have here a separate incident previous to that recorded in Mt. 16 : 18. Just as Simon has already recog-nized Jesus as the Christ, so does Jesus without more delay recognize Simon as ' the Rock.' The Hebrew form ' **Cephas,**' which is translated into its Greek equivalent ' Peter,' is used elsewhere in the N.T. only by St. Paul. A change of name was thought to imply a change of life and of character, e.g. Abram, Jacob, Levi. Peter's father is given as ' John ' (21 : 15) rather than Jonas, a Greek abbreviation, which is the name in Mt. 16 : 17. Our Evangelist would probably explain Jesus' acquaintance with Peter's name and family relationships by his own supernatural knowledge rather than by any com-

munication from Andrew. This power of 'second sight' is stressed again and again (1 : 48, 2 : 24–25, 4 : 18, etc.).

Next day Jesus determined to leave for Galilee ; there he 43 met Philip and told him, 'Follow me.' Now Philip be- 44 longed to Bethsaida, the same town as Andrew and Peter ; he met Nathanael and told him, 'We have found him 45 whom Moses wrote about in the Law, and also the prophets —it is Jesus, the son of Joseph, who comes from Nazaret.' 'Nazaret !' said Nathanael, 'can anything good come 46 out of Nazaret ? ' ' Come and see,' said Philip. Jesus saw 47 Nathanael approaching and said of him, ' Here is a genuine Israelite ! There is no guile in him.' Nathanael said 48 to him, 'How do you know me ? ' Jesus answered, 'When you were under that fig tree, before ever Philip called you, I saw you.' 'Rabbi,' said Nathanael, 'you 49 are the Son of God, you are the king of Israel ! ' Jesus 50 answered, 'You believe because I told you I had seen you under that fig tree ? You shall see more than that.' He said to him, ' Truly, truly I tell you all, you shall see 51 heaven open wide and *God's angels ascending and descending* upon the Son of man.'

The sudden transference of the scene to Galilee in the midst 43 of the account of the calling of the disciples is a little strange. Possibly our Evangelist is making a concession to the prevalent Synoptic tradition according to which the call of all the disciples took place there (Mk. 1: 16). Also prophecy demanded that Galilee should be the scene of Jesus' revelation of himself as Messiah (Is. 9: 1, Mt. 4: 12–16 : cf. 2: 11). The mention of Jesus' determination to leave for Galilee probably implies that he did so, and that it was there he met Philip, who was the first disciple 'found' by Jesus himself. The more advanced critics consider that our author confuses the Apostle Philip with 'the Evangelist' of the same name, and that Philip is specially chosen for mention here because 'the Evangelist' was well known in the Asiatic communities in which our Gospel would be current. (For other references to Philip and hints concerning his character see 6 : 5, 12 : 21, 14 : 8, and Introduction, p. lxi.)

The summons ' **Follow me** ' is not merely an invitation to accompany Jesus home, but both in this Gospel and in the Synoptics is a solemn formula for calling to discipleship (Mt. 8 : 22, 9 : 9, 19 : 21, Lk. 9 : 59, and see note on 1 : 37, 44 21 : 19). Philip **belonged to Bethsaida,** which, we are told, was also **the town of Andrew and Peter,** though the Synoptists connect the latter pair with Capharnahum (Mk. 1 : 29). The meaning of the name Bethsaida is ' Fishertown,' the only hint that the Gospel contains, apart from the Appendix, that the earliest disciples were fishermen. The town lay on the east bank of Jordan a short distance from its entrance into the Sea of Galilee and was rebuilt by the tetrarch Philip and named Julias, in honour of the daughter of Augustus. Some authorities, however, think that there were two towns of this name, and that the one here mentioned is defined in 12 : 21 as ' Bethsaida of Galilee ' in order to distinguish it from Bethsaida Julias. The movements of Jesus in 6 : 16-22 are also supposed to prove the existence of two Bethsaidas, in which case Philip's town may have been a suburb of Julias on the west bank of Jordan or farther along the coast at 'Ain Tabigha. But on the whole it is probable that there was only one town of the name (see Sir G. A. Smith, *Historical Geography of the Holy Land,* p. 457).

45 ' One lighted torch serves to light another ' (Godet), and so Philip next **met Nathanael,** a fellow-countryman from Cana of Galilee (21 : 2) ; but possibly the Redactor merely deduces this from the fact that Jesus is found at Cana in Galilee (2 : 1) immediately after his call. The identity of Nathanael is one of the riddles of the Gospel, the discussion of which will be best reserved till the end of the paragraph. Philip, unlike the downright Andrew, introduces Jesus in roundabout fashion as ' **him whom Moses wrote about in the Law** (Deut. 18 : 15), **and also the prophets,'** a circumlocution which implies ' the Messiah ' (cf. Lk. 24 : 27, Acts 3 : 22, 24, and note on 1 : 21). The fact that Jesus is here called **the son of Joseph** has been accepted as proof that the Evangelist was

unacquainted with, or did not subscribe to, the doctrine of the
Virgin Birth ; but the relationship between Jesus and Joseph
must in any case have been taken for granted (see note on
1 : 13 and cf. 6 : 42).

For the prejudice against Nazaret revealed in Nathanael's 46
rejoinder, ' **can anything good come out of Nazaret ?** ' various
explanations have been given : it is in Galilee, against which
the same prejudice is shown in 7 : 52 ; it is a small insignificant
village not even mentioned in the Old Testament ; its people
were ignorant and disreputable—a charge for which there is
no independent evidence whatever ; Nathanael, hailing from
the neighbouring village of Cana, was biased by the petty
jealousy so characteristic of small communities. But perhaps
the most probable explanation is that the Evangelist, by an
anachronism, is reading back into the early days of Jesus'
ministry the prejudices of his own day, when Nazaret would
be held in disrepute both among Jews, as the place of Jesus'
origin, and among Christians, because of Jesus' rejection there
recorded in Mk. 6 : 4.

Philip rather than argue bids Nathanael ' **Come and see** '—
' the best remedy for preconceived opinions ' (Bengel), ' the
true solution of religious doubts ' (Westcott), ' the simplest and
profoundest apologetic ' (Godet). At first sight of Nathanael
Jesus remarks to his companions, ' **Here is a genuine Israelite !** ' 47
In spite of the Evangelist's undoubted anti-Jewish bias (see
note on 1 : 19) the term ' Israelite ' is here used as a title of
honour, as in Rom. 11 : 1 ; 2 Cor. 11 : 22, and here we have
one of those apparent contradictions so characteristic of the
Gospel : it is to be explained by noting that our author makes
a distinction between the true community of Israel, at last
realized in the Christian Church, and the Jews as a religious
party opposed to the Church. Rev. 2 : 9 illustrates exactly
the same distinction. In harmony with this twofold attitude
of the Evangelist towards his own people are Jesus' next
words : ' **There is no guile in him** ' (Ps. 32 : 2, Rev. 14 : 5).
Nathanael, the genuine Israelite, is honestly willing to test the
truth of the Gospel, as contrasted with the counterfeit Jews
of 8 : 44 who, while priding themselves on their birthright as

Israelites (8 : 39), are in reality possessed by the devil of falsehood. The words also contain an allusion to Jacob who, on
receiving the title ' Israel ' (Gen. 32 : 28), was proclaimed to
be no longer a ' supplanter ' or ' deceiver ' (Gen. 27 : 35–36), but
a ' conqueror of God,' that is, one who, like Nathanael here,
relies for victory not upon guile but upon wrestling with God
in prayer.

48   Nathanael is surprised that Jesus should thus sum him up
in a moment : possibly his blunt honesty desires no empty
compliments, whereupon Jesus replies, ' **When you were under
that fig tree . . . I saw you.**' ' To sit under one's fig-tree '
was a proverbial expression meaning ' to be at home,'
which perhaps confirms our conclusion (43) that the call of
Philip and Nathanael took place after Jesus' arrival in
Galilee and perhaps at Cana, where Nathanael's home was
(21 : 2). Augustine tells us (*Confessions, VIII,* 12, 28) that
his conversion also took place under a fig-tree, which on
account of its shady foliage would be a favourite place for
meditation. Jesus' words seem at first to imply a miraculous
power of vision from a distance ; but the extraordinary impression they make on Nathanael shows that he regards them
as a proof of something still more wonderful, of the divine
intuition already illustrated at 42. He is amazed not at a
mere feat of physical long-sightedness, but at the divine clair-
voyance which is able to read at a glance both the scene and
the subject of his secret meditation, and by relating the two
has discovered an index to his character as a ' genuine Israelite
in whom there is no guile.' For it is possible that the mention
of the fig-tree is meant to have some bearing on Jesus' verdict
on Nicodemus. It was ' under his fig-tree ' that prophecy
pictured the ideal Israelite of the Messianic age as sitting
(Micah 4 : 4, Zech. 3 : 10). Nathanael may be supposed to
have been meditating on the coming of the Messiah, and
Jesus' mention of the fig-tree in conjunction with his expression ' a genuine Israelite ' would call Messianic associations
to his mind, and thus convince him that Jesus has read his
secret thoughts. Can one who enters thus mysteriously into
the Messianic dreamings of a complete stranger be any other

than the Messiah himself? Accordingly he at once hails 49
Jesus as ' Son of God ' and ' king of Israel,' two of the highest
titles which could be applied to the Messiah, for the first of
which compare 11 : 27, and for the second 12 : 13. Messiah
is alike the elect of God and the theocratic chief of the chosen
people. The two titles are combined in Ps. 2 : 6-7. In the
use of the phrase ' king of *Israel*,' we perhaps have another
hint of the distinction made by our Evangelist (see ver. 47)
between the divine community of *Israel* and the *Jews* as a
hostile religious party. ' King of *Israel* ' is a title of supreme
honour, but in 18 : 33 ff. Jesus scorns the title ' King of the
Jews.' The title ' Son of God ' on Nathanael's lips no doubt
bears merely its theocratic significance of ' Messiah ' ; but
regarded as expressing the thought of the Evangelist through
the lips of Nathanael it is pregnant with the full metaphysical
and mystic meaning characteristic of the Gospel (cf. 34 above
and note on ver. 14). Faith's perfect fruit ripens in a moment,
and we can say truly enough with Godet, ' Nathanael's faith
will never possess *more* than it embraces at this moment. It
will only be able to possess it more distinctly. The gold-
seeker puts his hand on an ingot ; when he has coined it,
he has it better, but not more ' : a good illustration of the
Evangelist's limited sense of the development of faith.

Jesus' question implies not blame of Nathanael's too easy 50
credulity, but rather joyful surprise at such ready faith ;
for the full significance of the word **Believe** in the Gospel
see note on 3 : 15. Jesus' promise, made not only to
Nathanael but to the whole circle, that **you shall see more
than that,** is fulfilled in the next chapter, where the miracle
of omniscience just recorded is followed by a miracle of
creative power, from the popular point of view an even
greater marvel, the changing of water into wine. The phrase 51
' **Truly, truly,** ' occurs in the N.T. only on the lips of Jesus :
hence the title ' the Amen ' (Rev. 3 : 14). The double form
of the phrase is peculiar to this Gospel. In the promise of
a vision of ' **heaven open wide and God's angels ascending and
descending upon the Son of man,**' an allusion has been variously supposed to the recorded appearance of angels at the

Temptation, the Agony (Lk. 22 : 43), the Resurrection, the Ascension. But it is more probable that the prediction is an echo of Mt. 26 : 64 than that there is a reference to any particular angelophany recorded in the Synoptics. Just as John had seen the heaven open (32–34), so should the disciples in the days to come ; but now heaven is more than moment-arily opened ; it is open and remains open (note the perfect tense in the original, well brought out by our translation ' wide open '). For the ' open heaven,' as symbolical of the near approach of God, compare Is. 64 : 1, Acts 7 : 56. The order of the words ' angels ascending and descending,' an apparent reversal of the natural order, is the same as in Gen. 28 :12, and proves that there is a reminiscence of Jacob's vision. The thought is that the angels are ever at men's side on earth, and therefore ' they first bear the prayer up to God before they bring down the answer from Him ' (Westcott). What Jacob saw in a dream the disciples shall experience in reality, for with the incarnation of the Logos living communication has been established between earth and heaven, which are now no longer two, but one whole (cf. Eph. 1 : 10, Col. 1 : 20). The angels in our verse are no less than symbolical mediators of the miraculous power of God Himself, which is now so fully revealed in the works of the Messiah that it ' brings God to man and makes earth a Bethel, and the gate of heaven ' (Dods).

' Son of man ' is in the Synoptics the favourite title used by Jesus of himself, probably because it contained a veiled claim to the Messiahship. A full discussion of the origin of the title belongs rather to Synoptic criticism, and would be out of place here. It was probably borrowed from the famous Messianic passage Dan. 7 : 13, a verse which is directly reflected in Mt. 26 : 64. Our Evangelist is true to the Synoptic tradition in using this title as Jesus' description of himself. Others may call him ' Son of God ' and ' king of Israel,' thus stressing his relation to God and to His Chosen People : Jesus, as one ' who is to remove the sin of the world,' prefers to emphasize his relation to mankind in general, and therefore calls himself the ' Son of man.' For

It should be noted that, as compared with the Synoptic use, the title in our Gospel has undergone a certain modification. The Synoptists employ it to hint at Jesus' Messiahship, our Gospel primarily to emphasize the reality of his manhood, though no doubt there is still the underlying suggestion of mystery and unique dignity. Thus our verse implies a contrast between the present humanity of the Christ and the true glory of his divine nature which will one day be revealed, while nearly every occurrence of the title in our Gospel is in passages which suggest that he who to-day appears to be merely the ' Son of man,' will one day be manifested in power and glory as ' Son of God ' (compare 6 : 62, 12 : 23, 13 : 31, 5 : 27, etc.).

Two questions remain : firstly, who is Nathanael ? Three solutions are put forward. First, if he be regarded as one of the Twelve, he should probably be identified either with Bartholomew, on the ground that the latter is coupled with Philip by the Synoptists (Mk. 3 : 18, etc.), while Nathanael is similarly coupled with Philip in our Gospel ; or with Matthew (or possibly Matthias), on the ground that the two names have a similar derivation—' gift of God.' ' Bartholomew ' is itself a patronymic meaning ' son of Ptolemy,' and it is claimed that the disciple's personal name may quite well have been Nathanael. Secondly, at the other extreme, there is the view that Nathanael is a purely ideal figure, the representative of those true ' Israelites ' who have professed faith in Christ in opposition to the ' Jews ' of 8 : 44. He is the symbol of the perfect disciple. Thirdly, and midway between the two extremes, is the theory that in Nathanael we have a symbolical counterpart of a real person, either the ' Beloved Disciple ' who, according to the point of view of the critic, may or may not be the author himself, or even, as has been speciously argued, St. Paul. The latter, like Nathanael, professed his faith in Christ only after he had met him face to face ; yet he had been preordained to Christ's service while still under the shadow of the law (typified by a fig-tree in Lk. 13 : 6 ff.), just as had Nathanael under his fig-tree. Paul also, like the ' genuine Israelite,' prided himself that ' I

E

also am an Israelite' (Rom. 11 : 1), while the promise made
to Nathanael of the vision of 'heaven wide open' suggests
the ecstasy of Paul who 'was caught up to the third heaven'
(2 Cor. 12 : 2). Probably the Evangelist brings forward
Nathanael as a figure half real, half ideal. As the fifth disciple
to be called he corresponds to Matthew (Mk. 2 : 14), whose
name, 'Gift of God,' he has taken. His call is also curiously
reminiscent of that of the other famous tax-collector of the
Synoptic tradition, Zacchaeus. The latter is called down
from his sycamore tree, Nathanael from under his fig-tree,
the one to be greeted by Christ with the words 'here is a
genuine Israelite,' the other with the words (Lk. 19 : 9),
'Zacchaeus here is a son of Abraham.' But the figure of
Nathanael, whoever he be, has undoubtedly been idealized :
he is the model disciple, and as such represents the viewpoint
of the Evangelist himself.

Lastly, what of the relation of this section to the Synoptic
tradition ? Just as Jn. 1 : 19–28 and 29–34 are the equivalents of Mk. 1 : 5–8 and 9–12 respectively, so is it natural to
see in 1 : 35 ff. the Johannine parallel to Mk. 1 : 16–20.
But it is obviously impossible to harmonize the two accounts,
if indeed they refer to the same occasion. Place, time, persons
and circumstances are all different. Accordingly in the
interests of harmony Westcott and others argue that our
account refers to a meeting of Jesus with his first disciples
preliminary to their formal call recorded at Mk. 1 : 16, which,
it is held, implies a previous acquaintanceship. This possibility cannot be altogether ruled out. But that our Evangelist
regards this occasion as the actual 'call' of the disciples is
far more probable, as appears from the use of the recognized
formula 'follow me,' and also from the fact that the disciples
are henceforth found in Jesus' company without any more
definite call being recorded. We conclude that John has
replaced the earlier account by one modified to suit his own
purpose, in order to emphasize the passing over of the
disciples from the Old Master to the New. Whereas in the
Synoptic account Jesus leaves the Baptist immediately after
his baptism, and the forty days in the wilderness, the tempta-

tion and a period of preaching in Galilee (Mk. 1: 13–15, to which there is no parallel in our Gospel) intervene before the call of the disciples, in our Gospel he remains for three days (vers. 29, 35, 43) in the neighbourhood of the Baptist, actually collecting his disciples from among the latter's followers. According to John it is the recognition of Christ's Messiahship and Divine Sonship which draws his first disciples to him ; indeed, his object in narrating their call is to emphasize the testimony it affords to that Messiahship which the Baptist has just proclaimed. Starting from the presupposition, which is without doubt historically probable, that Jesus would find his first disciples among the adherents of the Baptist, John combines this idea with material drawn from the Synoptics, reading back the faith of his own time into the profession of the earliest disciples, and thus producing an account which is, strictly speaking, not accurate history, but admirably serves the purpose of his apologetic. The main theme of this introductory section is, as already noted, the passing over of the disciples from the Old Master to the New (vers. 7, 8, 15, 20, 25–27, 30).

ACT I. THE NEW GOSPEL AND THE OLD

Section I. The Relation of the New to the Old

Illustration (i) : *Water turned into Wine* (2: 1–11)   2.

Two days later a wedding took place at Cana in Galilee ; the 1
mother of Jesus was present, and Jesus and his disciples 2
had also been invited to the wedding. As the wine ran 3
short, the mother of Jesus said to him, ' They have no
wine.' ' Woman,' said Jesus, ' what have you to do 4
with me ? My time has not come yet.' His mother 5
said to the servants, ' Do whatever he tells you.' Now 6
six stone water-jars were standing there, for the Jewish
rites of ' purification,' each holding about twenty gallons.
Jesus said, ' Fill up the jars with water.' So they filled 7
them to the brim. Then he said, ' Now draw some out, 8
and take it to the manager of the feast.' They did so ; 9
and when the manager of the feast tasted the water

47

which had become wine, not knowing where it had
come from (though the servants who had drawn it knew),
10 he called the bridegroom and said to him, 'Everybody
serves the good wine first, and then the poorer wine
after people have drunk freely ; you have kept the good
11 wine till now.' Jesus performed this, the first of his
Signs, at Cana in Galilee, thereby displaying his glory ;
and his disciples believed in him.

In contrast to the Synoptists, according to whom Jesus
opened his public ministry by teaching in Capharnahum (Mk.
1 : 21), John sets in the forefront a miracle which presents
peculiar difficulties. It is recorded by none of the Synoptists ;
unlike the better attested miracles it is performed in the realm
of inorganic matter by a process which it is hardly possible
to conceive ; finally, and this is of chief importance, from the
ethical point of view it is unintelligible and purposeless.
Strauss terms it truly ' a miracle of luxury,' than which nothing
could be less in harmony with the spirit of Jesus. From these
difficulties relief can be obtained only by resorting to an
interpretation more or less allegorical. But this is not to
deny that behind John's account there may lie an actual
historical incident, for the fact that an incident is capable of
being allegorized is no proof that it has no basis in history.
That the original account, taken over it may be from the
memoirs of 'the Witness,' has been embellished by the
Evangelist in the interest of his symbolism we may admit
all the more readily in the case of a Galilean episode, and
therefore one at which it is unlikely that ' the Witness' was
himself present. In any case for the proper understanding
of the section it is not the historical basis of the miracle
that is of importance but the elaborate symbolism which
the Evangelist builds up upon it.

The theme is the transmuting of the water of the old
Jewish ceremonial into the wine of the new Christian Gospel :
the stone vessels represent the old Judaism whose content
Christ has transformed from a mere ceremonial cleansing the
exterior (water) into a spiritual life renewing the heart (wine).

The O.T. bestowal of water (Exod. 17 : 5-7) is paralleled by the N.T. bestowal of wine. *Water* appears throughout as the 'symbol of the symbolical' (Holtzmann) as opposed to that which belongs to the realm of 'Spirit and reality' (cf. 3 : 5, 4 : 13-14). Thus John the Baptist, as the representative of the age of symbol, baptizes with water (1 : 26), while Jesus, who was 'the *real* Light' (1 : 9), baptizes with the holy Spirit (1 : 33).

Wine, on the other hand, is the symbol of the new spiritual Gospel. The use of such a symbol would be suggested by many passages in the Synoptics. Thus the Gospel is the new wine that bursts the old bottles (Mk. 2 : 22) ; the Baptist fasts, but the Son of man drinks wine (Mt. 11 : 18-19) ; wine is the symbol of the new covenant and of heavenly joy (Mk. 14 : 24, 25) ; the Kingdom of God is a Vineyard (Mk. 12 : 1-9), just as Jesus himself is the 'real Vine' (Jn. 15 : 1).

Suggestive also is the frequent use by the Synoptists of *wedding* metaphors in connexion with the teaching of the Kingdom. Thus the Kingdom is compared to a feast (Mt. 8: 11), and to a royal marriage (Mt. 22 : 2) : Jesus is the Bridegroom and the disciples the guests (Mk. 2 : 19-20; compare Jn. 3 : 29, where Jesus is the Bridegroom and the Baptist the 'best man ') ; elsewhere the Church is the bride (2 Cor. 11 : 2, Rev. 21 : 2), and the bond between Christ and the Church that of wedlock (Eph. 5 : 32).

In Mk. 2 : 19-22 the wine-symbolism and the wedding-symbolism are combined in one paragraph, and some critics suppose that this passage alone may have suggested to John the entire scenery of the miracle at Cana.

It should be noted finally, in favour of an allegorical interpretation of this section, that one of the chief 'miracles' performed at the Dionysian Mysteries seems to have been the changing of water into wine. Possibly we have a hint of the same idea in the ritual of the Feast of Tabernacles, when wine was mixed with water brought with elaborate ceremonial from the Pool of Siloam.

'The third day' in Greek always means 'the day after to-morrow,' that is, two days later (cf. Lk. 13 : 32) ; the point of departure is no doubt the day of Nathanael's call. Loisy notes that ' according to the Redactor's artificial chronology' Jesus ' manifested forth his glory ' on the seventh day, seven being the number of perfection. Chapter 1, verses 19, 29, 35, 41, 43, each marks the beginning of a new day, and two days later the miracle occurs. He holds that the passages dealing with the Baptist are later insertions, and that therefore in ' the fundamental document ' three days only were alluded to : the first would mark the call of Andrew and Peter, the second the call of Philip and Nathanael, while the miracle at Cana would take place literally on ' the third day.' **Cana of Galilee** should probably be identified with the village of Chirbet-Kana, which lies some twelve miles north of Nazaret, rather than with the Kefr-Kenna of the older tradition which is distant only four and a half miles north-west. If this identification be correct, then the qualification ' of Galilee ' is probably intended to distinguish it from the Phoenician Cana, situated in the territory of the tribe of Asher (Jos. 19 : 28) about eight miles south-east from Tyre. If it be insisted that this Cana also belonged to Galilee in the wider sense, then we must conclude that the words ' of Galilee' merely mark the transition from Peraea in this passage, and from Judaea at 4 : 46. In this case it is even possible that it is the Tyrian Cana to which our Evangelist refers, and indeed the note of time at 4 : 52 seems to favour this identification.

2   The fact that **the mother of Jesus was present** at the wedding does not necessarily imply that her permanent home was now at Cana. At verse 12 she leaves the place along with Jesus. There has been much speculation as to why Jesus and his disciples happened to be invited to the wedding, but in the case of a narrative so full of symbolism one is inclined to agree with Loisy that ' nothing is more vain than to speculate about the historical conditions of a fact which does not belong to strict history.' A wedding festival might last for a week (Gen. 29 : 27), and it would be on one of the last days that

3 **the wine ran short,** a serious matter, for, as a Jewish saying puts it, ' without wine there is no joy.' **The mother of Jesus** (perhaps symbolical of the O.T. Church, Rev. 12 : 1) appeals

to Jesus with the words ' **They have no wine** ' : the old legal religion ' lacks wine,' all the life energy is gone from it. Bengel supposes that Mary's words are a hint to Jesus to withdraw with his disciples and so relieve the embarrassment caused by the shortage of wine. Rather by calling attention to the need Mary indirectly challenges Jesus to help (cf. 11 : 3) : now is the time to manifest that miraculous power foreshadowed at 1 : 51. But Jesus is at once on his guard ; the words are those of a tempter ; they savour too much of Satan's suggestion in Mt. 4 : 3 (cf. note on 6 : 15). ' **Woman,**' 4 said Jesus, ' **what have you to do with me ?** ' The term 'woman' in the original has none of the harshness it suggests in English, but is perfectly respectful and even intimate ; Jesus even addresses his mother by it from the Cross (19 : 26) in ' a moment of unutterable tenderness ' (Godet). The rebuff lies in the words that follow : ' **What have you to do with me ?** ' (For the form of phrase cf. 2 Sam. 16 : 10, etc., Mk. 1 : 24, etc.) ' Your point of view, your aims and interests are quite different from mine.' The old ties of home must now be replaced by higher ties ; Jesus is now independent of every human influence, and even his mother is nothing to him in the accomplishment of his divine mission. We may compare Lk. 2 : 49, Mk. 3 : 33, thoughts which here become as it were forged into a sword which ' pierces through Mary's soul ' (Lk. 2 : 35). Jesus' apparent harshness has provoked endless discussion ; but when it is remembered that the words must ultimately be construed allegorically all difficulty disappears. The expression loses its last hint of offence when it is realized that John is picturing to us not a clash of wills between son and mother, but a conflict of two contradictory types of faith. The Divine Logos and the Theocratic Church are set over against each other. ' The motive of my actions,' says the Christ, ' is not to be sought for in the spirit of the old faith. I am not to be regarded as a wonder-working Messiah, as you, the representative of the old faith, judge me, but as the dying Son of God proclaimed by the new faith.' It is this last thought that is hinted at in Jesus' next words, ' **My time has not yet come.**' (For the phrase compare 7: 30, 8: 20, and for the converse idea 12 : 23, 13 : 1, 17 : 1.) The words which on the surface seem to refer to the time for Christ to display his miraculous power and thereby ' manifest forth his glory ' (ver. 11) have, as in all the parallels quoted above, a secondary and deeper reference to his death. The time for granting his mother's request and changing water into wine has not yet come, for it is an axiom of our Gospel that the transformation of the symbolical into the ' real ' can only come about with the bestowal of the Spirit, which in turn cannot take place till after Jesus' death (7 : 39).

Our Gospel several times emphasizes Jesus' unwillingness to be ' rushed,' especially by the claims of those he loved. (Compare specially 7 : 3, 6, and 11 : 5–6.) ' In all three cases human affection sought to bring pressure to bear on Jesus in connexion with his vocation, and in each case the interference is resented and repelled. Jesus does the will of God, and not the will of man ' (R. H. Strachan). Yet in each of the three cases Jesus ultimately yields. If in this case it appears inconsistent to perform the miracle immediately after insisting that the time for so doing had not yet come, the explanation is that in the intention of our author both the ' time ' and the ' Sign ' (ver. 11) have a significance quite other than one would judge from the letter of the narrative.

5 Mary, perhaps hoping from the qualification ' not *yet* ' that Jesus' refusal is not final, **said to the servants**—possibly symbolical of the Christian ministry—' **Do whatever he tells you,**'
6 words reminiscent of Gen. 41 : 55. The **six stone water-jars**, standing either actually in the banquet room or in the vestibule, would each contain **about twenty gallons,** or about 120 gallons in all, the Greek *metretes* being equivalent to eight or nine gallons. Similar jars have actually been discovered at Cana in modern days. These jars would be used for **the Jewish rites of ' purification,'** that is, for the washing of the guests' hands and of the various utensils as required by the ordinary social customs of the day (Mk. 7 : 3–4). Here they are symbolical of the old Jewish faith, whose content Christ was to transform from an outwardly purifying ritual to a life-giving religion instinct with spiritual power. John tells us that the jars were

filled to the brim in order both to emphasize the lavishness of 7
Jesus' gift and also to suggest that there was no room left for
adding anything to the water : the genuineness of the miracle
is thus certified. Commentators have been needlessly concerned to explain why Jesus placed such a large quantity of
wine at the disposal of the company. John's intention is
simply to emphasize the superabundant liberality of Christ's
bestowments : he gives his gifts ' from his fulness ' (1 : 16),
and ' in no stinting measure ' (3 : 34). From the words
' draw some out ' some have supposed that it was only the water 8
so drawn which was changed into wine : Jesus is thus relieved
of any responsibility for encouraging excess, but surely at
the cost of obscuring the main point of the symbolism which
is to emphasize the fulness of Christ's grace. The wine would
be taken to the manager of the feast in order that he might
taste it before it was served to the guests. This official is
not, as some have supposed, the ' chairman ' at the banquet,
Horace's *arbiter bibendi* or ' toastmaster,' but rather the
maître d'hôtel or chief steward, or indeed ' head waiter,'
who was responsible for the service of the meal. The note
that, when he tasted the wine, he did so not knowing where 9
it had come from, suggests that his judgment was therefore
quite unbiased. The reality of the miracle is thus emphasized. The custom of serving the good wine first is not 10
clearly alluded to elsewhere, though parallels have been sought
in Pliny, Martial and Cassius Iatrosophistes : the words are
intended as a pleasantry, and are not to be taken too rigorously.
Lk. 5 : 39 is sufficient comment. The Evangelist, with characteristic lack of interest in the story for its own sake (cf.
Introduction, p. xliii), does not tell us either the reply of the
bridegroom or the effect of the miracle upon the guests. It is
enough that the wine has been praised by the best judge and
the miracle thereby attested.

The point of verse 11 is not that this is the first ' sign ' 11
performed in Galilee (that at 4 : 54 being the second), but
rather that this miracle is of primary significance as being
the *first of all Jesus' Signs*, and therefore the one by which
he first *displayed* his glory. For glory see note on 1 : 14 :

the claim made there is warranted by the miracle recorded here. There are three main terms used in the Gospels of Jesus' miracles: 'acts of power' (never used in this Gospel), 'works' and *signs*. 'Works' is the word usually but by no means always used by Jesus himself in our Gospel, but 'signs' is the term which best suits the point of view of the Evangelist, for it emphasizes the evidential value of miracle for faith. In our Gospel the motive of compassion, so evident in the Synoptic accounts (Mk. 1: 41), is almost lost sight of, and Jesus' miracles become rather exhibitions of divine power whereby he 'displays his glory' and inspires belief in his claims (cf. 9: 3). Hence the miraculous element is deliberately enhanced. The nobleman's son is healed from a distance by a mere word, the blind man is blind from birth, Lazarus has lain in the grave four days: the miracle thus becomes a more convincing 'sign' of Jesus' 'glory' and a more effectual incentive to faith (see Introduction, p. xv f.). To our Evangelist the miracles are also 'signs,' in the sense that they are symbolical, important not for their own sake, but as types of spiritual truth. Each of the seven miracles recorded is selected designedly for the sake of the spiritual teaching to which it leads up: e.g. the Feeding of the Five Thousand is a 'sign' that Jesus is the 'Bread of Life,' the Healing of the Blind Man a 'sign' that he is 'the Light of the World,' the Raising of Lazarus a 'sign' that he is 'the Resurrection and the Life.' Thus the present miracle is a 'sign' that one has appeared who will introduce a new and spiritual worship. On the strength of this 'sign' his disciples believed in him. The Synoptists always represent miracle as preceded and conditioned by faith (Mk. 2: 5, Mt. 13: 58, etc.): in our Gospel, on the other hand, belief is the consequence of miracle (4: 53, 14: 11, etc.). Yet nothing is here said of the effect of the miracle upon the company at large: it is only the disciples who are said to believe, which suggests that even our Evangelist considers miracle to have significance only for those who already have some measure of faith.

One other question remains: how far ought this section to be read in connexion with the Feeding of the Five Thousand (chap. 6) and with it related to the ritual of the Last Supper as a symbolical illustration of the drinking of Christ's blood ? The Evangelist undoubtedly intends his narrative of the distribution of the loaves to be understood as symbolical of the eating of Christ's flesh, and 6 : 53–56 seems to require a parallel illustration of the drinking of his blood. The distribution of the wine to the guests would then represent the shedding of Christ's blood, and the whole incident would be read as a symbolical elaboration of Mt. 26 : 28. The two miracles in question are, however, placed so far apart in the text of our Gospel that any reference in this section to the Last Supper is probably quite secondary, the Evangelist's main intention being to set in the forefront of the Gospel the thought of the supplanting of the Old by the New. This is the theme of the whole section 2 : 1–4 : 42, which deals with the New Birth (3 : 3–8), the supplanting of the Baptist by the New and greater Master (3 : 22–30), the exaltation of a New worship above the Old (4 : 20–24) : to this whole series the two incidents of the Marriage at Cana and the Cleansing of the Temple serve as ' title-page vignettes ' (Holtzmann). The section 2 : 1–11 well illustrates the ingenuity and independence of the Evangelist who gathers together, probably around a nucleus of actual history, widely scattered Synoptic material, and out of it creates an entirely new picture to subserve his own apologetic aims. He no doubt intends his narrative to be accepted as at any rate approximately true history. Yet it is not facts but their spiritual significance which interests him ; in his own words (6 : 63) : ' What gives life is the Spirit : flesh is of no avail at all.'

Illustration (ii) : Cleansing of the Temple (2 : 12–22)

After this he travelled down to Capharnahum, with his mother 12 and brothers and his disciples ; they stayed there for a few days.

After this Jesus travelled down from the hill country of 12 Cana to Capharnahum, which lay near the shore of the Sea of Galilee nearly 700 feet below sea-level. The exact site of the town is uncertain, but it is probably to be found not at Tell-Hum, as early Christian tradition held, but at Khan Minyeh, situated at the north end of the plain of Gennesaret, at the point where the Damascus Road leaves the lake-side. Capharnahum would thus be an important trading centre (Lk. 5 : 27). Mk. 3 : 21 suggests that Jesus' family may have resided there, which would explain the reference here to his mother and brothers. The latter, whose names are given (Mt. 13 : 55) as James, Joses, Simon and Judas, were either the sons of Joseph by a former marriage, or more probably the sons of Joseph and Mary, and younger brothers of Jesus. Capharnahum is elsewhere (Mt. 9 : 1) called Jesus' 'own town.' Notice that from this point Jesus is represented as accompanied as a matter of course by his disciples, though no further detailed account of their call has been given (see note at end of chap. 1). Jesus remains only a few days at Capharnahum in view of the near approach of the Passover.

This visit to Capharnahum may correspond to that mentioned in Mt. 4 : 13. It is possible that our Evangelist may have introduced it merely out of respect to the Synoptic tradition. But the apparent aimlessness of verse 12, when considered by itself, adds probability to the supposition that he has incorporated it from the historical memoirs of 'the Witness.' 'If the Gospel is all an artificial composition with a dogmatic object, why should the author carry his readers thus to Capernaum—for nothing ? ' (Sanday).

At this point Moffatt inserts the section 3 : 22–30 on the ground that Jesus' journey (3 : 22) 'into the country of Judaea' requires Galilee as its point of departure. The section is certainly misplaced in its present context, but on the whole it seems preferable to place it immediately before chapter 4, where see note (p. 88).

13 Now the Jewish passover was near, so Jesus went up to Jeru-
14 salem. There he found, seated inside the temple, dealers in
15 cattle, sheep and pigeons, also money-changers. Making a scourge of cords, he drove them all, sheep and cattle together, out of the temple, scattered the coins of the

brokers and upset their tables, and told the pigeon-dealers, 16
‘ Away with these ! My Father’s house is not to be turned
into a shop ! ’ (His disciples recalled the scripture saying, 17
I am consumed with zeal for thy house.) Then the Jews 18
accosted him with the words, ‘ What sign of authority
have you to show us, for acting in this way ? ’ Jesus 19
replied, ‘ Destroy this sanctuary and I will raise it up in
three days.’ ‘ This sanctuary took forty-six years to build,’ 20
the Jews retorted, ‘ and you are going to raise it up in
three days ! ’ He meant the sanctuary of his body, 21
however, and when the disciples recalled what he had 22
said, after he had been raised from the dead, they believed
the scripture and the word of Jesus.

(For the general question of Jesus’ visits to Jerusalem see 13
Introduction, p. xiv.) The passover here mentioned is the
first of the three which, according to John, fell within the limits
of Jesus’ ministry, the second occurring at 6 : 4, and the third
at 11 : 55. The passover (Exod. 12) was celebrated at the
vernal equinox. John characteristically calls it the Jewish
passover (cf. 2 : 6, 5 : 1, 7 : 2, etc.), either because he writes
mainly for Hellenistic readers or possibly in order to distinguish the feast from the Christian Easter celebration.

Christ’s visit to the temple is ‘ a commentary on Mal. 3 : 1 ff.’ 14
(Westcott), and is clearly intended to have Messianic significance. In the outer Court of the Gentiles a regular market was
established where worshippers might obtain the animals
necessary for sacrifice. Here too were the tables of the
money-changers who found a lucrative business in the exchange
of the Roman currency into the Jewish, which alone might be
paid into the temple treasury. A small fee was exacted for
changing a shekel into the half-shekels required for the pay-
ment of the annual ‘ temple-tax ’ of half a shekel (Exod. 30 : 13 ;
Mt. 17 : 24). That profiteering was rife in the temple market
is proved by Edersheim, who relates that on one occasion,
through official intervention, the price of a pair of doves was
brought down from 15s. 3d. to 4d.

John alone mentions the scourge of cords. Jewish tradition 15

held that the Messiah at his coming would bear a lash for the chastisement of evil-doers, which suggests that the scourge is to be regarded rather as an emblem of authority than as a weapon of offence. The words **he drove them all, sheep and cattle together** are so phrased in the Greek as to suggest that the tradesmen themselves were not subjected to violence. Some hold that Jesus is here represented as dealing
16 more gently with the **pigeon-dealers** than with the other traders, possibly because they supplied the requirements of the poorer worshippers. But naturally it would be impossible to ' drive out ' the birds in their cages, and therefore Jesus bids their owners ' **Away with these !** ' The words ' **My Father's house** ' (cf. Lk. 2 : 49)—not ' our Father ' or ' your Father '—contain a veiled Messianic claim. ' Jesus felt himself to be the Son of Him who in a unique way had consecrated this place for His temple, and he exercised the authority of a Son against the turmoil which defiled his Father's house ' (Weiss). The Synoptists give Jesus' words as ' My house shall be called a house of prayer, but you make it a den of robbers ' (Mt. 21 : 13), apparently a composite citation of Is. 56 : 7 and Jer. 7 : 11. Here the taunt, ' **My Father's house is not to be turned into a shop** ' recalls Zech. 14 : 21, ' There shall be no more the Canaanite (the typical trader) in the house of the Lord of Hosts.'

17   John characteristically records the twofold effect of Jesus' act according to the moral predisposition of the witnesses. **His disciples,** on the one hand, **recalled the Scripture saying,** ' I am consumed with zeal for thy house ' (Ps. 69 : 9), that is to say, they recognized in their Master's reforming zeal a trait of the Messiah : from 15 : 25, 19 : 28, Acts 1 : 20, Rom. 11 : 9, 15 : 3, it is clear that Ps. 69 was generally given a Messianic significance. In the Greek the form of the word translated ' **I am consumed** ' is strictly future, whence some have supposed an allusion to the Passion : ' l'auteur a pu songer à la passion et à la mort de Jésus comme objet éloigné de la prophétie ' (Loisy). In this reference to the effect made on the disciples Sanday finds ' a bit of autobiography ' (for
18 **his disciples recalled** cf. ver. 22 and 12 : 16). The Jews,

on the other hand, who do not see that such an act as Jesus' carries with it its own moral justification and is in itself a 'sign,' demand of Jesus, ' What sign of authority have you to show us, for acting in this way ? ' Notice that they do not question the justice of his act : they merely demand his authority for thus exercising the *jus reformandi*. Jesus, they realize, has put forward Messianic claims : let him then produce his credentials and give visible proof of his divine authority. Jesus, following the analogy of Mt. 12 : 38-40 (the sign of Jonas), refuses any immediate proof, but holds out 19 the prospect of one great 'sign' which will be his warrant for all previous acts of authority : there will be no sign to-day, but to-morrow will show : ' Destroy this sanctuary, and I will raise it up in three days.'

The following four verses afford one of the cruces of Johannine interpretation. We will for the moment postpone the larger problems and deal merely with the letter of the text, remembering, however, that there runs throughout the verses a twofold reference to the temple building and to the body of Christ regarded as a spiritual sanctuary.

In the words ' Destroy this sanctuary ' we have a ' prophetic ' imperative, whereby Jesus' foes are challenged to do their worst. On the supposition that the words ' I will raise it up ' refer to the Resurrection, it may be noted that John regularly thus ascribes it to the power of Christ himself (10 : 17-18), while elsewhere in the N.T. it is the Father who raises the Son (Rom. 4 : 24, 8 : 11, Acts 3 : 15, 4 : 10). Possibly this follows from John's Logos-philosophy, according to which it was not the whole Person of Christ which died and rose again, but only the body which perished and was afterwards raised to life by the imperishable Logos. The expression ' in three days ' may mean not ' on the third day,' but ' within the period of three days,' that is, ' within a very short time '—the exact day not being defined.

The Jews take Jesus' words to refer to the temple buildings, 20 and, contrary to the impression left by the Synoptic account (Mk. 14 : 58, etc.), apparently consider them ' more absurd than blasphemous ' (Loisy). ' This sanctuary took forty-six years

to build, and you are going to raise it up in three days ! '
Herod's temple was begun in 20–19 B.C., and was completed
under Herod Agrippa II in A.D. 64. Forty-six years from the
former date would bring us to A.D. 27–28, 'which suits the
chronology of the Life of Christ as well as any date could do '
(Sanday). 'The coincidence is sufficiently striking' (Lightfoot) to suggest that John may have had first-hand evidence,
in the memoirs of ' the Witness,' for the words here recorded.
'It is most unlikely that a Greek teased himself with this
troublesome investigation, and then allowed his antiquarian
knowledge to slip out in such a way that no one would take
any notice of it' (Drummond). True the temple was not
actually completed at this date, but the words need mean no
more than that the temple had ' already been forty-six years
under construction.' But whether or no ' the Witness ' has
preserved the words as originally spoken in connexion with
the temple, it is probable that the Evangelist, true to the twofold line of thought running through the passage, sees in them
a symbolical reference to the age of Jesus. Starting from the
allusion in 8 : 57 to Jesus' age as ' not yet fifty,' Loisy thinks
that our Evangelist has made his age correspond to the seven
' year-weeks' of Dan. 9 : 25–27. He begins his ministry at the
age of forty-six: the ministry is prolonged for ' half a week '
(3½ years), so that at his death Jesus would be nearly fifty,
and his exaltation would take place in the ' year of Jubilee.'

21 The Evangelist here inserts one of those explanatory comments so characteristic of the Gospel (see Introduction, p. xliv) :
he meant the sanctuary of his body. Christ is thus made to
claim that he is the ' real ' sanctuary of God, in whom all
previous dreams of a dwelling-place of God among men are
realized (cf. 1 : 14). Paul frequently compares the human
body to a temple. In 2 Cor. 5 : 1 he speaks of ' this earthly
tent of mine ' ; in 1 Cor. 6 : 19 his readers are reminded that
' your body is the temple of the holy Spirit within you.'
Hence he in whom ' the entire Fulness of deity has settled
bodily ' (Col. 2 : 9) may well claim to be the ' real ' temple.
According to John the underlying meaning of Jesus' words is
' Kill me, and I will rise again from the dead ! '

John's reference to the subsequent reflections of the disciples 22 shows us how he himself came thus to interpret Jesus' words. Had not his claim been justified by the event ? Jesus had been raised from the dead. Accordingly John, who is typical of all disciples, believed the word of Jesus, that is, he assented to the claim implied in that word, and believed the scripture, namely, those passages in which a resurrection of the Messiah seemed to be foreshadowed, e.g. Ps. 16 : 10, Hos. 6 : 2, etc.

In considering the foregoing section two questions must be kept separate : first, supposing the narrative to have a basis in history, what were the actual words spoken by Jesus and what was their inner intention ? second, taking the words as we actually have them in the text, what is the primary significance which the Evangelist intends them to bear ? Consider the historicity of the incident first. That some such saying as that reported in verse 19 was actually spoken by Jesus is fairly clear from the evidence of the false witnesses (Mk. 14 : 58) and the references in Mt. 27 : 40 and Acts 6 : 14. The evidence at the trial distorts Jesus' challenge into a threat. According to John Jesus challenges his opponents to destroy ' this sanctuary,' in order that he may have the opportunity to ' raise it '—the same sanctuary ; according to the false evidence Jesus threatens himself to ' destroy this temple made with hands ' that in three days he may ' build *another* temple not made with hands.' Thus the general impression left by Jesus' words was that they referred to the temple buildings ; and, as it was with regard to an action in the temple buildings that Jesus had been challenged, it is certainly more natural that the ' sign ' with which he answers the challenge should have the same primary reference to the temple buildings. It is impossible to recover the exact form of Jesus' words. He evidently said something which lent itself to misconstruction, something which, at least on the surface, appeared to refer to the temple buildings. But can Jesus have intended his words (not necessarily as we have them here, but as they were actually spoken) to carry a secondary reference to his resurrection ? Though it would be easy enough for the disciples to read such a meaning into his words after his death, Jesus himself is hardly likely to have spoken thus in riddles, or to have been understood even by his disciples had he done so. He could not have alluded thus to his resurrection before even warning them of his approaching sufferings and death. If the incident is placed, as by our Gospel, at the beginning of the ministry, this consideration is almost decisive. But if the Synoptic setting of the incident (see below) is correct, then the certainty of death must have been at this moment clearly before Jesus' eyes, and his words may well have contained a veiled allusion to what lay before him. But it seems clear from the disciples' behaviour after the crucifixion that Jesus can hardly have thus definitely predicted the exact day of his resurrection. On the whole, critical opinion tends to the conclusion that, whatever Jesus' actual words both on this occasion and on that described in Mt. 12: 38–40, the sign intended was not primarily the Resurrection, though this intention was very early read into the words by the Church.

The exact significance which the Evangelist intends the words, as he here gives them, to bear is a second and quite different question. The fact that the whole incident is apparently introduced as a second illustration of the supplanting of the old faith by the new makes the following the most probable interpretation: Jesus sets over against the desecration of the temple by the devotees of the old religion his own promise of the raising up of a new and spiritual religion. 'Continue these practices,' he says, 'till you have reduced your religion to a mockery, and on its ruins I will raise up in a very short time (" in three days ") the worship of God " in Spirit and in reality " (4: 24).' True, according to this interpretation the new 'sanctuary' thus raised up would, strictly speaking, not be 'it,' i.e. the same sanctuary, but 'another,' as in Mk. 14: 58. But on this point see below: 'the old Church is transfigured and not destroyed' (Westcott). Is then the reference to the Resurrection to be ruled out altogether and verses 21–22 assigned to the Redactor as out of harmony with the Evangelist's thought? It may be so;

in the case of several similar ' comments ' it is undoubtedly so (cf. 4 : 2, 18 : 9, etc.). But John is notoriously fond of a ' double entendre ' ; and a secondary reference to the Resurrection, though it might be a misinterpretation of the strictly literal meaning of Jesus' words, would be quite in line with the Evangelist's method. We may quite well have here, not an interpolated comment by the Redactor, but a comment by the Evangelist himself, possibly upon matter which he is incorporating from the memoirs of ' the Witness ' (cf. Introduction, p. xli). Moreover, in these early sections John has been illustrating the gradual growth of faith in the disciples' hearts (cf. especially 1 : 50, 2 : 11, 2 : 22), and may well have thought to utilize this incident not only as an illustration of the supplanting of the old faith by the new, but also as the medium whereby he might place in the forefront of his Gospel his conception of that full resurrection faith of which 20 : 26-29 is the most perfect expression. It may be noted that this interplay of two lines of thought, that relating to the temple and that relating to the physical body of Christ, is rendered the more easy by the common Pauline analogy whereby the Church, the Christian counterpart of the temple worship, is equated with the mystical ' Body of Christ ' (Col. 1 : 18, 24 ; Eph. 1 : 23). Thus the ' temple not made by hands ' (Mk. 14 : 58) in the sense of the mystical body of Christ, the spiritual Church which is the expression of the new faith, becomes a mediating conception which links together and unites into one thought two ideas apparently so disparate as ' this temple made by hands ' and the actual physical body of Christ. We see too how it is possible for John, with the Pauline analogy in mind, to think of the new spiritual religion which Jesus is to raise up as in truth the same ' sanctuary ' as that which has been destroyed (' I will raise *it*,' not ' *another*,' as in Mark). ' The old Church is transfigured and not destroyed ' (Westcott), because ' if it is in the person of the Messiah that the Temple is laid in ruins, it is in his person also that it shall be raised again ' (Godet).

Finally, what is the relation of this section to the Synoptic account, which places the incident of the temple cleansing at the close of the ministry, and finds in it the motive for Jesus' arrest ? Note that John retains the Synoptic connexion of the incident with a question concerning 'authority' (Mk. 11 : 15-18, 28), but unites the latter with the request for a 'sign,' which the Synoptists give in a different context (Mt. 12 : 38-40). John's account cannot be reconciled with that of the Synoptists, unless indeed Jesus twice 'cleansed' the temple, at the beginning and at the close of his ministry. Though in the interests of harmony this view has been maintained, we must agree with Stanton that 'when in different ancient documents we find two accounts in many respects so similar referring to different times, it is on the whole most probable that we have to do with different traditions about the same event' (op. cit., p. 235).

There is no hint in the Synoptics of any knowledge of an earlier cleansing, nor in John of a later. Which dating then is historically correct ? Preference has sometimes been given to John on the ground that the Synoptists, as a result of their omission of this earlier visit to Jerusalem, may have misplaced an incident which belonged originally to the earlier date. But it seems more natural that the saying which (Mk. 14 : 58) was brought up in evidence against Jesus at his trial should have been spoken immediately before the catastrophe. Furthermore, it was only the presence in Jesus' train of a large number of Galilean pilgrims which made the act possible. At the beginning of the ministry Jesus' Messianic claims had not won sufficient recognition to make possible such an act of violence under the very eyes of the Sanhedrim. On the other hand, supposing the Synoptic chronology to be correct, it is easy to understand John's motive for thus antedating the incident. He no longer requires it to lead up to the *dénouement*, for this purpose is served in our Gospel by the Lazarus story ; rather does he utilize it as an eminently suggestive inaugural act. Jesus is represented as beginning his work of religious reform in the fittest and most obvious place. John's 'one consideration is that if Jesus is to offer himself to Israel as the Christ he

should do so at once, at the Passover, before the assembled
nation in his " Father's house " ' (Bacon, p. 395).

Theme (i) : *The New Birth—in relation to Pharisaism*
(2 : 23-3 : 13 ; 3 : 31-36)

**When he was in Jerusalem at the festival of the passover, 23
many people believed in his name, as they witnessed the
Signs which he performed. Jesus, however, would not 24
trust himself to them ; he knew all men, and required 25
no evidence from anyone about human nature ; well did
he know what was in human nature.**

To this section 2 : 23-25 form a preface indicating in general 23
terms the results of Jesus' stay in Jerusalem. We are reminded that the incident just narrated occurred immediately
before the festival of the passover. Pilgrims went to Jerusalem shortly before the festival in order to purify themselves
(11 : 55), and on the 13th Nisan, the eve of the festival, this
purification was completed by the removal of leaven from
every house. John probably intends us to understand that the
day on which every Israelite purified his house was that on
which Jesus purified ' his Father's.' During the festival
season, when Jerusalem would be crowded, **many people
believed in his name,** that is, they believed Jesus to be what
he professed to be, namely, the Messiah, **as they witnessed**
(day by day—the word is emphatically present tense) **the
Signs which he performed.** John has not recorded any
such ' Signs ' in Jerusalem up to this point ; but the narrative
makes no claim to be exhaustive. Note that while in the
Synoptics Jesus almost needs to be constrained to work
miracles, our Gospel represents him as freely employing them
as proofs of his divine authority. A close relation is obviously
intended between the words ' believed ' and ' witnessed ' :
John hints that the people's faith ' has little more duration
than the sight ' (Godet). It is one of John's curious inconsistencies that, while he insists on the evidential value of
miracle, he yet disparages faith based upon miracle (4 : 48,

65

20 : 29), as nothing more than what Luther calls 'milk faith.' Miracle cannot produce true faith, though it may consolidate it 'by unveiling to it completely the riches of its object' (Godet).

24   There is a play of words in verse 24, rendered possible by the elasticity of the concept of 'faith' in our Gospel (cf. 3 : 15 note). Though many trusted in his name, Jesus **would not trust himself to them**, that is, he had no faith in their faith. The meaning is, not merely that Jesus refused to have personal intercourse with his would-be adherents, but rather that he refused to enter into a moral and a spiritual relationship with them, as he had done for example with Nathanael, because on their part, a faith based merely on 'Signs' implied no moral relationship to him. True discipleship demands such a relationship ; but as they did not give themselves morally to him, he did not give himself morally to them' (Luthardt). A commentary on this statement is afforded by 6 : 14 f., where Jesus rejects homage based upon false beliefs and hopes (cf. Mt. 7 : 21 ff.).

25   John justifies Jesus' mistrust of his fellows by the fact that **he knew all men** (21 : 17). Because he knew the nature of 'all' he did not 'trust himself' to the 'many' mentioned above. The same thought is then characteristically (cf. 1 : 3 note) repeated negatively : **he required no evidence from anyone about human nature, for** well did **he know** ('he' is emphatic—'of himself, without need of any human medium') **what was in human nature**. This faculty of Jesus, wherein we have the supreme illustration of 'the gift of distinguishing spirits' (1 Cor. 12 : 10 ; cf. 1 Jn. 4 : 1) is repeatedly emphasized by our Evangelist. It has been held that John does not claim supernatural knowledge for Christ, but simply a higher degree of that insight, born of experience, which may be possessed by all men. Thus the word here used for 'know' signifies an acquired and not an innate knowledge. And yet this trait appears so often in our Gospel (cf. esp. 1 : 48, 4 : 18, 6 : 61, etc.) that it is difficult to believe that John does not ascribe to Jesus, in virtue of his Logos nature, a supernatural knowledge which quite transcends that moral and

spiritual insight into the inner life of others which even the
Synoptists claim for him (Mk. 2 : 8). ' An impression is borne
home to us, in every episode of the history, that while he
tabernacled with men he was more than human—that he
was a heavenly being who could exercise at will the pre-
rogatives of God ' (E. F. Scott, *The Fourth Gospel*, p. 166).

.3

Now there was a Pharisee named Nicodemus, who belonged 1
   to the Jewish authorities ; he came one night to Jesus 2
   and said, ' Rabbi, we know you have come from God to
   teach us, for no one could perform these Signs of yours
   unless God were with him.' Jesus replied, ' Truly, truly 3
   I tell you, no one can see God's Realm unless he is born
   from above.' Nicodemus said to him, ' How can a man 4
   be born when he is old ? Can he enter his mother's
   womb over again and be born ? ' Jesus replied, ' Truly, 5
   truly I tell you, unless one is born of water and the Spirit,
   he cannot enter God's Realm. What is born of the 6
   flesh is flesh : what is born of the Spirit is Spirit. Do 7
   not wonder at me telling you, " You must all be
   born from above." The wind blows where it wills ; 8
   you can hear its sound, but you never know where it
   has come from or where it goes : it is the same with
   everyone who is born of the Spirit.' Nicodemus answered, 9
   ' How can that be ? ' Jesus replied, ' You do not under- 10
   stand this ?—you, a teacher in Israel ! '

Though as a rule Jesus ' did not trust himself ' to men, 1
he showed his insight into human nature by his occasional
compliance no less than by his habitual reserve. In the case
of Nicodemus he makes an exception, the more remarkable
because the latter is a Pharisee, who belonged to the Jewish
authorities, that is, a member of the Sanhedrim, and as such
one of the ' official opposition ' to the Christ-party (cf. note
1 : 19). Nicodemus is not mentioned by the Synoptists,
and is otherwise unknown, though the Talmud frequently mentions as one of Jesus' followers a person of this name still
living at the time of the destruction of Jerusalem who possibly

may be identified with the present character, or at least may have provided the original for the character-study. (For other references in the Gospel see 7 : 50, 19 : 39.) Nicodemus provides the Johannine parallel to the ' Rich Young Ruler ' (Mk. 10 : 17 ff., etc.) In both cases the discussion centres upon the difficulty of entering the Kingdom (Mk. 10 : 23–25), while the immediately preceding verses in Mark (10 : 15) touch on the subject of ' re-birth.'

2   Nicodemus is represented as coming **by night,** probably out of ' fear for the Jews ' (19 : 38), though it may be that he desired the privilege of a private interview. Possibly the Evangelist regards the darkness of the night as symbolical of Nicodemus' ignorance. Some even suspect a reference to 3 : 20, but Nicodemus cannot fairly be reckoned among those who, in an ethical sense, ' hate the light.' He is rather the representative of the ' light half-believers ' of 12 : 42, and he desires to compromise neither himself nor his colleagues in whose name, as well as in his own, he says, **' Rabbi, we know you have come from God to teach us.'** (For the conciliatory mode of address compare Mk. 12 : 14, and for the thought that Jesus' teaching is ' from God,' Jn. 7 : 15–16. For the title ' Rabbi ' see note on 1 : 38.) Nicodemus belongs to the category of those mentioned in 2 : 23, whose faith in Christ is based merely upon his miracles. In his opening words we seem to hear echoes of the argument of Gamaliel (Acts 5 : 38–39), who, like Nicodemus (7 : 50), defends the cause of Christ without identifying himself with it.

3   Nicodemus' admission that Jesus has ' come from God to teach ' is virtually a challenge to Jesus to make his unique teaching known. It is to this challenge that Jesus replied— answering not the immediately preceding words but the question which he knew to be on the tip of his visitor's tongue: this, to judge by Jesus' reply, was that of Nicodemus' Synoptic prototype (Mk. 10 : 17), ' Good teacher, what must I do to inherit life eternal ? '

Jesus' reply gives us the thesis of the characteristic Johannine discourse which follows : **' No one can see God's Realm unless he is born from above.'** Jesus seeks in the first place

to correct Nicodemus' undue emphasis on *miracle* ; he desires
to lead him from a trust based on ' Signs ' to one which is
ethically and spiritually mediated ; to one who sees in por-
tents a proof that God's Realm is at hand he replies, as he
did to the questioning Pharisees (Lk. 17 : 20–21), ' the Reign
of God is not coming as *you* hope to catch sight of it—for the
Reign of God is *within you* '—it can be realized only by the
renewal of the inward, personal nature.

The phrase ' **see God's Realm** ' is noteworthy. It is unlikely
that any contrast is intended between ' *see* God's Realm '
here and ' *enter* God's Realm ' in verse 5, as if the latter
applied to the genuine ' citizen of the Kingdom,' the former
only to ' the mere intelligent spectator of its constitution and
character ' (Westcott). The word **see** is used as in Lk. 2 : 26,
Acts 2 : 27, 1 Pet. 3 : 10, with the sense ' to have experience
of.' ' *Realm of God* ' is a Synoptic expression (it occurs
only three times in our Gospel : 3 : 3, 5 ; 18 : 36) ; John's
ordinary usage would lead us to expect him to say here, ' No
one can *see life* unless he is born from above ' (cf. 3 : 36).
Curiously, while John here employs the Synoptic word
' Realm,' in the corresponding Synoptic passage (Mk. 10 : 17)
the favourite Johannine word ' life ' occurs, though doubtless
without the full mystical content which it always bears in
our Gospel. A comparison of Mt. 7 : 14 and 7 : 21 suggests
that the way to ' find life ' is to ' enter the Kingdom.' Hence
for our present purpose the ' *realm of God*,' and ' *life* ' may
be regarded as almost synonymous terms. Though John
here employs the former, his usual conception of ' life '
colours the significance which he gives to it. Even ' life '
in the heavenly ' realm ' implies the necessity of ' birth,' for
procreation and birth are everywhere the presuppositions
of life.

The would-be citizen of **God's Realm** must then be **born
*from above***, or ' born *anew* ' (Gk. *anothen*). The word may
be used with both meanings, and which is the sense intended here can be decided only by reference to the context.
In favour of the translation ' from above ' is John's usage in
3 : 31 ; 19 : 11, 23, with which we may compare Mk. 15 : 38

James 1 : 17, 3 : 15. In favour of the sense 'anew' is Nicodemus' reply in verse 4, and the general bearing of the section,
the intention of which appears to be to illustrate the nature
of the 'New Faith' by the necessity of a 'New Birth.' On
the other hand the immediate context favours the translation
'from above': the condition of entrance into the heavenly
realm is a heavenly birth, a 'birth from above.' John's
choice of an ambiguous word and its use with a *double
entente* is probably deliberate. For the dramatic development of the scene it is necessary that Nicodemus should
understand the word literally as referring to a *second* physical
birth: but the Evangelist intends us to interpret his words,
in the light of such passages as Mk. 10 : 15, Mt. 18 : 3, in the
ethical sense of a birth *from above*. He thus transforms the
pagan ideas of 'rebirth' which were prevalent when he wrote.
The entrance upon eternal life is conditioned not by a magical
renewal of the physical nature to be obtained by prescribed
rites, but by a birth *from above*, from God, who alone can give
men 'power to become his sons.' John's conception of the
New Birth stands directly related to the teaching both of
Jesus and of Paul. On the one hand we hear echoes of Jesus'
words (Mt. 18: 3): 'Unless you turn and become like children,
you will never get into the Realm of heaven at all,'—'the
same essential thought of a new life taking its departure from
an entire break with the past' (E. F. Scott). On the other
hand we are reminded of the Pauline doctrines of a heavenly
'adoption' (Rom. 8: 15, Gal. 4: 5 ff.), and a 'new creation'
(2 Cor. 5: 17, Gal. 6: 15; cf. Col. 3: 9–10). The closest
parallel to John's thought is in 1 Pet. 1: 3, 23.

On the supposition that in verse 3 we have the actual
words of Jesus, analogies have been sought in such O.T.
passages as Deut. 10: 16, or Ezek. 11: 19. But such parallels
are very imperfect, and it is easier to suppose that the Evangelist, under the influence of his Ephesian environment, is
reflecting the language of the Mystery Religions. The conception of 'rebirth' as a condition of 'salvation' was widely
current; even the Jews spoke of Gentile proselytes baptized
into their religion as 'new-born'; at Rome those initiated

into the Taurobolium and Kriobolium of the Great Mother and Attis were termed ' renati in aeternum.' Isis too had her ' renati,' while the rite of ' rebirth ' was the principal content of the Mithras-mysteries. Tertullian tells us that the heathen were baptized ' in regenerationem ' (cf. Rom. 6 : 1–11). John of course transforms the whole conception, but his thought undoubtedly clothes itself in terminology which reflects the current usage of his day.

Nicodemus misses the point of Jesus' challenge, for he has **4** not the insight to see below the analogy by which it is expressed. He understands Jesus' words in their literal sense : ' **How can a man be born when he is old ? Can he enter his mother's womb over again and be born ? '** Or can it be that Nicodemus' reply is not so much stupid as wistful ? Does he understand well enough that it is of a spiritual rebirth that Jesus speaks, but argues that such a radical change of heart, after a man's habits of thought and life are fixed ('**when he is old**'), is no more conceivable than the physical miracle by which Jesus symbolizes it ? To discuss the exact force of '**when he is old**' is superfluous, for clearly a man's old age neither adds to nor takes from the impossibility of his ' entering his mother's womb over again.' Possibly there may be an allusion to Nicodemus' own age : more probably the words merely express conversely Jesus' thought of becoming ' like a child ' (Mk. 10 : 15). Indeed, the whole Nicodemus-section awakens so many Synoptic echoes that little save the setting can be regarded as strictly original to our Evangelist, whose purpose in this verse is not so much to report a historical conversation as to illustrate the Pauline truth that ' the unspiritual man rejects the truths of the Spirit of God ; to him they are sheer folly, he cannot understand them ' (1 Cor. 2 : 14).

Jesus' reply is to follow up his assertion of the *necessity* of **5** the new birth with a definition of its *conditions*. The verse is an elaboration of verse 3. Instead of ' see ' we have **enter** : ' born from above ' is expanded into '**born of water and the Spirit.**' It is not, says Jesus, of a physical birth that he speaks, a birth ' from the womb,' but of an ethical and mystical rebirth 'from water and the Spirit.' How are we to understand these last words? Probably not as a description, under two collateral symbols, of the creative power of God (for 'water' in such a sense cf. 4 : 14, 7 : 38, and for 'wind' 3 : 8. So Loisy), but rather as an echo of 1 : 33, where 'water' and 'Spirit' are contrasted with special reference to the rite of Baptism (cf. Mt. 3 : 11, Acts 1 : 5). John's 'water' baptism was symbolic only: Jesus, who also employed the symbol (3 : 22), though perhaps giving it a subordinate place (4 : 2), brought also to men the 'spiritual' reality for which the symbol stood (1 : 33). The Evangelist here emphasizes the significance of Baptism perhaps because the Pharisees, of whom Nicodemus was the representative, had refused the rite (Lk. 7 : 30). At the same time he guards against a superstitious view of the sacrament by conjoining 'water' with 'Spirit.' The entrance into the Kingdom of God is a spiritual act of which the outward rite is only the seal; a higher agency must co-operate with the material element; water is but the vehicle and instrument of the Spirit: 'The entrance to the Church is through a sacrament not outward only, but spiritual also' (Westcott). Yet 'water' and 'Spirit' are here so closely co-ordinated that it is hardly true to say that the former stands for *mere* symbol. For the Evangelist even the symbol has real efficacy: water, by cleansing (Ps. 51 : 2, 7; Zech. 13 : 1, Eph. 5 : 26), supplies the negative side, as the Spirit, by quickening, supplies the positive side, of the new creation. (Compare Ezek. 36 : 25–27, Titus 3 : 5 for this twofold aspect of regeneration, and see note on 1 : 33.) This implied reference to the Christian rite of Baptism, though strictly speaking an anachronism on Jesus' lips, comes naturally enough from the pen of one who consistently writes with the conditions of the Church of his own time in view.

6   'Birth from the Spirit' is necessary because man's natural origin is not 'Spirit' but 'flesh,' and according to the universal law that like springs from like (cf. Aristotle, *Eth. Maj.*, 1, 10: 'Every nature generates its own *substance*,' not merely perpetuates its own qualities; similarly here we have the

substantive ' flesh,' not merely the adjective ' fleshly '),
' what is born of the flesh is flesh,' and only ' what is born of the
Spirit is Spirit.' Man's natural birth therefore can produce
only ' flesh.' Entrance to the Kingdom thus demands as its
condition not only an ethical change, as in the Synoptic
demand for repentance, but a metaphysical transmutation of
nature (cf. Scott, op. cit., p. 281). In the Pauline phraseology
' flesh ' (Gk. *sarx*) is the symbol of the sin-ward side of
human nature (' Though it does not of itself include the idea
of sinfulness it describes human nature on the side which
tends to sin '—Westcott), and together with the ' sensuous '
(Gk. *psychikos*) side is contrasted with the ' Spiritual '
(Gk. *pneumatikos*), which alone can ' inherit the Realm of
God ' (1 Cor. 15 : 50).

Nicodemus having expressed **wonder** at this necessity, Jesus 7
repeats that not even the foremost representatives of religious
Israel (plural **you**) are exempt from it : Nicodemus would
cease to wonder could he but understand that it is as impossible to explore the ways of the Spirit as to trace the foot-
steps of the wind and to guess ' where it comes from or where it 8
goes ' (Loisy notes that John applies the same thought to
Jesus, 7 : 27-28, 8 : 14, 9 : 29-30). ' The operation of the
regenerating principle is not bound to any rule, but is revealed
only by its divine effects in the human soul ' (Godet). Similarly, Socrates says (*Xen. Mem.*, 4, 3), ' the winds are invisible
though their effects are plain ; the soul of man is itself unseen ;
therefore despise not the unseen but honour God.' Colour
is added to the illustration by a play on words impossible to
reproduce in English, the Greek *pneuma* like the Hebrew
ruach bearing the double meaning of ' wind ' and ' Spirit.'
The point is that the Spirit, like the wind, is self-creative, and
accountable to itself alone (1 Cor. 12 : 11, ' as he pleases '), and
its workings are not unnaturally puzzling to Nicodemus, for
they are understandable only in the light of an experience
of which he as yet knows nothing (1 Cor. 2 : 14). How far
is this demand for a new birth—an echo of the Synoptic idea
that man may become perfect (Mt. 5 : 48)—consistent with
the original Johannine view, which appears to contemplate

not the changing of sinners into saints, but the division of men
once for all into those who have and those who have not
been partakers of the divine generation (1 : 12–13) ?

9　Nicodemus, realizing now that it is of a supernatural process
that Jesus speaks, asks, 'How can that be ?' Jesus ironically
10 expresses surprise at his perplexity: 'You do not understand?—
you, *the accredited* teacher (the article is emphatic) in Israel!'
This conception of the creative might and spontaneous action
of the Divine Spirit and its opposition to 'the flesh' is no new
doctrine, but should be easily recognizable to an expert in the
Scriptures from passages such as Jer. 31: 33, Ezek. 36: 26–28,
Ps. 139: 7.

11 'Truly, truly I tell you, we are speaking of what we do under-
　　stand, we testify to what we have actually seen—and yet
12　　you refuse our testimony. If you will not believe when I
　　speak to you about things on earth, how will you believe
13　　if I speak to you about things in heaven ? And yet the
　　Son of man, descended from heaven, is the only one who
　　has ever ascended into heaven.'

11　Nicodemus lapses into silence, and the passage passes into a
monologue by Jesus, which in turn merges into the reflections
of the Evangelist ; from this point Nicodemus recedes into
the background, and interest centres upon Jesus and in and
through him upon his Church in the midst of an unbelieving
world. Though for another two or three verses the words
are still ostensibly those of Jesus, and merge almost insensibly
into those of the Evangelist, from verse 11 onwards Jesus is,
in fact, not the speaker but the subject of the Evangelist's
meditation. Thus when he says ' *We* are speaking of what we
do understand,' the use of the plural is not merely rhetorical,
nor a linking up of Jesus with John the Baptist, nor, as some
old expositors held, an allusion to the three Persons of the
Trinity ; rather it reflects Christ's consciousness of his universality, hints that the Christ Spirit is now incarnate in the
Church. Jesus' words have passed insensibly into a declaration of the community: the writer, as the representative of

that community, testifies that he has himself been conscious
of a change wrought within him through the Spirit of Christ,
and that he has actually seen a similar change in the lives of
others.   The claim of 1: 14, 19: 35, 21: 24; 1 Jn. 1: 1–3; 3 Jn.
12 is here put on Jesus' own lips—but it is the Risen Jesus
speaking through the voice of his Church.   'And yet,' in spite of
such credentials, 'you refuse our testimony.'   The reference in
'you' is firstly to the Pharisees of whom Nicodemus is the
representative, and secondly to those in the Evangelist's own
day of whom he is the type (cf. 1: 10–11).

Nicodemus' lack of spiritual discernment has proved him in- 12
capable of understanding 'things on earth': how then can he be
expected to believe when Jesus speaks of 'things in heaven'?
The force of these two phrases is much disputed.   The meaning
must obviously be gathered from the immediate context, and
it seems at first most natural to see in 'things of earth' a
reference to the subject under discussion, i.e. the 'second
birth.'   Is it possible that this regeneration, as a process
at any rate experienced on earth, can be thought of as
'earthly,' in contrast to the consummation foreshadowed in
1 Jn. 3: 2?   Hardly, when regeneration already has its own
earthly counterpart in the natural birth, while Jesus expressly
speaks of it as due to the Spirit and as being 'from above.'
Possibly the reference is not exclusively to regeneration but
to the whole content of 'our testimony' (11).   Then, as Godet
puts it, 'Jesus contrasts the events which transpire on the
theatre of human consciousness, and which man can test by
self-observation, with divine counsels and plans which can
only be known by means of a revelation.'   But perhaps the
following would be an explanation more characteristic of our
author.   In Lk. 16: 11 the riches of heaven are called 'true'
riches, that is 'real' as opposed to symbolical, from which it has
been conjectured that in our passage the contrast suggested by
'things of heaven' and 'things of earth' may be the same as
that drawn in 16: 25, where to 'speak earthly things' is to
'tell in figures,' to make use of symbol as Jesus has here done
with his analogy of the wind, while 'to speak heavenly things'
is to drop the use of symbol, which makes understanding easier

to the child, and deal in terms of pure thought—'to let you know plainly about the Father.'

13 In the face of such teaching by Christ the world remains sceptical; 'and yet' if anyone can claim credence he can, in virtue of that unique relationship to 'heavenly things' which enables him alone to speak of them at first hand; for he is 'the only one who has ever ascended into heaven.' The question asked in Deut. 30: 11–12, Rom. 10: 6 is here answered. A knowledge of God, which could have been acquired by men themselves only by an ascent into heaven— which is an impossibility—has been communicated through 'the Son of man, descended from heaven.' (For this co-ordination of the ideas of 'ascent' and 'descent' compare 16: 28, Eph. 4: 10.) It is the descent of Christ from God which is here emphasized, with reference to such passages as 1: 14, 16: 28, etc. If the words are to be accepted strictly as an utterance of Jesus himself, the meaning can only be that the Son, descended from heaven in the Incarnation, has received a divine revelation through a mystic fellowship with 'things in heaven' (as experienced, e.g., at the baptism, when 'the heavens opened'), which is here called 'an ascent into heaven,' in virtue of which he lives, even in the course of his human life, in immediate intuition of divine things. Such would then be the meaning of the disputed clause (see A.V.) omitted in our translation '*which is in heaven*.' 'Heaven' is not so much a locality as a condition of being which can be experienced even on earth; the words would be equivalent to the phrase (in 1: 18) 'upon the Father's breast,' which might similarly be interpreted of a mystical fellowship experienced on earth. But the verse, though put on Jesus' lips, is probably to be taken rather as a reflection of the Evangelist in the light of Christ's subsequent death and Resurrection. 'Ascended into heaven' can then be taken, more simply, as a definite allusion to the Ascension as an event of history (cf. 6: 62, 20: 17). '*Which is in heaven*' (a phrase which may possibly be genuine but would be readily omitted because of the difficulty of referring the words to Jesus himself) would then be an echo of Dan. 7: 13, 1 Cor.

15 : 47–48, where the ' Son of man ' is thought of as a purely
heavenly being, and the meaning would be not that ' he used
to be in heaven and has left it,' nor that ' he still holds mystic
fellowship with heaven,' but that he has returned to heaven
as exalted, and thence inspires through his Spirit the teaching
of his Church ; 1 : 18 is also more naturally interpreted thus.
Baldensperger finds the force of the words ' the only one ' in a
supposed allusion to the Baptist Sect who held that Elijah
was incarnate in John the Baptist, who had thus ascended
and returned in John's person as a revealer of heavenly things.

From this point to the end of the chapter the text shows
unmistakable signs of disarrangement. The obvious continuation of verses 12–13 is verse 31, where the contrasted
ideas of ' heaven ' and ' earth ' are again picked up. There
is general agreement that verses 22–30 are out of place, this
section as a rule being transposed to follow 2 : 12. A better
position is after 3 : 36, where see note. But the sequence of
chapter 3 would be greatly improved if 14–21 were also removed
from their present context, verses 13 and 31 being thus
brought into immediate juxtaposition. The only point of
connexion between 13 and 14 is the very artificial one afforded
by the cognate ideas contained in ' ascended into heaven '
and ' lifted on high.' The whole section 14–21 should, it is
suggested, be transposed to follow 12 : 32, 3 : 14–15 taking the
place of 12 : 33 (which is obviously a gloss), and 3 : 16–21
being inserted between 12 : 34 and 12 : 35–36. By this rearrangement the sequence of chapter 12 is also greatly improved, while 3 : 14–21, which in its present context has always
been felt to end very abruptly and unsympathetically, finds
the most appropriate possible climax in 12 : 35–36. (See
note following 12 : 32.)

We pass therefore straight to 3 : 31.

For convenience, however, the commentary on 3 : 14–21,
together with a note on its setting in chapter 12 is inserted,
within brackets, at this point.

[' Indeed the Son of man must be lifted on high, just as Moses 14
lifted up the serpent in the desert, that everyone who 15

16   believes in him may have eternal life. For God loved the
     world so dearly that He gave up His only Son, so that
     everyone who believes in him may have eternal life, in-
17   stead of perishing. God did not send His Son into the
     world to pass sentence on it, but to save the world
18   by him. He who believes in him is not sentenced ;
     he who will not believe is sentenced already, for having
     refused to believe in the name of the only Son of God.
19   And this is the sentence of condemnation, that the Light
     has entered the world and yet men have preferred darkness
     to light. It is because their actions have been evil ;
20   for anyone whose practices are corrupt loathes the light
     and will not come out into it, in case his actions are
21   exposed, whereas anyone whose life is true comes out into
     the light, to make it plain that his actions have been divinely
     prompted.'

This section, which is out of place in its usual context, admirably supplements the conversation recorded in 12 : 30 ff.,
which is clearly incomplete as we now have it.   The question
of the people in 12 : 34 : ' Who is *this* Son of man ? ' requires an
immediately previous use of the title by Jesus.   This would be
obtained by inserting 3 : 14–15 after 12 : 32 (12 : 33 has the
appearance of a gloss which has taken the place of 3 : 14, and
indeed is explanatory of it rather than of 12 : 32).   Moreover,
12 : 35 contains Jesus' answer to 12 : 34 only on the supposition
that he shirks the question.   The real answer to 12 : 34 is
supplied by 3 : 16–21, which should be inserted here, 12 : 35–36
affording a most appropriate climax to the paragraph, which
in its usual position in chapter 3 ends most abruptly.   Notice
that the allusion in 3 : 14 to Christ's sacrificial death is prepared for by 12 : 24–25, that the reference to ' judgment ' in
12 : 31 is followed up by a development of the same idea in
3 : 18 ff., and that the theme of God's universal love for all
the world, which rings throughout the passage 3 : 16 ff., is in
complete harmony with the situation brought about by the
visit of the Gentile Greeks (12 : 20 ff.).   For the sequence of
the text as rearranged see commentary *in loco*, chapter 12

Immediately following 12 : 32 we therefore insert 3 : 14-15, which continue the veiled allusion to the Cross in 12 : 32. The ultimate triumph of the crucified Christ is as certain as the divine decree, whereby first '**the Son of Man** *must* **be lifted on high**' (' must ' is emphatic : see note below).

' **Lifted on high** ' is a phrase with a double meaning. In Luke 14 (10 : 15, 14 : 11, 18 : 14) it is used in opposition to the idea of ' humbling' (cf. also 2 Cor. 11 : 7, James 4 : 10, 1 Pet. 5 : 6). But here, as also in 8 : 28 and 12 : 32, there is a direct reference to the ' lifting up ' on the Cross. It is characteristic of our Evangelist to relate Christ's exaltation to his death. Compare his use of the words ' glory ' and ' glorify' (note on 1 : 14 and 13 : 31). See also Is. 52 : 13, and especially Acts 2 : 33 and 5 : 31, both of which passages are immediately preceded, in 2 : 23 and 5 : 30, by a reference to the Crucifixion (cf. also Lk. 24 : 26). The exaltation on the Cross is the first step of the ascent to the throne.

Christ then *must* be ' lifted up '—' **just as Moses lifted up the serpent in the desert,**' the reference being to Num. 21 : 8-9, which was read by the Alexandrian School as a type of the Crucifixion. Probably it is not so much the comparison of Christ with the serpent which is emphasized as the divine necessity (*must ;* cf. Mt. 16 : 21, Lk. 24 : 26) of the ' lifting up ' whereby salvation is mediated. At the same time there is real force in the words ' just as ' . . . *thus*, upon a stake, in contrast to the glorious Messianic exaltation promised by the Pharisees. Again, unlike the god at the esoteric Mysteries, Christ like the serpent was not shown to a few selected persons, but was exalted where all the world might see him and ' be drawn to him.'

The Israelites were saved by *looking at* the serpent, a thought to which we have an exact parallel in 6 : 40. Here we are told that ' **everyone who** *believes* **may in him have eternal life.**' 15 (Note that ' in him ' should be taken not with ' believes '— which would require a different Greek preposition—but with ' have ' ; cf. 1 : 4.) It is important to grasp the peculiar Johannine force of the word ' believe,' but not always easy to do so, for the Evangelist ' has but one word to denote all the different stages of belief' (Sanday, *Criticism of the Fourth Gospel*, p. 161). It is noticeable that he never uses the word in its substantive form 'faith,' probably because the word had been appropriated in a technical sense by the Gnostic theology, and our writer wishes to guard himself from any possible confusion of his teaching with that of the heretical systems. But under its various verbal forms the idea of 'believing' dominates the whole Gospel. In general we may admit that the 'believing' insisted on by John 'is something much narrower and poorer than the Pauline "faith." It implies not so much an inward disposition of trust and obedience, as the acceptance of a given dogma. To "believe" is to grant the hypothesis that Jesus was indeed the Christ, the Son of God.' But at the same time John's conception of faith is something more than mere intellectual assent, because 'the act of belief . . . is the summing up in an intellectual judgment of a previous religious experience. The confession that Jesus is the Son of God implies that you have been drawn to Jesus, and have recognized his saving power and the divine character of his life.' Once again 'assent is demanded not merely to a bare fact, but to the claim of a person, and it therefore partakes in some measure of the character of trust (cf. 12 : 44, 14 : 1). . . . Since a living Person is the object of the act of belief, that act, in itself a mere intellectual one, becomes involved with moral elements' (quotations from E. F. Scott, *The Fourth Gospel*, pp. 268–70). Note that while in the Mystery Religions the culminating rite through which 'life' was communicated was the vision of the Godhead (Gk. *epopteia*), our Evangelist here deliberately omits this thought (though the gazing of the people at the serpent presented an obvious parallel), and makes 'life' conditional upon a 'believing' which, as we have seen, has real moral content. Even 6 : 40 adds the necessity of 'believing' to that of 'seeing.' Moreover, John, like Paul, makes life conditional upon union with Christ : for Paul life may only be had 'in Christ Jesus' ; John's believer 'has *in him* eternal life' (cf. 15 : 4). This life is spoken of as eternal, not so much as contrasted with the temporary prolongation of life which was the reward of looking at the serpent, but rather as having its origin in the higher, eternal world. 'Eternal' is a qualitative and not merely a quantitative conception: it refers to the character and not merely to the duration of life. This life is not a future promise, but a present possession of the believer, in virtue of that act of faith which has put him in touch with the realm of 'the eternal' (cf. also note on 10 : 15, 14 : 9).

Here, according to our rearrangement, there follows 12 : 34 : **So the people answered, 'We have learned from the Law that the Christ is to remain for ever ; what do you mean by saying that the Son of man must be lifted up ? Who is this Son of man ? '** If the usual order of the text be retained (12 : 35 immediately following 12 : 34), then in replying to the people 'Jesus vouchsafes no direct solution of their difficulty' (Dods). If, as suggested above, we here insert 3 : 16–21, Jesus no longer appears to shirk the question. **Then Jesus said to them** (the opening words of 12 : 35), '**I** will tell you who this Son of man is and why he must be lifted up. It must be so, **for God so loved the world . . .'** God's love embraces all the *world,* not merely 'elect believers' (Loisy), though the following clause limits the gift of life to these. Our Gospel accepts the universality of Christianity more fully than any other N.T. book. (For the twofold sense of the word '**world**' see note on 1 : 10.) It is here regarded as the arena in which the salvation of believers is wrought out and as such the object of God's universal love. (Compare 4 : 42, 6 : 33, 12 : 47, and contrast 17 : 9, 14–16, etc.) This world-embracing love of God is proved by the fact that '**He gave up His only Son** ': the meaning is not merely that God 'sent' His Son (1 Jn. 4 : 9), but that He 'gave him up to *death* ' (cf. Rom. 8 : 32), with an obvious reference to Gen. 22 : 2. It is as a sin-offering that the Son of man is to be 'lifted up.'

God's love is limitless, but it can only be appropriated by faith ; accordingly love's gift is confined to '**everyone that believes in him,**' the promise being that all such shall '**have eternal life instead of perishing.**' In the Greek the tenses are significant. 'Perishing' is spoken of as a momentary event, 'eternal life' as an enduring possession.

17   We are here met with another of those apparent contradictions which are a constant difficulty in the interpretation
of the Gospel—the Evangelist's seemingly inconsistent statements concerning the place held by Christ in the world's
'judgment.' In many passages Christ claims supreme power
of judgment (cf. 5 : 22, 5 : 27, 9 : 39, 12 : 31). Here, as
in 12 : 47 (another proof that this section belongs to chapter
12), we are told that '**God did not send** ("the word, which contains the root of 'apostle,' suggests the thought of a definite
mission and a representative character in the envoy"—Westcott) **His Son into the world to pass sentence on it, but to save
the world by him.**' In contrast to the Jews' vindictive conception of the purpose of Messiah's coming, and possibly also
with an allusion to the Baptist's excessive emphasis on
'judgment,' it is here stated that judgment is not the motive
but rather the inevitable consequence of Christ's coming.
Christ comes to pass sentence on the world 'as little as the sun
comes to throw a shadow,' but 'judgment like the shadow is
the natural consequence of the world's constitution and
circumstances' (Holtzmann). The apparent contradiction
is thus reconciled: 'The judgment is on Christ's part in-
voluntary, for his whole desire is to draw men unto him and
save them. But none the less it is a real judgment' (Scott,
p. 215). Christ's appearance compels men by their attitude
to him to show themselves up in their true colours, and thereby they pass sentence on themselves: '**he who believes in
18 him is not sentenced ; he who will not believe is sentenced
already, for having refused to believe in the name of the only
Son of God.**' Just as a man who disparages a great work
of art condemns not the masterpiece but himself, so does the
unbeliever stand self-condemned. Note that for John such a
man 'is sentenced *already*'; judgment is taken out of the
future and carried back into the present with the result that,
though sometimes John appears to approximate to the
Synoptic view of a judgment 'at the last day' (cf. 5 : 28–29,
12 : 48), in reality this judgment is for him merely the
summing up of a process which is already going on. Each
of us has already pronounced a clear enough verdict on

our own moral tendency, and the Judge will only have to confirm it.

It should be noted that the Greek word here translated 'sentenced' (*krinein, krisis*) bears the double sense of 'to judge'—usually adversely—and 'to separate.' The process referred to in verses 17–18 is perhaps not so much 'condemnation' as the 'separation' of those who are to be partakers of life and those who are not. Salvation is offered to all: some by faith appropriate it, others by disbelief reveal their natural unfitness to receive it. In other words ' it needs to be observed that this judgment is not, in the first instance, an ethical one. Rather it connects itself with John's semi-Gnostic distinction of two great classes in the human race, those who are from above and those from below, children of light and children of darkness. The work of Christ was to sift out, as by a magnet, the purer element in mankind from the lower and grosser' (Scott, p. 215). Yet this statement must be modified in so far as we have seen that for John the act of ' belief' has real moral content. This idea of the predisposition on the part of men themselves either for or against Christ may almost be said to take the place in John's thought of the Pauline doctrine of divine election (cf. notes on 5 : 21 ff.).

This thought is carried on in the following verse, the point 19 of which is that ' judgment is not an arbitrary sentence but the working out of an absolute law' (Westcott). How it is that this ' sentence of condemnation ' is passed John illustrates by the use of the word *light* (which here occurs for the first time since the Prologue, and, as there, in conjunction with the word ' life '), a characteristic Johannine term which unites the two ideas of ' knowledge of the truth ' and ' moral integrity.' ' Light ' is ' holiness clearly revealed to the human conscience ' (Godet) (cf. Introduction, p. xxxviii). The emphasis here is not so much on the fact that men have rejected salvation when it was at their very doors as on the fact that the entrance of ' the Light ' into the world has provided the occasion for men's own self-condemnation on the evidence that they have ' preferred darkness to light.' The coming of Christ has compelled men to range themselves on one side or the other (cf. 12 : 48—yet

another link between this passage and chap. 12). Previously
men sinned through ignorance : they now do so by deliberate
choice. To say ' Evil be thou my good ' is to ' sin against the
Holy Ghost,' and thereby pass on oneself an irrevocable sentence of condemnation. The reason for so strange a preference
is that **' their actions have been evil '** ; that is, their whole moral
conduct is corrupt, and they therefore shun the light ; for sin
they must, but even a bad man does not care to sin in the full
light of day. Hence it is a universal law of psychology that
20 **' anyone whose practices are corrupt** (or rather ' paltry,'
' worthless,' ' such as will not stand the test ' ; cf. 2 Cor. 5 :
10) **loathes the light and will not come out into it, in case his
actions are exposed '** (cf. 16 : 8, Eph. 5 : 13, 1 Cor. 3 : 13).
A bad man hates the light because it shows up his *true character* not only to his own conscience but also to his fellows.
21 The converse is equally true : **' anyone whose life is true comes
out into the light.'** The A.V. has ' doeth the truth.' (Cf.
1 Jn. 1 : 6.) The phrase occurs in the O.T. (Gen. 32 : 10,
47 : 29, Neh. 9 : 33), but whereas there it denotes little more
than conduct conformable to one's nature or position, here
(as a result of the deepening of the concept of ' truth ' by
John) it denotes conduct conformable to the divine reality as
revealed in conscience. To ' do truth ' is to make ' truth '
in its full Johannine sense (see 1 : 9), the determining factor
in one's actions, ' to aim at reality—in the first place as regards
ourselves ' (R. H. Strachan). The man with such an aim does
not fear the light, but **' comes out into the light, to make it plain
that his actions have been divinely prompted '** ; for otherwise
they could not stand the test. That is, when a man's aim is
to see himself and let others see him as he really is (' doeth the
truth '), he welcomes the most searching scrutiny, all the
more so if his conduct is sound through and through ; for he
knows that when light falls on ' truth ' the only result is to
show up its genuineness. To ' have one's actions divinely
prompted ' (A.V. ' wrought in God ') is almost a synonym for
' doing the truth,' and means to act always with a true appreciation of what the action means to God.

Notice how this paragraph emphasizes the relation of the

will to the understanding. However 'intellectual' John's conception of faith may be, only the man who 'does the truth' is able to 'come to the light' and finally 'believe.' 'Light,' which for John means goodness revealed to the intellect, is closely related to 'truth,' which means goodness revealed to the conscience and will. If 'right action is true thought realized' (Westcott) the converse is equally valid that a man can understand the truth only when he is willing to do the right. (Cf. 7 : 17: 'If any man will do his will, he shall know of the doctrine.') How much of our modern 'unbelief' is due not at all to the 'intellectual perplexities' of which we hear so much, but to the fact that our wills shirk the moral constraint which Christ lays upon us. By thus insisting that 'enlightenment' is attainable only by way of ethical goodness John once again repudiates Gnostic doctrine, and takes his stand on Jesus' own teaching: 'Blessed are the pure in heart, for they shall see God.'

Here follows 12 : 35–36, wherein the paragraph reaches the fittest possible conclusion with a practical exhortation 'to redeem the time.']

The connexion with 3 : 13 is now picked up.

'He who comes from above is far above all others ; he who 31 springs from earth belongs to earth and speaks of earth ; he who comes from heaven [is far above all others. 32 He] is testifying to what he has seen and heard, and yet no one accepts his testimony. Whoever does accept 33 it, certifies to the truth of God. For he whom God has 34 sent utters the words of God—God gives him the Spirit in no sparing measure ; the Father loves the Son and has 35 given him control over everything. He who believes in 36 the Son has eternal life, but he who disobeys the Son shall not see life—God's anger broods over him.'

'He who comes' was a customary title of Messiah: John, 31 by adding the words 'from above,' carries on the thought of verse 13, and thereby identifies 'the Son of man' with the promised Messiah. In virtue of his heavenly origin he speaks with an authority 'far above all others' (cf. 8: 23, Acts 10: 36, Rom. 9: 5), who, being 'sprung from earth' continue to 'belong to earth,' and accordingly 'speak of earth'—the last words referring not so much to the content of their message as to its source: their words come with no greater authority than a mere earthly source of information can bestow. Christ, on the other hand, in virtue of the fact that he 'comes from heaven'

32 can claim the unique authority of one who 'is testifying to what he has seen and heard.' Just as verse 31 picks up verse 13, so does verse 32 pick up verse 11. Though Christ speaks with supreme authority as one who has first-hand knowledge 'yet no one accepts his testimony.' That is to be expected from people of like spirit with Nicodemus (ver. 12), who have not yet experienced the heavenly birth, and whose thoughts therefore move only in the sphere of earthly things (1 Jn. 4: 5). Notice that this verse would come most unnaturally after verse 26, 'everybody goes to him'—another argument in favour of placing the section 3: 22–30 at the end of the chapter.

33 And yet, after all, the rejection of Christ's testimony has not been quite universal, and 'whoever does accept it, certifies to the truth of God,' or more literally, 'sets his seal to God's trustworthiness.' Just as the affixing of a seal guarantees the validity of a document, so does the man who accepts Christ's testimony to the extent of being willing to put his personal seal upon it, thereby give his guarantee to the trustworthiness of God; for Christ is God's ambassador, and as such represents God (8: 26, 28, etc.), so that to trust Christ is to trust God. Conversely disbelief in Christ 'makes God a liar' (1 Jn. 5: 10). Christ is 'the "yes" that affirms all the promises of God' (2 Cor. 1: 20, and notice the similar use of the word 'seal' in 2 Cor. 1: 22. Lightfoot quotes a fine old Jewish saying, 'the seal of God is truth.' Compare also 6: 27).

34 To accept the testimony of the ambassador is to certify to the truth of God because 'he whom God has sent utters the words of God' (7: 16, 8: 28, 12: 49, 14: 10, etc.), so that to trust the Ambassador is to trust Him who sends him, all

the more so that the former comes as a ' plenipotentiary';
for ' God gives him the Spirit in no sparing measure.' Though
in the Greek both subject and indirect object are omitted,
this is undoubtedly the force of the words, for the following
verse makes it clear that the Father is the giver and the Son
the receiver. True, the omission gives the statement the
appearance of a general proposition, but it is one which (with
obvious reference to 1 : 32–33) applies especially to Christ.
The words ' not by measure ' (A.V.) mean not ' beyond all
certain reckoning,' but rather ' beyond the measure experienced by all who are sent by God.' The thought is that for
each of His messengers God has given a measure of His Spirit
proportionate to his task, and that this is surpassingly true
of Christ, who has a unique mission, and of whom it can therefore be said in a unique sense that he is one ' **whom God has
sent.**' Christ *is* sent in a unique sense because of the unique 35
love-relationship between Father and Son, in virtue of which
he has received a full commission in contrast to the fragmentary revelation vouchsafed to earlier prophets, who,
though also ' sent by God,' yet enjoyed but a fitful and imperfect experience of the Spirit (13 : 3, 17 : 2 ; Mt. 11 : 27,
28 : 18 ; contrast Mt. 13 : 17, Heb. 1 : 1–2) : ' **the Father loves
the Son and has given him control over everything.**'

When such an ambassador appears each man's attitude to 36
him determines his eternal destiny : ' **he who believes on the
Son has eternal life,**' that is, as a present possession (cf. 5 : 24),
while ' **he who disobeys shall not see life,**' not even if he waits
an eternity for it (note the similar contrast in tenses in 3 : 16).
It is significant that even for John the antithesis of faith is
not merely intellectual unbelief, but ' disobedience.' Unbelief may be a dissent from truth either of the intelligence
(Acts 14 : 2) or of the will (Rom. 11 : 30). For John the
will plays an important part in the act of faith (cf. notes on
3 : 15 and 3 : 21) ; for faith *is* an act, and similarly here
' disbelief is regarded in its activity ' (Westcott) as disobedience. When a man is guilty of such, ' **God's anger broods
over him,**' that is, he is punished by the *enduring* wrath of
God. God's anger is said to ' abide on him ' (A.V.), either

because it is thought of as *already* directed upon unregenerate man even before his act of disobedience (cf. 3 : 18, Rom. 1 : 18, esp. Eph. 2 : 3 : such men are ' objects of God's anger by nature '), or because God's anger is regarded as a *never-ending* reaction of the divine nature against sin.

Theme (ii) : The New Master—in relation to the Baptist
(3 : 22–30)

22 After this Jesus and his disciples went into the country of Judaea, where he spent some time with them baptizing.
23 John was also baptizing at Aenon near Salim, as there was plenty of water there, and people came to him and
24 were baptized (John had not yet been thrown into prison).
25 Now a dispute arose between John's disciples and a Jew
26 over the question of ' purification ' ; and they came and told John, ' Rabbi, the man who was with you on the opposite side of the Jordan, the man to whom you bore testimony—here he is, baptizing, and everybody
27 goes to him ! ' John answered, ' No one can receive
28 anything except as a gift from heaven. You can bear me out, that I said, " I am not the Christ " ; what I said
29 was, " I have been sent in advance of him." He who has the bride is the bridegroom ; the bridegroom's friend, who stands by and listens to him, is heartily glad at the sound of the bridegroom's voice. Such is my joy, and
30 it is complete. He must wax, I must wane.'

At this point, rather than after 2 : 12, we insert the section dealing with the renewed testimony of the Baptist to Christ. The reference to *baptizing* and the Baptist-disciples' jealous questioning concerning the comparative efficacy of Jesus' baptism and John's come more naturally after than before the discussion on the ' second birth ' with its emphasis upon the need for baptism (3 : 5). Furthermore, 3 : 25–30 provide a most appropriate introduction to 4 : 1, which verse has much more point if immediately preceded by 3 : 26 : ' everybody goes to him.'

22 Jesus now left the *town* of Jerusalem and went into the

country-side **of Judaea.** (For this use of the Gk. *ge* in the
sense of the country districts as opposed to the town compare
the similar use of *chōra* in Mk. 1 : 5 and Jn. 11 : 54-55.)
There is no need to assume that Jesus is moving from some
place outside Judaea (e.g. from Galilee) into that province
as is urged by those who place this section after 2 : 12, at
which point Jesus is in Galilee. Escaping then from the city
crowds Jesus **spent some time with his disciples baptizing.**
In the light of 3 : 5 it is quite probable that the Evangelist
regards Jesus' baptizing not merely as a preparatory rite
like John's, but as that perfect baptism ' with water and the
Spirit,' which is the essential condition of the new-birth.
By a characteristic anachronism the full Christian rite of
Baptism, which was introduced into the Church only after
Jesus' death (cf. 7 : 39), is thought of as being administered
by the Founder himself. That this statement caused some
embarrassment to future readers is shown by 4 : 2, where
see note.

In order to bring Jesus and John face to face once again 23
for purposes of comparison, we are told that **John was also
baptizing at Aenon near Salim.** There is some doubt about
the exact position of these villages. It is just possible that
the names are symbolic, John's baptism at Aenon (' springs ')
near to Salim (' peace ') signifying the baptism ' preliminary
to that of the true Melchisedek, the Prince of Peace ' (Loisy ;
cf. 14 : 27, 20 : 19-23). But this is very far-fetched, and
Salim is probably to be placed four or five miles east of
Shechem, where to-day there is a small village of the
same name. There is also an Ainun some eight miles
distant to the north-east by north, and between the two
places lies the Farah valley, where there is **plenty of water.**
By some objection has been taken to the distance between
these two sites, and also to the fact that Aenon would be in
Samaritan territory, where it is felt that John would not be
likely to minister. Furrer accordingly suggests an alternative site in Ain-Fara, some seven miles north-north-east from
Jerusalem.

The statement that **John had not yet been thrown into prison** 24 is either a gloss by a later scribe, who noticed the discrepancy of the Johannine with the Synoptic chronology, or more probably a deliberate correction by the Evangelist himself of Mk. 1 : 14, Mt. 4 : 12, whereby he justifies his statement that Jesus and John were baptizing side by side. Efforts have been made to reconcile the chronology by the argument that Jesus' return to Galilee narrated in Mk. 1 : 14 is not reached in our Gospel till 4 : 3, such earlier activities of Jesus in Galilee as are mentioned in our Gospel being antecedent to the opening of the Marcan account. (But for this see note at end of chap. 1.) Tradition is wholly against the supposition that at any time Jesus' ministry overlapped John's. Our Evangelist's correction of the Synoptic account is prompted by apologetic motives. The Johannine *mise-en-scéne* serves to provide a final opportunity for placing Jesus and John side by side in such a way that John's witness to the Christ may be renewed and Jesus' superiority to his forerunner dramatically set forth.

25 The occasion for the Baptist's final testimony is provided by **a dispute between John's disciples and a Jew** (not ' the Jews ' as A.V. ; a still more attractive conjecture is ' with Jesus '), who as a typical representative of the general public, prejudiced against both Jesus and John alike, would be an impartial judge of their respective claims. The argument is **over the question of ' purification.'** Verse 26 makes it plain that the general topic of discussion was 'Baptism,' both John's and Jesus' baptism being thus classed as a rite of ' purification,' and thereby brought into connexion with the Jewish ceremonial (cf. 2 : 6). It is superfluous to discuss at length the particular point in dispute : several suggest themselves. If Jesus be Messiah, why then does John, whose baptism is merely preparatory to Messiah's coming, still continue to baptize ? If Jesus be Messiah, why is he merely repeating the preparatory rites of his forerunner instead of supplanting symbol by reality ? But more probably we are meant to understand that the dispute is about the comparative efficacy of Jesus' baptizing and John's. The Baptist's 26 disciples, when **they came and told John** about their discussion,

were evidently in a jealous mood: 'here he is, baptizing, and everybody goes to him ! '—clearly an exaggeration springing from wounded pride. This assumption also fits in better with John's answer in the following verse that jealousy is beside the mark, for ' no one can receive anything except as a 27 gift from heaven,' that is, all true success in spiritual work can come from God alone, and Jesus' popularity is therefore a mark of God's favour. (For the expression 'from heaven'' compare Mk. 11: 30, and for the thought Jn. 3: 2, 6: 65, 19: 11, and especially Acts 5: 38–39.)

' Recollect too,' continues John, ' what my testimony to 28 this man was, and you will see how unreasonable is this jealousy': 'I said, "I am not the Christ ; . . . I have been sent in advance of him."' The reference is to 1: 19 ff., especially verses 20 and 23 ; but whereas in 1: 23 John quotes Is. 40: 3, here his words are rather an echo of Mal. 3: 1.

The marriage simile springs from the current O.T. con- 29 ception of the bond subsisting between Yahweh and Israel (Is. 54: 5, Hos. 2: 19 f., etc.), and is a reflection of the Synoptic passage, Mk. 2: 18 f. The marriage bond between the Christ who comes in place of Yahweh, and the Christian Church, which is Israel renewed, is about to be sealed (cf. 2 Cor. 11: 2, Eph. 5: 32, Rev. 19: 7, etc.). The very tact that the people are rallying to Jesus is proof enough that he is the Christ, for ' he who has the bride is the bridegroom.' The Baptist himself is but ' the bridegroom's friend,' whose part it was, according to Jewish custom, not only to participate in the wedding ceremonial, and to preside at the wedding feast (doubtless there is an echo here of 2: 1 ff.), but also to arrange the details of the marriage contract—a particularly apt illustration of the part played by John the Baptist. The ratifying of the contract, so far from giving cause for jealousy, is the consummation of John's life-work. So far from grudging Jesus his supreme dignity John is ' heartily glad at the sound of the bridegroom's voice.' The last words refer to no particular part of the wedding ceremonial, but are merely expressive of wedding rejoicing in general (cf. Jer. 7: 34, 16: 9, 25: 10). At the recognition of Jesus as Messiah John rejoices as one whose mission is fulfilled, and who asks no more, for his joy is complete (cf. 15 : 11, 16 : 24, 17 : 13).

30   Just as the morning star, herald of the dawn, must fade before the rising sun, so must John the herald give way to Christ himself : ' He must wax, I must wane.' It is interesting to note that while at Christmas the day begins to lengthen, on St. John's day, which the Church appropriately celebrated at the summer solstice, it begins to wane.

Theme (iii) : *The New Worship—in relation to the Samaritans* (4 : 1–42)

The interest is now transferred from Jesus' relations with the Baptist to the opening of his wider ministry. But the comparison between ' water ' and ' the Spirit,' under which symbolism the Evangelist emphasizes the distinction between the New Gospel and the Old, is still maintained.

4.

1 Now when the Lord learned that the Pharisees had heard of Jesus gaining and baptizing more disciples than John
2   (though Jesus himself did not baptize, it was his disciples),
3   he left Judaea and went back to Galilee. He had to pass
4   through Samaria, and in so doing he arrived at a Samaritan
5   town called Sychar ; it lay near the territory which Jacob
6   had given to his son Joseph, and Jacob's spring was there. Jesus, exhausted by the journey, sat down at the spring, just as he was. It was about noon.

1   Now when the Lord learned that the Pharisees had heard of Jesus gaining and baptizing more disciples than John : the reference to the Pharisees is unexpected and the language is clumsy and involved, and shows signs of editing, as so often at the point of juncture before or after a section which has fallen out of its original context (see Introduction, p. lxvii). Possibly the text as we have it is the result of a combination of the original words of the Evangelist and the Redactor's editing. Except at 6 : 23 and 11 : 2, both of which are parenthetic statements and may also be due to the Redactor,

the term **the Lord** is used of Jesus in this Gospel only after
the Resurrection. As verse 2 is probably also an addition by
the Redactor, we may perhaps assume that the Evangelist
originally wrote : ' When therefore Jesus knew that he was
making and baptizing more disciples than John, he left Judaea,
and went away again into Galilee.' According to the Evangelist the reason for Jesus' departure is that he may not appear
to be a rival to John : the Redactor, to whom rather than to
the Evangelist himself is probably due the persistent exaltation
of Jesus at the expense of the Baptist (see Introduction, p. lxvi),
changes the motive by an abrupt allusion to ' the Pharisees.'
Jesus withdraws because the Pharisees show signs of alarm at
the increasing number of his adherents, and he desires to avoid
a collision with them, for ' his time was not yet come ' ;
the Jewish party are not to be thought of as favouring John
(though no doubt the ' Baptist sect ' at Ephesus, to which
the Redactor may vaguely allude, would be largely composed of Judaizing opponents of orthodox Christianity) ;
but they are still more jealous of his greater successor. Notice
that all whom Jesus baptizes at once become **disciples,**
for the Evangelist regards this baptizing not merely as a
preparatory rite parallel to that of John, but as the full
Christian sacrament foretold in 1 : 33, whereby men are sealed
by the Spirit as members of the Church. He is thereby guilty
of an anachronism which alike anticipates Jesus' commission
to baptize given in Mt. 28 : 19, and clashes with the idea that
it was not till after Jesus' death that the Spirit was given
(7 : 39) and therefore, by inference, that spiritual baptism
could be dispensed. It is probably because he is conscious of
this difficulty that the Redactor adds the modification in
verse 2 that **Jesus himself did not baptize, it was his disciples. 2**
The anachronism, indeed, still remains, but it is less glaring
when a ministerial function subsequently fulfilled by the
Twelve is ascribed to them even during Jesus' lifetime—
but not actually assigned to the Master himself. It may be
noted too that by his correction the Redactor once again subtly
emphasizes Jesus' superiority to the Baptist. The latter
himself baptized with water : Jesus, whose function was to

H

baptize with the Spirit, like Paul (1 Cor. 1: 14–17) left the
mere outward rite to his disciples.   From this point of view the
twelve are thus early regarded almost as ministerial ' officials '
(see E. F. Scott, *The Fourth Gospel*, p. 137).   It may be noted
that, though John is by general consent regarded as the great
N.T. teacher on the subject of the sacraments (mediaeval
artists regularly pictured him with the Cup, while Peter
held the keys and Paul the sword), it is characteristic of this
Gospel to minimize the importance of the mere outward rite.
The mechanical act is nothing apart from the Spiritual gift
which constitutes its inner meaning ; and it was to bestow this,
not to perform rites, that Christ came.   Indeed, the whole of
this section, with its implied contrast between the barren
Samaritan rites and the ' free gift of God ' through Jesus, is
a working out of this thought.   (Compare also the treatment
of the Lord's supper, and see note on 6 : 63.)

3   Jesus then, as a result apparently of the dispute recorded in
3 : 25 ff., left Judaea and went back to Galilee, which he had left
at 2 : 13, according to our Gospel after a previous brief ministry
there (1 : 43–2 : 12), whereas according to the Synoptists
(Mk. 1: 14, Mt. 4: 12) the Galilean ministry opened at this
4 point.   John takes advantage of the fact that he had to pass
through Samaria to introduce, as a link between the early
Judaean incidents and the ministry in Galilee, a picture of
Jesus in contact with a non-Jewish people.   The Evangelist's
universalist outlook (cf. 3 : 15–16), and the fact that he writes
at a time when Christianity had become mainly a Gentile
religion, demand that he should correct at an early stage in
his Gospel the impression made by such sayings as Mt. 10 : 5,
Mk. 7 : 27, and the objection that, according to the earlier
accounts, Christ's own ministry had been limited to the Jews.
The following narrative almost certainly rests on some
authentic record ; but even ' real history has its ideal side :
otherwise it would only be an accumulation of facts without
significance ' (Godet) ; and John means to imply that Jesus
himself anticipated the first extension of the Christian Church
beyond Jewish boundaries.   Jesus had to travel through
Samaritan territory, because the main pilgrim road from

Jerusalem to Galilee ran that way, and otherwise a détour through Peraea would be necessary (Mk. 10 : 1). Josephus uses the very words of our Evangelist : ' Those who wish to go away quickly (from Galilee to Jerusalem) must needs go through Samaria.' A similar visit, but on the way south, is mentioned in one of Luke's ' travel-narratives' (Lk. 9: 51 ff). Samaria or Shomron was built by Omri as the capital of the Kingdom of Israel (1 Kings 16 : 24), and gave its name to the surrounding country. Destroyed by Hyrcanus, it was rebuilt by Herod and called Sebaste ; in the time of Christ the territory of Samaria was included in the tetrarchy of Archelaus under the Procurator Pontius Pilate.

Jesus then **arrived at a Samaritan town called Sychar,** a 5 place unknown to the O.T., which at one time was commonly identified with Shechem (Gen. 33 : 18) or Sychem (Acts 7 : 16), subsequently Neapolis, now Nablûs. It is suggested that the name Sychem may have been altered in derision by the Jews to Sychar, which means ' city of drunkards' (cf. Is. 28: 1). But this identification is now abandoned, and Sychar (called in the Samaritan Chronicle ' Ischar ') is to be placed at the site now called ' Askar, a few ruins and hovels at the foot of Mount Ebal, about one mile and three-quarters east-north-east from Nablûs and little more than half a mile north from Jacob's Well ' (G. A. Smith, *Historical Geography of the Holy Land,* p. 371). This site is **near the territory which Jacob had given to his son Joseph** at Shechem (Gen. 33: 18, 48 : 22—where ' shechem ' is the Hebrew word translated ' portion '— Jos. 24 : 32) and half a mile to the south, at the point where the great north road through Samaria forks, is **Jacob's spring.** 6 The writer obviously has a definite geographical background before him, and the place-names are even less likely to be merely symbolical than are Aenon and Salim (3 : 23), though it may be that the exact position of the sites should be fixed with a like degree of latitude. The tradition regarding Jacob's well does not depend upon the O.T. Why was a well dug there at all in a district abounding in copious streams ? Was it that Jacob, a stranger in the land, might avoid disputes with his neighbours about water-rights ? Loisy well notes that Jacob's well 'symbolizes the ineffectual regime of legal purifications as compared with that of the living water, Christian baptism, the source of immortal life.'

Jesus, exhausted by the journey, sat down at the spring, just as he was—without more ado, 'not on a throne, not on a cushion, but simply, as he was, on the ground' (Chrysostom). As so often (11 : 35, 19 : 28, 1 Jn. 1 : 1–3, 4 : 2, etc.) our writer strongly emphasizes the real humanity of Jesus probably in opposition to the prevalent views of the 'Docetists' who regarded Jesus as a 'phantom' without any true material existence. It was about noon (the sixth hour ; see note on 1 : 39), when the heat would be at its height and the well deserted (evening being the usual hour for the drawing of water), thus providing an opportunity for an undisturbed *tête-à-tête*. In the exact note of time we may perhaps trace the hand of 'the Witness.'

7 And a Samaritan woman came to draw water. Jesus said to
8 her, 'Give me a drink' (his disciples had gone to the
9 town to buy some food). The Samaritan woman said, 'What ? You are a Jew, and you ask me for a drink—me, a Samaritan ! ' (Jews do not associate with Samaritans.)
10 Jesus answered, ' If you knew what is the free gift of God and who is asking you for a drink, you would have asked him instead, and he would have given you " living "
11 water.' ' Sir,' said the woman, 'you have nothing to draw water with, and it is a deep well ; where do you get
12 your " living " water ? Are you a greater man than Jacob, our ancestor ? He gave us this well, and he drank from it,
13 with his sons and his cattle.' Jesus answered, 'Anyone
14 who drinks this water will be thirsty again, but anyone who drinks the water I shall give him will never thirst any more ; the water I shall give him will turn into a spring of water welling up to eternal life.'

7 And a Samaritan woman came to draw water. Why, we ask, during the heat of the day and at half a mile's distance from her home in Sychar ? Possibly on her way home from

work in the fields (4 : 35). Why draw from the well when there are abundant supplies of running water nearer the village ? Possibly because of ' the fondness of tradition which . . . drew Jacob's fanatic children to its scantier supplies ' (G. A. Smith, p. 374) ; for the same reason, John may have felt, that men cling to dead ritual when they might draw from the Spirit of the living Christ.

Jesus creates his own opportunity by a simple request, ' Give me a drink,' for ' Jesus knows well that the way to gain a soul is often to ask a service from it ' (Godet). His reason for appealing to the woman is that his disciples, who otherwise would have drawn water for him, **had gone to the town to 8 buy some food** (cf. Lk. 9 : 52), thus showing that they, as well as their Master, were superior to the Rabbinic prejudices, according to which ' to eat the bread of a Samaritan is as eating the flesh of swine.'

' The woman is one of those whose hold on religion is a slender one, viz., a knowledge that divisions exist among religious people ' (R. H. Strachan), and recognizing Jesus as a Jew, possibly by something distinctive about his dress or accent, she expresses wonder that he should thus disregard the customary barriers not only of sex but even of religious caste (cf. Acts 10 : 28). ' **What ? You are a Jew, and you ask me for a drink—me, a Samaritan woman !** ' Here follows an explanatory note that **Jews do not associate with Samaritans, 9** probably added by the Redactor, it may be when he translated the Gospel for the use of Gentile readers (Introduction, p. lxvi f.). The hostility between the two peoples, which lasts to the present day, dates back to the colonization of Israel by the Assyrians (2 Kings 17 : 24), from which resulted the opposition of the Samaritans to the Jews at the Return (Ezra 4, Neh. 6), and finally the building of a rival temple on Mount Gerizim.

Jesus tries to find some point of contact whereby he can 10 meet the woman's spiritual need : he says in effect : ' You speak of giving and taking between two such as you and me ; if you had the insight to distinguish between earthly and heavenly riches and understood my power to pass on God's free gift to you, then *you* would have been the first to ask

and I the first to give.' ' She would have become the petitioner and not have wondered at the petition' (Westcott).
' The free gift of God ' is either to be taken as an indefinite
expression meaning ' the freeness of all God's giving,' or
else points more definitely to the gift by God of His own Son
(3 : 16), or, more probably in this context, to the gift of the
holy Spirit which is the Father's peculiar ' good gift ' (Lk.
11 : 13). The words **' living water '** may have been suggested
by the scene before Jesus' eyes as he spoke, the contrast
between the stagnant water of the old well and the running
water which flowed close by. The primary meaning of
' living water ' is spring water as opposed to that contained
in cisterns (Gen. 26 : 19, Lev. 14 : 5). Already in the O.T.
the expression is used in a figurative sense (Jer. 2 : 13, 17 : 13,
Zech. 14 : 8), and here ' living water ' is symbolical of a
spiritual life which never grows stagnant but has the property
of perpetually reproducing itself. (Cf. 7 : 37–39, which in
turn is an echo of Is. 55 : 1.) In a desert country running
water is the most precious of God's gifts ; indeed, the favourite
name for a spring in Asia Minor is ' Huda-verdi ' or ' God
hath given ' ; it is thus a fitting symbol of ' God's free gift.'

11   As so often in our Gospel (2 : 20, 3 : 4, etc.) Jesus' companion picks up his words in a material sense and by another
question gives him the chance to develop his theme.   **' Sir,
you have nothing to draw water with, and it is a deep well.'**
The present depth of the well is said to be some one hundred
feet, and formerly it must have been much deeper. Note that
the watering-place is here called a ' well,' while in verse 6 it
is a ' spring.' As a matter of fact it is a deep ' pit ' lined with
rough masonry. But ' Robinson says there is a spring in
it, Conder that it fills by infiltration. If either of these be
correct, then we can understand the double titles given to it
in the narrative' (G. A. Smith, p. 374).   **' Where do you get
12 your " living water " ? Are you a greater man than Jacòb
our ancestor ? He gave us this well, and he drank from it,
with his sons and his cattle.'** The woman says in effect:
' If you can't get water from the well and yet have another
and a better kind of water, then you must be one greater

even than Jacob, who felt the need of the well and found it good enough for himself and copious enough to satisfy both his family and his flocks.' The Samaritans set great store by their claim to descent from Jacob through Joseph, the representative of the northern tribes of Ephraim and Manasseh. (Compare the similar boast of ' the Jews ' in 8 : 33, 39, 53.)

Jesus corrects the woman's misconception that the question 13 is still merely the quenching of *physical* thirst by showing her that he is speaking not of ' this water ' in a material sense of which ' anyone who drinks . . . will be thirsty again, but of the water I shall give him, of which anyone who drinks . . . will 14 never thirst any more.' Unlike the water of Jacob's well, which at best merely satisfies the need of the moment, Jesus offers a spiritual draught which will banish thirst for ever (cf. 6 : 35). A saying surely which provokes thought. Should the growth of our spiritual life be towards complete satisfaction (as pictured here) or towards a more and more intense thirst after holiness (Ps. 42 : 2, etc., Mt. 5 : 6) ? Even in the life of heavenly perfection there will be thirst to be quenched (Rev. 7 : 17, 21 : 6, 22 : 1). The truth is that Christ both excites the desire for spiritual good and also satisfies it. ' Thou, O Christ, art all I *want*, More than all in Thee I *find*.' Christ satisfies a man not by banishing his thirst, which would be to stunt his soul's growth,[1] but by bestowing upon him by the gift of his Spirit an inward source of satisfaction which perennially and spontaneously supplies each recurrent need of refreshment : ' the water I shall give him will turn into a spring of water welling up to eternal life.' The gift which Christ offers is no material

---

[1] We have the converse truth in Eccl. 24 : 21, when Wisdom says, ' Those who eat me will always hunger for me again ; those who drink me will always again thirst for me.'

Compare Faber :

" The lack of desire is the ill of all ills ;
Many thousands through it the dark pathway have trod :
The balsam, the wine of predestinate wills
Is a jubilant pining and longing for God."

water which at best springs from the earth and returns to the earth, but the Spirit which is the secret of eternal life. An ordinary fountain may spring heavenward, but the force of gravitation draws it back to earth: this spiritual fountain leaps upward till it attains to eternal life. ' The thoughts of worldly men are for ever regulated by a moral law of gravitation, which like the physical one holds them down to earth' (Charles Dickens). Christ gives the inward power whereby this spiritual law of gravitation is overcome. Henceforth man may have within himself a spiritual force which will raise him to eternal life. Note that our Gospel, by emphasizing not merely the tradition of Jesus' teaching, but rather the spontaneous and self-renewing power of his everpresent spirit, has above any other N.T. writing secured to Christianity a principle of inward life and ever-fresh development.

15 ' Ah, sir,' said the woman, ' give me this water, so that I need
16 not thirst or come all this road to draw water.' Jesus said to her, ' Go and call your husband, then come back
17 here.' The woman replied, ' I have no husband.' Jesus said to her, ' You were right in saying, " I have no
18 husband " ; you have had five husbands, and he whom you have now espoused is not your husband. That was
19 a true word.' ' Sir,' said the woman, ' I see you are a
20 prophet. Now our ancestors worshipped on this mountain, whereas you Jews declare the proper place for
21 worship is at Jerusalem.' ' Woman,' said Jesus, ' believe me, the time is coming when you will be worshipping the
22 Father neither on this mountain nor at Jerusalem. You are worshipping something you do not know ; we are worshipping what we do know—for salvation comes
23 from the Jews. But the time is coming, it has come already, when the real worshippers will worship the Father in Spirit and in reality ; for these are the wor-
24 shippers that the Father wants. God is Spirit, and His worshippers must worship Him in Spirit and in reality.'
25 The woman said to him, ' Well, I know messiah (which

means Christ) is coming.   When he arrives, he will 26
explain it all to us.'   ' I am messiah,' said Jesus, ' I who
am talking to you.'

The woman, whose chief desire appears to be ' to have her 15
life made more comfortable ' (Godet), and who still imagines
that Jesus is speaking of some magic water which, being
within the recipient, can satisfy without the labour of drawing,
says half in earnest half in jest, ' Sir, give me this water, so
that I need not thirst or come all this road to draw water.'
Jesus' reply seems lacking in logical sequence. Westcott 16
thinks that the woman's last words contain a veiled reference
to her home, and imply that in them ' the speaker passed
beyond herself. . . .   The greatest gift was not complete unless
it was shared by those to whom she was bound.'   Accordingly
' Christ . . . bids her summon him to whom it was her duty
to minister.'   A less far-fetched explanation is that Jesus
finding her not only spiritually obtuse but even inclined to
be flippant, tries to sober her by confronting her with the
shady side of her own life and thereby to reach a part of her
nature wherein he can awaken some response.   He therefore
bids her ' Go and call your husband, then come back here.'
No doubt here and in verse 18 John thinks of Jesus as using
his supernatural knowledge (note on 2 : 25). The woman, 17
surprised and embarrassed at this sudden turn in the conversation, tries to extricate herself by fencing—' I have no
husband,'—but only gives Jesus an opening to confound
her still more with the words, ' You were right in saying, 18
" I have no husband " ; you have had five husbands, and he
whom you have now espoused is not your husband. That
was a true word.' Owing to the frequency of divorce the
woman may well have had five legitimate husbands ; but
her present consort is a mere lover.   Those who (e.g. Loisy)
regard the woman merely as a type of the Samaritan people
see in the five husbands the gods of the five nations settled
in Samaria by the Assyrians (2 Kings 17 : 24–34), the sixth
presumably being the God of Israel, whom they ' do not
know' (verse 22), and who is therefore to them at least no

true husband (cf. Ezra 4: 2–3). The Samaritans worship
the true God, but with irregular rites. This theory, at first
sight improbable, has weight lent to it by the turn taken
by the conversation in the very next verse, where there
emerges this very question of the validity of the Samaritan
worship. Otherwise we must suppose that in her anxiety
to avoid the dangerous ground on to which Jesus is leading
her the woman tries once again to change the subject. Certainly her retort shows no consciousness of sin, but only
19 surprise at Jesus' uncanny insight. ' Sir, I see you are a
prophet '—for such insight, and not merely foresight, is the
chief characteristic of the prophets. Perhaps a reference
to religion, a prophet's own province, will entice Jesus on
to safer ground. She therefore ' directs attention from her
own case by proposing to him a point of controversy'
(Astié, quoted by Godet). Mount Gerizim, lying directly
before her eyes, readily suggests a subject—a burning topic
then, and indeed even to-day, when some two hundred men,
the remnants of the Samaritan Church, still carry on the cult
upon the mountain.

20 ' Our ancestors,' says the woman, ' worshipped on this
mountain,' that is, on Gerizim. At Deut. 27: 4, where the
site of the first offering is stated to be Ebal, the Samaritan
text reads ' Gerizim,' the mountain from which the blessings
were pronounced (Deut. 11: 29, 27: 12). The rival temple
erected here by the Samaritans after the return from the
exile had been destroyed by Hyrcanus in 129 B.C., and in Jesus'
day was lying in ruins. By ' our ancestors ' may be meant
either the Israelites of Joshua's days, who, according to the
Samaritan reading of Deut. 27: 4, worshipped on Gerizim ;
or—with a more definite contrast with ' you Jews '—' our
forefathers ever since the time of Nehemiah ' when Sanballat
built the rival temple ; or, possibly, ' the patriarchs,' from
whom in common with the Jews the Samaritans claimed to
be descended (note on 4: 12). The woman would then be
contrasting the immemorial practice of the patriarchs who
worshipped on mountain-tops, and therefore by inference on
Gerizim, with the more recent localized cult ' at Jerusalem,

where you Jews declare the proper place of worship is.'
According to a Samaritan tradition it was on Gerizim that
Abraham prepared for the sacrifice of Isaac ; here also he
met with Melchizedek. Note that the woman asks no
definite question, but she implies, ' Which point of view is
right ? '

The gist of Jesus' answer is that it is not the Church to 21
which we go, but the spirit in which we go that counts.
His words reflect the thought of such passages as Is. 66 : 18–23,
Jer. 3 : 16, Mal: 1 : 11 : with the revelation which Christ
brings ' the time is coming when you will be worshipping
the Father neither on this mountain nor at Jerusalem.' The
word ' Father ' is the key-word. Once the true nature of
religion is realized, all sectarian rivalries are forgotten. It is
the object of worship which determines its conditions ; once
God is revealed to be the universal Father, and such is the
content of Christ's revelation, the limitations of place are
done away, and both the knowledge and the worship of
God are mediated by purely spiritual means. Jesus thus
expressly abrogates Deut. 12 : 5, which in the eyes of such
as the Samaritan woman would be the seal set upon Jewish
exclusiveness. ' Nowhere does the Evangelist's spiritual
universalism shine more brightly than in the discourse to the
Samaritan woman. . . . Until one has fully realized what
Jerusalem was to the Jews, how completely it represented
their national religion, their pride of race, their past history,
and their hopes for the future, one cannot fully understand
at what cost of self-suppression, and through what painful
following of the higher light any Hebrew could reach that
utterance. When the author of the Apocalypse writes of the
future, his highest hope is to see a new Jerusalem : the
Evangelist is willing to see Jerusalem for ever eclipsed '
(Percy Gardner, *The Ephesian Gospel*, p. 222 f.). By the time
John wrote, the temple at Jerusalem, like its rival on
Gerizim, was lying in ruins.

It is not the place of worship which is of account, but its 22
object and its spirit: as regards its object, ' **You are worshipping something you do not know.**' The neuter pronoun

refers to God abstractly as the object of worship rather than to God as a Person. (For the force of **know** in the Gospel, see note on 8 : 19, 10 : 15.) The Samaritans, who are typical of the heathen world, worship they know not what in the characteristic manner of Gentiles (Acts 17 : 23). Of the O.T. Scriptures the Samaritans acknowledged the Pentateuch only, and were thus without the knowledge of God as revealed by the prophets and in the history of His chosen people. The Jews' worship, on the other hand, is intelligent : ' **we are worshipping what we do know—for salvation comes from the Jews** ' (cf. Rom. 3 : 1–2, 9 : 4–5, Ps. 76 : 2). We have the exact opposite of this thought in 8 : 54–55, where Jesus says to ' the Jews ' : ' You say, " He is our God," but you do not understand Him.' For this reason it has been supposed that in the words ' **we are worshipping what we do know**,' John, speaking through Christ's lips, intends to contrast the *Christian* manner of worship with all other religions, including both the Jewish and the Samaritan. But the following words ' **salvation comes from the Jews** ' surely make this quite impossible. The contrast here is between the unintelligent Samaritan rites and the Jewish religion regarded as *the soil from which Christianity sprang*. ' The peculiar relation between this people and God ' springs from the fact that ' according to the divine plan the history of this people must issue in the salvation of the world ' (Godet). Though all such sectarian distinctions are about to be transcended in Christ, Jesus frankly confesses himself a Jew, and claims superiority for his faith (cf. verse 9 and notes on 1 : 11 and 2 : 16). By thus insisting upon the permanent worth of the O.T. revelation John perhaps intends to combat the Gnostic doctrine that the God of the O.T. was a lower God and the ancient revelation worthless. Judaism is the only religion hitherto in which the truth has partially been revealed, and which is therefore fitted to be the ' mother ' of Christianity (cf. Rev. 12 : 5, and note on 19 : 27). The apparent inconsistency of 8 : 54–55 is explained by the distinction already noted (see note on 1 : 19 and esp. 1 : 47), which our author draws between the true community of Israel at last realized

in the Christian Church and 'the Jews' regarded as a
religious party opposed to the Church.

But though of all faiths hitherto the Jewish is the highest, 23
'the time is coming' when every difference, such as that
between Jew and Samaritan, will lose its significance; indeed,
with the appearance of Christ that time 'has come already,
when the real worshippers,'—that is, those whose ideas of worship pass beyond limitations of time and place and *symbolic*
rites and ceremonies, which belong to the sphere of the flesh, to
the *reality* which lies beyond the symbol and belongs to the
sphere of the Spirit—will be raised above all limitation and all
symbolism, and 'will worship the Father in Spirit and in reality';
that is, worship will manifest itself *in the sphere of the Spirit*
(Rom. 1 : 9, Eph. 6 : 18), in a man's inner life, as opposed to
worship at any particular site, for ' the wind blows where it
will' (3 : 8), and spiritual worship cannot be bound to any
one place ; and it will be worship of God *as He really is,*
that is, worship with first-hand knowledge as opposed to that
mediated through symbolism ; hitherto men have seen
' only the baffling reflections in a mirror,' but henceforth ' it
will be face to face ' (1 Cor. 13 : 12). Here the word ' reality '
further defines ' Spirit,' as in 1 : 17 it defines ' grace.'

Thus ' the rival claims of Gerizim and Jerusalem are not
determined by the Lord ; for they vanish in the revelation
of a universal religion' (Westcott) which being 'in Spirit'
will correct the defect of Jewish worship which was too
largely symbolical, and being 'in reality' will correct the
defect of Samaritan worship which was vitiated by an imperfect knowledge of God. It should be noted perhaps that this
passage does not condemn outward forms of worship as such,
but only the sectarian spirit which counts them sufficient
cause for division.

The necessity for such ' spiritual' and ' real' worship
springs from the very nature of the object of worship : ' these
are the worshippers that the Father wants,' for ' God is Spirit.'
It is the nature not the personality of God which is de- 24
scribed (cf. note on 1 : 1, ' the Logos was divine '). The
nature of God is spiritual, as distinguished from the earthly,

material nature of man, and, as only Spirit can hold converse with Spirit (3 : 6), 'His worshippers must worship Him in Spirit and in reality,' for even the worship of the temple becomes an irrelevance unless it is accompanied by worship in the inward sanctuary of the heart. (Compare 1 Kings 8 : 27, Is. 66 : 1, Micah 6 : 6–8, Mk. 14 : 58, Lk. 17 : 21, Acts 7 : 48, 17 : 25.)

25   It has been commonly held that the woman's reply—'Well, I know messiah is coming ; when he arrives, he will explain it all to us '—implies that she is ready to be taught and that ' her spirit longs for the full light to be brought by the Messiah' (Godet). But the scene becomes much more dramatic if we suppose that she remains stubborn and flippant up to the point of Jesus' startling pronouncement in the following verse. She is still smarting under Jesus' innuendo (ver. 18), and now tries to break off the conversation with the remark that she is content to leave the solving of all these riddles to ' Messiah.' The Samaritans based their expectations of Messiah upon Deut. 18 : 18, and looked for him to come not as a Davidic king, or political leader, but rather as one who would restore and reform the cult upon Gerizim and convert both Jews and heathen to it. Josephus tells us that during the later years of Pilate's procuratoiship there was a rising of the Samaritans under the influence of these Messianic expectations, so that it is possible that they were at their height during Jesus' ministry, and may have been actually stimulated by him. It is objected that a Samaritan woman would not use the term ' Messiah ' as a proper name, for the Samaritans used the name ' Hashab,' ' the Converter,' or ' El Muhdy,' ' the Guide.' But the Jewish term may well have been popularized among the Samaritans by Jewish apostates who are said to have been numerous at this time. In any case John makes no claim to be reporting the actual words of the conversation. The explanatory parenthesis (which means Christ) is of course an addition, probably by the Redactor, for the benefit of his Hellenist readers. (Cf. note on 1 : 41.)

There follows the tensest and most dramatic moment in

the whole of N.T. narrative. The woman has persistently
sought to hold Jesus at arm's length ; to escape Jesus'
scrutiny she has invoked ' Messiah,' only to find herself
utterly confounded by his rejoinder, ' I am messiah, I who 26
am talking to you.' Christ will not allow her to postpone
the solving of her difficulties : they can be solved now ; her
decision must be made now ; the Messiah whom she awaits
is here. (For the question of the historicity of this declaration
by Jesus of his Messiahship so early in his ministry (contrast
Mt. 16 : 20) see note at the end of this section.)

At this point his disciples came up ; they were surprised 27
that he was talking to a woman, but none of them said,
' What is it ? ' or, ' Why are you talking to her ? ' Then 28
the woman left her water-pot, and going off to the
town told the people, ' Come here, look at a man who 29
has told me everything I ever did ! Can he be the
Christ ? ' They set out from the town on their way to 30
him. Meanwhile the disciples pressed him, saying, 31
' Rabbi, eat something.' But he said to them, ' I have 32
food, of which you know nothing.' So the disciples 33
asked each other, ' Can anyone have brought him something to eat ? ' Jesus said, ' My food is to do the will 34
of Him who sent me, and to accomplish His work. You 35
have a saying, have you not, " Four months yet, then
harvest " ? Look round, I tell you ; see, the fields are
white for harvesting ! The reaper is already getting his 36
wages and harvesting for eternal life, so that the sower
shares the reaper's joy. That proverb, " One sows and 37
another reaps," holds true here : I sent you to reap a 38
crop for which you did not toil ; other men have toiled,
and you reap the profit of their toil.'

At this point we have a good illustration of John's char- 27
acteristic lack of interest in a story for its own sake, apart
from the doctrinal truth which it is intended to illustrate (see
Introduction, p. xliii). Jesus' conversation with the woman
has reached its climax ; but just as we are looking for the

dénouement in the woman's conversion she ' evaporates from
the stage.' Was she, or was she not converted? As in
the case of Nicodemus and of the Greeks (12 : 20) we are not
told. Meantime the interest of the narrative passes over
to the disciples who at this point came up, and were surprised
that Jesus was talking to a woman. It was contrary to custom
for a Rabbi to converse with a woman, whose sphere was
held to be not learning but the home. It was a saying of the
doctors that it was ' better that the words of the law should
be burnt than delivered to women,' and that ' each time that
the man prolongs converse with the woman he causes evil
to himself, and desists from the Thorah and in the end inherits
Gehinnom' (*Pirke Aboth*). But though surprised, like the
woman herself (ver. 9), that Jesus should thus despise the
barriers both of sex and of national caste, the disciples are
either too shy or too respectful to ask ' What is it that
you want with the woman? Or, if you want nothing, Why
are you talking to her? '

28 In the phrase the woman left her water-pot, commentators
have suspected symbolism, but they have drawn from it
directly contradictory inferences. The pitcher is abandoned
either because the woman is thought of as leaving the water
of life behind, or, on the other hand, because, now having
that water within herself, she no longer requires her pitcher.
Godet sees in her action ' a pledge of her speedy return, the
proof that she goes to seek someone.' The words are simply
a vivid touch intended to emphasize the speed with which
the woman hurries off to the town to spread her news and
bring out her neighbours to put this possible Messiah to the
29 test. ' Come here, look at a man who has told me everything I ever did,'—merely the exaggeration characteristic of
a gossip, though some commentators have read into the
words a hint that her many marriages were due not to the
husbands' deaths, but to her own contrivance. ' Can he be
the Christ? '—a question framed as if in expectation of a
negative answer (cf. Mt. 12 : 23): ' Surely this can't be the
Christ!' She is still more than half doubtful, and wishes
to have her own impressions confirmed by her neighbours,

who, stirred by curiosity, set out from the town on their way 30
to Jesus. Meantime the interest passes to the disciples,
who meanwhile—that is, in the interval while the woman 31
was still away and her fellow-townsmen had not yet arrived
—offered Jesus the food just brought from the village and
pressed him, saying, ' Rabbi, eat something.' ' To the prosaic
invitation of the disciples Christ makes a mystical response '
(Loisy). He has been buoyed up by the joy of work and
the evident promise of speedy results. Spiritual exaltation
or pressure of work not seldom rendered Jesus oblivious of
his bodily needs (Mt. 4 : 2, Mk. 3 : 20, 6 : 31); he replies,
' I have food of which you know nothing,' words which the 32
disciples interpret in a literal rather than the intended
spiritual sense : ' Can anyone have brought him something to 33
eat ? ' or rather, ' Surely no one can have brought him anything to eat—in Samaria of all places ! ' The disciples'
misunderstanding is a favourite artifice of the Evangelist
(cf. 3 : 4, 4 : 15, etc. ; also Mk. 8 : 16) to give point to Jesus'
explanation which follows : ' My food is to do the will of 34
Him who sent me, and to accomplish His work,' i.e., ' the means
whereby I sustain my being lie in the endeavour to fulfil
the will of my Father, which is the true purpose of my mission.'
Jesus implies that spiritual life alone is true life, real life, and
to nourish this is more important than merely to sustain
our bodily existence which has worth only so far as it is
the symbol and medium of spiritual endeavour. (Cf. 6 : 27,
Mt. 4 : 4.) We have interesting parallels in Browning's *Fra
Lippo Lippi* ' to find its (the world's) meaning is my meat
and drink,' and Sophocles, *Electra*, 363, ' For me be it food
enough that I do not wound my own conscience.' Our
Gospel lays much emphasis upon the will of God, a word which
may almost be said to take the place of the Synoptic term
' kingdom ' as expressive of the sovereignty of God (cf. 5 : 30,
6 : 38-39, 6 . 40, 7 : 17, 9 : 31, etc.). The expression His
work refers not only to the conversion of the Samaritans,
which is the task of the moment, but to the whole of Jesus'
vocation (cf. 5 : 36, 17 : 4).

In the verses that follow we seem to have echoes of Mt. 35

9 : 37–38, Lk. 10 : 2, and of the Parable of the Sower. The difficulty of tracing a consistent sequence of thought throughout 35–38 has led to the conjecture that we may have here a ' conglomerate ' passage composed of sayings originally uttered on various occasions, and subsequently brought together on account of their similarity of subject, in this case sowing and reaping. Needless difficulty has been caused by the supposition (e.g. by Westcott) that ' the sower ' of 36 is not Jesus but his predecessor the Baptist. By avoiding this error a tolerable sequence may be secured.

Jesus justifies his exalted mood by pointing out with what marvellous rapidity fruit is springing up from the seed sown at the well side. ' **You have a** (proverbial) **saying, have you not, " Four months yet, then harvest " ? '** Some have taken these words as an actual remark of the disciples overheard by Jesus and taken as his text, and have seen in them a hint that the visit to Samaria took place four months before harvest, that is, in December or January. But verses 6–7 suggest the season of heat, and in any case the words sound unmistakably like a proverb. The proverb in Mt. 16 : 2 is similarly introduced by the phrase ' ye say.' In the Greek the form of the words is metrical, which suits the supposition that we have here a popular adage, or at any rate a quotation from an unknown context used in a proverbial sense. The words can hardly be intended to mark accurately the usual interval between seedtime and harvest, for in Palestine the sowing begins in October and the harvest in April—an interval not of four months but of six. ' **Four months** ' is simply expressive of any short interval ; the proverb, as generally used, would teach the need of patience, while also encouraging with the hope that after no long interval results will follow effort—*but an interval there is bound to be* (Cf. Eccl. 11 : 1, 2 Tim. 2 : 6). Jesus' meaning would then be this : In the ordinary course of nature men have to wait ere they can reap a harvest from their sowing. But here is an exception : so speedy has been the result of my spiritual sowing that seedtime and harvest have been miraculously brought together : ' **Look round, I tell you ; see, the fields are white for harvesting ! '**

It is but a few minutes since Jesus sowed the first seed in the woman's heart, and yet in that stream of Samaritans hurrying out of the village towards him he sees a harvest already ripe for reaping. If, as we suppose, the Evangelist has built up this scene out of reminiscences of ' the Witness,' we may well suppose that the metaphor of sowing and reaping was suggested to Jesus by the country-side on which he was looking : the district is still famous for its corn. Lightfoot writes: ' When we once realize the scene, when in imagination our eye ranges over that vast expanse of growing corn—so unusual in Palestine, however familiar in corn-growing England—we are at once struck with the truthfulness and the significance of this allusive parable.' (For the phrase ' lift up your eyes . . .' compare Is. 49: 18 ff., a passage which offers interesting parallels in thought and language.)

The sowing is but newly begun, and yet ' **the reaper is already 36 getting his wages and harvesting for eternal life** ' : whereas usually the harvester has to wait months before he can get to work, in *this* case he is *already* getting his reward, and is gathering a harvest of souls into the store-house of eternal life. But who is the reaper—Jesus or his disciples ? If Jesus, as is certain, is ' the sower ' in the words that immediately follow, then it would seem more natural to see his disciples in ' the reaper ' both here and below. But the disciples have so far not put their hand to the Samaritan harvest. But neither indeed has Jesus. Probably the word is used simply in a general sense, the meaning being : ' The work of reaping, bringing with it reward for the toil of sowing, is already beginning,' so that it may be truly said that in this case ' **the sower shares the reaper's joy** ' : that is, the sower has not yet left the field when the crops are ripe for harvesting, so that, without any interval of waiting, he actually has his share in the joy of harvest. Sowing was proverbially regarded as a work of painful toil, harvesting as a joyous festival (Ps. 126: 5–6, Is. 9: 3), but on this occasion, so rapidly has the seed borne fruit that the sower finds himself taking part in the harvest festival. He ' sees of the travail of his soul, and is satisfied ' (Is. 53: 11). **The sower** here is clearly Jesus himself—if indeed anything more definite is implied than that the quick response of the Samaritans has brought it about that sowing-toil and harvest-joy are almost instantaneous. The ' reaper ' will then be both Jesus himself and his disciples, both the ' labourers ' and the ' Lord of the harvest ' who sends them forth (Mt. 9: 37–38). The whole force of the passage is ruined by supposing with Westcott that Christ is ' reaper ' alone, those who preceded him, e.g. the prophets and John the Baptist, being the ' sower.' Jesus, in our Gospel as in the Synoptics, is the Sower *par excellence*. (For Jesus' joy at the prospect of harvest compare Lk. 10: 21 ff., Jn. 12: 23 ff.)

37 The difficulty in tracing the sequence of thought at this point has been due to a failure to realize that in the next two verses we have not so much the actual words of Jesus spoken at the time in question, but rather a comment by the Evangelist, put indeed upon the lips of Jesus, but really spoken from the point of view of his own day. Freely paraphrased the sequence is this ; the Evangelist comments as one writing at the beginning of the second century ; ' I say that in this exceptional case " the sower shares the reaper's joy " ; for, in spiritual work as a general rule, the proverb, " One sows, another reaps," holds good, and we have an illustration of its truth in the fact that Jesus has sent us his missionaries to harvest a crop at the sowing of which not we but others toiled.' ' That proverb, " One sows, another reaps," holds good here.' Where ? Certainly not in Jesus' experience narrated in the preceding verses, for his opportunity of playing the part of sower and reaper simultaneously is the exception which proves the rule stated in the proverb. The Greek pronoun, which has been translated here, in our Gospel refers regularly to something which follows (cf. 9: 30, 15: 8). An illustration which gives reality to a mere saying follows in verse 38. Proverbs are often popular cynicism crystallized, and in its original sense this one might easily be cynical and despairing in its tone (cf. Job 31: 8 ; and for the proverb in general Deut. 6: 11, Josh. 24: 13, Micah 6: 15, Is. 65: 21–22, Mt. 25: 24, and Plutarch—quoted by Dods : ' It was objected to Pompey that he came upon the victories of Lucullus, and

gathered those laurels which were due to the fortune and valour of another ') ; yet when referred to spiritual work it has its true side ; and here is an illustration : ' **I sent you to** 38 **reap a crop for which you did not toil.**' The Sower of the parable here appears as he who sends out the reapers, the ' Lord of the harvest ' (Mt. 9 : 38). The past tense ' sent ' supports the contention that the words are written from the point of view of the future, not spoken by Jesus himself with reference to the original choice of the Twelve as ' apostles,' in which choice such a ' sending ' might be held to be implicit. To put on Jesus' lips the reflections of a later age is a common Johannine artifice : another good example is 17 : 18. The Evangelist reflects that well might Jesus say to the Christian teachers of his (John's) own time, ' **other men have toiled, and you reap the profit of their toil.**' Here is an exception to the rule laid down in, e.g., 2 Tim. 2 : 6 : ' The farmer who has done the work must have the first share of the fruit.' Who is meant by ' **other men** ' ? Those who accept 37–38 as strictly the words of Jesus himself see a reference to John the Baptist or even to the earlier prophets. But if we are to abide strictly by the historical setting, it is rather into Jesus' own personal labours that the disciples are about to enter. Jesus sowed the seed at the well side : they are about to reap the harvest. The use of the plural ' other men ' is better explained as due to the future viewpoint from which the verses are written. The Evangelist is thinking of all those first Christian missionaries into whose labours he and his fellow-workers at the beginning of the second century have entered. Some critics see a reference to the Evangelist Philip as the original converter of the Samaritans (Acts 8 : 5–8), or to St. Paul, who had ' laboured more abundantly than they all ' (1 Cor. 15 : 10). Though it is needless thus to particularize, it is most probable that the writer has in mind the first Christian mission to the Samaritans as recorded in Acts 8, on which passage Holtzmann (quoting Bugge) remarks that, in fulfilment of the prophecy of Jn. 4 : 21, the Samaritans abandon the worship on Gerizim and yet are not brought to Jerusalem, an envoy being sent to them (Acts 8 : 14).

39 Now many Samaritans belonging to that town believed in him
  on account of the woman's testimony, ' He told me
40   everything I ever did.' So when the Samaritans arrived,
41   they pressed him to stay with them ; he did stay there
  two days, and far more of them believed on account of
42   what he said himself. As they told the woman, ' We
  no longer believe on account of what you said ; we have
  heard for ourselves, we know that he is really the Saviour
  of the world.'

39 The Evangelist now sums up the result of Jesus' mission to
Samaria. **On account of the woman's testimony** (ver. 29)
many Samaritans belonging to that town believed in him, with
40 the result that, **when they arrived** at the well side (a reference
back to ver. 30), **they pressed him to stay with them** ; and he
did stay there two days—a very brief stay, perhaps thus limited
by John out of deference to the Synoptic tradition according to
which (Mt. 10 : 5) Jesus actually forbade the evangelization of
Samaria. With the hospitality here shown by the Samaritans
contrast Lk. 9 : 53. Their incipient ' faith ' is due in the first
place to curiosity and the desire to see more miracles ; but a
41 truer faith is revealed later when **more of them believed** not on
account of the woman's story, but **on account of what he
said himself.** True faith is the result of personal experience
(' **we have heard for ourselves ; we know** ') based upon Jesus'
42 witness to himself, not the result of mere hearsay or idle gossip
(' **what you said** '—the woman's ' talk ' being contrasted with
Jesus' ' word '). The Samaritans, through personal contact
with Jesus, have had the same revelation made to them as had
the woman in verse 26 : they ' **know that he is really the Saviour
of the world.**' This title is clearly put upon the Samaritans' lips
by the Evangelist himself, for it is a Johannine expression
(1 Jn. 4 : 14) which seems to have its roots neither in Judaism
nor in the Synoptic tradition, but rather in the soil of the
later Gentile Church : it savours of the terminology of the
Mystery Religions.

 This early avowal by the Samaritans of the Messiahship
of Jesus can hardly be accepted as historical, but should be

regarded as an anticipation of history such as we have in 1 : 41, 49. The only consideration which might have induced Jesus thus early to break through a reserve, which elsewhere he maintains to all save the innermost circle of his disciples, and openly to declare himself Messiah, is, as Stanton (p. 227) suggests, that ' there was not indeed among the Samaritan population, cut off as it was from the life of the Jewish people, the same danger that mischief would arise from false expectations as there was in other districts where he preached.' But this weighs little against the inherent improbability that Jesus would reveal to a flippant woman a secret which he withheld for long even from his closest friends. This consideration leads up to the question of the historicity of the whole incident. It is true, as even Renan admits, that ' most of the circumstances of the narrative bear a striking stamp of truth.' Yet there is much in the dialogue which it is difficult to accept as an accurate report of an actual conversation. Quite apart from the difficulty caused by Jesus' avowal of his Messiahship, it must be admitted that neither could Jesus' revelation of the spirituality and universality of his Gospel be intelligible to a heathen woman, nor the subtle allusions of verses 35–38 to the disciples ; indeed, the latter become understandable only when read, as we can read them, from the point of view of a later generation. In any case there can hardly have been any reliable report of the conversation with the woman even if it took place—for there was no eye-witness present (ver. 8)— unless indeed Jesus himself recounted it verbatim, or the disciples went to the woman for information, both of which suppositions are unlikely. The possibility, however, cannot be entirely ruled out that the Beloved Disciple, not being strictly one of ' the disciples ' of verse 8 (see Introduction, p. xlvi), may have been present as witness. As for the general setting of the narrative, there is much here too which suggests the presence of an eye-witness. Nowhere in the Gospel are the topographical allusions more accurate : the great high-road passing through Samaria through which ' he must needs go ' on his way from Judaea to Galilee, the deep well, the reference to the overhanging heights of Gerizim, the illustrations drawn from the ripening corn, for which the locality is noted. And yet we cannot but feel that the *tout ensemble* of the scene is thoroughly artificial. If the sites mentioned are literally and historically accurate, why should the woman, whether she lived in Sychem or Askar, have come to Jacob's well for water, especially as verse 11 seems to hint that the well was not generally used ? Critics remark that springs are a favourite site for important occurrences in Eastern life (Gen. 24 : 11 ff. ; 1 Sam. 9 : 11 ; 1 Kings 17 : 10), and that this explains John's choice of a venue, to which Dods makes the telling rejoinder : ' In other words, wells are common meeting-places, therefore this meeting at a well cannot have taken place ! ' And yet the difficulty remains. Indeed, Synoptic passages such as Mt. 10 : 5 almost forbid us to accept this section as strict history, while it is most improbable that the disciples would so far offend against Jewish prejudices as they do in verses 8 and 31. Once it is admitted that the narrative is largely artificial there is of course endless scope for symbolical interpretation, and one feels that this has been carried to extremes. Is it really likely that by the ' five husbands ' John intends to symbolize the gods of the five nations settled in Samaria by her conquerors (though the five nations seem to have had *seven* gods : contrast 2 Kings 17 : 28–31 with idem, verse 24, and cf. Josephus, *Ant. IX.*, 14, 3), or that under any circumstances he would intend by the paramour Yahweh Himself ? Hardly less far-fetched is the suggestion that the lover symbolizes the Samaritan religious leader Simon Magus, whom Acts 8 : 9–13, 18–24, brings into intimate connexion with the original conversion of the Samaritans, or Dositheus, who is mentioned along with Simon as another Samaritan heretic. The probability is that the Evangelist is here utilizing reminiscences preserved by ' the Witness ' of a somewhat similar scene, and that, to serve his own didactic purpose, he builds up the section as we have it out of hints supplied by other sources already at his disposal. We have echoes of Mt. 9 : 37–38, and of the Parable of the Sower. We note too how, in dependence on Luke, John exaggerates Jesus' kindly feelings towards the Samaritans, of which we have hints in the earlier Gospel (Lk.

9 : 52–55, 10 : 30–37, 17 : 11–19). Holtzmann notes that this section, together with the Nicodemus section, takes the place in our Gospel of the Synoptic ' Sermon on the Mount.' But whereas in the Synoptics Jesus, like a second Moses on a second Sinai, delivers a higher law which fulfils the old law to the letter (Mt. 5 : 17–18), according to John the old law passes away altogether and becomes new (cf. 2 Cor. 5 : 17). Like Paul, John would consider the old Jewish faith to be un-spiritual and exclusive (Gal. 3 : 3, 4 : 3–7 ; 2 Cor. 3 : 6–8, 17), whereas in the spiritual faith of Christ national divisions are done away (Jn. 4 : 21, Gal. 3 : 28). The section is therefore to be treated, like the Nicodemus section, as another illustra-tion of the triumph of the new faith over the old. Just as a new birth must follow the old, so must the old religion of sense and symbol pass over into the new religion of ' spirit and truth.' The triumph of the new faith is summarized in a personal triumph of its originator Jesus, who at the beginning of his ministry here receives the recognition which historically he claimed only at the end of his career.

Section II. The Appropriation of the New Gospel

Illustration (i) : The Officer's Son healed : Christ restores Life
(4 : 43–54)

A new section begins at this point. Hitherto the theme has been the relation of the New Gospel to the Old, the superiority of Christianity to the older religions. This was introduced by two appropriate illustrations, the changing of water into wine and the cleansing of the temple, and was developed along three lines. We now pass to the ' appropriation of the New Gospel,' this theme, like the former, being introduced by several suitable illustrations drawn from incidents which the Evangelist has selected from the store at his disposal on account of their didactic value.

When the two days were over, he left for Galilee (for Jesus 43 himself testified that a prophet enjoys no honour in his 44 own country) ; on reaching Galilee, he was welcomed 45

by the Galileans, who had seen all he did at the festival in
Jerusalem—for they too had gone to the festival.

46 Once more he came to Cana in Galilee, where he had turned
the water into wine. There was a royal official, whose
47 son was lying ill at Capharnahum ; when he heard that
Jesus had arrived in Galilee from Judaea, he went to
him and begged him to come down and cure his son, who
48 was at the point of death. Jesus said to him, 'Unless you
49 see signs and wonders, you never will believe.' The
official said, 'Come down, sir, before my boy is dead.'
50 Jesus told him, 'Go yourself, your son is alive.' The man
believed what Jesus told him, and started on his journey.
51 And on the road his servants met him with the news
52 that his boy was alive. So he asked them at what hour
he had begun to improve ; they told him, 'Yesterday at
53 one o'clock the fever left him.' Then the father realized
that it had left him at the very time when Jesus had said
to him, 'Your son is alive ' ; and he became a believer
54 with all his household. This was the second Sign which
Jesus performed again after leaving Judaea for Galilee.

43 Verse 43 picks up verse 3 : When the two days (ver. 40) were
44 over, Jesus left for Galilee (for he himself testified that a prophet
enjoys no honour in his own country). The saying occurs,
Mk. 6 : 4, Mt. 13 : 57, Lk. 4 : 24, with reference to the ill-
welcome Jesus received at Nazaret. John emphasizes the
fact that Jesus himself quoted the proverb, probably because
otherwise he would have hesitated to apply it to the Christ.
But what locality is here intended by his own country?
Most interpretations are based upon the supposition that the
natural motive for Jesus' departure (for presumably gives
the motive) would be the wish to go *to* a place where he would
be honoured *from* a place where he was not being honoured.
Hence the conclusion that 'his own country' must be Judaea,
which Jesus has left at verse 3. He goes to Galilee presumably
in the hope of finding a more receptive audience. But this
theory must be rejected : not only must the Evangelist have
been aware that the saying which he quotes from the Synoptics

was spoken with reference to Nazaret, but he himself elsewhere regularly regards Nazaret as Jesus' birthplace (1 : 46,
19 : 19) and Galilee as his native country-side (2 : 1, 7 : 52).
Moreover, a glance back to 4 : 3 reminds us that Jesus' motive
for leaving Judaea was *not* that he might obtain elsewhere
honour which he was not meantime receiving. On the contrary his success was becoming embarrassing, and threatened
to involve him in collision with the Pharisees (3 : 26, 4 : 1),
so that he withdrew in order to escape publicity. John now
tells us that he goes to his ' own country ' of Galilee knowing
that there at least he will not be ' lionized,' **for a prophet
enjoys no honour in his own country**. But the sequel was not
exactly what he anticipated : **on reaching Galilee, he was** 45
**welcomed by the Galileans, who had seen all he did at the
festival in Jerusalem,** that is, his ' cleansing ' of the temple and
the miracles alluded to in 2 : 23. After his successful mission
in Jerusalem Jesus seems of some account even to his own
fellow-countrymen, who belong to the class of ' believer '
mentioned in 2 : 24-25, and manifest the type of faith criticized
by Jesus in 4 : 48. We conclude therefore that ' his own
country ' (Gk. *patris*) is here used in the broader sense of
' birthland,' not in the narrower sense of ' birth-place ' (as
in Mk. 6 : 4), and is applied to the province of Galilee.

Other solutions may be briefly mentioned. Early com-
mentors take the verse as an explanation of Jesus' neglect of
Nazaret while he goes on to Cana. Meyer thinks that the
meaning is that Jesus, having first substantiated his Messianic
claims in Judaea, now returns with new credentials to his
own country in the hope that now at length he may be able
to surmount the vulgar prejudice to which the proverb gives
expression. Loisy suggests that ' his own country ' is merely
a general expression for the whole of Palestine, the Ancient
Kingdom of Jesus' own people, and thus may be considered to include *Samaria*. The verse gives Jesus' reason
for leaving Samaria. He feels that it is unfitting that—in
contradiction to the proverb to which he has set his own
approval—he should be so highly honoured in any part of that
' country ' where his incarnate life is to be spent. His re-

ception in Samaria seems almost a violation of a divine decree
expressed in 1:11. He shrinks from receiving during his
earthly life honours which he feels are due to him only as Risen
Lord. Ingenious but too far-fetched! No explanation is
entirely satisfactory, and it may be that the verse is misplaced
or has been interpolated here under a misconception that
Judaea was Jesus' ' own country.'

46 **So once more Jesus came to Cana in Galilee.** Why to Cana?
It is just possible that Jesus' family lived here (note on 2:1),
but there is no evidence. As a matter of history the miracle
about to be recorded probably took place at Capharnahum.
But our Evangelist stages the scene at Cana, because this was
the place **where Jesus had turned the water into wine.** The
first miracle at Cana provided the illustration with which the
Evangelist introduced the previous section of his Gospel:
now with his usual love of symmetry he brings Jesus back to
Cana in order that he may open the present section with an
illustration drawn from the second miracle performed at the
same place. In verse 54 he deliberately emphasizes the
parallelism. The choice of Cana rather than Capharnahum as
the scene of the miracle serves the double purpose of giving
balance to the narrative and of heightening the miracle
by increasing the distance at which the cure was performed.
**There was a royal official, whose son was lying ill at Caphar-
nahum,** the place (for which see note on 2:12) where, according
to the Synoptics (Mt. 8:5-13, Lk. 7:1-10), the miracle
actually took place. Josephus' use of the Greek word
basilikos shows that it means not a kinsman of the king
(A.V. ' nobleman ') but one of his military officials: hence the
' centurion' of Matthew and Luke. The ' king' would be
Herod Antipas who, though strictly only a ' tetrarch,' was
allowed the courtesy title of ' king.' It is suggested that the
father of the sick boy may have been ' Chuza, Herod's
steward' (Lk. 8:3) or ' Manaen' (Acts 13:1)—apparently
for no better reason than that these happen to be the only
two of Herod's courtiers whose names we know! Note
that while Luke calls the sick lad a ' slave' (*doulos*) and
Matthew uses the ambiguous word ' boy' (*pais*, used by

John in ver. 51), John tells us that he was a ' son ' (*huios*).
The father when he heard that Jesus had arrived in Galilee from 47
Judaea, went to him and begged him to come down (the road
from Cana to Capharnahum being a descent to the Lake-side)
and cure his son, who was at the point of death, the same expression as Luke's (7 : 2), whose narrative our Evangelist
clearly has in view. If Jesus' reply—' Unless you see signs and 48
wonders, you never will believe '—seems undeservedly harsh,
the explanation is that it is ' not an answer to the father's
request, but a reflection of Jesus occasioned by it ' (Godet).
The words are a warning rather than a rebuff, and are aimed
not so much at the father as at his fellow-Galileans : theirs is
the faith which believes only when it sees ; he, on the contrary, is shown by the sequel to be one of those ' who believe
though they have never seen ' (20 : 29). The combination
' signs and wonders' occurs in the Gospels only here and in
Mk. 13 : 22, Mt. 24 : 24, but is common in Acts. The two
words ' severally mark the two chief aspects of miracles :
the spiritual aspect, whereby they suggest some deeper truth
than meets the eye, of which they are in some sense symbols
and pledges ; and the external aspect, whereby their strange-
ness arrests attention ' (Westcott). (For another apparently
harsh retort by Jesus to a request to heal see Mk. 9 : 19.)

Undaunted by Jesus' seeming unwillingness, the official said, 49
' Come down, sir, before my *child* (*paidion :* a more tender
note this time) is dead.' He will take no refusal ; it is enough
for Jesus to ' come down,' for if he does so healing is certain—
a faith like that of Mk. 9 : 24. But now, as if in dismissal,
Jesus told him, ' Go yourself, your son is alive.' The last words
are repeated twice before the end of the chapter (51, 53), and
emphasize the appropriateness of this miracle as an introduction to the theme of *Christ, the Bread of Life.* Jesus has
healed simply by a word, as indeed he was asked to do according to the Synoptic version (Mt. 8 : 8, Lk. 7 : 7). Accordingly
we are told that, though Jesus' claim to have healed from a
distance must have been a new trial to his faith, yet, without
seeing any miracle, the man believed what Jesus told him 50
(literally, ' believed *the word* '), and set out on his journey.

His faith, in contrast to the Galileans' of verse 45, is comparable with that of the Samaritans of verse 41.

51 Meanwhile the officer's servants, noting an improvement in the boy's condition, had set out to reassure their master, and on the road they met him with the news that his boy was
52 alive. So he asked them at what hour he had begun to improve. The Greek phrase here translated ' improve ' seems to have been a technical medical expression : Arrian also uses it with reference to a sick man. To the father's question the servants reply, ' Yesterday at one o'clock (i.e. in the afternoon) the fever left him.' In Matthew's account the lad was suffering not from fever but from paralysis. The time which is here stated to have elapsed between the healing of the boy and the meeting of the father with the servants is greater than would be expected, for the generally accepted site of Cana (see note on 2 : 1) is not more than about 15 miles from Capharnahum. Critics have been much exercised to explain the discrepancy. Various excuses have been invented for the father's dilatoriness ! His beast may have been tired, or he may have had business to do for Herod ! Westcott seeks to shorten the interval by supposing that the hour intended is (contrary to all usage) 7 p.m., while others suppose that from the point of view of one speaking after sunset any hour before sunset might be regarded as ' yesterday.' But all such discussions are really beside the mark. It may be that ' the seventh hour ' has a symbolical intention, seven being the perfect number, and therefore suitable for use in connexion with a miracle of the Christ. In any case it is certain that John is not the least concerned with problems of time and distance. It is enough for him that the healing occurred simultaneously with the word of Jesus, and that
53 the father realized that the fever had left his son at the very time when Jesus had said to him, ' Your son is alive.' John adds that so impressed was the officer by this miraculous coincidence that he became a believer with all his household (cf. Acts 10 : 2, 16 : 34, etc.). Again we are reminded that in our Gospel the word ' believe ' covers many gradations of faith. In this man's case faith had been present even before

the certification of the miracle (50) ; now that faith is confirmed. Previously he had trusted in a promise ; now he
believes in the absolute sense, that is, that Jesus is the Christ.
(See note on 3 : 15.)

The account concludes with the note that this was the 54
second Sign which Jesus performed again after leaving Judaea
for Galilee. (For the purpose of this remark see note on
ver. 46 above.) The meaning is not that this is the second
miracle performed by Jesus in Galilee, but that for the second
time Jesus' return to Galilee from Judaea is marked by a
miracle at Cana. A second series of miracles, with an
appropriate didactic discourse appended, begins with this
healing at Cana, just as the earlier section of the Gospel was
introduced by the account of the Cana wedding feast.

The paragraph 4 : 46-54 provides a close parallel to 2 : 1-11,
with which, as we have seen, the Evangelist pointedly links
it. Note that in both narratives Jesus replies to a request
for help with apparent harshness (2 : 4, 4 : 48), the petitioner
continues to trust (2 : 5, 4 : 49), and finally Jesus grants the
request with unexpected fulness.

Note finally that, in addition to the points already mentioned, our narrative differs from the account of Mt. 8 : 5-13,
Lk. 7 : 1-10 (the incident does not occur in Mark) in the
following particulars. Unlike the ' centurion ' John's ' royal
official ' appears to be not a heathen (though the contrary
has been urged in the interests of identifying the Synoptic
and the Johannine stories) but rather a Galilean Jew. Again
Jesus here expresses no surprise at the man's faith, as he
does in the Synoptic account : the Johannine outlook would
hardly permit this. It is also characteristic of John to heighten
the effect of the miracle by making it appear that it was performed at a greater distance than is the case according to the
Synoptists. As a result of this change in the conditions
under which the cure takes place, the Johannine officer appears
as the representative of an even higher type of faith than
does the Synoptic centurion. At first the latter's faith might
seem the higher, for (Mt. 8 : 8) he believes that a word from
Jesus is enough, whereas the officer urges Jesus to go with

him in person (Jn. 4 : 47). But in the sequel the officer's faith rises superior even to the centurion's in proportion as the distance at which he trusts that Jesus can heal is greater. The centurion's home was close by, this man's in another town. Yet, in vivid contrast to his fellow-countrymen of verse 45, ' he believed in the word.' Holtzmann suggestively remarks that herein he becomes the type of the true believers of later days—the actual readers of our Gospel—who continue to trust, though they are distant in time from Jesus' miracles, as he was in space.

Illustration (ii) : The Five Thousand fed : Christ sustains Life (6 : 1–15)

It is likely that at this point a dislocation of the text has taken place, and that chapter 6 ought to precede chapter 5. In its present position 5 provides us with a Jerusalem interlude which interrupts the Galilean ministry. The opening words of 6, ' after this Jesus went off to the opposite side of the sea of Galilee,' connect admirably with 4 : 54, and are perfectly natural if Jesus is at the moment of departure (as at 4 : 54) near the Sea of Galilee ; but they are not appropriate after 5 : 47, which leaves Jesus in Jerusalem. Further, the opening words of chapter 7, ' After this Jesus moved about in Galilee ; he would not move in Judaea, because the Jews were trying to kill him,' are not appropriate to the position at the end of 6, when Jesus is *already* in Galilee ; but they would follow perfectly immediately after the account of the visit to Jerusalem in 5, the reference to the attempt of the Jews to kill Jesus being then an echo of 5 : 18 and 7 : 19–20 (7 : 15–24 being restored to its original position at the end of 5. See note *in loc.*). This rearrangement also has the advantage of simplifying the vexed problem of the unnamed feast of 5 : 1, as the latter may now be regarded as the Pentecost following the Passover of 6 : 4. The order of events is then as follows : after the miracle at Cana (4 : 46–54) Jesus for a time continues his ministry in Galilee (chap. 6) ; then, after a crisis there (6 : 60–71), he goes to Jerusalem for Pentecost (5 : 1), but is compelled by Jewish hostility (5 : 16, 18 ; 7 : 19) to return to

Galilee (7 : 1) ; he then returns finally to Judaea in time for the Feast of Tabernacles (7 : 2). It may be noted also that as a result of the rearrangement the Johannine account falls more nearly into line with the Synoptics. The visits of Jesus to Jerusalem before the Crucifixion provide one of the chief points of discrepancy between our Gospel and the others. But by postponing the visit of 5 : 1 until after the events of chapter 6, it is possible to regard it as taking place subsequently to the close of the Galilean ministry as narrated by Mark, so that, if it be admitted that the visit of 2 : 13 preceded the opening of the Galilean ministry as described by the Synoptists (but on this see note at end of chap. 1 and at 3 : 24), it follows that this ministry, so far as it is recorded by the Fourth Gospel, remains unbroken by any visit to Jerusalem.

Against the proposed rearrangement it may be urged that the crisis of the Galilean ministry described at the end of chapter 6 comes too early if placed before chapter 5, its appropriate setting being immediately before Jesus' final departure from Galilee at 7 : 10, in which position it provides a fitting conclusion to the first Section of the Gospel. This argument has some force, particularly so if the rearrangement results in the first Section of the Gospel ending abruptly at 7 : 24 (7 : 15-24 belonging, as noted above, to chapter 5). But, as will be seen below, we propose to transpose 8 : 12-20— a paragraph clearly out of place in its present position—to follow 7 : 24 as a fitting climax to the first Section of the Gospel.

Note finally that there is some indication that parts of chapter 6 may be due to a later hand than the body of the Gospel (see note on 6 : 28), in which case the confusion would be due to interpolation rather than to dislocation. It is possible, on the other hand, that a deliberate displacement may have taken place as the result of the Redactor's editing. The original order may have been as we propose to rearrange : the Redactor, out of a desire for an artificial symmetry, may have transposed the chapters into their present position. He thereby secures that for the second time (cf. 2 : 13) Jesus proceeds to Jerusalem with the laurels of a mighty act performed at Cana fresh upon him, while each of three Galilean miracles (the wine at Cana, the healing of the official's son, the feeding of the multitude) is followed by a feast and a ministry at Jerusalem.

6.

1 After this Jesus went off to the opposite side of the sea of
2 Galilee (the lake of Tiberias), followed by a large crowd on account of the Signs which they had seen him perform
3 on sick folk. Now Jesus went up the hill and sat down
4 there with his disciples. (The passover, the Jewish festival,
5 was at hand.) On looking up and seeing a large crowd approaching, he said to Philip, 'Where are we to buy
6 bread for all these people to eat ? ' (He said this to test Philip, for he knew what he was going to do himself.)
7 Philip answered, ' Seven pounds' worth of bread would not be enough for them, for everybody to get even a
8 morsel.' One of his disciples, Andrew the brother of
9 Simon Peter, said to him, ' There is a servant here, with five barley-cakes and a couple of fish ; but what is that among so many ? ' Jesus said, ' Get the people to lie
10 down.' Now there was plenty of grass at the spot, so
11 the men lay down, numbering about five thousand. Then Jesus took the loaves, gave thanks to God, and distributed them to those who were reclining ; so too with the fish,
12 as much as they wanted. And when they were satisfied, he said to the disciples, ' Gather up the pieces left over,
13 so that nothing may be wasted.' They gathered them up, and filled twelve baskets with pieces of the five
14 loaves left over from the meal. Now when the people saw the Sign he had performed, they said, ' This really
15 is the Prophet who is to come into the world ! ' Whereupon Jesus perceived they meant to come and seize him to make a king of him ; so he withdrew by himself to the hill again.

1 After this Jesus—leaving Cana and taking ship probably at Capharnahum, to which place he returns at verse 17—

went off to the opposite side of the sea of Galilee, to a spot on the north-east coast of the Lake, perhaps a little south of Bethsaida, near which place (Lk. 9 : 10) the miracle took place. (For the position of Bethsaida see G. A. Smith, *Historical Geography*, p. 457.) The description of the Lake as the lake of Tiberias (cf. 21 : 1), is an indication of the later 2 date of our Gospel. The name does not occur in the other Gospels, nor is it used by writers of the first century A.D., Strabo, Pliny and Josephus all employing the designation ' lake of Gennesar,' or ' Gennesaritis.' It is found, however, in the Greek writer Pausanias, who wrote in the middle of the second century, and regularly in the Talmud. The town of Tiberias, which ultimately gave its name to the Lake, was built by Antipas, and named in honour of Caesar ; in the time of Jesus, if built at all, it would be quite new. The use by John of both the old name and the new is a hint that the Gospel was written during the period of transition from the one form to the other, and would suit a date at the very end of the first century or beginning of the second.

Though Jesus had retired in search of rest and solitude (Mk. 6 : 31), he was followed by a large crowd, who probably made their way round by foot across the Fords of Jordan (Mt. 14 : 13). Mark implies that the crowd's motive was to hear Jesus' preaching (6 : 34), Matthew that they brought their sick to be healed (14 : 14), Luke combines both motives (9 : 11) ; our Gospel implies that the crowd, true to their reputation (4 : 48), follow chiefly out of curiosity on account of the Signs which they had seen him perform on sick folk. Meanwhile Jesus, desiring quiet, went up the hill and sat 3 down there with his disciples. Compare Mt. 15 : 29, where the scene of the second feeding of the multitude (the 4,000) is placed upon a hill, whereas the first feeding apparently took place on the level land near the shore. John combines traits from both accounts. We also have an echo in this verse of the Matthean introduction to the ' Sermon on the Mount ' (Mt. 5 : 1), and in the words on looking up (verse 5) an echo of the Lucan introduction (Lk. 6 : 20). By the hill is meant the plateau-land above the Lake, not any particular summit.

4 What is the point of the remark that **the passover, the Jewish festival, was at hand**? It is something more than a mere note of time, and may be intended to explain the presence of so many people on the march. Yet pilgrim caravans would hardly travel without supplies, nor would they be likely to turn aside thus from the main route, much less to double back to Capharnahum, as we are told they did later (22–25). The words are probably symbolical and 'designed to give a clue to the understanding of the spiritual lessons of the miracle which are set forth in the discourse which followed' (Westcott). John conceives that Jesus, in the miraculous meal, provided a substitute for the approaching festival, at which he did not intend to be present in person, and thereby implies that the Christian Sacrament of the Lord's Supper (which as we shall see is symbolized throughout the whole of chapter 6) is destined finally to supplant the Jewish Passover, for 'Christ our paschal lamb has been sacrificed' (1 Cor. 5 : 7). This is the second Passover mentioned in our Gospel, the first being at 2 : 13.

The narrative which follows is based upon the two Synoptic accounts of a miraculous feeding (Mk. 6 : 34 ff. and parallels ; Mk. 8 : 1 ff. and parallels). There is less cause here than in other parts of the Gospel to suppose that the Evangelist is relying upon the independent evidence of 'the Witness' (note ver. 28 below). In characteristic fashion he selects from the mass of Synoptic material dealing with the Galilean ministry an outstanding miracle which will serve to introduce the symbolical exposition of the meaning of the Lord's Supper which follows. Accordingly there are details in his account of the miracle which can be understood at their full value only in the light of the discourse with which the chapter ends.

5   Jesus, then **seeing a large crowd approaching, said to Philip, 'Where are we to buy bread for all these people to eat?'** The peculiarity of the Johannine account is that the anxiety about food originates with Jesus himself, not with the disciples as in the Synoptic account (Mk. 6 : 36–37). Historically Mark's narrative is the more probable : nightfall reminds the disciples that the people have been all day without food, a

much less artificial contingency than that Jesus, as soon as he saw the crowd, should begin to feel concern about how they are to be fed. But considered symbolically John's alteration is full of significance : Christ ever takes the initiative, and his gifts to his own are all of free grace. John alone at this point mentions Philip by name. Have we here the recollection of an eye-witness ? Possibly, for it has been pointed out that Philip belonged to this neighbourhood (12 : 21), and might be expected to know where food might be obtained. John loves to add vividness to his narrative by specifying individuals by name (e.g. see 18 : 10). He seems to have had a special interest in Philip (1 : 43–44, 12 : 21), possibly because the Evangelist of the same name (see note on 1 : 43) was known in the district where John wrote. Lest Jesus' question should seem inconsistent with the supernatural insight so often emphasized in the Gospel (note on 2 : 25) John explains that **he said this** 6 **to test Philip**—a man who believed only when he saw (14 : 8)— **for he knew what he was going to do himself.** Philip, ' a good man of business—more ready to rely on his own shrewd calculations than on unseen resources ' (Dods), answered that ' **seven pounds' worth of bread would not be enough for them.'** 7 The ' denarius ' was worth about 9½*d.*, and was the ordinary daily wage of a working man (Mt. 20 : 2). The same sum is mentioned by Mark (6 : 37) ; was it the contents of the common purse at the moment ? Rather the sum is a rough calculation of what it would cost ' **for everybody to get even a morsel.'** Mark implies that this sum would suffice ; John, as usual heightening the effect, says that not even this would be enough.

One of his disciples, Andrew the brother of Simon Peter, 8 introduced as if for the first time, in spite of 1 : 40—said to Jesus, ' **There is a servant here, with five barley-cakes and a** 9 **couple of fish.'** The details agree with the Synoptic account (Mk. 6 : 38 and parallels), but John alone mentions the slave-boy who brought the food, and adds that the loaves were of barley. Possibly these two features, and also the words ' **what is that among so many ? '** are borrowed from 2 Kings 4 : 42–44. Elisha's barley loaves are called ' bread of the first-fruits,' which Lev. 23 : 9 ff. treats of in connexion with the

Passover. John may intend a symbolical reference to the paschal loaves, and Loisy suggests that the boy typifies the 'auxiliary minister' at the early Christian eucharistic services. Barley loaves were the food of the poor, and the worst form of bread. (See Ezek. 13: 19, Judges 7: 13, and compare Livy: 'he ordered barley bread to be given to the cohorts who had lost their standards.') Christ is shown to be one who produces mighty results from the slenderest possible means.

10   Jesus said, ' Get the people to lie down.' Now there was plenty of grass at the spot, so the men lay down, numbering about five thousand. As to the number there is again agreement with the Synoptists, and if there is any emphasis on the word men, it is assumed that the women and children partook over and above (Mt. 14: 21). Like Mark and Matthew, John notes that the spot was grassy : ' the level plain on the east of the Jordan, the Butaiha, so fertile that some have claimed it for Gennesaret, still helps us to understand how " there was much grass in the place " ' (G. A. Smith). Are we to conclude that John, like the Synoptists, pictures the miracle as taking place on the grassy shores of the Lake—in spite of the ascent of verse 3 ? (See note on ver. 15.)

11   Then Jesus took the loaves, gave thanks to God, and— himself, apart from any mediation by the disciples (contrast Mt. 14: 19, to which reading the *Textus Receptus* assimilates our text)—distributed them to those who were reclining, the bread to all as a necessity, so too with the fish, as much as they wanted. The lowly personal service of Jesus is similarly emphasized in 13: 1 ff., possibly in contrast to the current teaching of the Stoics, to whom the thought of being ' servant of all ' was repugnant and pity actually a vice. Jesus asks a blessing on the meal, like the head of the household at the Passover Feast, while the sacramental atmosphere of the scene is intensified by John's use of the solemn word *eucharistesas* (cf. 1 Cor. 11: 24) in place of the more common word *eulogein* used by the Synoptists (Mk. 6: 41 and parallels ; Mk. 8: 6, Mt. 15: 36, however, use the word *eucharistesas* in the account of the second miraculous feeding). For our Gospel this scene, together with the ' Foot-washing ' in chapter

13, takes the place of the Synoptic account of the Institution of the Lord's Supper. John alone records that when they 12 were satisfied, Jesus said to the disciples, ' Gather up the pieces left over, so that nothing may be wasted,' thus emphasizing the sacredness of the sacramental bread. The words sound almost like an instruction for the conduct of the eucharistic liturgy. Accordingly the disciples gathered them up, and filled twelve 13 baskets with pieces of the five loaves left over from the meal— presumably one basket for each disciple, though ' the Twelve ' are first mentioned as such at 6 : 67. The fragments of fishes are not mentioned because, though the fish too was commonly used as a symbol of life, it is from the bread only that a symbolical lesson is drawn in the following discourse, and bread only that is used as an ' element ' at the sacrament. Note that after this miracle there was bread to spare, just as there was wine to spare at Cana, the abundant fulness of the life offered by Christ thus being emphasized. The question of the relation of the two miracles in the mind of the Evangelist has already been discussed. (See p. 54 f.)

While the Synoptists tell us nothing about the impression 14 made upon the crowd when they saw the Sign Jesus had performed, John records their verdict that ' This really is the Prophet who is to come into the world ! ' The last words were applied to the Logos in 1 : 9, and ' the coming One ' was a phrase commonly used of the Messiah (Ps. 118 : 26). For ' the Prophet ' cf. Deut. 18: 15 ; in 1 : 21 he is distinguished from Messiah, but the distinction was not strictly observed, and here the thought seems to be that Jesus is Messiah himself. (See note on 1 : 21.) This view is confirmed by the statement that Jesus perceived they meant to seize him to make a king of him, 15 that is, to proclaim him Messiah. The Greek word used for ' seize ' is the same as occurs in Matthew's words (11 : 12) : ' the Realm of Heaven suffers violence, and the violent *press into* it.' The Synoptists do not record this attempt to make Jesus king. John, by introducing the incident, prepares the way for Jesus' words to Pilate (18 : 36) : ' My realm does not belong to this world.' The nearest parallel in the Synoptics is the temptation narrative (Mt. 4 : 8 ff.), from which—unless

indeed we have here the independent account of ' the Witness'
—John may possibly have borrowed the incident. The offer
of the kingship to Jesus here upon ' the hill ' reminds us of the
' high mountain ' of the third temptation, just as Jn. 2 : 3
recalled the first temptation. The Christ of the Fourth
Gospel never allows his hand to be forced (cf. 2: 3–4 ; 7 : 3, 6 ;
10 : 18) ; ' his hour had not yet come,' and therefore he
withdrew by himself to the hill again. Mark (6 : 46) and
Matthew (14 : 23) both mention that Jesus at this point ' went
up the hill to pray,' naturally enough if, as the Synoptists
imply, the miracle took place by the shore of the Lake. But
according to John (ver. 3) Jesus climbed the hill before the
miracle, which presumably took place on the high ground ;
no descent has been mentioned, and there is no higher point
on the flat plateau to which Jesus might have ascended for
prayer. John apparently borrows this final clause from the
Synoptic account without noticing that it confuses his own
narrative ; the word **again** loosely covers up the difficulty
of this double ascent.

Illustration (iii) : Christ walks on the Water : the ever-present
Saviour (6 : 16–21)

16 When evening came, his disciples went down to the sea, and
17   embarking in a boat they started across the sea for Caphar-
    nahum. By this time it was dark, Jesus had not reached
18   them yet, and the sea was getting up under a strong wind.
19   After rowing about three or four miles they saw Jesus
    walking on the sea and nearing the boat. They were
20   terrified, but he said to them, ' It is I, have no fear ' ;
21   so they agreed to take him on board, and the boat instantly
    reached the land they were making for.

16   When evening came, his disciples went down to the sea—
another hint that John supposes the miracle to have taken
place on the high ground. Is this the evening of the same or
the following day ? John seems to place the miracle earlier
in the day, and to imply that the disciples left the same evening.

According to the Synoptists it was already evening (Mk.
6 : 35 and parallels) when Jesus fed the crowd : yet, in spite
of a second mention of the coming of evening (Mk. 6 : 47,
Mt. 14 : 23), they too seem to mean that the departure took
place the same evening ('straightway,' Mk. 6 : 45). The
disciples left Jesus to follow, and embarking in a boat (some 17
MSS read, as Mk. 6 : 45, ' *the* boat,' which would imply that
it was the same boat in which they had previously crossed
from Capharnahum) started across the sea for Capharnahum.
According to Mark Jesus told the disciples to go on ahead
northwards up the coast towards Bethsaida, perhaps intending
himself to follow on foot, and to be picked up by the boat at a
spot on the shore near that town. (See note below on ver. 19.)
By this time it had become dark, Jesus had not reached them
yet,—the pluperfects seeming to imply that the disciples,
perhaps by arrangement, had waited for Jesus before starting,
and set sail only because the sea was getting up under a strong 18
wind and they feared that further delay would make the
crossing dangerous. John is here out of agreement with Mark,
according to whom the disciples had definite instructions to go
on ahead, and not to Capharnahum but to Bethsaida. While
Mark and Matthew say that the boat was ' in the middle of the 19
sea,' John, with his love of precise detail, tells us that after
rowing about three or four miles they saw Jesus walking on the
sea and nearing the boat. The ' stade ' was roughly 200
yards. Mark tells us that the hour was ' about the fourth
watch of the night,' that is, shortly before daybreak : John
seems to imply an hour at dead of night, thus intensifying the
symbolical effect of the story. The words translated walking
on the sea might quite well mean ' walking *by* the sea '
(cf. 21 : 1, ' by the sea of Tiberias,' 6 : 21 ' at the land ' ;
Greek *epi* with Genitive). The meaning would then be
that the boat was clinging to the shore because of the
storm, and that the figure of Jesus, waiting for the boat
to pick him up, suddenly loomed up on the beach. This
would fit in with the hint dropped by Mark that Jesus
sent on the disciples towards Bethsaida with the intention of
rejoining them there before crossing together to the other side

of the Lake.   The meaning of verse 21 would also be simplified.
It is just possible that some such incident may be the origin
of this wonder-story about Jesus—one of the most difficult to
accept literally.   Nevertheless, the translation ' walking on the
sea ' is justified here beyond question in the light both of the
Synoptic narratives, where Matthew even adds the parallel
incident of Peter walking on the water, and also of the disciples'
manifest astonishment.   Had John merely implied that the
disciples caught sight of Jesus on the beach he would hardly

20 have added that **they were terrified.**   Mark explains their fear
by saying that ' they thought it was a ghost ' : John, perhaps
on account of his strong anti-docetic views, omits this.   Jesus'
answer is given in the exact words of Mk. 6 : 50, ' **It is I,
have no fear.**'   For the phrase ' It is I ' (Gk. *egō eimi*),
so common in the Gospel, see 4 : 26, 8 : 24, 28, 58 ; 9 : 9,
13 : 19, 18 : 5, 6, 8 ; Mk. 13 : 6 ; Lk. 21 : 8.   Reassured by

21 the Master's voice the disciples **agreed to take him on board.**
The narrative then ends abruptly, for while Mark and Matthew
both tell of the stilling of the storm and imply that the boat
had some distance to go before coming to shore at Gennesaret
(Mk. 6 : 53, ' When they had passed over '), John merely notes
that **the boat instantly reached the land they were making for.**
The Lake at its widest part is some seven miles across ; but
if the passage was merely across the northern bay a row of four
miles would bring the boat close in to Capharnahum.   Some
critics find in John's conclusion confirmation of the view that
Jesus was in fact standing on the shore.   Verse 21 may then be
translated ' They wished (giving the Greek verb its natural
meaning) to take him into the boat, and immediately (before
they had time to do so) the boat ran aground.'   But if this is
John's meaning we would expect ' *but* immediately.'   And
though the imperfect tense of the verb favours the sense that
the disciples merely *wished* to take Jesus into the boat but did
not do so, the alternative rendering ' they were willing ' is quite
legitimate : at first they hesitated through fear, but at the
sound of Jesus' own voice **they agreed to take him on board.**
Also the land in question is obviously Capharnahum, which
' they were making for ' (ver. 17), not some point on the east

coast where, it is suggested, Jesus might have been waiting to be picked up. John agrees with the Synoptists that Jesus actually came to the boat over the water, and his statement that the boat immediately reached land is intended to heighten the miracle by providing a graphic illustration of Ps. 107 : 30. ' The moment Jesus set foot in the barque he imparted to it . . . that victorious power over gravity and space which had been so majestically displayed in his own person ' (Godet).

It may be noted that the insertion by John at this place of the miracle of Jesus walking on the water is governed not only by its analogous position in Mark, where it follows the feeding of the five thousand, but also by its fitness to serve as an introduction to the sacramental discourse on ' the bread of life.' The miracle in part meets the objection of verses 52 and 60, by hinting that Jesus' corporeality was of a peculiar kind which transcended the limits both of gravity and of space. The way is thus prepared even for the miracle foreshadowed in verse 62. It is possible too that John may be seeking to combat exaggerated ideas current in his own day as to the exclusive presence of Christ in the Eucharist alone : ' The storm-tossed ship symbolizes the Church, and Jesus communicates himself to its needs in a fashion that transcends limitations of sense. . . . Not only in the Eucharist, but amid the storms of life does Jesus appear. His is a real spiritual presence everywhere ' (R. H. Strachan).

Theme : The Partaking of Christ the Bread of Life (6: 22-27)

Next day the crowd which had been left standing on the other 22 side of the sea bethought them that only one boat had been there, and that Jesus had not gone aboard with his disciples, who had left by themselves. So, as some boats from Tiber- 23 ias had put in near the spot where they had eaten bread after the Lord's thanksgiving, and as the crowd 24 saw that neither Jesus nor his disciples were there, they embarked in the boats themselves and made for Capharnahum in search of Jesus. When they found him on the 25 other side of the sea, they said, ' Rabbi, when did you get here ? ' Jesus answered them, ' Truly, truly I tell you, it 26

is not because you saw Signs that you are in quest of me,
27 **but because you ate these loaves and had your fill. Work
for no perishing food, but for that lasting food which
means eternal life ; the Son of man will give you that,
for the Father, God, has certified him.'**

22 The Evangelist having conducted Jesus and his disciples
to the western side of the Lake, now turns back to the people
who had been miraculously fed, and gives us a somewhat
artificial summary of the motives which induced them also to
cross the Lake. **Next day,** that is, on the day following the
multiplication of the loaves, **the crowd which had been left
standing on the other** (eastern) **side of the sea bethought them
that** (on the previous day) **only one boat had been there,** that is,
the boat in which the disciples had departed, **and that Jesus had
not gone aboard with his disciples, who had left by themselves**
for the western shore. Jesus then could not have crossed by
boat. But had he gone on by foot, to be picked up by the
disciples, or was he still in seclusion near at hand ? This
doubt is cleared up in verse 24. Meanwhile, a means of
following Jesus, should it be necessary so to do, providentially
23 presents itself, **as some boats from Tiberias had put in near the
spot.** As these boats had come not from Capharnahum but
from Tiberias, their occupants would be unaware that Jesus
had already landed before dawn at Capharnahum. As
Tiberias was on the west coast, south of Capharnahum, and
during the night a strong west wind had been blowing (Mt.
14 : 24, ' the wind was against them ' as they crossed west-
wards), we may surmise that the boats had been compelled
by the gale to land on the side of the Lake opposite to their
home port. We are told that they had put in **near the spot
where the people had eaten bread after the Lord's thanksgiving,** an apparently unnecessary reminder of the miracle
which serves nevertheless to link up the discourse which
follows with the miracle which has served as its introductory
illustration. (For the term ' the Lord ' see note on 4 : 1.) **The**
24 **crowd** then as they **saw that neither Jesus nor his disciples were
there,** that is, when they had made sure that Jesus was not

still lingering near by and that his disciples had no intention of returning for him, at length embarked in the boats themselves, and made for Capharnahum in search of Jesus. It is super-fluous to ask how it happened that there were sufficient boats on the spot, with owners accommodating enough, to convey so large a crowd across the Lake. As Mark and Matthew tell us that immediately after the miracle Jesus had himself dismissed the main body of the people, it may be that only a compara-tively few enthusiasts had remained. But John is not con-cerned with such questions. His object is to transport the crowd across the sea so that the same people who were miraculously fed may provide an audience for the sacramental discourse, and to do this so speedily that the crowd arrives in Capharnahum before Jesus could reasonably be supposed to have had time to make his way round by foot. The reality of the miracle of Jesus walking on the water is thus presented to the crowd and the way prepared for their dramatic surprise in the following verse, where we read that when they found 25 him on the other side of the sea, they said, ' Rabbi, when did you get here ? '—and by implication ' *How* did you get here ? ' ' They came seeking him, but were surprised to find him ' (Dods). They are confronted with yet another ' Sign,' yet even so they do not understand the significance of the presence of Jesus there before their eyes any more than they appreciated the true meaning of the miracle of the feeding. Hence the point of Jesus' rebuke, ' Truly, truly I tell you, it is not because 26 you saw Signs that you are in quest of me, but because you ate these loaves and had your fill.' Jesus pays no heed to the crowd's question, but points out the unspiritual motive behind their pursuit of him. Their recent experiences had appealed to them only in so far as their bodily appetites had been satisfied. The word used is properly applied to the giving of fodder to animals, though in later Greek it is freely used of human beings (Mt. 5 : 6, etc.). They had indeed seen ' signs ' —whether the reference be to the two miracles just narrated or to Jesus' miracles in general, as in verse 2—but they had missed their true significance. They thought only of material nourishment, not of that spiritual ' life ' which was Christ's

true gift. They had eyes only for the symbol, not for the
reality which lay behind—in fact, even the symbol appealed to
them only because it brought with it bodily satisfaction.
Instead of seeing 'in the bread the sign,' they had 'in the sign
beheld only the bread' (Lange). We may compare the
disciples' misunderstanding in Mk. 8: 17–21, after the second
miracle of feeding. John probably has this incident in view
for, as we have seen, he borrows traits from both Synoptic
miracles.

27 Jesus therefore seeks to point his audience from the symbol
to the reality : **'Work for no perishing food, but for that lasting food which means eternal life.'** The word for 'work'
(*ergazesthe*) is unusual in this sense of 'work to procure,' but its
use renders possible the play on words to be noted in verse 28.
All material food is **perishing** ; its satisfaction is merely
transitory ; even the divine manna would not keep (Exod.
16: 20) ; yesterday Jesus had multiplied loaves for the people,
yet ' they were already hungry again, and had toiled after him
for miles to get another meal' (Dods). Indeed, material life
itself is but a protracted death process (1 Cor. 6: 13). Let the
people rather seek that better 'food' which remains per-
manently in the man who receives it as the principle and
perennial source of 'eternal life.' (Compare 4: 14.) And such
food may be had for the asking for **'the Son of man will give
you that.'** It was to give this, not merely to multiply loaves
that the Son of man (cf. 1: 51) came. Jesus does not say 'the
Messiah' lest he should reawaken the false expectations of
verse 15 : he uses for himself a title which alike expresses his
sympathy for all *human* needs, and also hints to the initiated
that he *is* Messiah.

To bestow this spiritual food upon men is the chief object
of Christ's mission, **'for the Father, God, has certified him,'**
that is, commissioned him for this very purpose. (For the word
'certified' or, to give the word its literal meaning, 'sealed,'
see note on 3: 33.) To set one's seal to anything is to authenticate its genuineness ; thus a sovereign will give his seal to his
vicegerent (Gen. 41: 42). God has set His seal upon Christ
not only in his miracles but also in that miracle of incarnation

whereby the Logos was consecrated and commissioned to his life-giving mission. Some see in the word ' seal ' a reference to the stamping of loaves with the name of the maker ; others to the custom that when a person ordered a banquet he gave his seal to the steward commissioned to provide it.

The discourse which follows presents many problems, most of which will be best discussed at the end of the section. At this point it may be noticed that, on the assumption that two scenes are distinguished—the seashore (ver. 25) and the synagogue (ver. 59)—and also two audiences—the crowd (ver. 22), and the Jews (vers. 41 and 52), it has been suggested that we have here a conflation of two separate discourses an address to ' the crowd ' on the seashore and a controversy with ' the Jews ' in the synagogue. Thus Chastand allots to the seaside verses 26–27, 31–35, 41–42, 47–58, and to the synagogue verses 28–30, 36–40, 43–46, while Loisy would distinguish verses 26–27, 32–33, 47–48, 51, 53–58 as ' a poem on the bread of life,' independent of the rest of the dialogue. It may be that the Witness' notes of two addresses spoken on different occasions have been worked up by the Evangelist to suit his didactic purpose, and grouped together as bearing on the same subject. (For a similar conglomerate passage we might compare 10 : 1–18.) But in view of the whole character of this chapter it would be dangerous to assume that we have here anything approaching the words actually spoken by Jesus, so that detailed conjecture as to place, occasion and audience seems somewhat superfluous.

One is tempted, however, to suspect that part at least of verses 28–33 may have been interpolated. The connexion of verse 28 with what precedes is not very clear, consisting indeed in little more than the play on the word ' work.' Verse 34, on the other hand, would follow well enough immediately after 27 (we should have exactly the same connexion as between 4 : 14 and 15 ; there, ' the water I shall give . . . Sir, give me this water ' ; here, ' the Son of man will give you that food . . . Sir, give us that bread '). Finally the demand for a ' Sign ' in verse 30, though it may be partially explained along the lines attempted below, comes very unnaturally from the lips of those who have just been miraculously fed, especially as the 'Sign' demanded is one comparable to the gift by Moses of the manna, a miracle which had, in fact, been as nearly as possible reproduced by Jesus already. It is possible that verses 28–33 may have been inserted by the Redactor with his usual desire to approximate the narrative to that of the Synoptists, who (Mk. 8:11, Mt. 16:1) immediately after the feeding of the four thousand record a similar demand for a 'Sign.' But according to Mark it is the Pharisees, not the crowd who have been fed, who ask for it, and in this fact we perhaps have a hint as to the origin of such parts of the present discourse as seem to belong more naturally to a controversy with the Jewish leaders than to an address to a popular audience. This is, however, purely conjecture, and the verses must be dealt with as they stand.

28 Then they asked him, 'What must we do to perform the
29 works of God?' Jesus replied to them, 'This is the work of God, to believe in him whom God has sent.'
30 'Well, then,' they said, 'what is the Sign you perform,
31 that we may see it and believe you? What work have you to show? Our ancestors ate manna in the desert: as it is written, *He gave them bread from heaven to eat.*'
32 Then said Jesus, 'What Moses gave you was not the bread from heaven; it is my Father who gives you the
33 real bread from heaven—for the bread of God is what comes down from heaven and gives life to the world.'
34 'Ah, sir,' they said to him, 'give us that bread always.'
35 Jesus said, 'I am the bread of life; he who comes to me will never be hungry, and he who believes in me will never be thirsty again.'

28 The people apparently imagine that in bidding them 'work for no perishing food,' Jesus is calling upon them to aim at a higher *ethical* standard, which will express itself in the *performance* of acts pleasing to the will of God, and therefore, with a play on the word 'work,' they ask him, 'What must we do to perform the works of God,' that is, the works which

God commands ? (For a similar use of the Genitive, cf. Rev.
2 : 26.) The crowd have no conception of 'life' as a gift:
it is something which must be worked for. Religion for
them is not the living of a divinely given 'life,' but the performance of sundry religious duties. Jesus had indeed just
bidden them 'work for lasting food,' but it was for food
which 'the Son of man will *give*.' 'The believer's work does
not earn a recompense at the last, but secures a gift' (Westcott). We are reminded of the scribe's question (Mk. 12 : 28),
'What is the chief of all the commands ? ' But whereas in
Mark Jesus sums up the whole law in the law of love, here he
replies that 'the work of God' consists not even in the
keeping of the whole law, but in an *act* of *faith*: '**This is the** 29
work of God, to believe in him whom God has sent.' The religious life-relationship depends not on the performance of
the law and the consequent acquiring of merit, but on a
freely offered faith. It should be noted that in the Greek
final construction, '**to believe**' 'marks not only the simple
fact of believing, but the effort directed to and issuing in this
belief' (Westcott). (Cf. 4 : 34.) There is a sense in which 'to
believe' is to perform a work. The influence upon our
writer of Paul's doctrine of 'justification by faith' is obvious.
The verse too provides an interesting point of union between
Paul and James. ' *Faith* is the highest kind of *work*, for by
it a man gives himself; and a free being can *do* nothing
greater than to give himself' (Godet). As J. Réville puts it,
' What a pity that St. Paul had no knowledge of these words
when the Jerusalem disciples were giving him the cold
shoulder or even excommunicating him in the name of loyalty
to their Master for having said exactly the same thing.'

The words ' **him whom God has sent** ' are an obvious allusion 30
to the Messiah (cf. 3 : 17, 17 : 3), and it now dawns on the
people that Jesus is thus designating himself; they therefore
call on him to authenticate his claims: ' **Well, then, what is
the Sign you perform, that we may see it and believe you ?** '—
for these folk faith is not, as defined in the last verse, an act
of trust in a person, but merely assent to that person's message,
an assent, too, based entirely on the testimony of the senses.

How like much popular 'faith' even to-day!—'**What work have you to show?**' The play on the word 'work' is continued. Here is a *tu quoque* to Jesus' demand of 27 and 29: 'You bid us do the work of God; well, what have *you* done?' This demand for a 'Sign' comes strangely from those who just the day before had had proof of Jesus' power in the miraculous feeding. It is true that a similar demand for a 'Sign' is reported by the Synoptists (Mk. 8: 11, Mt. 16: 1) immediately after the feeding of the four thousand, but there the demand is made by the Pharisees who were not witnesses of the miracle. For John, on the contrary, the interest of the present situation depends on the assumption that Jesus is now addressing those whom yesterday he fed. The symbolical language of verse 27 loses all force unless addressed to those who had been sharers in the 'perishing food' of verse 11. The spectators of yesterday's miracle are to-day asking what 'Sign' Jesus can perform to prove his authority. Moreover, they give a hint of the form they 31 desire this 'Sign' to take: '**Our ancestors ate manna in the desert: as it is written** (Exod. 16: 4, Ps. 105: 40, Ps. 78: 24–25, Neh. 9: 15), "**He gave them bread from heaven to eat.**"' Now Jesus has just performed a miracle which might be deemed to repeat sufficiently closely the O.T. wonder which the people quote, and we might suppose that the people admit this (as indeed they did by their exclamation in verse 14), but imply that, if Jesus is Messiah, then he must outdo Moses and perform another miracle greater still. Did not Jesus himself hint that he could do so when he said (27) 'the Son of man will give you that *lasting food*'? The people, we might say, have but raised their claims to the level of that promise. But there is evidence to show that Jewish theology regarded the giving of the manna as *the* miracle *par excellence*, the *non plus ultra* even for the Messiah. In fact, the Rabbis taught that Messiah would prove his authority by repeating just this miracle by which, they held, Moses had proved his. 'As was the first Redeemer,' so ran the Midrash, 'so shall be the final Redeemer; as the first Redeemer caused the manna to fall from heaven, even so shall the second Redeemer cause the manna to fall.' In the light of this it seems more likely that John pictures the people as insinuating that Jesus has not yet equalled Moses' miracle. He may have fed them once by multiplying ordinary loaves and fishes ; but he has not, like Moses, given them bread from *heaven*, though he has hinted that he can do so (ver. 27). Let him fulfil his promise, and thereby authenticate his claims. Even in the Synoptics a similar demand is made for a ' sign *from heaven* ' (e.g. Mk. 8 : 11), for some super-miracle to put, as it were, God's own seal upon Jesus' ordinary miracles. Indeed, John's chief purpose, writing as he does with the Jewish-Christian controversies of his own day in view, is to illustrate the Pauline saying (1 Cor. 1 : 22) that ' Jews demand miracles.' In the days of his flesh, as in the Evangelist's own day, Christ could produce no credential so conclusive but that the Jews would demand one more conclusive still.

To this demand for a further ' Sign ' Jesus replies that he is speaking of a gift far more marvellous than any given by Moses ; for, even supposing that manna be regarded as the heavenly gift *par excellence*, ' **it was not Moses (but God) who 32 gave you this bread from heaven.'** Jesus' questioners had quoted the words, ' He gave them bread from heaven to eat,' as if Moses were the giver ; but in the original context (on Moses' own showing, Exod. 16 : 15) the giver is not Moses, but God. Moreover, Jesus adds, it is only in a symbolical sense that manna can be called ' bread from heaven ' : ' **It is my Father who gives you the** *real* **bread from heaven,'** that is, the bread ' which fulfils absolutely, ideally, the highest conception of sustaining food' (Westcott) (for ' **real** ' see 4 : 23). Notice the contrast implied between what Moses ' *gave* ' and what the Father ' *gives*.' The supreme miracle is not in the past, but in the present. Once again the New Faith is shown to be superior to the Old ; now, as never before, the true spiritual nourishment may be had for the asking, ' **for the bread of God 33 is what comes down from heaven and gives life to the world.'** The spiritual nourishment offered by the Father through Christ and in Christ's own person (though this is not definitely stated till ver. 35) is ' **real** ' for two reasons : first, it is ' **from**

heaven' in a sense far truer than the symbolical sense in which
manna may be said to be 'from heaven'; secondly, whereas
the manna sustained only the Israelites, this bread 'gives life
to the whole world.' In connexion with John's comparison
of Christ with the manna, we may quote an interesting parallel
from Philo, according to whom the Logos had his type in the
manna: 'The Logos distributes to all the heavenly food of the
soul, which is called manna' (*Qu. rer. div.*, 39). 'You see,
then, what the food of the soul consists in—in the Word of
God, given continually like the dew' (*Leg. alleg.*, iii, 59).

34   To this the people reply, exactly as did the Samaritan
woman (4: 15) when Jesus offered her the 'living water':
'**Ah, sir, give us that bread always.**' Though the word
'**always**' is in an emphatic position, it is not necessary to
assume that a contrast is implied with the single meal provided
by Jesus the day before, as if the people were merely asking
for a continuous daily supply of the food then provided. The
words are simply a literary artifice intended, like 4: 15, to
lead up to the momentous pronouncement which immediately
follows. Instead of speaking about this bread, let Jesus *give*
it, for it will be welcome at all times. We are reminded of
the Synoptic phrase (Mt. 6: 11, Lk. 11: 3), 'Give us to-day
our bread for the morrow.' But here Jesus does not merely
bid us pray for it; he declares himself to *be* that bread.

35 Jesus said, '**I am the bread of life,**' that is, the bread which
supplies or communicates life. In response to the request to
give this bread, Jesus replies that he himself *is* this bread, and
that communion with him will result in perfect satisfaction:
'**he who comes to me will never be hungry, and he who believes
in me will never be thirsty again.**' (For the phrase 'I am,'
introducing a Messianic claim, see notes on 4: 26, 6: 20, and
for other pictorial figures used in conjunction with it cf.
especially 8: 12, 10: 7, 9; 10: 11, 14; 11: 25, 14: 6,
15: 1, 5.) The spiritual need which cries for satisfaction is
expressed by the double figure of 'hunger' and 'thirst'
(cf. Is. 49: 10; Mt. 5: 6; Rev. 7: 16), whereby it is implied
that Christ is not only the 'bread of life,' but also the 'water
of life,' as in 4: 14, where see note. The double metaphor

prepares the way for the climax of the symbolism in verses 53-56, with their reference to mystical and sacramental ' eating ' and ' drinking.' Note that the appropriation of this ' life ' is expressed not by a word suggestive of mere physical action, such as ' take,' but by ' come to me,' ' believe in me,' both expressions hinting a protest against a purely materialistic conception of sacramental grace, while the former (cf. 5 : 40) emphasizes the spontaneity which is so characteristic a factor in John's idea of faith.

' But, as I told you, though you have seen me, you do not 36 believe. All those will come to me who are the Father's 37 gift to me, and never will I reject one of them ; for I 38 have come down from heaven not to carry out my own will but the will of Him who sent me, and the will 39 of Him who sent me is that I lose none of those who are His gift to me, but that I raise them all up on the last day. It is the will of my Father that everyone who sees the 40 Son and believes in him should possess eternal life, and that I should raise him up on the last day.'

The theme of verse 35 is picked up again at verse 47, verses 36-40 being in the nature of an aside, while 41-46 are an interlude, possibly a later interpolation. The people have asked for a ' Sign ' to substantiate Jesus' claims : ' But, says Jesus, as I told you (we can point to no definite saying, but the 36 reference is probably to the thought of verse 26), though you have seen me, you do not believe.' Jesus himself is the most convincing of all ' signs ' ; they have seen his power visibly set forth in his life and work, and yet in spite of every inducement to faith they still refuse to believe, and each new gift offered to them serves but to emphasize their lack of receptivity. And yet the reason for their unbelief is clear enough : the motive which has brought them after Christ is a purely sensual one (26), whereas it is only a divinely given impulse which can truly bring men to Christ—' All those (but only 37 those) will come to me who are the Father's gift to me.' (Cf. 65, and for the idea that believers are the Father's gift to the Son, cf. 17 : 2, 6, 12, 24.) Are we to think of this ' giving ' as an act of eternal election—an echo of the Pauline doctrine of ' predestination '—or of present grace ? If the latter, then the ' giving ' is equivalent to the ' drawing ' of verse 44 : if the former, then the ' giving ' is preparatory to the ' drawing.' In any case it is only a divinely inspired impulse which can turn to Christ those who *come to him* : for the individual will has its part to play even in the case of the elect. Accordingly Jesus singles out of the mass of the elect the individual with the responsive will, and promises that such will never be excluded from the number of his disciples—' never will I reject one of them.' (For the idea of ' rejection,' cf. 9 : 34, 12 : 31.) It should be noted that in this verse the object of the ' Father's giving ' is expressed in Greek (as also in 39) by a comprehensive neuter, the thought of the believer's individuality being thus subordinated to that of the Father's grace (cf. 17 : 10). When the Father gives, the Son never rejects the gift, for, says Jesus, Father and Son have but 38 one will : ' I have come down from heaven not to carry out my own will but the will of Him who sent me ' (cf. 5 : 30, Mk. 14 : 36). ' Come down ' carries on the metaphor of the ' bread from heaven ' (33) and contains a direct reference to the incarnation (1 : 10, 14). Christ welcomes all who come to him because the Father's will is above all a will to save 39 both in this world and the world to come, because ' the will of Him who sent me is that I lose none of those who are His gift to me, but that I raise them all up on the last day.' ' Where the Father leaves off the work the Son carries it on : the last act of the Father was to give believers to the Son ; the Son's first act is not to allow them to be lost, that is, to meet with death, but to welcome them ; his final act, after he has carried his work through all its stages, is to raise them up ' (Holtzmann). The phrase ' on the last day ' occurs only in our Gospel (vers. 40, 44, 54 ; 11 : 24, 12 : 48) ; yet such an idea of a final day of resurrection and of judgment (5 : 28, 29) has little place in John's scheme of thought, according to which life and judgment alike are present and inward rather than future and dramatic. We have here one of those apparent contradictions so characteristic of the Gospel (see

note, p. 29), when John appears to desert his own point of
view and fall back on a primitive eschatology. Unless, indeed,
the aside (vers. 36–40), together with the interlude (vers. 41–46),
are to be boldly assigned to the Redactor, we have here one
of those inconsistencies which ' only serve to remind us that
John, with all his originality of thought, was still partly
bound to the past. Along with his own conception, he strove
to make room for the belief that had impressed itself on the
Church at large, of which he was a member ' (E. F. Scott,
The Fourth Gospel, p. 216). But in any case John's chief
purpose here is to insist that the Father's will finds expression
in the Son's whole redemptive mission. Hence the condition
of that life, which it is the Father's will to bestow, is that men
should respond to the appeal of that mission : **' It is the will** 40
of my Father that everyone who sees the Son and believes in
him should possess eternal life, and that I should raise him up
on the last day.' Note that the believer's response is now described not by the idea of ' coming,' as in 37, but—by way of
emphatic contrast with the people's unresponsiveness in 36—
by the idea of ' seeing *and* believing.' (For the emphasis upon
the necessity of faith as well as of vision, see note on 3 : 15.)
The last clause of the verse, with its sudden change of subject,
is grammatically awkward, and gives further ground for the
conjecture that these references to a resurrection on the last
day may be an addition of the Redactor.

Now the Jews murmured at him for saying, ' I am the bread 41
which has come down from heaven.' They said, ' Is 42
this not Jesus the son of Joseph ? We know his father
and mother. How can he claim now, " I have come
down from heaven "? ' Jesus replied to them, ' Stop 43
murmuring to yourselves. No one is able to come to me 44
unless he is drawn by the Father who sent me (and I will
raise him up on the last day). In the prophets it is 45
written, *and they will be all instructed by God* ; everyone
who has listened to the Father and learned from Him,
comes to me. Not that anyone has seen the Father—he 46
only, who is from God, he has seen the Father.

Verses 41–46 are, like 28–33, a controversial interlude, and
interrupt the main thread of the discourse, which is picked
up at 47. We note too that the Galilean crowd fades out of
41 sight, and we are told: **Now the Jews murmured at him** (as
did their ancestors in Exod. 16: 7–9 against Moses at the
time of the giving of the manna) **for saying, ' I am the bread
which has come down from heaven.'** Jesus had not used
these exact words, but they are a fair summary of the content
of verses 35 and 38. Are we to understand by **the Jews**
the deputation from Jerusalem which, according to Mark
(7: 1), challenged Jesus immediately after the feeding of the
five thousand ? More probably the term is used quite generally, as so often in the Gospel, to signify the ' official opposition ' to Jesus, in which sense it may include even Galileans.
(See note on 1 : 19.) The Jews have the same difficulty in
accepting Jesus' claim to a heavenly origin as had Nicodemus
the possibility of a ' birth from above ' (3: 4). The ground
of their incredulity is that they know Jesus' earthly origin :
42 **' Is this not Jesus the son of Joseph ? We know his father
and mother. How can he claim now** (that is, after living so
long as one of ourselves) **" I have come down from heaven " ? '**
We may compare the scene in the synagogue at Nazaret
(Mk. 6: 3), which John has transferred to the synagogue at
Capharnahum (ver. 59). The words **' We know his father
and mother '** may imply merely knowledge of who his
father and mother were, not necessarily acquaintance with
persons both of whom are presumed to be still living. From
the fact that Jesus is called **' the son of Joseph '** it has been
held that John intends to controvert the doctrine of the
Virgin Birth, surely a rash conclusion from words assigned
to unbelieving Jews. At the same time it is clear that
John places no value on the doctrine : ' It is his habit, when
he finds any account or statement in the earlier biographies
which seems to him unworthy of the Son of God, to alter it
to make it more appropriate. If he had objected to the
statement of the paternity of Joseph, it is almost certain
that he would have found a way of avoiding such statement '
(Gardner, *Ephesian Gospel*, p. 287.) (See also note on 1 : 13.)

As in the case of Nicodemus (3 : 5), Jesus does not stay to 43 answer an objection born of misunderstanding, but after a word of rebuke, ' Stop murmuring among yourselves,' repeats with renewed emphasis what he has already said (37-39). It is beside the mark to attempt to remove such intellectual difficulties as are expressed in 41-42, for they are the result of unbelief, not, as the Jews pretend, the cause of it. The real ground of their unbelief (and is it not the ground of much of our unbelief ?) is not a perplexed mind, but an unsurrendered will. A man can be led to faith in Christ only by a divine impulse brought to bear upon his will. As Jesus has already told them (37), ' No one is able to come to me 44 unless he is drawn by the Father who sent me.' We feel that in these words John has in view something more than the immediate situation, and is endeavouring to remove the perplexity which must have existed among Christians of his own day on account of the failure of Christianity to win the Jews. We may compare Paul's argument in Rom. 9 : 1 ff., and the somewhat similar thought contained in Jesus' own words in Mk. 4 : 11-12, Jn. 12 : 40. If Christ is not wholly triumphant, it is because there are some whom God has not yet ' drawn ' to Him—a tender word reminiscent of Jer. 31 : 3 (' with lovingkindness have I drawn thee '). We may, if we will, call this ' Predestination ' ; but to ' say that a certain number are not " given " or " drawn " to Christ by God is simply the Jewish way of saying that unbelief in Christ in many cases is unintelligible, but yet must have its place in the eternal purpose of God ' (R. H. Strachan). The concluding words of the verse, ' and I will raise him up on the last day,' again have the appearance of a redactional addition.

Scripture too bears witness to the truth that faith must 45 be traced back ultimately to the action of *God* Himself, for ' In the prophets (i.e. in that portion of the Scriptures known as ' the prophets,' cf. Acts 7 : 42, 13 : 40), it is written, " and they will all be instructed by God." ' The argument requires that the emphasis should be on *God* as the ultimate cause of believing discipleship. The quotation is from Is. 54 : 13, and we may compare Jer. 31 : 33-34, Micah 4 : 2, 1 Thess. 4 : 9,

1 Cor. 2 : 13, 1 Jn. 2 : 27. And yet the divine impulse which results in faith does not relieve men from the necessity of intellectual effort ; God influences men's wills faithwards ('draws them'), but He does so by first asking them to use their minds ('instructed by God') : accordingly, adds Jesus, **'everyone who has listened to the Father and learned from Him, comes to me.'** Before a man can be a believing disciple of Jesus, he must first be a hearer and a learner in the school of God. With the words 'listened . . . and learned,' cf. Mt.

46 13 : 23, 'hears the word and understands it.' There follows a characteristic 'aside' or 'parenthetic comment,' in which the Evangelist safeguards the necessity of Christ as mediator between God and man. It must not be thought, as, e.g., the Gnostics held, that such divine instruction can proceed from an immediate vision of God : **'Not that anyone has seen the Father—he only, who is from God, he has seen the Father.'** Christ alone possesses an immediate knowledge of the Father, and therefore he alone can communicate true knowledge (cf. 1 : 18, 3 : 13, 14 : 6, Mt. 11 : 27), and that because he alone has come to earth from God (3 : 31–34, 7 : 29). The thought, though in contrast with the immediately preceding verses, is quite in harmony with the viewpoint of the Gospel as a whole, and the words should almost certainly be regarded, not as a redactional insertion, but rather as a reflection of the Evangelist himself, who seeks to guard against the danger of the previous verse being misunderstood, to the detriment of the truth that the Father can be known only through the Son. Such a 'parenthetic comment' would become more natural could we suppose that it is interjected by the Evangelist in the midst of material which he is in process of incorporating from the notes of 'the Witness.' But such a conjecture is precarious in the case of the present chapter.

47 'Truly, truly I tell you, the believer has eternal life. I am
48 the bread of life. Your ancestors ate manna in the
49 desert, but they died ; the bread that comes down from
50 heaven is such that one eats of it and never dies. I am

the living bread which has come down from heaven ; 51
if anyone eats of this bread, he will live for ever ; and
more, the bread I will give is my flesh, given for the life
of the world.'

The theme broken off at 35 is now resumed. The intervening section has dealt with the unbelief which stands in the
way of the appropriation of life, and has emphasized the
truth that the faith which is a condition of life is not merely
an ethical ' work of God ' (28–29), but the result of an inwardly
working divine impulse. Christ now harks back to the
promise of 35 : when such faith is present, then ' Truly, truly 47
I tell you, the believer has eternal life,' and this life can be
communicated now through a personal relationship, for ' I 48
am the bread of life.' The people had insinuated that the
only authentic ' bread from heaven ' was the manna given
through Moses (31). But, says Jesus, it is clear that such
manna cannot have been the real ' bread of life,' for ' Your 49
ancestors ate manna in the desert, but (in spite of all their
eating) they died ; (whereas) the bread that comes down from 50
heaven is such that one eats of it and never dies.' This translation is much to be preferred to the R.V. : ' This (i.e. the
bread I offer) is the bread which cometh down out of heaven
that a man may eat thereof and not die.' We have here a
play upon the word ' die ' (cf. Mt. 10 : 39) which in 49 is used
of physical death and in 50 of spiritual death. But such a
distinction would be less clearly present to Jewish thought,
according to which the physical death of 49 would be something more than mere physical dissolution, bringing with it
separation from God in the colourless life of Hades, while
the spiritual life of 50 would also imply continued physical
existence culminating in a bodily resurrection. The claims
made for the manna, says Jesus, have been proved false by the
result ; on the other hand, in contrast to the manna, ' I am 51
the living bread which has come down from heaven,' a claim
which can be proved true by all who care to put it to the
test, for ' if anyone eats of this bread, he will live for ever.'
Notice the significant alteration of ' bread of life' to 'living

bread': Christ is not merely the bread which gives life; he is that, because he is bread which has in itself an everlasting store of life (cf. 'living water,' 4: 10, 7: 38). Manna, not itself being 'living,' but 'perishing food' (27), could impart life only for a season: Christ being 'living,' containing in himself the very principle of life, can impart life for ever (cf. 5: 26, and 6: 57). Note that now for the first time Jesus definitely claims that in his own person he is the bread 'which has come down from heaven': in 33 and 50 he did so only by implication. At the same time the negative thought 'shall not die' gives place to the positive and more emphatic 'will live for ever.' Also for the first time the content of this personal life in Christ is spoken of in so many words as something to be 'eaten'; whereas hitherto, when Jesus has definitely spoken of himself as the 'bread of life,' the appropriation of that life has been described by the terms 'coming' and 'believing' (35). The way is thus prepared for the significant sacramental pronouncement, to which the whole discourse has been leading up, 'and more (marking the climax), the bread I will give is my flesh, given for the life of the world.' The thought passes from what Christ *is* to what he *gives*. Just as the Father 'gave' the Son (3: 16), so now does the Son 'give' his flesh, and now, as then, it is not merely for the deliverance of one nation (as in the Paschal feast), but to give life to the whole world. The crucial point is the intention of the word 'flesh.' Westcott holds that it merely 'describes human nature in its totality regarded from its earthly side,' and that the reference here is to the whole manifestation of Christ in the flesh (1: 14, 1 Jn. 4: 2), the purpose of which was to bring new life to the world (17: 2); 'the thought here is of support and growth, and not of atonement.' But in that case nothing new is added to what has already been said, and a more satisfying explanation is that we have a reference not only to the incarnation, but to the atonement. 'I will give' points to the future, and the word *given* 'for the life of the world' (if indeed it is to be retained in the text, which is doubtful; but in any case it must be understood) would be used, as in 3: 16, with the sense 'gave up to *death*, to be sacrificed' (cf. also 1:29, 1 Jn. 4:10), though John habitually regards the death of Christ not as a sacrificial atonement, but rather as the means whereby the life-principle or the holy Spirit is liberated into all the world (16:7). But no explanation is adequate which fails to recognize that John's main purpose in thus identifying the life-giving bread with Christ's *flesh* is at last to bring into prominence the sacramental bearing of the whole discourse. This becomes abundantly plain in the following verse, where the idea of drinking Christ's blood is added to that of eating his flesh. It should be noted, moreover, that throughout the present context (32, 34) the word 'give' has been used in the sense of bestowing nourishment on men, not of offering up a sacrifice to God, as would be necessary here were the primary reference to Christ's atoning death. Note too the resemblance of the thought to Mk. 14:24, Mt. 26:28.

The Jews then wrangled with one another, saying, 'How can he 52 give us his flesh to eat?' So Jesus said to them, 'Truly, 53 truly I tell you, unless you eat the flesh of the Son of man and drink his blood, you have no life within you. He who feeds on my flesh and drinks my blood possesses 54 eternal life (and I will raise him up on the last day), for 55 my flesh is real food and my blood is real drink. He 56 who feeds on my flesh and drinks my blood remains within me, as I remain within him. Just as the living 57 Father sent me and I live by the Father, so he who feeds on me will also live by me. Such is the bread which 58 has come down from heaven: your ancestors ate their bread and died, but he who feeds on this bread will live for ever.' This he said as he taught in the synagogue 59 at Capharnahum.

The discourse now reaches its climax, and an incredulous question, as so often in John (e.g. 3:4), prepares the way for a momentous pronouncement: The Jews then—accepting 52 Jesus' words in a material sense and able to make nothing of them—wrangled with one another, saying, 'How can he give

us his flesh to eat ? ' The Jews' exasperation and Jesus'
claims alike come to a head. While on their part the ' murmuring ' of 43 becomes a ' wrangle,' Jesus' claims are summed
up in a definite challenge which, so far from answering his
opponents' difficulties (cf. ver. 43), appears rather to add to
them by repeating in a still more precise and literal manner
53 the ideas at which they had taken offence: ' **Truly, truly I
tell you, unless you eat the flesh of the Son of man and drink
his blood, you have no life within you.**' The title ' Son of
man ' is used, as often in this Gospel, in a context which
alike suggests the divine mystery and the true humanity of
Jesus' personality (see note on 1 : 51). Our exegesis of this
difficult verse will depend on the interpretation already
placed on the word ' flesh ' in verse 51, where we held that
there was a quite definite allusion to the sacrament of the
Lord's Supper. The use here of the double symbolism of
' eating his flesh ' and ' drinking his blood ' seems to establish
the sacramental bearing of the passage beyond question.
Those who deny the reference to the Eucharist hold that the
addition of the phrase ' drink his blood ' is intended merely
to bring into prominence Christ's atoning death: ' To eat the
flesh is to contemplate by faith the holy life of the Lord . . .
to drink the blood is also to contemplate his violent death, to
make it our own ransom, to taste its atoning efficacy ' (Godet).
But in view of the fact that we have now had reproduced in
this chapter the whole terminology of the sacramental ritual
as given in Mt. 26 : 26–28, it can hardly be denied that John
has the sacrament quite definitely in view. If it be objected
that John uses the term ' flesh ' (*sarx*) instead of ' body '
(*sōma*) as used by the Synoptists and Paul, we may reply
that John is emphasizing the necessity of appropriating the
whole personality of Christ, the constituent parts of which,
according to O.T. phraseology, would be ' flesh ' and ' blood.'
Later N.T. usage shows that ' flesh ' was a favourite word in
the dogmatic writings of the time (1 Pet. 3 : 18, 4 : 1 ; 1 Tim.
3 : 16. Cf. also Barnabas 5 : 6, Hermas Sim. V, 6 : 5–7).
' Flesh ' is used instead of ' body ' in the sacramental ritual
by Justin and Ignatius. But though John alludes primarily

to the sacrament, a reference to the atoning death is of necessity implied. The soul's sustenance and satisfaction, which is symbolized in the sacrament, is found in Christ not only as living and working, but as dying. ' A communion service, where men realize the mystery that Jesus died for them, is the summit of Christian experience ' (Strachan). At the same time it should be noted that John habitually links the sacrament much less closely to the Passion than does Paul. Thus the Institution, instead of taking place ' on the night he was betrayed ' (1 Cor. 11 : 23), is dissociated from Passion Week and connected here with the life-giving miracle of the feeding of the multitude, while the place held in the Synoptics by the Institution is filled in our Gospel by the incident of the foot-washing, which symbolizes not Christ's death, but his spirit of lowly service. That the Church of the second century closely connected the miraculous feeding with the sacrament is clear not only from the writings of the time, but also from the paintings of the Roman Catacombs. We conclude then that, taken at its face value, verse 53 amounts to an assertion that ' life ' can belong only to the members of the Church of Christ who have made confession of their faith by partaking of the Christian Sacrament. Yet the words even as they stand are probably meant to bear a spiritual as well as a literal interpretation, to express the truth that, just as Jesus' food was to do the will of God (4 : 34), so can we obtain spiritual sustenance only by making our will and life one with Christ's. Can the literal and spiritual intention of the words be reconciled ? (See note after 63.)

Verse 54 expresses in positive terms the reward of the man 54 who fulfils the conditions stated in 53, while the word ' eat ' gives place to ' feed upon,' the latter implying not a single but a continual appropriation of the divine life : ' He who feeds on my flesh and drinks my blood possesses (as a present bestowal) eternal life—and I will raise him up at the last day ' (notes on 40, 44)—a promise which is certain of fulfilment, ' for my flesh is real food and my blood is real drink,' as 55 opposed to that earthly or ' perishing ' food which is merely symbolical but not ' real.' Note that the climax of John's sacramentalism is reached at this point where the 'life' which elsewhere follows from faith (40, 47; 3: 15, 16, 36) is promised as the result of an 'eating' and 'drinking,' whereby the disciple attains to a mystic union with his Master: 56 **'He who feeds on my flesh and drinks my blood remains within me, as I remain within him.'** The believer is 'in Christ' (1 Jn. 3: 6, 24) and Christ is 'in him' (15: 4-7). Paul also sometimes gives us the one thought, sometimes the other (e.g. compare 2 Cor. 5: 17 with Col. 1: 27). 'There is so to speak a double personality. The believer is quickened by Christ's presence, and he himself is incorporated in Christ' 57 (Westcott). But if it be true that communion with Jesus gives life, it is because Jesus has himself access to the source of life, for, says Jesus, **'just as the living Father sent me and I live by the Father** ('by' expresses not the purpose of Christ's life, the thought of 4: 34, but the ground of his life: it is due to the purpose of God that he lives), **so he who feeds on me will also live by me.'** The mystic union of the believer with Christ is a reflection of that of Christ with the Father who, because He is *living* (i.e. 'has life in Himself,' 5: 26) can give life, just as can Christ in virtue of the fact that he is the *living* bread (51). Compare Paul's thought (1 Cor. 3: 23), 'You belong to Christ, and Christ to God.' Note that in this verse we have the expression 'feeds on *me*,' which is even more emphatic than 'feeds on my flesh and drinks my blood.' On the other hand the double idea of 'eating and drinking' has again given place to the single thought of 'feeding upon '—a hint perhaps that to John it is the spiritual truth behind the sacrament that has real significance, not the mechanical ritual of receiving two elements, but the spiritual appropriation of Christ's personal life (cf. note on 63). So too in the following verse, which sums up the whole argument, there is no reference to the second symbol, and Christ becomes 58 simply 'the Bread of Life': **'Such (the reference being to the whole description 51-57) is the bread which has come down from heaven.'** The discourse then ends as it began with a pointed contrast between Christ and the manna: **'your ancestors ate their bread and died, but he who feeds on this**

bread will live for ever.' The construction in the Greek is a
little irregular, and in English is best simplified as above.
The antithesis exactly repeats that of 49–50. The analogy
between Christ and the manna is paralleled in 1 Cor. 10 : 3 f.,
where Paul sets the gift of grace by Christ over against the
gift of manna by Moses. Note also the word 'murmur,'
Jn. 6 : 41, 1 Cor. 10 : 10.

There follows a note fixing the occasion of the discourse : 59
This he said as he taught in the synagogue (or rather ' in full
synagogue,' the article being omitted just as we say ' in
church ') **at Capharnahum.** There is a similar note at 8 : 20.
Presumably this refers to the whole section from 26 ; alternatively from 41. (For the problems raised here see notes
on 27 and 41.) Apparently John has in mind Jesus' preaching,
according to the Synoptists, at Nazaret (see note on 42) in
the local synagogue ; but as it is impossible to carry the
crowd of 25 to Nazaret, he makes the lake-side town of
Capharnahum serve his purpose. It may be that the verse
is an addition of the Redactor, who thus clumsily tries to identify with the Synagogue sermon of Mk. 6 : 2 f. our present
discourse which, according to the Evangelist's original pre-
sentation, was spoken on the seashore (25).

After what has been said it must be clear that in this
discourse we have no verbatim report of Jesus' words, but
rather a homily by the Evangelist (though possibly based on
fragmentary sayings of Jesus preserved by ' the Witness ') in
which he puts by anticipation into the mouth of Jesus himself
allusions to the Christian sacrament of the Lord's Supper
similar to the reference to Christian Baptism already noted
at 3 : 5. It is incredible that Jesus could have addressed
teaching so advanced to an audience largely composed of the
common folk of Galilee, or that it should have been compre-
hensible to them had he done so ; such a discussion is incongruous in Jesus' lifetime, when the Lord's Supper had not yet
been instituted, but suits the Evangelist's own time when the
sacrament had become one of the central objects of the attack
on Christianity. In verse 52 there are put into the mouth
of ' the Jews ' objections to the Christian sacramental ritual

of the Evangelist's own day.   The Jew of the beginning of the
second century, dwelling as he did in the atmosphere of the
Greek Mystery Religions, may well have been tempted to ask
whether, when the Christian spoke of 'eating the flesh and
drinking the blood of the Son of Man,' he meant anything
essentially different from what the heathen Greeks around
him meant when they spoke of 'eating' their God at a
sacrificial meal.   At the 'Bouphonia' or 'Ox-murder' at
Athens, for example, to quote Miss J. R. Harrison (*Ancient
Art and Ritual*, p. 89), 'the ox was slain with all solemnity, and
all those present partook of the flesh . . . What they wanted
from the Bull was just that special life and strength which all
the year long they had put into him and nourished and
fostered.   That life was in his blood.   They could not eat that
flesh nor drink that blood unless they killed him.   So he
must die.   But it was not to give him up to the gods that they
killed him, not to " sacrifice " him in our sense, but to have him,
keep him, eat him, live by him and through him, by his grace.'
Did the Christian, asked his Jewish neighbour, mean anything higher than this ?   John's purpose—though even he is
perhaps not wholly untouched by this heathen-mystery conception of the appropriation of life—is (as will come out more
clearly at verse 63) to combat this purely material notion of
the Christian sacrament, while at the same time insisting on
its real efficacy.

Conclusion : The Crisis in Galilee   (6 : 60–71)

60 Now many of his disciples, on hearing it, said, ' This is hard
61   to take in !   Who can listen to talk like this ? '   Jesus,
     inwardly conscious that his disciples were murmuring at
62   it, said to them, ' So this upsets you ?   Then what if you
     were to see the Son of man ascending to where he formerly
63   existed ?   What gives life is the Spirit : flesh is of no avail
     at all.   The words I have uttered to you are spirit and life.
64   And yet there are some of you who do not believe ' (for
     Jesus knew from the very first who the unbelieving were,
65   and who was to betray him ; that was why he said ' I tell

you that no one is able to come to me unless he is allowed
by the Father ').
After that, many of his disciples drew back and would not 66
associate with him any longer.   So Jesus said to the twelve, 67
' You do not want to go, too ? '   Simon Peter answered 68
him, ' Lord, who are we to go to ?   You have got words
of eternal life, and we believe, we are certain, that you are 69
the holy One of God.'   Jesus answered them, ' Did I not 70
choose you, the twelve ?   And yet one of you is a devil ! '
(He meant Judas the son of Simon Iscariot ; for Judas 71
was to betray him—and he was one of the twelve.)

In the Synoptics also (e.g. Mt. 11 : 26 ff., 16 : 13 ff.) we have 60
hints that Jesus became conscious that a sifting-out process was
inevitable even among his professed followers.   Not only had
the ' Jews ' become hardened in opposition, but many of his
disciples, on hearing it, said ' This is hard to take in !   Who
can listen to talk like this ? '   The word disciples is here used
not of the Twelve (who appear at 67) but in the broader sense
of Jesus' followers and adherents from whom the Twelve were
chosen as an inner circle (Mk. 3 : 7, 13–14).   To these Jesus'
words—the reference, as seems clear from 62, being specially
to 58—are hard, not as being difficult to understand but as
being difficult to tolerate.   Nor is the stumbling-block in their
case so much Paul's ' offence of the Cross ' as the fact that
he whom they thought to be Messiah was now, like some heathen
mystery-monger, stooping to such riddles as ' eating flesh '
and ' drinking blood,' the latter thought in particular being of
course an abomination to Jews.   Once again John echoes
the thought of his own day, just as Origen later alludes to
Jewish taunts about ' Thyestean Feasts ' (*Celsus VI*, 27).
The remark that Jesus was inwardly conscious that his 61
disciples were murmuring is intended once again to emphasize
his supernatural insight.   (Cf. Mk. 5 : 30 and note on 2 : 25.)
His reply is reproachful :   ' Then what if you were to see the 62
Son of man ascending to where he formerly existed ? '   The
thought of Jesus' ascending corresponds to that of his ' coming
down from heaven ' in the ' hard saying ' of 58, while the

title 'Son of man' again (cf. 53) serves to connect Christ's humanity with an activity which is purely divine. This thought of Christ's return to his pre-existent state is elsewhere variously expressed by John under the thought of a return to the Father (7 : 33, 13 : 3, 16 : 5, 28), an ascent to the Father (20 : 17) and an ascent to heaven (3 : 13). The Evangelist does not necessarily think of this ascent as visible to the senses, for the word 'see' (*theōrein*) is frequently used of mental or spiritual vision (4 : 19, 8 : 51, 12 : 45, 14 : 17, 17 : 24). (For John's view on 'the Ascension' see p. 359 f.)

But what is the intention of Jesus' reply? Not surely to minimize the first difficulty by confronting his questioners with a difficulty greater still, as if the meaning were, 'you are upset by this : how much more would you be upset if you saw me ascend! . . .' Rather does Jesus hint that 'the future will solve the riddle of the present' (Luthardt), and the meaning is : 'if you were to see the Son of man ascend . . . would you still be upset at this demand that you should feed upon him as upon a bread of life which has come down from heaven? Would it not rather make it easier for you to understand in what sense it *is* possible for you to eat and drink his flesh and blood? Once you have " seen " me ascend to where I formerly existed and have experienced the power of the exalted spiritual Christ, it will become self-evident that no mere material eating and drinking could mediate the life of that Christ, and that as a matter of fact my words were never intended to bear that material interpretation at which you take offence.' (Cf. 16 : 7, where spiritual illumination is consequent upon Christ's return to the Father.) It is interesting to note that the Marcan passage in connexion with which our passage must be read (see note at end of chapter) ends with the same ascension imagery (Mk. 8 : 38- 9 : 1). It will be remembered also that the point of introducing the miracle of the Walking on the Water was to prepare the way for the idea that Christ's body was untrammelled by the limits of time and space, and that consequently his flesh and blood were non-corporeal and spiritual substances to be appropriated not in a material but in a spiritual sense. The following verse drives home just this thought : ' Surely it is evident that all I have said *must* 63 be understood in a spiritual sense ; material flesh cannot possibly have the power to beget spiritual life, for only spirit can beget spirit (3 : 6)—'**What gives life is the Spirit : flesh is of no avail at all.**' (Cf. 1 Pet. 3 : 18, 1 Cor. 15 : 45, and especially 2 Cor. 3 : 6 ff., in which passage it is made clear (ver. 17) as it is here (62) that ' the Spirit ' is personified in the glorified Christ.)

Christ's words then are not to be interpreted in a literal and material sense, for ' **the words I have uttered to you are spirit and life** ' ; they are to be accepted in a spiritual sense, but more than that, they have in themselves power to mediate spiritual life. Just as Christ is an incarnation of ' the Word ' so would John seem to regard Christ's words almost as an emanation of himself sharing his own life-giving power. (For the peculiar significance attached by John to Jesus' **words** cf. 5 : 24, 8 : 31, 47 ; 12 : 48, 15 : 7, 17 : 8.) Just as in the O.T. the word of God is not a mere utterance but rather a vehicle of power conveying to the man to whom it comes a portion of God's own Spirit, so Jesus' words ' are not so much the expression of his thought as the emanation of his actual being and power ' (E. F. Scott). So great is the power of Jesus' *words* that they may almost be equated with the *works* of God (14 : 10).

Than verse 63 there could be no clearer statement of the purely spiritual nature of the believer's communion with his Lord ; the problem is how to reconcile this with 53-56, which appear to insist with equal clearness that the only guarantee of ' eternal life ' is in that sacrament wherein the believer partakes under material symbols of the flesh and blood of Christ. Some would cut the knot by excising 52-59 as an interpolation. But this is a counsel of despair, and it is better frankly to recognize that we have here side by side two inconsistent lines of thought which John tries, not with complete success, to harmonize. After appearing to sanction ritualism in 53-56 he provides the antidote in 63, as we saw to be the case in his allusion to Baptism (see note on 3 : 5). Verse 63 gives us John's own characteristic point of view, while in 53-56 we have one of those concessions to popular ideas which we have

noted elsewhere in the Gospel (e.g. note on 39). In 53–56 we
see reflected popular conceptions of the sacramental mystery
which had become so ingrained in the faith and ritual of the
Church that John did not care to ignore them, while 63 shows
us his desire to interpret and spiritualize these conceptions
and thus save the Church from superstitious materialism.
At the same time it must be admitted that John himself
is not untainted by those very ideas which he seeks to correct,
as also was Ignatius when he wrote (Eph. 20) of the
Christian as ' breaking one bread, which is the medicine of
immortality and the antidote that we should not die.' Just
as John's ideas of ' life ' (see chap. 3) are metaphysical as well
as moral, so are his ideas of the sacraments material as well
as spiritual. The material elements for John do really represent the flesh and blood of Christ, who is present in them not
merely by way of symbol but actually. In mitigation of
John's apparent inconsistency it may be said that the two
points of view would not be so clearly distinguishable to the
Evangelist as to ourselves ; the thought of the day would
recognize no such complete antagonism as do we between
matter and spirit, else Paul could hardly speak of a ' spiritual
body' (1 Cor. 15 : 44). For John the material side of the
sacrament might be an unquestioned reality, while its peculiar
worth, as is true also in the case of miracle and even of
historical incidents in general, would be in the underlying
spiritual truth. A similar inconsistency might be traced even
in Paul. (Note e.g. the emphasis upon the material side of the
sacramental ritual in Rom. 6: 3–5, 1 Cor. 10 : 16–21, 11 : 27–
29, Gal. 3 : 27.) Probably neither Paul nor John would conceive of communion with the Church apart from participation
in those mystic acts by which that communion was symbolized.

64 ' My teaching,' says Jesus, ' is hard only because you give
to it a sense repugnant to its spirituality . . . and yet (in spite
of this explanation) **there are some of you who do not believe.'**
There follows another reference to Jesus' supernatural insight.
In contrast to the surprise of Mk. 6: 6 Jesus is represented as
knowing the hearts of the disciples and especially of the traitor
(cf. 13 : 27) from the beginning—**for Jesus knew from the very**

first (for the phrase cf. 15 : 27, 16 : 4) who the unbelieving were
(cf. 2 : 25), and who was to betray him.   Jesus was not surprised
at his followers' disloyalty, for he knew that there must be
unbelief save where a divine purpose ' draws ' to discipleship :
That was why he said, ' I tell you that no one is able to come 65
to me unless he is allowed by the Father ' (37, 44–45).   As in
the parallel Synoptic passage (Mt. 16 : 17) it is not ' flesh and
blood ' but ' my Father in heaven ' who reveals the truth.
Here again is an apologetic for the failure of Christianity
among the Jews both in Jesus' own day and in John's : it
was God's will, and Christ himself felt no surprise ; why then
should we ?

   ' So the great number of disciples (60) disappears as sudden- 66
ly as it appeared ' (Loisy), for after that (i.e. either ' as a result
of this ' or ' from this time ') many of his disciples drew back
(for the phrase cf. Mk. 13 : 16 and for the thought Ps. 44 : 18)
and would not associate with him any longer.   So Jesus
said to the twelve—here mentioned for the first time but 67
assumed by John to be familiar to his readers—' You do not
want to go, too ? '   The question does not imply doubt on
Jesus' part, which from the point of view of 64 he could not
feel, but is an invitation to the Twelve to declare their loyalty.
Accordingly Simon Peter—speaking as in the Synoptics as the 68
representative of all (cf. 13 : 6, 24, 36 ; 21 : 3)—answered him,
' Lord, who are we to go to ?   You have got words of eternal
life,' that is, not merely words concerning eternal life, but
words issuing in eternal life, a direct reference to 63.   Peter's
confession in Mk. 8 : 29 is here so modified and expressed in
Johannine language as to explain what sort of an attraction
it was which drew men to Jesus and held them to him.   The
words of Jesus, which ' upset ' mere adherents (61), to the true
disciple become the source of eternal life (cf. 1 Cor. 1 : 18).
Having heard these words, says Peter, ' we believe, we are 69
certain, that you are the holy One of God.'   (Cf. 17 : 8 where
Jesus' words convince his hearers of his peculiar relationship
to God—there that God ' sent him,' here that he is ' the Holy
One of God.'   For this title for the Messiah cf. 1 Jn. 2 : 20,
Rev. 3 : 7, Mk. 1 : 24.)   It is equivalent to ' the Son of God '

with special stress on the ethical side of the relationship (cf.
10 : 36 where the two ideas of holiness and sonship are brought
together) and so is exactly parallel to the invocation used
by Peter in Mt. 16 : 16. The words 'we believe, we are
certain' are in the Greek in the perfect tense, the force being
that the disciples' minds are already made up so that no claim
however startling can shake their conviction. For the
relation of faith to knowledge in the thought of John see note
on 3 : 15, 10 : 38, 17 : 3, 8. Knowledge may either precede
faith (1 Jn. 4 : 16), or as here follow it—more naturally, for
'faith begins as an experiment and ends as an experience.'
Here the order has no significance, the double expression being
simply a strong asseveration of conviction. (Cf. esp. note on
10 : 15.)

70   John is careful to guard against the supposition that Jesus
was deceived by this declaration of an apparently unanimous
loyalty · accordingly we are told that Jesus answered them
(for Peter spoke as representative), 'Did not I choose you?
(Mk. 3 : 14, Lk. 6 : 13, Jn. 13 : 18, 15 : 16, 19). And yet—
in spite of a double election, by God first (65) and then by
Jesus—one of you is a devil ! ' (For devil cf. 8 : 44 ; 13 : 2,
1 Jn. 3 : 8, 10. ' The fundamental idea seems to be that of
turning good into evil' (Westcott). Judas is a devil because he
is one through whom the devil acts (13 : 2, 27)—a tool of the
devil. Can it be that we have here an echo of Jesus' rebuke
to Peter in Mk. 8 : 33 ?—' Get behind me, you Satan ! '
Luke hesitates to apply the word to Peter and simply omits the
incident : John, who in this paragraph is dwelling more on the
treachery of the one than the faith of the eleven, goes farther
and calls not Peter but Judas ' devil.' John will not admit
that Jesus chose Judas in ignorance of the fact that he would
turn traitor (6 : 64, 13 : 18), and accordingly adds an explana-
71 tory note : He meant Judas the son of Simon Iscariot ; for
Judas was to betray him—and he was one of the twelve, the
last words marking the heinousness of the treachery. This
anticipation of the betrayal is antedated as compared with
Mark's account, where it occurs after the *second* prediction
of the passion (Mk. 9 : 31). Here and in 13 : 26 it is Judas'

father who is called 'Iscariot'; in 12 : 4 and 14 : 22 it is
Judas himself. The generally accepted derivation of the name
is 'Ish Keriyoth,' 'a man of Keriyoth,' a village either of
Judah (Josh. 15 : 25) or of Moab (Jer. 48 : 24). Another suggested derivation is 'man of lies,' but this would not be so
naturally applied to both father and son as would the place-
name.

The dependence of this concluding paragraph on the
Synoptics and the fact that one of the most serious dislocations of the Gospel text has taken place at this point (i.e.
chap. 5 has been transposed from after to before chap. 6)
suggests that here, as in other Peter-passages (13 : 36 ff.,
18 : 15 ff.), the Redactor has been at work. In any case it
is clear that the paragraph is based on Mk. 8 : 27 ff., Mt.
16 : 13 ff. Note, however, that John, like Luke (9 : 18 ff.),
makes the Confession follow immediately after the miraculous
feeding and its dependent discourse, although the defection
which comes to a head in 66 might be expected to require a
longer time to mature. But while Luke simply omits the
incidents which intervene in Mark, John by subtly linking up
65 with 37 and 44 makes it appear that there was no interval.
John says nothing of the various popular estimates of Jesus as
given in Mk. 8 : 28, though it may be that in verse 14 we have
an echo of Mark. Again John, once more following Luke,
does not mention the protests of the Twelve at Jesus' prediction of his death. The thought of death is implicit in verse 51
and the Twelve are assumed to assent to it. Indeed, John never
dwells on 'the offence of the Cross.' Finally note that John's
motive in recording the Confession differs from the Synoptists'. According to the latter this is the first open acknowledgment of Jesus' Messiahship by the Twelve. But according to John that acknowledgment has already been made
(1 : 41, 49), and as a result the bestowal of the name 'Peter'
is also transposed to chapter 1 and omitted here. John's
motive is to show that concurrently with the growth of faith
there was also a hardening of disbelief. His emphasis is not
so much on Peter's faith as on Judas' treachery. A winnow-
ing process was necessary in the inner circle (66-71) as in the

outer (60–65). Indeed, there is a close parallelism between these two paragraphs of the concluding section: compare 60 with 67, 63 with 68, 64 with 71.

SECTION III. THE RESULT OF THE NEW GOSPEL

Illustration : The Lame Man healed on the Sabbath (5 : 1–16)

The third section of the First ' Act ' of the Gospel sums up generally the result of the appropriation of the New Gospel: religion for the disciple of Christ means not restraint but life. The Master who gives new life also frees from old restrictions (5 : 11)—in virtue of his authority as one who is ' equal to God' (5 : 18). This theme, as usual, is introduced by an Illustration: The healing of an invalid on the Sabbath (5 : 1–16).

1　After this there was a festival of the Jews and Jesus went up to Jerusalem. If with some authorities we read '*the* festival,' it is natural to suppose that a Passover is intended, this being for the Jews *the* festival *par excellence* (2 : 23, 6 : 4). But the definite article should probably be omitted, when we are left with the following alternatives: Purim in March, Passover in April, Pentecost in May, Tabernacles in October, Dedication in December. Critics have generally favoured Purim or Passover on the ground that 4 : 35 indicates a date in spring ; but see note *in loc.*, where we concluded that there was no clue as to the season. If chapter 5 be retained in its position before 6, it is best to suppose that Passover is meant. This would then be the second Passover mentioned before that of the Passion, the first being at 2 : 13 and the third at 6 : 4, and the name of the feast may have been suppressed here in order to bring the Johannine account more into harmony with the Synoptics, where Jesus' ministry lasts but one year. If, however, we transpose chapter 5 to a position after 6, we may regard the present feast as the Pentecost immediately following the Passover of 6 : 4. (See note at beginning of 6.) In the original the name Pentecost was probably mentioned here ; but the subsequent transposition of chapters 5 and 6 would result in an allusion to Passover (6 : 4) between Pentecost

(5 : 1) and Tabernacles (7 : 2), and the name Pentecost may have been omitted to avoid a chronological difficulty.

In the account of the miracle which follows we have clear 2 echoes, sometimes verbal (esp. 8-9), of the Synoptic healing of the Paralytic (Mk. 2 : 1-12) ; while the situation as regards the Sabbath is parallel to that of Mk. 3 : 1-6. John seems to have borrowed traits from both incidents. As the miracle is introductory to the main theme which follows, we may expect in the account symbolical allusions to the outworn legal dispensation which is to be supplanted by the new Gospel of Life.

Now in Jerusalem there is a bath beside the sheep-pool, which is called in Hebrew Beth-zatha. In the word is we may possibly have a hint that the Evangelist is drawing on the Witness' memoirs, though the present tense does not necessarily imply that the words were written before the destruction of Jerusalem in 70 A.D., any more than the past tense in 11 : 18 implies that Bethany and Jerusalem had since vanished from the earth ! The site of the miracle is still doubtful. The words in the Greek run, ' there is—near the sheep '—(*probatike*—an adjective, for which some noun must be supplied) ' a pool called B.' Most commentators have understood the ' sheep-*gate* ' (referring us to Neh. 3 : 1, 32), which is close to the north-east corner of the City. But possibly it is easier to understand ' sheep-*pool*,' the word being suggested by the reference to ' the pool called B.' which immediately follows. Another suggestion is that *probatike* may be not an adjective meaning ' sheep,' but a substantival reproduction of the Aramaic *Perobatayah* meaning ' Baths.' The translation would then be ' there is near the Baths a pool called in Hebrew B.' The name also is uncertain and has come down to us in three forms : (*a*) Bethesda (for which textual evidence is inferior) with the meaning either of ' house of mercy ' or of ' house of emission.' (*b*) Beth-zatha, which has good MSS. authority and is generally accepted. The word suggests ' house of the olive,' and was the name of the quarter of the City north of the temple, called by Josephus ' the New Town.' (*c*) Bethsaida, or ' house of fishing '—well supported by MSS., but inappropriate of Jerusalem and improbable. As for the site: (1) If we read ' Beth-zatha,' and take *proba-tike* to refer to the sheep-gate or sheep-pool, we must look for a site north of the temple near the Sheep-gate, and may choose: (*a*) the Twin Pools near the north-west corner of Antonia, or the ' Birket Israin ' by the modern Gate of St. Stephen, both of which pools might be ' disturbed ' by the emptying out of the washings from the Temple. This would also suit the reading ' Bethesda,' in the sense of ' house of emission.' Both these sites are supported by tradition. (*b*) The Twin Pools at St. Anne's, near the north-east corner of the City, where the remains of arches and ' porticoes ' have actually been discovered. Tradition since the Crusades favours this spot. (2) If we may read ' Bethesda,' and take *probatike* as a proper name, meaning ' Baths,' without reference to the ' sheep ' locality, then a site south of the temple is permissible, and we may choose (*a*) the Virgin's Well or ' Gihon' (meaning ' the Gusher'), which still has a reputation for healing disease, or (*b*) Siloam, which is also disturbed by the rush from Gihon. The ' disturbing ' of the water would then be due to the bubbling up of a natural spring, which is much the most natural explanation of verses 3, 4, 7, and would also suit the name ' Bethesda ' in the sense of ' house of emission.' The difficulty is that while the reading ' Beth-zatha ' seems most probable, the northern district offers no site where the water is disturbed by a natural spring. For the whole question see Sir G. A. Smith, *Jerusalem*, vol. ii, pp. 564 ff.

3   Wherever this pool be, it has five porticoes—built perhaps as a shelter for invalids as at the medicinal baths of Tiberias ; hence perhaps ' house of mercy '—where a crowd of invalids used to lie, the blind, the lame, and folk with shrivelled limbs

4 [waiting for the water to bubble. For an angel (cf. Rev. 16 : 5) used to descend from time to time (the idea being that the intervals were irregular and due to divine providence) into the bath, and disturb the water ; whereupon the first person who stepped in after the water was disturbed was restored to health, no matter what disease he had been afflicted

with.] The passage in square brackets is poorly supported, and is almost certainly a later addition. If the pool were disturbed by a natural spring the legend would easily arise that the healing properties of the water were due to the action of an angel. In the 'five porticoes' a symbolic allusion has been supposed to the five books of the Law, which so long had held but failed to heal the Jewish people. The same symbolism perhaps appears in the following words, **now one man was there, whose illness had lasted thirty-eight** 5 **years**—the period of the Israelites' wandering in the wilderness (Deut. 2 : 14), and also, it seems, the number of centuries during which, according to contemporary Jewish theology, men had already awaited the coming of the Messiah. Whether or no we read in this deeper symbolism the mention of the length of the man's illness (probably some form of paralysis as in the Markan incident, Mk. 2 : 1-12) serves alike to emphasize Jesus' compassion, the miraculous nature of the healing, and Jesus' courage in healing on the Sabbath. Why, if the sufferer has already lain for so long, can he not wait till the Sabbath is past ? **Jesus saw him lying, and knowing** 6 **—by divine intuition—he had been ill for a long while he said to him, ' Do you want your health restored ? '** The question might seem to answer itself, but it would serve to awaken that receptive spirit without which no healing miracle is possible (Mk. 6 : 5 f.) ; for the human will must co-operate with the divine. **The invalid replied,** that his long illness 7 was due not to lack of will to be healed, but to lack of opportunity : **' Sir, I have nobody to put me into the bath, when the water is disturbed ; and while I am getting down myself, someone else gets in before me.'** It has been held, without reason, that this reply assumes the authenticity of verse 4. The point is that, in order to profit by the healing properties of the spring, it was necessary to step in immediately after the bubbling up ; possibly there was room only for one invalid near enough to the medicinal spring to receive benefit from it before its special properties were lost by its mingling with the ordinary pool-water. **Jesus said to him, ' Get up,** 8 **lift your mat, and walk.'** The 'mat' would be the light

pallet on which he would be carried out daily, like the lame man in Acts 3 : 2, while the fact that in response to Jesus'
9 command **instantly the man got well, lifted his mat, and started to walk,** alike proves the reality of the cure and provides the occasion for the clash with the Jews which immediately follows. (Note the close parallelism with Mk. 2 : 11–12.)

Now it was the Sabbath on that day—the crux of the whole
10 situation : **so the Jews** (here probably the members of the Sanhedrim ; cf. 1 : 19) **said to the man who had been cured, 'this is the Sabbath, you have no right to be carrying your mat.'** Their authority would be such passages as Jer. 17 : 21,
11 Neh. 13 : 15, Num. 15 : 32 ff. **To this he replied, ' But the man who healed me, he told me, " Lift your mat, and walk." '** He excuses his action by appealing to the authority of him who gave him the power to do it, and thereby provides us with the key to the proper understanding of this whole section : the Christ who gives new life also has the power to free from the restraint of the old law. But the Jews are concerned not with the cure but with the breaking of the
12 Sabbatical regulations, and therefore **they questioned him, 'Who was it that told you, " Lift it and walk " ?**—and thereby
13 encouraged you to break the Sabbath ! ' **But the man who had been healed did not know who it was, for (owing to the crowd on the spot) Jesus had slipped away,** not wishing to
14 create a stir. **However, later on Jesus met him** (literally ' found him ' probably with the idea of set purpose as in 1 : 43, 9 : 35) **in the Temple,** where presumably he had gone to give thanks. The Marcan paralytic when healed goes to his own house (Mk. 2 : 11) : this man, symbolical perhaps of the whole nation, goes to the sacred house of his people where the stage is set for Jesus' controversy with the upholders of the old order. Here then Jesus met him **and said to him, ' See, you are well and strong ; commit no more sins, in case something worse befalls you.'** (Cf. 8 : 11, and for the idea that physical illness has an ethical cause Mk. 2 : 5–10— another link between this passage and its Synoptic parallel.) While Jesus' warning assumes that the disease had been the

effect of sin, 9: 1-3 reminds us that illness does not *alway.*
presuppose the sin of the individual in question. We have
here an echo of Paul's thought that while Christ frees us
from the law's restrictions (Gal. 5: 1), this deliverance must
not become an incentive to sin (Gal. 5: 13; cf. Rom. 6: 1-18).
By ' something worse ' is implied either a relapse into worse
illness (Mt. 12: 45) or more probably the loss of eternal
salvation (Heb. 10: 26 ff). **Meanwhile, having now learned 15
the name of his benefactor, off went the man and told the
Jews it was Jesus who had healed him,** his motive for giving
the information being not, as has been suggested, pique at
Jesus' allusion to his ' sin,' but rather the desire either to
vindicate himself or to spread Jesus' fame ; compare the
testimony of the blind man in chapter 9. All unwittingly
he did Jesus a disservice, **and this was why the Jews persecuted 16
Jesus, because he did things like this on the Sabbath,**—the
imperfect tense in the Greek implying that Sabbath-breaking
had become a habit with Jesus. According to Mark also (3: 6)
it was a cure on the Sabbath which provoked the Pharisees'
first plots against Jesus. It has been pointed out that in
the time of the Evangelist and in a place like Ephesus, where
the Jews were in a minority, the question of Sabbath obser-
vance can hardly have been very acute, and the fact that
our Gospel here and also in chapters 7 and 9 emphasizes so
strongly the Jews' resentment at Jesus' cures on the Sabbath
makes it necessary to suppose a substratum of tradition,
possibly the memoirs of ' the Witness,' beneath the work of
the Evangelist, which reflects generally the thought and the
problems of his own day. (Cf. Percy Gardner, *The Ephesian
Gospel*, p. 227.)

Theme : Religion not Restraint but Life
(5: 17-47, 7: 15-24, 8: 12-20)

**The reply of Jesus was, ' As my Father has continued working 17
to this hour, so I work too.'** But this only made the 18
Jews more eager to kill him, because he not merely broke
the sabbath but actually spoke of God as his own Father,

19   thereby making himself equal to God. So Jesus made this answer to them : ' Truly, truly I tell you, the Son can do nothing of his own accord, nothing but what he sees the Father doing ; for whatever He does, the Son

20   also does the same. The Father loves the Son and shows him all that He is doing Himself. He will show him

21   still greater deeds than these, to make you wonder ; for as the Father raises the dead and makes them live, so the

22   Son makes anyone live whom he chooses. Indeed the Father passes judgment on no one ; He has committed the judgment which determines life or death entirely to

23   the Son, that all men may honour the Son as they honour the Father. (He who does not honour the Son does not

24   honour the Father who sent him.) Truly, truly I tell you, he who listens to my word and believes Him who sent me has eternal life ; he will incur no sentence of judgment,

25   he has already passed from death across to life. Truly, truly I tell you, the time is coming, it has come already, when the dead will listen to the voice of the Son of God,

26   and those who listen will live ; for as the Father has life in Himself, so too He has granted the Son to have

27   life in himself, and also granted him authority to act as

28   judge, since he is Son of man. Do not wonder at this ; for there is a time coming when all who are in the tombs

29   will listen to his voice and come out, the doers of good to be raised to life, ill-doers to be raised for the sentence of judgment.

30 I can do nothing of my own accord ; I pass judgment on men as I am taught by God, and my judgment is just, because my aim is not my own will but the will of Him who sent me.'

17   In face of this threat of persecution the reply of Jesus was, ' As my Father has continued working to this hour, so I work too.' The connexion is a trifle artificial, in so far as in the following verses Jesus appears to justify himself not, as is demanded by the immediate context, for having encouraged the invalid to break the Sabbath, but, as in Lk. 13 : 14 ff.,

for having himself engaged in an illegal activity. But the
emphasis throughout is not so much on the action itself as
on the truth that it is due to a unity of being and activity
between Son and Father. The Sabbath regulations were
based on the doctrine of God's rest on the seventh day
(Gen. 2 : 1-3, Exod. 20 : 11, 31 : 17). But, says Jesus, this
rest must not be interpreted as literal idleness. Even for
God ' not rest but worthy labour is the soul of life,' for
He must continue to sustain creation (Mt. 5 : 45), and
it cannot be conceived that He will ever suspend a function
which is characteristically His own. ' God never stops
working,' says Philo (*De alleg.*, ii), ' for as it is the property
of fire to burn and of snow to be cold so of God to work.'
The question of reconciling God's continual activity with His
Sabbath rest much engaged the Rabbis. ' Why does God
not keep the Sabbath ? May not a man wander through
his own house on the Sabbath ? The house of God is the
whole realm above and the whole realm below ' (' Shem. R.,'
30). The idea also seems to have been held that the perfect
' rest ' would not be till the end of time (cf. Heb. 4 : 9 ff.).
God, says Jesus, has continued to be active right up to the
moment of this cure, so that in it is to be seen the work of
God Himself. Even on the Sabbath God must continue His
beneficent activity, and, says Jesus, ' I must do the same.'
He thereby claims as it were to be the organ of the perpetual
activity of the Father (though hardly in so wide a sense as
1 : 3), and declares that this unique relation to God makes
him even ' Lord of the Sabbath ' (Mk. 2 : 28).

Such is Jesus' defence : **but this only made the Jews more** 18
eager to kill him, because he not merely broke the sabbath,
but actually spoke of God as his own Father—in a unique
sense quite other than that in which all men may be said
to be ' sons of God ' (1 : 12) ; compare ' his own Son ' (Rom.
8 : 32)—**thereby** (adds the Evangelist, stating his own
inference rather than the Jews') **making himself equal to
God.** In the last words we have the very essence of the
Johannine theology, which here, as in 10 : 33, is vigorously
disputed by the Jews. We may compare in the parallel

Synoptic passage (Mk. 2 : 7) the Jews' resentment at Jesus' claim to forgive sins, a function belonging to God alone. In our Gospel Jesus never actually claims to *be* God, but repeatedly that he perfectly *represents* God (e.g. 10 : 30, 14 : 9).

The relationship between Father and Son is variously conceived in our Gospel as a unity of nature whereby the one is immanent in the other (10 : 30–38, 14 : 9–11), as a common activity whereby the Father acts through the Son and shares His functions with him (3 : 35, 17 : 10, 4 : 34), as a dependence of the Son upon the Father, wherein he fulfils the Father's commands (5 : 30, 6 : 38, 57; 8 : 26, 10 : 18, 12 : 49, 14 : 31, 15 : 10). In a word, the Son's relation to the Father, as hinted in the phrase ' the Logos was *with* God ' (1 : 1, where see note), is one of ' free dependence ' (Godet). This is brought out in the next verse, the importance of the pronouncement being stressed both by the solemn formula ' truly, truly,' and by the double statement in both negative and positive terms (cf. 1 : 3, 3 : 18, etc.).

19 So Jesus made this answer to them, ' Truly, truly I tell you, the Son can do nothing—i.e. is *morally* powerless to do anything—of his own accord, nothing but what he sees the Father doing ; for whatever He does, the Son also does the same.' On the one hand the Son is dependent on the Father, for his actions are but a reflection of the Father's ; on the other hand the Son is the representative of the Father, for it is through the Son that the Father's activity is expressed. The words ' what he *sees* the Father doing ' are significant. The Son is not like some O.T. prophet who must be instructed concerning each point as it arises ; rather has he an immediate *intuition* of what is the Father's will, of ' what the Father is doing.' The idea seems to be that the Father's will is an ideal ' work ' (cf. 4 : 34), which is first ' seen,' grasped by divine intuition, by the Son, and then becomes realized in the Son's action, so that it may be said that ' whatever the Father does, the Son does the same.' The Father's will is the archetype of the Son's action (6 : 38, etc.). ' The Father of the universe,' says Philo (*Conf. lingu.*, 14), ' has brought the Logos into being as His eldest Son . . . ; and he who was

begotten, imitating the ways of his Father, and looking to His archetypal patterns, kept forming the separate species' (quoted by Scott, op. cit., p. 60). The general truth has of course direct application to the immediate circumstances as a vindication of Jesus' action in curing the invalid. He is but realizing the Father's ideal ; his apology is that of Luther at Worms : ' I cannot otherwise, so help me God ! '

This divine intuition whereby the Son is able to realize the Father's ideal is due to the fact that ' the Father loves 20 the Son '—a love-relationship which is here regarded not so much (as in 17 : 24) as a mystical relationship existing from eternity between the Father and the pre-incarnate Logos, but rather as a moral attribute, eternal indeed, but now realized in time in Jesus' human self-consciousness, so that even to the incarnate Logos the Father ' shows him all that He is doing Himself,' i.e. reveals the workings of His will to him, so that the Father's active will becomes the spring of the Son's action. (Cf. Mt. 11 : 27, and note that the same moral relationship is expressed in the sphere of ordinary humanity in Mt. 12 : 50.) And more than this, ' He will show him (the Son) greater deeds than these ' (cf. 14 : 12, where it is shown, once again in the sphere of human life, that a moral relationship, here of faith, results in a fuller participation in the ' works ' of God), i.e. soon the will of the Father revealed progressively to the Son will express itself in still greater deeds, ' deeds to make you wonder.' The awakening of wonder might seem to be an inadequate motive, but the emphasis is on the pronoun rather than on the verb—' deeds to make even *you*, who now scoff, turn to wonder '—while the motive is more fully expressed in verse 23. The place of ' wonder ' in religion is well illustrated by a traditional saying of Jesus preserved by Clement of Alexandria (*Strom.*, ii, 9, 45) : ' He that wonders shall reign, and he that reigns shall rest.' ' The man who cannot always wonder,' says Carlyle, ' is but a pair of spectacles behind which there is no eye.' John's mind leaps forward to the ' wonderful ' achievements of Christianity in later days, when Jesus' words seemed to be fulfilled in such incidents as Acts 4 : 13. The deeds that have been are

21 indeed but symbols of greater deeds to be, ' for as the Father
raises the dead and makes them live '—*the* function *par
excellence* of God (1 Sam. 2 : 6, 2 Kings 5 : 7, Deut. 32 : 39,
and the *Shemoneh Esreh*, ' Blessed art Thou, O Lord, who
quickenest the dead ')—' so the Son makes anyone live
whom he chooses,' thus proving that he indeed has the right
to ' make himself equal to God ' (18). The words ' dead ' and
' live ' are here used most comprehensively, and must be
understood both in a natural and in a spiritual sense. No
doubt there is a forward glance to the physical resurrection
of Lazarus (chap. 11), but that in itself is symbolical of the
spiritual ' resurrection ' of the elect, who are here differentiated
from the mass of mankind by the words, ' whom he chooses,'
and in 29 are described as those who are ' raised to life.' Just
as Jesus spontaneously ' chose ' the invalid man from the
crowd at Beth-zatha, so does he ' choose ' those whom he
makes live.'

Verses 21–29 are difficult on account of a seeming failure
to distinguish clearly between the idea of a present spiritual
' life,' and that of an eschatologically conceived physical
' resurrection.' It is possible to interpret 21–23 in a purely
general sense, 24–27 in an ethical and spiritual sense, 28–29
in a physical and eschatological sense. But there is no need
thus to differentiate, for such distinctions are modern, and
would hardly trouble our author. John, like Paul (Col.
2 : 12–13, Rom. 8 : 10–11, 1 Cor. 15 : 22), would regard the
ethical and bodily ' resurrection ' as *one* experience of being
' made alive '—the physical resurrection being but the
climax of the spiritual rebirth (note on 6 : 58). That the
emphasis throughout is on ethical renewal appears alike
from the introductory illustration—the healing of an impotent
man, not the raising of one dead in the physical sense—
and from the recurrence of the word ' already ' (24, 25).
At the same time ' there is no inconsistency between the
spiritual and the material quickening, both of which are
taught distinctly in the Gospel. In John there is no dualism.
The writer conceives of matter as penetrated with the
divine. Alike God and the Word of God move downwards

and outwards, through spirit to the material envelope and vesture of spirit' (Sanday, *Criticism of the Fourth Gospel*, p. 196).

The idea of 'judgment' (for which see notes on 3 : 17-21) 22 is now combined with that of 'life-giving,' the connexion being suggested by the phrase ' whom he chooses,' which appears to transfer to the Son the right to decide who is to live and who is to die: an authority is thus claimed for the Son, which Jew and Christian alike assigned to *God* alone. ' **Indeed the Father passes judgment on no one,**' that is, He prejudices the chances of none to eternal life (3 : 17), for the destiny of each individual will be determined by his attitude to Christ ; in this sense each man is ' judged ' by Christ, and it can be said that the Father '**has committed** *all* **judgment** (i.e. the judgment which determines both life and death, the word here including the idea of acquittal as well as of conviction, though the emphasis is usually on the latter idea, as in 24 and 29 and 3 : 19) **to the Son,**' the Father's motive in thus delegating His authority being '**that all men may honour the Son as they honour the** 23 **Father,**' the representative and plenipotentiary (note on 18) receiving the same honours as the Sovereign himself (cf. 20 : 28, Phil. 2 : 10, and contrast Mk. 10 : 18). But the intention here is rather to emphasize the converse truth that '**he who does not honour the Son does not honour the Father who sent him**' : to refuse honour to Christ, as did the Jews (18), is to dishonour God Himself (cf. 15 : 24).

Christ now shows how his ' judgment ' works itself out, and 24 how his functions as life-giver and judge are related : ' **Truly, truly I tell you, he who listens to my word** (6 : 63) **and believes Him who sent me has eternal life ; he will incur no sentence of judgment, he has already passed from death across to life** ' (cf 1 Jn. 3 : 14). The believing acceptance of Christ s word, as implying faith in the Father whose representative he is, issues in life (3 : 36, 17 : 3, etc.). The believer thus escapes ' judgment,' the purpose of which is to determine whether or no he is to ' have life ' ; ' the place of judgment is on the threshold between life and death ' (Godet) ; for through faith he has *already* been ' judged ' and acquitted, and has thus got past

the determining point and beyond the risk of an adverse
verdict, that is, out of the reach of 'death' (cf. 3 : 18, which
stresses the converse truth). His 'judgment' is behind him,
and already he is tasting of eternal life (Heb. 6 : 5). As
Loisy puts it : 'For him the final resurrection and the last
judgment are alike superfluous.'

25 Verse 25, like 28-29, has been regarded as an eschatological
addition, on the ground that 24, 26-27 provide a smooth and
logical sequence, whereas the verses in question introduce
confusion between 'the time' which 'has come already'
(25) and 'a time coming' (28). But see note on 21 above.
**'Truly, truly I tell you, the time is coming, it has come already,
when the dead will listen to the voice of the Son of God, and
those who listen will live.'** On the ground that 'the voice'
is to be identified with 'his voice' in 28, some hold that the
reference here is to the resurrection at 'the last day.' But
the words 'has come already' are decisive against this.
The verse has in view neither the final consummation nor
even such particular incidents as Mt. 27 : 52-53, or the
miracles of raising the dead recorded in the Gospels—except
in so far as the latter serve as concrete illustrations (note,
e.g., the close parallel between this verse and 11 : 43-44)—
but rather the truth, implied in the previous verse, that
the new order is breaking through into the old (cf. 4 : 23).
As the result of Christ's ministry the *spiritually* dead (Mt.
8 : 22, Lk. 15 : 24, Eph. 5 : 14, Rev. 3 : 1) will hear, and such
as give heed will 'live' in the spiritual sense of 21 and 24.
Indeed, 25 is but a repetition in a more pictorial form of 24,
both verses being introduced by the solemn formula. Note
the hint that there are two kinds of hearing : 'All the dead
hear, but not all give ear' (Weiss). 'The question, how can
the spiritually dead hear and believe ? is the question, how
could the impotent man rise in response to Christ's word ?
Perhaps psychologically inexplicable, it is, happily, soluble
in practice' (Dods).

The power to 'raise the dead and make them live' was
shown in verse 21 to be one which 'made Christ equal to
God' (18). This 'equality' is now emphasized once again

and made the justification for Christ's claims: '**For as the** 26
**Father has life in Himself, so too He has granted the Son to have
life in himself**'; and as the source of divine life, Christ has power
to bestow it. The thought is exactly parallel to that of 6 : 51,
57, where see notes. The quality ascribed in 1 : 4 to the pre-
existent Logos is here transferred to the Incarnate Son. The
emphasis is on the words 'in himself.' ' Here,' says Godet,
' is the boldest paradox uttered by the mouth of Jesus. It is
given to the Son to live *of himself*.' A paradox which, when
transferred to ourselves, will help perhaps by analogy to solve
the psychological riddle of verse 25 : ' We possess as a thing
given—the faculty of *self*-determination,' and it was by
exercising this in a moral decision (5 : 6) that the *impotent*
man attained to *power*.

As 25–26 has repeated 21, so does 27 recall the thought of 22. 27
Since to give or not to give life constitutes ' judgment,' it may
be said that in virtue of the gift of ' life in Himself,' whence
springs the power to give life, the Father has '**also granted him
(the Son) authority to act as judge**,' a function which he is well
qualified to exercise ' since he is Son of man.' We note that
(in contrast to 1 : 51, 3 : 13 and Mt. 9 : 6, where the thought is
closely parallel) the article is omitted before both ' Son ' and
' man.' The effect would seem to be to stress not so much the
Messianic significance of the title—though no doubt this is still
present—but rather its human colouring. It is Christ's true
humanity which makes him a fitting agent of God's judgment
(cf. Acts 17 : 31 and God's words in the *Testament of
Abraham* : ' I do not judge you ; but every man shall be
judged by a man '). But why ? Both in virtue of his
human sympathy and understanding (cf. Heb. 2 : 14–18,
4 . 15, where, however, it is intercession, not judgment, that is
in question) and also because it is by their attitude to the
incarnate Son who tarries among them and whose glory
they have seen (1 : 14) that men most surely pass judgment
on themselves.

At this point the thought at last becomes purely eschato- 28
logical, and looks forward to a ' resurrection ' which is both
bodily and future, as is clear from the allusion to ' tombs '

and to ' a time coming.'   ' **Do not wonder at this,**' that is, at the
claims already made ; the future will remove all doubt as to
Christ's present authority (cf. the argument of 6 : 62) ; ' **for
there is a time coming when all** (contrasted with ' whom he
chooses ' in 21 and ' those who listen ' in 25 : the resurrection
is now the universal one at the last day) **who are in the tombs
will listen to his voice and come out.**'   Contemporary Judaism
looked for the final resurrection as the supreme demonstration
of divine power ; the part to be played by Christ then will
vindicate his claim to ' make men live ' now. Note that
the signal for the final resurrection is not to be a ' trumpet '
(Mt. 24 : 31, 1 Cor. 15 : 52) but ' **his voice,**' which by recalling 25
perhaps suggests that the signal for resurrection even at the
last day is not some dramatic word of command, but the word
of the Gospel which is already being preached, and by their
attitude to which men are already being judged. The last
day will but witness the consummation of a process already
going on. Cf. 12 : 48, where we are told that a man's judge on
the last day will be Christ's word to which he is listening
to-day. Note that the perplexed ' wonder ' of this verse is
quite distinct from 'the reverential ' wonder ' of 20.

Whereas Paul, when in 1 Cor. 15 : 51 ff. he writes ' *all* of us
are to be changed,' appears to have in view only the resurrection of the saved, John, following the thought of Mt. 25 : 46,
shows that the issue of the general resurrection is twofold,
29 ' **the doers of good to be raised to life, ill-doers to be raised for
the sentence of judgment** ' : for the former, judgment being
already past (24), there is immediate entrance into life ; the
latter, who in life have refused to subject themselves to the
judgment of Christ's Gospel, must now do so (12 : 48), and will
go forth condemned. (Cf. also the thought of 3 : 20–21,
and for this curious outcropping of eschatology cf. note on
6 : 39.)

30   Verse 30 modifies the claim made in 22 by recalling 19 :
Jesus' right to judge is based on the unique relationship to the
Father defined in 19 : ' **I can do nothing of my own accord ;
I pass judgment on men as I am taught by God** '—the idea being
that Jesus *listens* to the Father's verdict (cf. 19, ' what he *sees*

the Father doing ') before he pronounces his own. ' Nor can Jesus' judgment err, because it is merely as the executor of the Father's will he judges' (Dods) ; Jesus has no personal bias : ' my judgment is just, because my aim is not my own will but the will of Him who sent me.' The meaning is not that Jesus has no distinct will of his own, but that *morally* speaking there was in him but a single will, for his own will was always subordinated to the Father's : ' Not what I will, but what thou wilt.'

Itestify to myself, then my evidence is not valid ; I have 31 Another to bear testimony to me, and I know the evidence 32 He bears for me is valid. You sent to John, and he bore 33 testimony to the truth (though I accept no testimony from 34 man—I only speak of this testimony, that you may be saved) ; he was a burning and a shining lamp, and you 35 chose to rejoice for a while in his light. But I possess 36 a testimony greater than that of John, for the deeds which the Father has granted me to accomplish, the very deeds on which I am engaged, are my testimony that the Father has sent me. The Father who sent me has also borne testimony 37 to me himself ; but His voice you have never heard, His form you have never seen, His word you have not kept 38 with you, because you do not believe him whom He sent. You search the scriptures, imagining you possess eternal 39 life in their pages—and they do testify to me—but you 40 refuse to come to me for life. I accept no credit from 41 men, but I know there is no love to God in you ; here am 42 I, come in the name of my Father, and you will not accept 43 me : let someone else come in his own name, and you will accept him ! How can you believe, you who accept 44 credit from one another instead of aiming at the credit which comes from the only God ? Do not imagine I am 45 going to accuse you to the Father ; Moses is your accuser, Moses who is your hope ! For if you believed Moses you 46 would believe me, since it was of me that he wrote. But 47 if you do not believe what he wrote, how will you ever believe what I say ? '

31 The logical sequence at this point is not very clear, and indeed the whole section 31–44, as is the case with several of the 'Baptist' passages (see Introduction, p. lxvi), hangs rather loosely in the context ; 30 would be more aptly followed by 45. Verses 31–44 are a unit in themselves, and form the most striking of those passages emphasizing the 'witness' to Jesus' claims (cf. 1 : 7 note) which ' may be regarded as in the first place apologetic, and contain the Evangelist's answer to current objections on the part of Jews and heathen' (E. F. Scott, *The Fourth Gospel*, p. 196). The passage is connected with the preceding verses generally in so far that the thought of the unique intimacy between Father and Son is carried on, and more particularly by the persistence of the language of a law-court: Christ, who appeared in the rôle of Judge, now comes forward as witness (note how in 8 : 14–15 the thought conversely passes from ' witness' to ' judgment '). **'If I testify to myself, then my evidence is not valid '** : legal usage among Jews, Greeks and Romans alike would not admit the testimony of a witness in his own case (cf. also Deut. 17 : 6, 19 : 15). ' If it were true,' says Jesus, ' that in making these claims I was bearing unsupported testimony to myself,

32 then you might well disbelieve me ; but the truth is that **I have Another to bear testimony to me, and I know the evidence He bears for me is valid,** my filial consciousness only corroborates the Father's own testimony (given in 36 ff.) ; it follows then that my judgment on myself is as *valid* as my judgment on others is *just,* for in both cases it is not really my own judgment but God's.' Hence it is no contradiction when in 8 : 14 (which as we shall see should immediately follow the present discourse) Jesus says, ' Though I do testify to myself, my evidence is valid.' In the words **'I know the evidence He bears for me is valid '** we have the Evangelist's favourite asseveration (19 : 35, 1 Jn. 5 : 9) put on Jesus' own lips. By **Another** is meant of course the Father, not John the Baptist, who is introduced in the next verse simply by way of contrast, as if to hint, ' if you thought John's witness worth having, how much more the Father's ! '

33 **' You sent to John, and he bore testimony to the truth ' :** the

reference is to 1 : 19 ff.   But, strictly speaking, John's testimony to Jesus was given not to the deputation from the Jews
but on the following day to his own disciples (1 : 29 ff.) :
' the reference is better suited for the readers of the Gospel than
for the audience of Christ' (Loisy).   While thus calling John
to witness Jesus makes it clear that he does so ' **though I accept** 34
no testimony from man '—not that he discredits it (the meaning
in 3 : 11, 32), but he discounts it as unnecessary for his own
assurance (cf. the thought of 2 : 25), however valuable it might
be for the confirmation of the faith of waverers.   Indeed, Jesus
mentions the matter not in his own interest, but in theirs :
' **I only speak of this testimony that you may be saved** ' (1 : 7).

We have in 35 the Johannine parallel to Mt. 11 : 7 ff.— 35
Jesus' verdict on the Baptist :   ' **he was a burning and a shining**
lamp,' not the self-luminous light (1 : 8, 8 : 12), but the lamp
which must first be kindled, and which can shine only by burning itself out, yet, even so, invaluable as a guide to lead men
to the true light (there is a possible allusion to Ps. 132 : 17 ;
for the figure cf. 2 Sam. 21 : 17, 2 Pet. 1 : 19, Rev. 21 : 23).
Such was John, ' **and you chose to rejoice for a while in his**
light,' ' like gnats playing in the sunshine ' (Hausrath), or like
children amusing themselves while the sun shines, with a picture
of whom Luke (7 : 32) concludes his account of Jesus' verdict
on the Baptist.   The thought is that the Jews ' instead of taking advantage of the precious moments during which the torch
burns to accomplish an indispensable task, do nothing but
dance and play the fool in its light till it goes out ' (Godet).

But though John might well be called to witness, ' **I** (picking 36
up 34) **possess a testimony greater than that of John** (i.e.
greater than John can bear to me), **for the deeds which the**
Father has granted me to accomplish, the very deeds on which
I am engaged, are my testimony that the Father has sent me.'
Jesus' ' works ' include not merely his miracles, but his whole
Messianic vocation (4 : 34, 5 : 19–20, 17 : 4).   The word
' granted ' contains the idea both of commission and permission,
while in the phrase ' granted me to accomplish' the Greek turn of
expression emphasizes the divine *purpose* : the mission is still
in process of fulfilment, but God's purpose is that it shall be

accomplished (19 : 30) ; the miracles ' are not given in the
form of works done, but of works to be done' (Godet). (For
Jesus' ' works,' as proof of his divine origin, cf. 10 : 25, 38,
14 : 11, and Mt. 9 : 2–8, 11 : 2–6, 20–24.) By the commission
to fulfil the Messianic function the Father has implicitly borne
testimony that He has sent Jesus. But Jesus can point also
37 to a more *immediate* divine testimony : ' The Father who sent
me has also borne testimony to me Himself.' Some see here a
reference to the divine testimony borne to Jesus at the
Baptism, when a *voice* was heard from heaven and the Spirit
descended in the *form* of a dove, details which, it is claimed,
give force to Jesus' next words, ' but His voice you have never
heard, His form you have never seen.' If this interpretation is
accepted, it will be necessary to put a full-stop at the end of
37, and hold that the thought of the divine testimony of
Scripture is not introduced till 38. Otherwise (mainly on the
ground that the words ' You have *never* heard ' are too vague to
refer to so definite an occasion as the Baptism) we must understand by the ' testimony ' of 37 that which stands written in
Scripture and may still be read (this would be the force of the
Greek perfect), while by the following words Jesus would
imply that his hearers have proved unresponsive to both of
the means of prophetic revelation recognized in Scripture,
that to sight (' form ') and hearing (' voice '), the vision and the
word. Others again (taking 37 and 38 as one sentence) understand the meaning to be that the whole of Scripture bears
testimony to Jesus ; but the Jews, on account of their
rejection of the Christ (38*b*), have missed the opportunity, which
otherwise they might have had, of hearing God's voice and
seeing His form, both alike expressed in the person of Jesus,
whose voice and form they might indeed always have detected
in the pages of Scripture, had they but ears to hear and eyes
to see (cf. 1 : 18, 6 : 46, 14 : 9 and Deut. 4 : 33). However
37 be interpreted, the meaning is that the Jews have missed
God's revelation hitherto, and in consequence they have not the
38 fruit of that revelation stored in their hearts to-day : ' His
word you have not kept with you ' ; it has not become a permanent possession, a ' Word which roots itself inwardly with

power to save your souls' (Jam. 1 : 21 ; and cf. 17 : 6, 1 Jn. 2 : 14, 3 : 15), 'because you do not believe him whom He sent.' Their attitude to him who is the theme of the whole Word of God is proof enough that they have not made that Word their own ; if their life had been nourished on that Word, then they must have been prepared to welcome him for whose coming the Word was a preparation. The Word here includes not only Scripture but 'the whole compass of divine revelation' (Holtzmann).

The Jews' refusal to accept the very One to whom the 39 Scriptures bear witness proves that all their study of the Scriptures is vitiated by a misunderstanding : **'You search the scriptures, imagining you possess eternal life in their pages,'** under the misconception that the mere study of the letter saves (cf. Jer. 8 : 8, Rom. 2 : 17–20), whereas the source of life is not in the Scriptures as such, but in him to whom they testify (2 Cor. 3 : 6)—'and **they do testify to me** (a parenthetical remark thrown in)—but (though you pore over the promises) 40 **you refuse to come to me** (who am the fulfilment) **for life.'** They reject Jesus' invitation (6 : 35) because they 'imagine' that they already 'possess life' in virtue of their diligent 'searching' of the Scriptures ; they are 'always curious to learn and never able to attain the knowledge of the truth' (2 Tim. 3 : 7). We are reminded of Jesus' lament over Jerusalem (Mt. 23 : 37).

The following verses would seem to be added by the Evangel- 41 ist lest it should be thought that Christ in thus stressing his own claims is seeking honour for himself. This Jesus disclaims : **'I accept no credit from men '** ; Jesus cares as little about men's good opinions as about their testimony (34) (distinguish the 'credit' here from the 'honour' of ver. 23, and cf. 7 : 18, 8 : 50) ; he feels no chagrin at their rejection of himself : it is their attitude to *God* which distresses him (cf. Lk. 12 : 10) —'**but I know there is no love to God in you.'** How could there 42 be any such love when 'here am I, come in the name of my 43 **Father, and you will not accept me '** ? (cf. 23). On the other hand, '**let someone else come in his own name, and you will accept him !** ' They reject one who holds a commission from

the Father (10 : 25), whereas they will be willing to welcome
one who comes not with a message from God but with some
new-fangled Gospel made to fit their own national aspirations
and vanity. The reference is probably neither to false prophets in general (Mk. 13 : 6, 21–22), nor to any individual Jewish Messiah (Acts 5 : 36–37)—Bar Cochba, who put himself
forward in A.D. 132–5, has been suggested, but even the final
redaction of the Gospel is probably earlier than this date ;
in any case a false Messiah would hardly come ' in his own
name' (Mk. 13 : 6)—but rather to the personal Antichrist who
was expected in the Evangelist's day (1 Jn. 2 : 18, 4 : 3 ; 2 Jn.
7 ; 2 Thess. 2 : 3 ff.).

44   Jesus' rejection by such is no surprise : **' How can you believe,**
you who accept credit from one another instead of aiming at the
credit which comes from the only God ? ' (for the last phrase
cf. 17 : 3 explained by 1 Jn. 5 : 20). How can the motives of
Jesus who ' accepts no credit from men ' be appreciated by
those whose one aim is to enhance their own dignity in the eyes
of their fellows (12 : 43, Mt. 23 : 5 ff.), forgetful that the true
Jew is ' a Jew who is one inwardly . . . praised by God, not
by man ' (Rom. 2 : 29) ?

45   Since Jesus cares nothing for men's opinions (41), his hearers
need not fear that angered by their disrespect he will accuse
them before God : **' Do not imagine I am going to accuse you**
to the Father ! ' Besides, there will be no need to do so, for
already there is one who accuses : **' Moses is your accuser,**
Moses who is your hope ' (39, 8 : 33 ff.). The Jews regarded
Moses as their mediator before God ; in his writings too they
found the promise of the hoped-for prophet (Deut. 18 : 15 ;
cf. Lk. 24 : 44, Rom. 10 : 5–8, Acts 3 : 22, 7 : 37). But by
rejecting him in whom those hopes were fulfilled, they had in
fact renounced their faith in Moses and lost the hope that was
46 grounded in that faith : **' For if you believed Moses you would**
believe me, since it was of me that he wrote.' Nay more, Moses
actually becomes their accuser ; for just as in Paul's eyes
the knowledge of the law makes a man a conscious sinner
(Rom. 7 : 7), so the fact that the Jews with the promises before
their eyes have spurned him who fulfils the promises lays them

open to the accusation of that Moses who wrote the promises. The thought is that the Jews have been disloyal to the spirit of the Mosaic faith, and so have lost their standing even as Jews. ' Every true Jew will naturally become a Christian, every bad Jew will instinctively reject the Gospel ' (Godet).

Had the Jews then been loyal to their professed faith in 47 Moses, they would have welcomed Jesus ; ' But if you do not believe what he wrote, how will you ever believe what I say ? ' If they refuse to believe in the writings which prophesy, how can they believe in the words which fulfil and realize that prophecy ? If one misconceives the sense of the O.T. one naturally cannot understand the N.T.

7.

> The Jews were amazed, saying, ' How can this uneducated 15 fellow manage to read ? ' Jesus told them in reply, 16 ' My teaching is not my own but His who sent me ; any- one who chooses to do His will, shall understand whether 17 my teaching comes from God or whether I am talking on my own authority. He who talks on his own authority 18 aims at his own credit, but he who aims at the credit of the person who sent him, he is sincere, and there is no dishonesty in him. Did not Moses give you the Law ?— 19 and yet none of you honestly obeys the Law. Else, why do you want to kill me ? ' The crowd replied, 20 ' You are mad. Who wants to kill you ? ' Jesus answered 21 them, ' I have only performed one deed, and yet you are all amazed at it. Moses gave you the rite of circumcision 22 (not that it came from Moses, it came from your ancestors), and you will circumcise a man upon the sabbath. Well, 23 if a man gets circumcised upon the sabbath, to avoid breaking the Law of Moses, are you enraged at me for curing, not cutting, the entire body of a man upon the sabbath ? Give over judging by appearances ; be just.' 24

At this point should be inserted the section 7 : 15–24, where the Sabbath-controversy is continued. In their usual position these verses are clearly out of place. They occur in the account of Jesus' visit to the Feast of Tabernacles in October.

Yet, without any explanation, particular reference is made (7 : 21) to the effect produced by ' one deed ' performed at the Feast of Pentecost the previous May, since when Jesus has been absent in Galilee (7 : 1). The emphasis again on *one* miracle (7 : 21) seems inconsistent with the people's testimony to Jesus' *many* miracles (7 : 31). Finally, 7 : 20 (' Who wants to kill you ? ') seems incongruous if placed immediately before 7 : 25 (' Is this not the man they want to kill ? '), though the latter verse is perfectly consistent with 7 : 1 (' the Jews were trying to kill him '). On the other hand, the thought of 7 : 15–24 is obviously a continuation of that of chapter 5. Apart from the main topic, the violation of the Sabbath, note how 7 : 16–17 is an echo of 5 : 30–32, 7 : 18 of 5 : 41 ff., 7 : 19 of 5 : 45 ff. The usual position of the section may be due to a copyist, on the look-out for a suitable place to insert a fragment already displaced from its true position, having noticed the apparent connexion between Jesus' ' teaching ' in 7 : 14 and the Jews' ' marvelling ' at his ' letters ' in 7 : 15. (For the whole question of the displacements in chapters 7 and 8 see an article by the present writer in the *Expository Times*, November 1921.)

15   The Jews were amazed, saying, ' How can this uneducated fellow manage to read ? ' or perhaps, for this better suits Jesus' reply, ' *Where does this uneducated fellow get his learning ?* ' (cf. Acts 26 : 24). According to the first rendering the Jews consider Jesus an illiterate, according to the second they are taunting him as one who has had no training in the Rabbinical schools and is therefore unversed in the traditional methods of Scripture interpretation. The Evangelist would see something intensely dramatic in this picture of the Jews confronted by the Incarnate Logos and yet treating him as an ' **uneducated fellow** ! ' Loisy well notes that in the Synoptics, though there too the Jews express wonder at Jesus' learning (Mk. 6 : 2), there is no trace of any unwillingness to rank him as a Teacher because he was not a graduate of the schools. But this objection may well have been raised in the course of the Jewish polemic against Christianity in the Evangelist's own day. Jesus' reply is that he has had an education they know not of,

he is not merely self-taught (5 : 30 f.) : 'My teaching is not 16 mine but His who sent me,' a greater Teacher than any Rabbi! Moreover, this teaching has a twofold attestation : and firstly that of every good man's conscience—'anyone who chooses 17 to do His will shall understand whether my teaching comes from God or whether I am talking on my own authority ' ; that is, when a man puts his will into line with God's will, he will feel that Jesus' teaching finds an echo in the aspirations of his own conscience ; he will therefore be convinced that such teaching is no man-made doctrine, but is inspired by God Himself, and has behind it the authority of God Himself. Knowledge of spiritual truth is possible only on certain ethical conditions : Jesus' teaching can be understood only by those who are prepared to practise it. (See also note on 3 : 21.) Such is the first attestation to the divine origin of Jesus' teaching ; moreover, it is the mark of a man who merely speaks his own mind that he will tend to glorify himself ; ' he who talks on his own authority aims at his own credit.' But Jesus does neither the one (5 : 30) nor the other (5 : 41) ; on the contrary the second attestation to Jesus' teaching will be found just here, that his motives are entirely disinterested and devoted ; for it will surely be admitted that ' he who aims 18 at the credit of the person who sent him, he is sincere, and there is no dishonesty in him.' (For this contrast between ' sincerity ' (A.V. ' truth ') and ' dishonesty ' (A.V. ' unrighteousness ') cf. Rom. 2 : 8, 2 Thess. 2 : 12.) To such a teacher they should listen as to God Himself.

' Not content to remain upon the defensive Jesus makes a 19 sortie ' (Loisy). The connexion would seem to be as follows : ' it is not surprising that you reject my teaching seeing that you reject Moses' also (cf. 5 : 45–47) : ' Did not Moses give you the Law ?—and yet none of you honestly obeys the Law. Else, why do you want to kill me ? ' i.e., if they had put into prac- tice the intention of their own law, they would see that judged by it Jesus had done nothing to merit death (5 : 18). Alter- natively, and perhaps more simply, we may suppose that the way is being prepared for the argument of 22–23 : ' Moses gave you the law, but none of you strictly keep it, for in one

particular (circumcision on the Sabbath) you regularly violate it ; why then do you seek to kill me, who merely did once
20 what you do every week ? ' **The crowd,** who are supposed to be ignorant of their leaders' designs against Jesus, scoff at the idea of a plot, and replied, ' **You are mad ! Who wants to kill you ? '** Literally the words mean, ' you have a devil ! ' (Cf. 8 : 48, 52 ; 10 : 20.) The same phrase is used in Mt. 11 : 18, Lk. 7 : 33 of the Baptist, and there, as here, means nothing more than that the victim is possessed by gloomy fancies, a very different thing from ' *being* a devil ' (6 : 70). (See also Mk. 3 : 21–22, where the comment of Jesus' friends that ' he is out of his mind ' is heightened by the scribes into the insinuation that ' he has Beelzebul.') It is noticeable that our Gospel omits all reference to Jesus' exorcism of ' devils.'

21 Jesus ignores the crowd's rejoinder, and himself takes the offensive : judged by their own practice how little cause they have for offence. ' As for what I have done,' he says, ' you all do it, and with much less at stake ! ' ' **I have only per-formed one deed '**—the healing of the impotent man—' **and yet you are amazed at it '**—because they regarded as a daring transgression of the Sabbath-law what was in fact an object-lesson in its true spirit. The Greek phrase translated ' at it,' is probably to be taken thus with the verb ' amazed.' If taken with the following verse (A.V. ' therefore ') the meaning
22 can only be, ' *Well then, let me tell you,* **Moses gave you the rite of circumcision (not that it came from Moses, it came from your ancestors), and you will circumcise a man upon the sabbath,'** that is, if the eighth day after birth happens to fall on a Sabbath. The parenthesis is probably inserted either by the Evangelist or the Redactor merely for the sake of accuracy. If part of Jesus' argument, it is best to explain thus with Godet : ' The ordinance of circumcision formed no part of the Decalogue. It was derived from ancient tradition, and inserted in his code by Moses in an incidental manner. Who then could have expected that such an ordinance would take precedence of one of the commandments of the Deca-logue itself, of the law of the Sabbath ? ' The principle that circumcision might be performed on the Sabbath is clearly

stated in the Mishna: 'Every work which can be done on the eve of the Sabbath does not set aside the Sabbath; but circumcision, which cannot be done on the eve of the Sabbath (i.e. if the eve be the seventh day after birth), sets aside the Sabbath.' '**Well, if a man gets circumcised upon 23 the sabbath, to avoid breaking the Law of Moses** (i.e. by the infringement of the regulation that a child must be circumcised on the eighth day), **are you enraged at me for curing, not cutting, the entire body of a man upon the sabbath?**' Jesus uses an argument *a fortiori* based upon his own principle that 'the Sabbath is made for man.' If it is permissible on the Sabbath to cure a single member (for circumcision was apparently held to exercise a 'curative' virtue upon the member affected: 'praeputium est vitium in corpore'), how much more to make sound a man's whole body. Or perhaps the contrast is not so much between partial healing and complete healing, but rather, as our translation suggests, between mutilation and perfect health, between restraint and complete liberty (cf. Gal. 5:3). It may be noted that John's choice of circumcision as an example of Sabbath-breaking to set over against Jesus' cure does not provide so forcible an argument as the illustrations given by the Synoptists (Mt. 12:3 ff., Lk. 13:15); for while circumcision, being a divine institution earlier even than Moses and sanctioned by his law, could awaken no scruples if performed on the Sabbath, the Synoptic examples of Sabbath-breaking, not having received express divine sanction, might do so. But from the Evangelist's point of view circumcision is a peculiarly fitting illustration, for it hints at the contrast, which is the key-note of this section of the Gospel, between the old Law which can only give a man outward purity at the cost of mutilating him and putting him under restraint and Christ who heals a man completely and gives him his perfect freedom.

Jesus now draws the moral: '**Give over judging by appear- 24 ances; be just.**' On the surface this implies that Jesus' healing of the impotent man was only an apparent violation of the Law: in reality it was an expression of the Law's true spirit. But doubtless there is a deeper meaning, intended for the critics of Christianity in the Evangelist's own day : Christianity is not, as might appear to the casual observer, the subversion of the Law, but, as Christ himself taught, its perfect fulfilment (Mt. 5 : 17)—the only just verdict.

8.

12 Then Jesus again addressed them, saying, ' I am the light of the world : he who follows me will not walk in darkness,

13   he will enjoy the light of life.' So the Pharisees said to him, ' You are testifying to yourself ; your evidence is

14   not valid.' Jesus replied to them, ' Though I do testify to myself, my evidence is valid, because I know where I · have come from and where I am going to—whereas you do not know where I have come from or where I am going to.

15
16   You judge by the outside. I judge no one ; and though I do judge, my judgment is true, because I am not by myself—there is myself and the Father who sent me.

17   Why, it is written in your own Law that the evidence of

18   two persons is valid : I testify to myself, and the Father

19   who sent me also testifies to me.' ' Where is your Father ? ' they said. Jesus replied, ' You know neither me nor my Father ; if you had known me you would

20   have known my Father also.' These words he spoke in the treasury, as he was teaching in the temple, but no one arrested him, because his time had not come yet.

7 : 24 standing by itself would form a very abrupt conclusion to the discourse at Pentecost ; as already suggested (note at beginning of chap. 6) we propose to insert here 8 : 12–20. In favour of its usual position as part of Jesus' teaching at the Feast of Tabernacles it is generally urged that the key thought ' I am the light of the world ' was suggested by the symbolism of that feast, when four golden candelabra were illuminated in the Court of the Women as a memorial of the Pillar of Fire in the wilderness. But the renewal of Jesus' address at 8 : 12 seems strange after the scattering of his audience at 7 : 53 (8 : 1–11 does not belong to the original Gospel). Burton therefore proposes appropriately enough to place this proclamation by Jesus of

himself as the Light of the world immediately after the healing of the man born blind (he arranges thus : 9 : 39–41, 10 : 19–21, 8 : 12–20). But the thought of the verses is so closely akin to that of chapter 5 and 7 : 15–24, and provides so appropriate a climax to the whole section that one can hardly resist the conclusion that 8 : 12–20 was originally part of this same discourse. Nearly every verse contains an echo of 5 and 7 : 15–24 ; in particular the thought of ' witnessing ' (5 : 31–39 ; 7 : 18 ; 8 : 12–14, 17–18), and of the resultant verdict (5 : 40–47 ; 7 : 17, 24 ; 8 : 15, 19), runs through all three passages. The line of thought is as follows : Testimony is borne to Jesus both by his own works and by his Father (5 : 32–37 *a*) ; but his opponents cannot appreciate this testimony because their powers of judgment are distorted (5 : 37 *b*–47) ; yet the man who brings this warped will into line with God's will *can* get insight (7 : 17) ; let not the Jews therefore allow their judgment on things spiritual to be biased by external prejudices (7 : 24). Note now the connexion at 8 : 12 : let men but look to Christ and they will find him ' the light of the world,' needing no external testimony (5 : 34), but self-evidencing in a far truer sense than John ' the lamp ' (5 : 35), and able therefore to lead them into true judgments (7 : 24, 8 : 12 *b*). (See also F. Warburton Lewis, *Disarrangements in the Fourth Gospel*, p. 17 ff.)

Then Jesus again addressed them, saying (words which 12 possibly should be omitted as a link put in after the paragraph had been displaced) **' I am the light of the world.'** Rather than being prompted by the symbolism of the Feast of Tabernacles the words are an echo of the Prologue (1 : 4–5, 9 ff., where the idea of the ' world ' is also prominent. Cf. also Is. 8 : 22–29 : 2, 42 : 6, 49 : 6, Mt. 4 : 15 ·16, 5 : 14–16.) According to tradition ' Light ' was one of the names of Messiah. **' He who follows me** (as the Israelites did the Pillar of Fire ?) **shall not walk in darkness** (1 : 5, 12 : 46)—where there is many a pitfall (1 Jn. 2 : 10–11)—**but shall have the light of life.'** The ideas of ' light ' and of ' life ' are associated as in 1 : 4, where see note ; that verse shows that ' light of life ' means not ' the light which gives life,' as in the phrase ' bread of life ' (6 : 35), but rather ' the light which results from the possession of life,' ' the light which emanates from life ' (Godet). As the Prologue has it, ' this life was the light for men.' The ' life ' which is the gift of Christ (6 : 27, etc.) expresses itself in ' light,' that is, in an insight into moral truth which will save men from blundering into false judgments (7 : 24). (See notes on 1 : 4, 3 : 19.)

13 So the Pharisees said to him—turning his own words (5 : 31) against himself—' **You are testifying to yourself ; your**
14 **evidence is not valid.'** Jesus replied to them, ' **Though I do testify to myself**—and therefore on my own showing (5 : 31) might seem to have no claim on your belief—**my evidence is valid, because I know where I have come from and where I am going to** (explained 13 : 3, 16 : 28)—**whereas you do not know where I have come from or where I am going to.'** On the surface Jesus' defence would appear to be : ' I admit the validity of my general rule (5 : 31) ; but ordinary rules cannot apply to one of divine origin and divine destiny such as I know myself to be ; and you, who do not share my self-consciousness, are not in a position to dispute my testimony to myself which is based upon that self-consciousness.' But Jesus' real defence is only reached at 16–18, where he repeats the argument of 5 : 32 that his ' witness ' is in fact not uncorroborated, for he has ' Another to bear testimony to him.' The present verse merely prepares the way for that defence by emphasizing that divine self-consciousness in virtue of which Jesus perceives in his own mission (cf. 5 : 36) the corroborative testimony of God Himself. Godet well comments : ' Christianity is entirely based upon Christ's consciousness of himself, and it is the heroism of faith to rest upon the extraordinary testimony which this Being gave to himself.'

The Jews, on the other hand, not having this divine insight,
15 judge by appearances (7 : 24) : ' **You judge by the outside** ' (cf. 2 Cor. 5 : 16, and as an example of such ' judgment,' 7 : 27). Jesus, on the other hand, even though he has all the qualifications for *penetrating* judgment, prefers not to act as judge himself—' **I judge no one** '—but rather to echo *God's* judgment

(5 : 30) ; and it is in virtue of this latter fact that '*if ever* 16 (not 'though') I do judge (and he cannot but do so constantly—3 : 18-19, 5 : 22 notes), my judgment is true, because I am not by myself—there is myself and the Father who sent me ' ; that is, ' I am conscious of a unique communion with the Father, in virtue of which mine is no mere individual judgment but one supported by the Father's judgment on which indeed it is based.' (Compare *Pirke Aboth*, iv, 12 : ' Judge not alone, for none may judge alone save *one*.')

Christ's evidence then is valid : ' Why, it is written in your 17 own Law that the evidence of two persons is valid ' (see note on 5 : 31, and cf. Deut. 17 : 6, 19 : 15 and Mt. 18 : 16, Heb. 10 : 28, 2 Cor. 13 : 1) ; and in this case there *are* two witnesses : ' I testify to myself, and the Father who sent me also 18 testifies to me.' The manner of the Father's testifying was given in 5 : 36 ff. Loisy notes that in addition to working out this subtle argument from the law of evidence the Evangelist also plays on the word ' judgment,' the sense of which throughout this passage is equivocal : ' the judgment of the Pharisees is a judgment of value without practical consequence : that of Christ is a sovereign decision, a divine decree from which there is no appeal ' (5 : 28-29).

Jesus' appeal to an absentee witness does not satisfy his 19 opponents : 'Where is your Father ? ' they said. The Jews know well enough *who* the Father is (5 : 17-18), but will be content with nothing short of a divine theophany. It is interesting to compare this question and Jesus' rejoinder with the similar request of Philip and Jesus' reply in 14 : 8 ff. In Philip's case the ethical conditions laid down in 7 : 17 are present, and Jesus therefore grants him a fuller revelation of spiritual truth ; in the present case Jesus can but reply that his hearers' lack of understanding of himself renders impossible a revelation of God which otherwise might have been theirs : Jesus replied, ' You know neither me nor my Father ; if you had known me you would have known my Father also ' (cf. 14 : 9). To ' know ' in our Gospel implies much more than a bare theoretical knowledge ; the idea also contains moral and religious elements ; for John, as for prophet and psalmist, to 'know the Lord' would mean also to trust him, and to enter into harmony with his will and purpose. Hence knowledge of the Father is impossible to those who refuse to submit their wills to Jesus.

20 The section ends with a note concerning the place where this discourse was delivered: **These words he spoke in the treasury, as he was teaching in the temple.** By the **treasury** is meant that part of the Women's Court where stood the thirteen boxes with funnel-shaped openings, in which was deposited money collected for the temple and various charitable purposes (Mk. 12 : 41 ff.). The Sanhedrim met regularly close by in the chamber ' Gazith,' between the Court of the Women and the Inner Court. Thus the point of the note is that Jesus was teaching within earshot of his enemies, **but no one arrested him, for his time had not yet come.** (For the last clause cf. 7 : 30, 44 ; 13 : 1, and note on 2 : 4.)

ACT II. THE CONFLICT OF THE NEW GOSPEL WITH THE OLD

Section I.—The Divine Origin of the Christ

Illustration : Jesus and his Brothers (7 : 1–14, 25–27)

7.

1 After this Jesus moved about in Galilee ; he would not move in Judaea, because the Jews were trying to kill him.

²⁄₃ Now the Jewish festival of booths was near, so his brothers said to him, ' Leave this and go across into Judaea, to let

4 your disciples witness what you can do ; for nobody who aims at public recognition ever keeps his actions secret. Since you can do these deeds, display yourself to the world '

5 (for even his brothers did not believe in him). Jesus said to

6 them, ' My time has not come yet, but your time is always

7 at hand ; the world cannot hate you, but it hates me

8 because I testify that its deeds are evil. Go up to the festival yourselves ; I am not going up to this festival,

9 for my time has not arrived yet.' So saying, he stayed on

10 in Galilee. But after his brothers had gone up to the festival, he went up too, not publicly but as it were pri-

196

vately.   At the festival the Jews were in quest of him, say- 11
ing, 'Where is he ? '   And the crowd disputed about him 12
hotly ; some said, ' He is a good man,' but others said,
' No, he is misleading the people.'   For fear of the Jews, 13
however, nobody spoke of him in public.

When the festival was half over, Jesus went up to the temple 14
and began to teach.   Then said some of the Jerusalemites, 25
' Is this not the man they want to kill ?   Yet here he is, 26
opening his lips in public, and they say nothing to him !
Can the authorities have really discovered that he is the
Christ ?   No, we know where this man comes from ; 27
but when the Christ does come, no one will know where
he comes from.'

The second main division of the Gospel is reached with Jesus'
entry upon his final ministry at Jerusalem, throughout which
the dramatic emphasis centres upon the conflict of the New
Gospel with the Old, of faith with unbelief.   But first John
records one last Galilean interlude : **After this**—for the 1
sequence of events see note on p. 124 f.—**Jesus moved**
about in Galilee ; he would not move in Judaea, because
the Jews were trying to kill him—a reference to 5 : 18,
7 : 19-20.   The imperfect tense **moved about** implies a stay
in Galilee of some length in contrast, e.g., to the brief visits of
2 : 1-12, 4 : 43-54.   At this point, unless it be between
10 : 21 and 22 (where see note), must be inserted the leisurely
teaching mission undertaken by Jesus on his way from Galilee
to Jerusalem and narrated in Lk. 9 : 51-19 : 28.   The word
here used (' move about ' ' walk,') is regularly used of just such
a going about of a teacher among his disciples.   Holtzmann
sees in this verse proof that John regards the Judaean ministry
as the rule, and a visit to Galilee as an exception which requires
to be justified.   Rather John implies that Jesus wished to
avoid a premature clash with the Jews (cf. 4 : 1-3, 43-44).
Now the Jewish festival of booths was near.   The Feast 2
of Booths or Tabernacles commemorated God's providence
towards His people while they dwelt in tents in the Wilderness,
and lasted for eight days (from 15th Tisri) in the second half of

October, during which period the people lived in tents in the open places of the city. It ranked second only to the Passover in importance, ' the holiest and greatest feast,' Josephus calls it, when any pious Jew might be expected to visit Jerusalem :
3 so his brothers (2 : 12) said to him, ' Leave this and go across into Judaea, to let your disciples witness what you can do.' Contrast the brothers' action according to Mk. 3 : 21, 31 ; here so far from restraining Jesus they urge him to bring matters to an issue. ' Let these wonderful deeds of yours be done not only in a corner (Acts 26 : 26), but in the limelight, where they may be seen by your disciples '—among whom apparently the brothers do not yet reckon themselves (5). ' Disciples ' include those who have professed a certain measure of faith in Jesus without necessarily attaching themselves to his person (6 : 60 ff.). Many such would naturally be found in Judaea (4 : 1), especially during festival seasons (2 : 23), when adherents from all parts would congregate. The brothers' challenge does not so much imply doubt concerning the reality of Jesus' works as hint that a change of method is necessary if the zeal of Jesus' followers is to be kept at high pitch. Jesus' present disciples, be they Jewish residenters or Galilean visitors, must be shown that he has power to make good his claims at the headquarters of the Jewish religion. Wellhausen and Schwartz see in this challenge to go to Judaea a relic of an earlier form of the Gospel, according to which Jesus had not previously visited Jerusalem. But the question is not of recruiting *new* disciples from an hitherto untried field, but of confirming the loyalty of his *present* disciples by advancing his claims in the most impressive setting.
4 ' For,' it is urged, ' nobody who aims at public recognition ever keeps his actions secret ' (cf. Lk. 8 : 16–17, 11 : 33, 12 : 2, Mt. 10 : 26) ; that is, one can't hide one's actions and yet hope to be prominent oneself. Jesus, they hint, is privately making claims which can be vindicated only ' in public ' (cf. 11 : 54). ' Make yourself *known*,' they urge, ' as that which by your actions you *profess* to be,' that is, as Messiah. But Messiah must fill the whole stage ; therefore, ' *since* you can do these deeds (granting his ability to do them, not ' *if*,' as A.V., which

would question it), **display yourself to the world '**—Jerusalem
being for the Jew the ' World-metropolis.' (For ' world '
cf. 12 : 19, 18 : 20 and note on 1 : 10. Here it means the
sum-total of heterogeneous humanity.)   **For even his brothers,**   5
who might be expected to be the first to believe, **did not believe
in him :** they demanded world-recognition first, whereas
' faith would have been content to wait ' (Westcott).

There are two reasons why Jesus cannot accept his brothers'   6
advice ; his case is entirely different from theirs : first, in this,
that while nothing depends upon *their* manifestation to the
world, everything depends upon *his* ;   they may choose their
own time, but he must wait a signal from God.   **Jesus said
to them, ' My time** (cf. note on 2 : 4, 7 : 30, 8 : 20, 13 : 31,
Lk. 9 : 51) **is not come yet, but your time is always at hand.'**
Moreover, the ground of this distinction between Jesus and his   7
brothers lies in a distinction deeper still—the relation of each
to ' the world,' that is, to the sum total of forces ranged against
Jesus and his cause (cf. 1 : 10, 14 : 17, 15 : 18–19, 16 : 20, 33,
17 : 9, 14) : **' the world cannot** (the word ' answers to the law
of moral correspondence '—Westcott ; cf. 20 : 9) **hate you**—
who share its point of view—**but it hates me** (15 : 18–19)
because I testify that its deeds are evil '—because in my light its
evil is shown up (3 : 19 f.).   We recall Jesus' similar retort to
his mother at 2 : 4.   **' The world '** has a different meaning for
Jesus and for his brothers. **' Go up to the festival yourselves '**—   8
they would go merely as pilgrims : Jesus, when he goes up,
must do so as Messiah ; therefore **' I am not going up to this
festival.'**   Jesus looks forward from ' *this* festival,' the Feast
of Booths, which as ' a festival of peculiar joy for work accomplished ' (Westcott) would not chime in with his present mood,
to that final Passover when, his work accomplished, ' his time '
would have arrived (12 : 23, 17 : 1).   To go up now would be
to be proclaimed Messiah prematurely, and that is to be
avoided, **' for my time has not arrived yet.'**

Porphyry remarks on Jesus' ' inconstancy ' when, after the   9
statement that **so saying, he stayed on in Galilee,** it is added
that **after his brothers had gone up to the festival, he went up** 10
too.   Rather does John intend to insist once more (as in

2 : 4, 7. where see note) that Jesus would never consent to take hurried action on another's initiative. The true reason for the delay, followed by an apparent change of plan, is that Jesus may be sure of his own mind and of God's will before he precipitates his arrest. Jesus' brothers symbolize the Jewish point of view, as does his ' mother ' in 2 : 4, and we have here a Johannine parallel to the 'Temptation' of Mt. 4 : 5–7, where Jesus is tempted to adopt the Jewish Messianic programme and secure recognition by a signal display of power. It is added that Jesus went up **not publicly but as it were privately,** by which we are to understand not that he refrained from teaching openly on arrival (cf. 18 : 20), but that he travelled on his own account, ' incognito,' and not with one of the pilgrim caravans. The fact is mentioned to emphasize that Jesus did not simply come into line with his brothers' advice.

11 **At the festival the Jews** (the Jewish authorities of 5 : 16–18 opposed to the 'crowd' of pilgrims mentioned in the next verse) **were in quest of him, saying, 'Where is he ? '** Again the meaning is not that Jesus remained ' incognito ' on arrival, but that he was not among the first of the pilgrims to arrive : 'the Jews' were impatiently awaiting his appearance. **And**
12 **the crowd** (of pilgrims and common folk) **disputed about him hotly.** The Greek word suggests that it was ' suppressed discussion in low tones, in corners and among friends ' (Dods). Some said, ' **He is a good man** '—his motives are pure—**but others said, ' No, he is misleading the people** '—he is arousing Messianic expectations for his own purposes (cf. Mt. 27 : 63,
13 Lk. 23 : 5). **For fear of the Jews, however, nobody spoke of him in public** : they were waiting for the authorities to declare their mind first.

14 Possibly Jesus had already been a day or two in Jerusalem, but now he appears at the temple : **When the festival was half over, Jesus went up to the temple and began to teach.** This would be on the fourth or fifth day of the festival which lasted eight days. On the ground that Jesus would probably teach thus on a *Sabbath* an attempt has been made to fix this date as the 15th October, A.D. 29. But ready

listeners would be found in the temple on any day during the festival week.

(Verses 15 to 24 have been inserted at the close of chapter 5.)

Then said some of the Jerusalemites—the residenters, as 25 opposed to the ' crowd ' of pilgrims, who might be expected to have information about the designs of their rulers against Jesus—**' Is this not the man they want to kill ?** (5 : 18, 7 : 1, 19). 26 **Yet here he is, opening his lips in public, and they say nothing to him ! Can the authorities really have discovered that he is the Christ ? '** They are surprised that Jesus should be allowed to speak so freely, unless indeed the rulers have changed their minds as the result of a discovery that he is really the Messiah. But this idea is quickly dismissed on the ground of the ancient dogma that Messiah would suddenly appear out of concealment. (Cf. Jn. 1 : 31, Mt. 24 : 26, and the apocalyptic ideas as expressed in 4 Ezra 7 : 28, 13 : 32, and Apoc. Baruch 13 : 32.) There is a Jewish saying that ' three things come wholly unexpected—Messiah, a god-send, and a scorpion.' Justin Martyr alludes to a tradition that not even Messiah would know his own mission until he was anointed by Elijah. With this in mind the people conclude, **' No, we** 27 **know where this man comes from,'**—an allusion to Jesus' assumed origin in Nazaret, which did not fulfil the Messianic requirements noted in verse 42 ; but the point is that this is no *sudden* appearance, Jesus is a man whose antecedents are known—**' but when the Christ does come, no one will know where he comes from.'** It may be noted that in thus assuming the point of view of the people according to which Jesus was born at Nazaret, the Evangelist is reflecting the real opinion of the time and not merely the belief of his own day which took for granted the nativity at Bethlehem. Is this trait due to ' the Witness ' ? But though the Evangelist here uses the ordinary language of current Messianic expectation, it must be remembered that for him the word **Christ** has outgrown its limited significance of ' Messiah,' and has become almost an equivalent for ' Son of God,' with which phrase indeed it is frequently co-ordinated (11 : 27, 20 : 31). This comes out in Jesus' reply.

Theme : Christ's Divine Commission (7 : 28–52, 8 : 21–59)

28 So Jesus cried aloud, as he was teaching in the temple, ' You know me ? you know where I come from ? But I have not come on my own initiative ; I am sent, and sent by
29 Him who is real. You do not know Him, but I know
30 Him, because I have come from Him and He sent me.' So they tried to arrest him ; but no one laid hands on
31 him, because his time had not come yet. Indeed many of the people believed in him, saying, ' When the Christ does come, will he perform more Signs than this man ? '
32 The Pharisees heard the people discussing Jesus in this way, so the high-priests and the Pharisees despatched
33 attendants to arrest him. Then said Jesus, ' I will be with you a little longer, then I go to Him who sent me ;
34 you will search for me but you will not find me, and
35 where I go, you cannot come.' The Jews said to themselves, ' Where is he going, that we will not find him ? Is he off to the Dispersion among the Greeks, to teach the
36 Greeks ? What does he mean by saying, " You will search for me but you will not find me, and where I go, you cannot come " ? '

28   So Jesus—as if reading their thoughts—**cried aloud, as he was teaching in the temple.** The words that follow may be taken either as an admission on Christ's part of the superficial truth of the popular estimate, as if he were to say, ' It may be that you do know my **earthly** origin, but . . .' ; or, more probably, his reply is an ironical question: '**You know me ? you know where I come from ?** ' Nay—I have a heavenly origin too, of which you know nothing—'**I have not come on my own initiative,**' commissioned by no higher authority, '**I am sent, and sent by Him who is real** '—by One who so fully exemplifies the ideal relations between Sender and Sent that Jesus' mission by God may be said to be the archetype of
29 every true human mission.   It is this unique relation to the

Sender, possessed by Jesus only, which alone qualifies to give
a judgment on Jesus' origin ; Jesus, and not his critics, must
be the judge of the genuineness of his commission from God :
**'You do not know Him, but I know Him, because I have come
from Him and He sent me.'** Jesus' critics do not know the
Sender, and therefore have no right to pass judgment on the
Sent (cf. 5 : 37–38, 8 : 14). They have an eye only for his
earthly parentage, but Jesus sees beyond the shadow to the
reality. (For the thought cf. Mt. 11 : 27.)

So they tried to arrest him, as at 5 : 17 f., after a similar claim 30
to a unique relationship to God ; **but no one laid hands on him,
because his time had not come yet.** Jesus' words of verses
6 and 8 had proved true in spite of his action in coming up to
Jerusalem which seemed to contradict them. Thus does
John emphasize again the absolute independence of Jesus
from all outward constraint ; his fate is wholly self-determined.
(Cf. 8 : 59, 10 : 39, and esp. 10 : 17.) But the immediate cause
of Jesus' present escape was that the people were of two
minds : **Indeed many of the people believed in him, saying,** 31
**' When the Christ does come, will he perform more Signs than
this man ? '** Perhaps there is a hint here of the thirst for
miracles of the Galilean section of the crowd (cf. 4 : 48).
' The mention of miracles accuses their faith of imperfection,
but it also condemns the incredulity of the other Jews '
(Loisy).

The Pharisees heard the people discussing Jesus in this 32
**way, so the high-priests and the Pharisees despatched attendants
to arrest him.** (See note on 1 : 24.) John uses the title
high-priests not only of those who held the office of high-
priest but of members of the hierarchical families ; for him
the ' high-priests ' practically correspond to the Synoptic
Sadducees. Jesus warns his enemies that by his death they 33
will simply bring about for him his glorification with the
Father, and for themselves the shutting of the doorway to
salvation : **Then said Jesus, ' I will be with you a little longer,
then I go to Him who sent me ; you will search for me '—**
' not in penitence nor yet in anger, but simply in distress ' (West- 34
cott)—**' but you will not find me.'** Having rejected the Christ

the Jews will awake too late to the sense of their need, but
the opportunity will not recur (cf. Is. 55 : 6, Lk. 17 : 22,
19 : 43 f.). Christ will have passed beyond their ken, and
they cannot follow him : ' and where I go you cannot come.'
Christ alone could have led them to his own dwelling-place
with the Father (14 : 3), whereas now they must ' die in their
sins ' (8 : 21). There is a note of melancholy here which
recalls Mt. 23 : 37.

35   The Jews, misunderstanding Jesus' allusion to his heavenly
destination, construe it malevolently : **The Jews said to
themselves, 'Where is he going that we will not find him?
Is he off to the Dispersion among the Greeks, to teach the
Greeks ? '** They jeeringly conjecture that rejected by the
true Jews of Palestine Jesus will betake himself to the Jews
scattered throughout the Gentile world, and make them a
base of operations for teaching the Gentiles—as did Paul.
From the Evangelist's point of view the words would seem a
remarkable prophecy of the actual course of Christianity.
Jesus' friendship with the Samaritans would lend colour to
this conjecture. But not even this notion satisfies the Jews.

36 **'What does he mean by saying, " You will search for me but
you will not find me, and where I go, you cannot come "? '**
' Christ's words cannot be shaken off. . . . A vague sense remains
that there is in them some unfathomed meaning ' (Westcott).
Christ unfolds this in 13 : 33–14 : 6.

At this point a somewhat drastic rearrangement of the text
suggests itself : the sections up to the end of chapter 8 should
probably be read in the following order (omitting, as no part
of the original Gospel, the *Pericope de adultera*, 7 : 53–8 : 11) :
8 : 21–59, 7 : 45–52, 7 : 37–44. The section 8 : 12–20 has
already been inserted after chapter 5 *plus* 7 : 15–24. Note
first that the sequence from 7 : 52 to 8 : 21 is not satisfactory.
Jesus can hardly have been present at the inquiry of the chief
priests and Pharisees into the failure of the officers to arrest
him (7 : 45–52). Yet at 8 : 21 he renews to this audience a
discourse exactly similar to that broken off at 7 : 36. Further,
8 : 21 admittedly resumes the argument of 7 : 34, ' Then Jesus
said to them *again* . . .' With the text as it stands the

Jews' question in 7 : 35–36 is left in the air, contrary to the
Evangelist's usual manner. Elsewhere we note that such
questions, provoked by some difficult saying of Jesus, are asked
deliberately to prepare the way for a second declaration by him.
(We may compare 13 : 33 ff. and 16 : 16 ff.) Accordingly,
after the question of 7 : 36, we expect an immediate rejoinder
from Jesus, and this we have in 8 : 21. One more transposition,
that of 7 : 45–52 before 7 : 37–44, makes the sequence perfect.
As the text stands, at 7 : 32 the officers are sent to arrest Jesus,
but it is not till a new day has dawned at 7 : 37 that they report
to their masters at 7 : 45. With the suggested rearrangement,
at 7 : 32 the officers are despatched, at 8 : 59 they allow Jesus
to escape, and in the very next verse, 7 : 45, they are called
to account for their remissness ; moreover, these events can
now be assigned to a single day. We are then left with
7 : 37–44 as an impressive climax to the whole section dealing
with Jesus' visit to the Feast of Booths, the paragraph closing
(vers. 43–44), as so often in the Gospel (cf. 6 : 66 ff., 10 : 19 ff.),
with a note of the impression made upon the people. While
we adopt this rearrangement it may be more convenient to
follow in the commentary the usual order of the text. (For
the whole question of the rearrangement of the text of chapters
7 and 8 see the *Expository Times*, November 1921.)

Now on the last day, the great day, of the festival, Jesus 37
stood and cried aloud, ' If anyone is athirst, let him come to
me and drink ; he who believes in me—out of his body, as 38
scripture says, streams of living water will flow ' (he meant 39
by this the Spirit which those who believed in him were to
receive :—as yet there was no Spirit, because Jesus had not
been glorified yet). On hearing this some of the people 40
said, ' This really is the Prophet ' ; others said, ' He is the
Christ ' ; but others said, ' No, surely the Christ does not 41
come from Galilee ? Does not scripture say it is *from* 42
the offspring of David, from David's village of *Bethlehem*,
that the Christ is to come ? ' So the people were divided 43
over him; some wanted to arrest him, but no one laid 44
hands on him.

37 To the original seven days of the festival (Num. 29: 12,
Deut. 16: 13) there had been added an eighth day, kept as a
Sabbath (Lev. 23: 36, Num. 29: 35, Neh. 8: 18), as a day of
special rejoicing, on which the people left their booths and thus
commemorated the permanent settlement in the Holy Land.
The first and the eighth days were the most solemn, the
'great days,' of the festival.   Josephus calls the eighth day
'the sacred close of the year.'   It is of this day that we read:
**Now on the last day, the great day, of the festival, Jesus stood
and cried aloud, 'If anyone is athirst, let him come to me
and drink.'** (Cf. 4: 10, 14; 6: 35, Is. 55: 1.) The eighth
day had taken on the characteristics of a harvest festival, and
some think that Jesus' reference to 'drinking' is suggested
by the Bachanalian rites commonly associated with such a
festival.   Much more probably we have a reference to the
symbolism of the feast, on each morning of which a golden
pitcher, filled with water from Siloam, was poured out as a
libation in the temple court.   Even if it be true that this
ritual was discontinued on the eighth day, 'the void caused
by the absence of a ceremony performed on the preceding
days would be felt' (Lange), and Jesus seeks to fill it by
pointing the people to himself, in whom their spiritual thirst
38 may be satisfied: '**He who believes in me—out of his body, as
scripture says, streams of living water will flow,**' not an exact
quotation from Scripture, but a free citation in which we may
have echoes of e.g. Is. 43: 18–21, 44: 3, 48: 21, 55: 1, 58: 11.
The meaning will then be: either, that he who first drinks
from Christ will henceforth have within himself a perennial
source of life—the exact thought of 4: 14—or, that he who
first drinks from Christ will in turn himself become the source
of life to others, just as Christ, by living on the Father, obtains
the power to feed others (6: 57).   To this we have a remarkable
parallel from the Talmud: 'Quando homo se convertit ad
Dominum suum, tanquam fons aquis vivis impletur, et fluenta
ejus egrediuntur ad omnis generis homines et ad omnes tribus.'
The difficulty is to see the force of 'out of his body,' which some
ingeniously explain as a metaphor from a fountain built in
the form of a human statue.   The meaning becomes much

clearer if we can refer the verse not to the believer but to Christ. This is possible if we translate, as the Greek admits, ' If anyone is athirst, let him come to me ; and let him drink who believes on me ; as scripture says, out of his body (i.e. the Messiah's, who in a quotation would naturally be referred to not in the first but in the third person) streams of living water will flow.' There is no place in ' Scripture ' where it is said that believers themselves become fountains of water. But if the verse be applied to Christ, an apposite reference is possible to Exod. 17 : 6, Ps. 105 : 41, an image used by the prophets, Ezek. 47 : 1, 12, Joel 3 : 18. The pouring forth of the water of Siloam at the festival was actually in commemoration of the Rock in the Wilderness, while 1 Cor. 10 : 4 shows that the image was used of Christ. The expression ' **out of his body** ' may now be explained as an anticipation of the scene in 19 : 34, which gives a symbolical illustration of this passage. Burney, however (*Aramaic Origin*, p. 109 ff.), suggests that the words are due to the confusion of the Aramaic *me'yin* (' bowels ') with *me'yan* (' fountain '), and would translate, ' as the scripture hath said, Rivers shall flow forth from the fountain of living waters ' (Zech. 14 : 8, etc.). Cyprian, among others, seems to have referred verse 38 to Christ, and in a letter from the Church of Lyons to Gallic Christians (A.D. 175), we read of a certain martyr ' besprinkled and strengthened by the heavenly fountain of the water of life that issues from the navel of Jesus.'

Once this interpretation is accepted the comment in the 39 following verse becomes quite apposite, and indeed expresses a characteristic thought of the Gospel : **he meant by this the Spirit which those who believed in him were to receive :—as yet there was no Spirit, because Jesus had not been glorified yet.** Strictly the meaning is ' as yet there was no *communication* of the Spirit,' for this John held to be impossible (16 : 17, 20 : 17 ; cf. Acts 2 : 32-33) except in conjunction with Jesus' ' glorification,' an idea which in our Gospel may almost be said to fore-shorten his death (11 : 4, 12 : 23, 13 : 31), resurrection and exaltation (17 : 1, 5, etc.) into one event. The Spirit was to take the place of Jesus (14 : 16), and therefore could not be

communicated while he was yet present in the flesh. Christ's
death thus becomes the condition alike of his ' glory ' and of his
full spiritual activity. There is probably no allusion to any
definite event such as Pentecost. Note that, just as in
4 : 13 f., 23 f., an allusion to the living water is explained by
reference to the Spirit, the reality of which water is but the
symbol (1 : 33).

40   There follows a summary of the varied impressions left by
Jesus' teaching on the people (cf. Mk. 8 : 27 ff.) : **On hearing
this**—not merely the immediately preceding claim, but the
whole tenor of Jesus' teaching at the festival—**some of the**
41 **people said, ' This really is the Prophet ' ; others said, ' He
is the Christ '**—two stages in the growth of belief (cf. 4 : 19, 29 ;
9 : 17, 38. For the distinction between ' the prophet ' and
' the Christ ' see note on 1 : 21, 6 : 14.) **But others said, ' No,
surely the Christ does not come from Galilee,'** which, accord-
42 ing to this Gospel (4 : 44), was Jesus' ' own country.' **' Does
not scripture say it is from the offspring of David, from
David's village of Bethlehem, that the Christ is to come ? '** The
tradition was based on such passages as Micah 5 : 2, Is. 11 : 1,
Jer. 23 : 5. David spent his boyhood at Bethlehem (1 Sam.
16 : 1, 4, etc.). It may be that Jesus' Galilean connexions
were urged as an objection to Christianity in the Evangelist's
own day, possibly by the ' Baptist Sect.' From the fact that
John gives no answer to this objection it has been assumed
that he did not accept the ' fictions ' of the early chapters of
Matthew and Luke. (But see note on ver. 27.) In truth,
to John the question was a matter of indifference ; for him,
as for Jesus himself (Mk. 12 : 35 ff.), the Christ is not David's
son but his Lord.

43   Once again (cf. 31) Jesus owes immunity to the lack of
unanimity on the part of his foes : **So the people were divided
44 over him ; some wanted to arrest him, but no one laid hands
on him.**

45 **Then the attendants went back to the high-priests and Pharisees, who asked them, ' Why have you not brought him
46   with you ? '** **The attendants replied, ' No man ever**

spoke as he does.' The Pharisees retorted, ' Are you 47
misled as well ? Have any of the authorities or of the 48
Pharisees believed in him ? As for this mob, with its 49
ignorance of the Law—it is accursed ! ' Nicodemus, one 50
of their number (the same who had come to him before),
said to them, ' But surely our Law does not condemn the 51
accused before hearing what he has to say and ascertaining
his offence ? ' They answered him, ' And are you from 52
Galilee, too ? Search and you will see that no prophet
ever springs from Galilee.' ·

For the true position of the following paragraph see note
before 7 : 37. It seems strange that the attendants despatched
at 32 (at least a day previously, for a new day begins at 37)
should only now return to report their failure : **Then the 45
attendants went back to the high-priests and Pharisees, who
asked them, 'Why have you not brought him with you ? '**
The high-priests and Pharisees are the Johannine equivalent
for the Sanhedrim. The authorities cannot understand why
their order has not been carried out. With our proposed
rearrangement the reason is stated at 8 : 59. Jesus had
miraculously slipped through their hands. They have been
thwarted, they know not how, by Jesus' divine ' self-determination,' and it only remains to plead in excuse that they have been
paralysed by Jesus' power of speech : **The attendants replied, 46
' No man ever spoke as he does.'** There is no real faith on the
attendants' part, yet their blind admiration serves as a foil
to the stubborn hostility of their masters : **The Pharisees 47
retorted, ' Are you misled as well ? '**—even you, whose duty
it is as officials not to reason why, but to obey. **' Have any 48
of the authorities**—the only capable arbiters in matters
religious (3 : 1)—**or of the Pharisees**—the guardians of
orthodoxy—**believed in him ? '** Those who do believe are
negligible. **' As for this mob, with its ignorance of the Law— 49
it is accursed ! '** Even though ignorant of the Law they come
under its curse through their violation of it ! The Pharisees
regularly contrasted with themselves, as students of the
Law, the ignorant mob or *am-haarets*. 'Sacerdotal anger is

fond of putting on esoteric airs ' (Godet). The Pharisees'
objection to Jesus is a throw-back from that of the Jews of
the Evangelist's own day, who would ridicule Christianity as
drawing all its converts from the poor and ignorant (1 Cor.
1 : 26 ff.). But though among Christians there were ' not
many' educated men, John hints that there were at least
some, though they might be timid ; for Nicodemus protests :
50 **Nicodemus, one of their number, the same who had come to
him before** (the A.V. ' by night ' seems to be an addition
51 after 19 : 39 ; for Nicodemus see 3 : 1 ff.), **said to them,
' But surely our Law does not condemn the accused before
hearing what he has to say and ascertaining his offence ? '**
The protest should have weight as coming from ' one of their
number,' i.e., one of the Pharisaic members of the Sanhedrim.
Are Jesus' accusers sure that in condemning him unheard
they are not themselves violating the Law ?   (See Deut. 1 : 16,
17 : 4, Exod. 23 : 1.)   The Pharisees' only reply is a sarcastic
52 pleasantry : **They answered him, ' And are you** (emphatic—
' you, who are so obviously a Jerusalemite ! ') **from Galilee
too ? '**—and therefore disposed to side with a fellow-countryman (cf. Mk. 14 : 70). ' **Search** (the Scriptures) **and you will
see that no prophet ever springs from Galilee.'**   According to
2 Kings 14 : 25, Jonah hailed from Galilee ; and what of
Elijah, Elisha, Hosea, Nahum, Amos ?   But the fact that the
tense of the word ' springs ' is present rather than perfect,
perhaps suggests that the reference is to the future rather
than to the past.   Galilee had few prophetic traditions, and
was not the district from which Messiah was to be expected.

An Interpolated Incident : Jesus and the Adulteress
(7 : 53–8 : 11)

This section interrupts the sequence of the narrative, and
though there is no reason to doubt that we have here an
authentic piece of evangelical tradition, both external and
internal evidence goes to show that it is no original part of the
Gospel.   It is omitted by all the oldest Greek MSS. except
one (D), and by a large number of the more reliable later

MSS.; while those which do contain it frequently either obelize the passage as doubtful, or even insert it in a different context, e.g. at the end of the Gospel, after 7: 36, or even after Lk. 21. There are also many textual variations. Early Fathers such as Origen, Theodore of Mopsuestia, Chrysostom, Cyril of Alexandria, Tertullian, Cyprian, did not read it as part of the Gospel, and though Jerome retained it in his Latin text and Ambrose and Augustine argue for its authenticity, this counts little against the weight of earlier evidence. The internal evidence is equally strong. Neither the language nor the tone of the narrative is Johannine: Greek words occur used nowhere else in John, and indeed the whole style and thought is much more akin to that of the Synoptists. This is the ' only narrative in the Fourth Gospel in which the utterances of Jesus do not serve the purpose of his own glorification, but are spoken entirely for the sake of the persons with whom he is dealing' (Schmiedel). It seems probable that we have here an authentic fragment of Synoptic tradition belonging to the days immediately before the Passion (one group of MSS. inserts it after Lk. 21, while Holtzmann suggests a position after Mk. 12 : 17 ; see note on 8 : 6) which failed to find a place in one of the canonical Gospels—perhaps because it offended the taste of the early Church and seemed subversive of moral discipline—but was preserved in one of the non-canonical Gospels (e.g. Eusebius states that the work of Papias contained ' the story of a woman accused before the Lord of numerous sins, a story contained also in the Gospel of the Hebrews '), whence presumably it found its way into our Gospel, and was inserted at this point perhaps as an illustration of 7 : 24 and 8 : 15.

And every one of them went home. Who? If the sentence 53 belongs to the original narrative, then apparently the Pharisees are meant, in which case ' the remark is an utterly idle one' (Godet) : if, as is more likely, it is part of the borrowed paragraph, then the phrase has no connexion with the previous scene, and we have no means of knowing to whom it refers, unless it be, as Holtzmann suggests, the audience of Mk. 12 : 17.

But Jesus went to the Hill of Olives—not elsewhere mentioned 1 in the Gospel, but the place to which, according to Luke (21 : 37, 22 : 39), Jesus repaired each evening during the last week. Note the similarity of the next verse to Lk. 21 : 38, 2 after which one group of MSS. inserts the paragraph : **Early in the morning he returned to the temple, the people all came to him, and he sat down** (Mk. 9 : 35, Lk. 4 : 20 ; in Jn. 7 : 37 Jesus ' stands ') **and taught them**—perhaps in Solomon's Portico (10 : 23). The Greek words both for ' early ' and for ' people ' (John uses ' crowd ') are Synoptic, not Johannine, as is also the title ' scribes ' in the next verse (John uses 3 ' high-priests,' 7 : 32) : **The Scribes and Pharisees brought a woman who had been caught in the act of committing adultery,** 4 **and making her stand forward they said to him, ' Teacher**— addressing him with an appearance of deference—**this woman was caught in the very act of committing adultery.'** The woman would in the ordinary course have been tried before the Jews' own court, but by bringing her to Jesus they 5 thought to lay a trap for him (6). **' Now Moses has commanded us in the Law to stone such creatures.'** Lev. 20 : 10, Deut. 22 : 22 give death (without any particulars) as the penalty of adultery ; Deut. 22 : 23 f. specifies stoning in the case of a betrothed virgin. But stoning was probably held to be implied in all cases (cf. Ezek. 16 : 38–41) in spite of the Talmudic dictum that death *simpliciter* meant ' strangling.' 6 **' But what do you say ? '** They said this to test him, in order to get a charge against him—hoping that with his habitual pity he would exonerate the woman and so lay himself open to the charge of contempt of the Law, while if he bade stone her he might be accused before Pilate of encroaching on the rights of the Roman authority which alone had the power of life and death. The test is exactly parallel to the other questions addressed to Jesus in the Synoptics (Mk. 12 : 13–34, in which section Holtzmann would place this narrative) and might be expected to place Jesus in a similar dilemma.

7 **Jesus stooped down, and began to write with his finger on the ground.** There is no point in asking what Jesus wrote, for the significance lay not in what was written but in the gesture itself. The action was meant not to give an answer,

but as a hint that no answer was to be given. It is the action of a man who is preoccupied, angered both at 'the shame of the deed itself and the brazen hardness of the prosecutors' (*Ecce Homo*), and holding his feelings under strict control. Jesus' gesture was a perfectly natural one, such as any one of us might find ourselves copying when sitting, perhaps with a stick in hand, in a preoccupied or pensive mood. Jesus, oriental fashion, would be sitting on the ground (2), so the action is not so strange as it sounds. (For a similar refusal on Jesus' part to act as judge cf. Lk. 12: 13 f.) But Jesus' questioners will not rest content with silence: **But as they persisted with their question, he raised himself and said to them, 'Let the innocent among you throw the first stone,'**—'innocent' not of all sin, else no man could be fit to judge, but of a similar sin—if not actually adultery, then at least some sin of unchastity, if not in deed, then in thought. Let them judge themselves before they presume to judge another. 'The wonderful art displayed in Jesus' answer consists in its removal of the question from the judicial sphere, in which his adversaries had placed it, to that moral province beyond which he did not for the present care to extend his authority' (Godet). The man to throw the first stone would take the place of 'the Witness' as laid down in Deut. 17: 7. **Then he stooped** 8 **down again and wrote on the ground**—as if to show that he had done with the matter. **And on hearing what he said,** 9 **they went away one by one** (the A.V. gives the true reason for their departure, 'being convicted by their own conscience,' but this is an addition), **beginning with the older men**—i.e. in order of precedence, not necessarily with the idea that the older men had the more tender consciences or had been guilty of more sins. So the company melted away **till Jesus was left alone with the woman standing before him**—one of the intensely dramatic moments of the Gospel (cf. 4: 26). **Looking up, Jesus said to her, 'Woman, where are they?** 10 **Has no one condemned you?'** 'Is no one prepared to accept my challenge and begin the stoning?' **She said, 'No one,** 11 **Sir.' Jesus said, 'Neither do I!'**—although, as alone being 'innocent,' Jesus, if any, might have condemned her (Rom.

8 : 33 f.). Jesus thus illustrates the truth of 3 : 17, 7 : 24, 8 : 15—the motive perhaps for the insertion of the incident, though the 'judgment' of these passages is a conception distinct from the 'condemnation' here. But though Jesus does not condemn the woman, he does condemn her sin, as is shown by his words of dismissal, 'Be off, and never sin again !' There is no positive declaration of forgiveness, as in Lk. 7 : 48–50. The woman is not 'justified' (Rom. 3 : 24), but by Jesus' 'forbearance' her sin had been 'passed over' (Rom. 3 : 25).

[8 : 12–20. This section has been commented on after 7 : 24. See note, p. 192 f.]

(For proposed rearrangement of text see note p. 204 f.)

21 Then he said to them again—thus picking up his hearers' question at 7 : 36, which verse this section should immediately follow—'I go away, and you will search for me, but you will die in your sin;—because you cannot find me as Saviour and Messiah (note on 7 : 33–34)—where I go, you cannot come '; 'and the issue was not failure only but death, and death in sin, for the search under false motives, with false ends, was itself sin' (Westcott). Contrast Jesus' words to his own disciples (13 : 33 ff.), in whose case the disability to 22 'follow' him is only temporary (13 : 36, 14 : 3.) So the Jews said, 'Will he kill himself ? Is that why he says, "Where I go you cannot come "?' Death would seem to be the only way along which such as they could not follow Jesus, for at least they have no desire to die for him ! Some (quoting Josephus) see an allusion to the hell of suicides whither pious Jews would refuse to follow this fanatic. It may be that we have here an echo of a possible objection brought against Christ in the Evangelist's day : so far from dying to fulfil God's purpose, he merely courted death like some Stoic suicide. The Jews' misunderstanding leads up, as usual, to a fuller explanation by Jesus : they cannot follow him because in origin, affinities, and outlook they and he belong 23 to different worlds : He said to them, 'You are from the world below, I am from the world above : you belong to

this world, I do not belong to this world ' (cf. 3 : 31). The
second half of the verse explains the first ; for ' this world'
' signifies human life as constituted independently of, and
consequently in opposition to, the will of God ' (Godet). Jesus
draws his own out of this world (17 : 6, etc.) ; the process by
which that separation takes place is faith (1 : 12) ; but the
Jews have not believed : ' So I told you, you would die in 24
your sins ; for unless you believe that I am, you will die in
your sins.' It seéms better here to take the words ' I am '
in an absolute sense and see in them a ' mystic formula '
(Loisy) complete in itself (cf. 8 : 28, 58 ; 13 : 19) and hinting
at Christ's participation in the deity of the Father (the
phrase being an echo of e.g. Exod 3 : 14, Deut. 32 : 39, Is.
43 : 10), rather than to translate, as does Moffatt, ' who I am,'
or to supply a predicate from the context (as may be done
in 4 : 26, 9 : 9, 18 : 5 f.), and interpret ' that I am Messiah '
(Meyer), or ' that I am from the world above ' (Dods, Holtzmann). The Jews still try to get a clear answer—They said, 25
' Who are you ? '—but instead of giving it Jesus replied,
first with an exclamation of exasperation, ' Why should I
talk to you at all ? ' (among a host of translations this is
undoubtedly the best ; for the spirit of the exclamation cf.
Mk. 9 : 19), and then with an enigma, ' I have a great deal to 26
say about you and many a judgment to pass upon you ; but
He who sent me is true, and so I tell the world what I have
learned from Him.' The meaning would seem to be either
' you incite me to pass hard verdicts upon you, but I restrain
myself, for there is only one real judge, and it is His verdict
and not mine (5 : 30) that I must pronounce to the world ' :
or perhaps better (for Jesus does proceed to say many harsh
things of his hearers), ' the verdict I have to pass is a hard
one, but, however unpleasant the hearing, it must be pronounced, for He to pronounce whose verdict I am sent is the
Truth, and I am here simply to declare what He reveals to
me !' Wellhausen supposes that the original reading may
have been : ' I have much to say about *myself* and much
testimony to bear to myself.' (Cf. 5 : 30-32, 8 : 14-16.)
Again the Jews ' misunderstand ' : They did not understand he 27

was speaking to them about the Father (cf. 8 : 18 ff.)—a comment by the Evangelist himself, not by the Redactor, for the Gospel abounds with similar allusions to an almost inconceivable dulness on the part of the Jews. Therefore Jesus proceeds to expound the Father by means of that mystic phrase ' I

28 *am* ' which hints at his oneness with God Himself: so Jesus said, ' When you have lifted up the Son of man, you will know then that I am (cf. Exod. 7 : 5, Is. 52 : 6)—that my being is to be interpreted by the Father's and the Father's by mine—and that (therefore) I do nothing of my own accord, but speak as the Father has taught me ' (5 : 30 f.) In ' lifted up ' there is a reference to the Cross as the beginning of Christ's ' glory ' (cf. 3 : 14; 12 : 32 f., and note on 7 : 39). It is in the Cross that Jesus' Godhead, his ' equivalence to the Father ' (5 : 18) will most clearly appear. The Cross not only reveals the nature of Jesus but the nature of God, not only the divinity of Jesus, but the Christlikeness of God. By contemplating the Cross the Jews will get their answer as to what Jesus means

29 by the Father. ' He who sent me is at my side ; He has not left me alone ; for I always do what pleases Him.' (Cf. 10 : 17 f., 15 : 10.) To share God's thoughts, to ' speak as He has taught,' we must first do His will (7 : 17). The last clause of the verse gives the evidence for the truth of the first two, rather than the cause (cf. Lk. 7 : 47) : the fact of the Father's presence is proved by the obedience of the Son's will. This is a much deeper truth than the converse, that consciousness of the presence is the reward of obedience—though both thoughts are equally true.

30 As he said this, a number believed in him. But we are soon shown how little such faith amounts to. As the discourse proceeds Jesus' hearers quickly lapse back to the point of view of ' the Jews,' and Jesus addresses them as such. At 37 they ' want to kill him ' ; at 44 ' their father is the devil ' ; at 59 they try to stone Jesus ; all of which emphasizes how superficial in John's view (cf. 2 : 23 f.) was any faith on the part of ' the Jews.' Indeed, though the conversation is

31 introduced with the words so Jesus addressed the Jews who had believed in him, saying—the controversial note is so

prominent throughout that we are tempted to suspect that the Evangelist has forgotten that the address begins as one to ' believers.' Possibly ' who believed in him ' may be a gloss, for from John's point of view ' Jews who believed ' is almost a contradiction in terms. As if to test this profession of faith Jesus says, ' **If you abide by what I say, you are really disciples of mine,**' that is, if they are not merely content with the first profession of faith but remain loyal to it ; to ' abide in ' teaching means to penetrate through from its letter to its spirit ; as a result ' **you will understand the truth, and the 32 truth will set you free.**' They will ' understand the truth ' because they are obedient to it (7 : 17) and have the knowledge which only experimental testing of it can bring (see esp. note on 10 : 15). Such knowledge makes a man ' free ': ' the man with astigmatism, or myopia, or whatever else it is, must get the glasses that will show him the real world, and he is safe, and free to go and come as he pleases. See the real in the moral sphere, and the first great peril is gone ' (T. R. Glover). The ' truth ' is ' the full revelation of the true nature of things ' (Godet), and such moral vision frees man from the power of evil. There is a striking parallel in Epictetus (4 : 7) : ' I am freed by God, I know His commandments, no one can any longer enslave me.' The Jews looked for Messiah to liberate them from the Roman yoke : Jesus offers them a better ' freedom.' But the Jews pick up his words as if they refer not to moral, but to civil and political, liberty : ' **We are Abraham's offspring,**' they retorted, ' **we 33 have never been slaves to anybody. What do you mean by saying, " You will be free " ? '** As ' Abraham's offspring ' they were ideally destined to rule all peoples, and each individual was subject to God alone. The Egyptian, Babylonian, Syrian and Roman conquests are ignored, though in 19 : 15 the people acknowledge their subjection. Jesus, in reply, shows that it is of *moral* liberty that he speaks. Note how the following verses reflect a whole series of Pauline ideas. **Jesus replied, ' Truly, truly I tell you, everyone who commits 34 sin is a slave '** (omit ' of sin ' as a gloss). (Cf. Rom. 6 : 16, 20 ; 2 Pet. 2 : 19, and the Stoic saying ' solus sapiens est liber.')

By John sin is conceived not as a positive principle, but rather as a privation or limitation of the full life which may be had in Christ. Godet explains the verse as meaning that the man who commits sin is ' a slave in the house of God,' i.e. ' fear and servility characterize his relation to God.' Both ideas may be combined, for ' the slave *of* sin becomes by that very fact a slave *with respect to* God.' Certainly in 35 it is God, 35 not sin, who is regarded as the Master. **' Now the slave does not remain in the household for all time ; the son of the house does.'** (For the argument, cf. Gal. 4 : 1–7, 21–31 ; Heb. 3 : 5–6.) Having been mastered by sin the Jews are slaves, and as such have lost the right, which originally they had as sons of Abraham, to a permanent place in the household of God. For it is only ' the son of the house ' who has such a right (a slave may be sold or dismissed at any time), and for the new religion, sonship is a matter of spiritual and moral, 36 not of physical, birth (3 : 5). **' So, if the Son sets you free, you will be really free.'** If *the* Son *par excellence*—Christ who perfectly realizes this filial relationship in the household of God—gives them such freedom, and the entrance to the household implied by it, as he has himself, they will be really free, in contrast to the false claim of 33. (Cf. Rom. 8 : 2, Gal. 5 : 1.) The Son of the house is the only one besides the Father who has the right to free the slaves. How this freedom is wrought out according to Paul is shown in Gal. 4 : 1–7. From John's point of view the Son frees because he is himself the truth (8 : 32, 14 : 6). The argument that follows is 37 exactly parallel to that of Mt. 3 : 9 ff. and Rom. 9. **' I know you are Abraham's offspring '**—by physical descent, **' yet '** not by spiritual birth, as is clear from the fact that **' you want to kill me, since my word makes no headway** (or ' holds no place ') **among you '**—an impossible remark to ' believers ' (31 note), and in fact unlikely in any real conversation even with unbelieving Jews. Jesus would hardly thus deliberately exasperate his hearers. But the words are natural enough if, under the guise of a discourse, the Evangelist is picturing the stubborn opposition of Judaism to the spread of Chris- 38 tianity. **' I speak of what I have seen with my Father, and**

you act as you have learned from your father.' The Jews'
opposition to Jesus was morally inevitable, for their difference
of outlook corresponds to a still more profound difference of
origin. If Jesus speaks as he is prompted by a clear intuition
of *his* Father's will (i.e. God's), it is to be expected that they
will treat him as is suggested to them by *their* father (i.e. the
devil, 44). (For Jesus' claim that his teaching depends on a
direct vision of God cf. 3 : 32, 6 : 46.) **They answered him,** 39
' Abraham is our father,'—and therefore our inherited disposition can be nothing but good ! **' If you are Abraham's
children,'** said Jesus, **' then** (according to the principle of 38)
do as Abraham did.' True sons of Abraham would share
Abraham's faith (Gen. 15 : 6, Jn. 6 : 29). Perhaps John
hints that the Jewish opponents of Christ in his own day
are to be classed among those ' who style themselves Jews—
no Jews are they, but a mere synagogue of Satan ! ' (Rev.
2 : 9). Abraham would have welcomed Jesus (56) : **' but** 40
**now you want to kill me, to kill a man who has told you the
truth, the truth I have learned from God.'** It is this identifying of himself and his message with God which, according to
John, is at the root of the Jews' hatred of Jesus (5 : 18, etc.) ;
thus their conduct is ' murder based on hostility to God '
(Dods) : **' Abraham did not do that. You do the deeds of** 41
your father ! '—so, whoever that father be, he is *not* Abraham !
   Apparently it now dawns on the Jews that it is spiritual
descent which is in question. ' You admit,' **they said to him,**
' our physical descent from Abraham. Well, our spiritual
descent, our peculiar relation to God so closely bound up
with the Abrahamic heritage, is just as unquestionable ' :
' We are no bastards : we have one father, even God ! ' There
has been no adulterous disloyalty to Yahweh (cf. Hosea 2 : 4,
etc., for the figure of speech) ; there is no idolatrous blood in
their veins. Yet the sudden change of subject on the part
of the Jews (from physical to spiritual descent) is a little odd,
and one feels that John is deliberately arguing up to the
climax at 44 and introduces ' God ' here as a foil to ' the
devil ' there. Jesus refutes this claim as he did the other (39),
' by laying down a moral fact by which their claims are

shattered' (Godet). They shall be known by their fruits:
42 the principle of 38 still holds good : **Said Jesus, ' If God were
your father, you would love me** (as your brother), **for I came
here from God** (my *origin* is divine ; 13 : 3, 16 : 28) ; **I did not
come of my own accord** (i.e. without a commission from
God), **I was sent by Him '** (my *mission* too is divine). Thus
the Jews' misunderstanding has a moral root in their evil
43 heredity : **'Why do you not understand my speech ?**—
Jesus' characteristic way of expressing himself—**Because
you are unable to listen to what I am saying,'** i.e. because they
shrink from the moral content of his message. The old truth
that our so-called *intellectual* difficulties more often than not
have their root in an unregenerate *will*. To use a modern
metaphor, our ' reception ' is poor because our moral ' set '
is not ' tuned to God's wave-length.' Thus is reached the
44 climax of Jesus' indictment : **' You belong to your father the
devil, and you want to do what your father desires ;**—above
all to compass the death of Christ—**he was a slayer of men
from the very beginning,'** that is, either ' since the devil by
tempting to disobedience first made men liable to death '
(Gen. 2, 17) ; or possibly ' since the first murder, that of Abel,
which was suggested by the devil' (cf. 1 Jn. 3 : 12, 15).
While Paul traces death to the sin of one man (Rom. 5 : 12 ff.),
John goes behind Adam to Satan, in whom (from a point of
view which has affinity with Persian dualism—a dualism often
noted in this Gospel, e.g. note on 1 : 5, 12) he sees the
personification of sin and death, as in Christ he sees the
personification of truth and life. **' And he has no place in
truth,'** that is, the truth is not the sphere in which the devil
moves ; his attitude to truth corresponds to his own inherent
nature : he shuns truth **' because there is no truth in him '**—
his nature is false through and through, so that **' when he
tells a lie, he is expressing his own nature** (Mt. 12 : 34), **for he
is a liar and the father of lies,'** or possibly ' and the father of
liars,' implying ' he is *your* father and *you* are liars ' (55).

[Some critics would translate the above verse, ' You belong
to the Father of the Devil,' i.e. to the Demiurge (as distinct
from the supreme God), with whom John, following the

Gnostics, is here supposed to identify the God of the O.T.
and of his hearers. The last words of the verse could then
be more simply translated: ' he (the devil) is a liar, and his
father (the Demiurge) is a liar also.' But there is no hint
of this idea in the rest of the Gospel, and the emphasis here
is upon the devil, not on his imaginary father. The Jews
are the children of the devil, not his brothers (1 Jn. 3: 10).]

Being children of falsehood the Jews cannot but mistrust 45
him who is the Truth: 'But as for *me*' (the position of the word
is emphatic, contrasting Christ with the devil)—' it is because
I tell the truth that you do not believe me,'—a reason for incredulity the reverse of the usual! 'Which of you can convict 46
me of sin?' Calvin remarks here that ' the defence should be
restricted to the circumstances of the case,' and not taken here
as a claim to entire sinlessness of life; but without doubt
John would understand the words in the latter sense (cf.
7: 18). ' Sin ' here means more than an ' error ' of inexact-
ness; logically, no doubt, we would here expect Christ to
disclaim not ' sin ' in general, but falsehood. But as ' truth '
in our Gospel is much more than the reverse of falsehood, so
many other sins besides that of falsehood would be considered
a violation of ' truth.' Only a man free of all moral wrong is
one who ' tells the truth.' Just as the Jews' misunderstanding
has a moral cause (42), so it is Jesus' moral perfection which
guarantees the truth of his words. 'If I tell the truth, why do
you not believe me?'—a question already answered in 44–45:
it is just because Jesus *does* tell the truth that they do not
believe. If, on the contrary, their moral parentage were
different, they *would* believe: 'He who belongs to God listens 47
to the words of God (6: 37, 44; 3: 21); you do not listen to
them, because you do not belong to God.'

To Jesus' denial to them of Abrahamic and divine descent 48
the Jews retorted that Jesus himself is no true Jew, and that it
is *he* who has devilry in his blood, thus turning back both
Jesus' charges on his own head: 'Are we not right in saying
you are a Samaritan (i.e. an outcast heretic, an enemy of his
own people), you are mad?' (lit. ' have a devil '; note on 7: 20;
cf. Mt. 12: 24–27, etc.). Edersheim points out that the

Aramaic word here rendered into Greek by 'Samaritan may have been *Shomroni*, which would literally mean 'child of Satan.' If so, still more point would be added to the taunt.

49 Jesus replied, 'I am not mad : I honour my Father and you dishonour me ' ; ' my actions are due not to madness, but to the desire to honour God ; how can you, who dishonour one
50 who honours God, yourselves be God's children ? ' 'However (I do not resent these insults, because) I do not aim at my own credit' (5 : 41). Yet none can lightly dishonour Jesus, for 'there is One who cares for my credit, and he is judge.' And it is only those who listen to Jesus who will escape that
51 Judge's condemnation: 'Truly, truly I tell you, if anyone holds to what I say, he will never see death '—an emphatic repetition of 5 : 24, where see notes. (For the expression 'see death,' cf. Lk. 2 : 26, Heb. 11 : 5.) Again the Jews misunderstand Jesus, taking his reference to 'death' in a literal sense:
52 The Jews said to him, ' Now we are sure you are mad. Abraham is dead, and so are all the prophets ; and you declare, "If anyone holds to what I say, he will never taste death ! " ' For ' taste death,' as a bitter cup which all must drink, cf. Mk. 9 : 1. But the Jews misquote Jesus, who said ' see death.' Strictly even a believer may ' taste death' (Heb. 2 : 9), though he has not the long, tense experience of it implied in ' seeing.'
53 'Are you greater than our father Abraham ? He is dead, and the prophets are dead. Who do you claim to be ? ' In claiming for his own words a power to conquer death which was not experienced, even in their own persons, by those who in the past were the organs of God's word, Jesus is surely setting up to be greater than they. Whom then does he take himself
54 for ? No more than at 25 does Jesus give a direct answer ; but again, as there, he emphasizes his unique relation to the Father. He repeats the truth of 5 : 31–32, substituting the idea of ' glory ' for that of testimony : it is only as the Father's ' commissioner ' that Jesus claims divine standing. Jesus replied, ' Were I to glorify myself, my glory would be nothing ; it is my Father who glorifies me.' ' Glorify' seems to be used here with two shades of meaning, first in the ordinary sense of self-praise, and then in the peculiar Johannine sense, for

which see 7 : 39. 'You say, "He is our God," but you do not 55 understand him' (5 : 37). Their misunderstanding of God is proved by the rejection of his commissioner. (Cf. also 4: 22.) 'I know him'—the Greek word ' know ' (as opposed to ' understand' which is used of knowledge acquired by observation) implying the direct intuition of one who in mind and will is one with God. 'Were I to say, "I do not know him," I would be a liar like yourselves.' In Jesus' case the lie would consist not in making such claims but in veiling them behind a false modesty. The Jews are liars because they claim to know God when they do not: conversely Jesus would be a liar if he confessed not to know God when he did. 'But I do know him and I hold to his word'—thus fulfilling the two conditions necessary for the possession of ' eternal life ' (17 : 3, 8 : 51).

Once again Jesus contrasts the Jews' attitude with that of 56 Abraham, whose parentage they claim: ' Abraham exulted that he was to see my Day,' i.e. the day of Christ's earthly manifestation (Lk. 17: 22 ff.). [Burney (*Aramaic Origin*, p. 111) thinks that the sense ' *longed* to see ' is required both by grammar and context, and suggests an original Aramaic verb, which can mean both ' long ' and ' exult,' of which he supposes our Greek to be a mistranslation.] Late Jewish thought depicted the patriarchs as rising from Sheol to greet the Messiah on his appearance (so Moses and Elias hail Christ at the Transfiguration). Even in his earthly lifetime Abraham may have been said, in the contemplation of such a covenant as Gen. 22 : 15 ff., to have ' seen the promises far away and hailed them' (Heb. 11: 13) as foreshadowing ' my day.' But when Jesus adds 'He did see it,' the meaning is not that Abraham had any such vision while still on earth (e.g. figuratively in the birth of Isaac; Gen. 21 : 1 ff.), but that he is *not* dead, as the Jews wrongly hold (52), but still consciously follows the fortunes of his people (cf. Mk. 12: 26 f.) ' and he rejoiced ' at Christ's coming, even while that people scorned it. To the Jews this seems to imply a claim to be Abraham's contemporary: Then said the Jews to him, 'You are not fifty years 57 old, and Abraham has seen you?' (or, as A.V., 'hast thou

seen Abraham ? '). ' Fifty years ' is perhaps a round number
used without any intention of stating Jesus' exact age. Jesus,
they say, is not yet past the prime of life. Lightfoot thinks
that the figure is determined by the age when Levites retired
(Num. 4 : 3, 39). Irenaeus evidently understands the passage
literally, for he quotes our Gospel as evidence that Jesus taught
till he was forty or fifty (Irenaeus, II. 22 : 5). For the theory
that the number is symbolical see note on 2 : 20. Jesus finally
answers his questioners with an absolute statement of his
58 pre-existence (for which see 1 : 1) : ' Truly, truly I tell you,' said
Jesus, ' before Abraham was born I am '—the present tense
marking a timeless existence and the mystic phrase (cf. 8 : 24,
28) once again emphasizing Jesus' oneness with God.
59 At this they picked up stones to throw at him ; but their
attempt to murder him was ' like the waves lifting themselves
up to drown the stars ' (Strachan): but Jesus concealed himself
and made his way out of the temple. The order of the words
is significant—not ' went out and hid himself,' but ' hid
himself and went out,' the idea evidently being that Jesus
miraculously disappeared, as indeed is hinted by the addition
in the A.V. ' going through the midst of them, and so passed
by.' Jesus, according to John, is inviolable (cf. 7: 30, 10: 39,
12 : 36). At this point Jesus symbolically abandons his own
people (the temple) and goes out to humanity (the man born
blind ; chap. 9).

SECTION II. THE DIVINE NATURE OF THE CHRIST

Illustration : The Blind Man healed (9 : 1–38)

1 **As he passed along he saw a man who had been blind from
his birth.** The reference is presumably to Jesus ' passing '
out of the temple (so the gloss in the previous verse), in which
case the incident would follow immediately after the controversy
in the temple. But Jesus would not thus attract attention to
himself immediately after his escape, and it is better to suppose
that the vague phrase ' as he passed along ' introduces a
fresh scene, about the exact setting of which the Evangelist

is quite careless. Possibly the incident is to be connected with the Feast of Dedication (10 : 22). The blind man was presumably begging at the temple gates (Acts 3 : 2). The fact that he was ' blind from his birth ' both emphasizes the incurable nature of the trouble, and also fits in with the figurative interpretation whereby the man is symbolical of those who by birth and upbringing have been strangers to the Jewish revelation : the Gentiles accept Christ's healing while his own people spurn him. **And his disciples asked him, 2 ' Rabbi, for whose sin—for his own or for his parents'—was he born blind ? '** The question was based on the doctrine, refuted by Jesus in Lk. 13 : 1–5, that every calamity must be due to some particular sin. The idea that the man may have been born blind in consequence of his own sin (unless we take it as a bewildered suggestion by the disciples without any thought of its exact implications) implies a doctrine of pre-existence (Jer. 1 : 5, Ps. 139 : 16, Eph. 1 : 4, and cf. Heb. 7 : 10) and the corresponding belief that a man's present condition is a reward or punishment for conduct in a previous existence (cf. Wis. 8 : 20, ' being good, I came into a body undefiled '). This is a Greek rather than a Jewish idea. That the blindness is due to the parents' sin is a characteristically Jewish idea (Exod. 20 : 5, Jer. 31 : 29). Note that while in Lk. 13 : 1–5 Jesus uses the problem of undeserved suffering as an incentive to repentance, here it is regarded chiefly as a means whereby he himself may be glorified. Jesus' reply indicates as usual that, according to our Evangelist, the motive behind his miracles is not so much pity as the desire to ' manifest his glory ' (cf. 2 : 11 note): **Jesus replied, ' Neither for his own sin 3 nor for his parents'—it was to let the work of God be illustrated in him.'** Yet elsewhere Jesus does not ignore the inevitable relation of sin to suffering (5 : 14, Mt. 9 : 2). As a result of the miracle the ' work of God ' would be ' illustrated ' in a twofold sense : on Jesus' part by a revelation of the healing power of God Himself (5 : 36, 10 : 37 f. 14 : 10) ; and on the man's part by a signal display of his faith in Christ (see esp. 6 : 28 f.). Symbolically the meaning is that God has allowed the world, before the Incarnation of the Light, to

remain in darkness, in order that the opportunity might be
provided for Him to reveal His glory in the Logos (cf. Acts
3 : 13, also after an act of healing), and for the world in consequence to profess its faith (9 : 39). For the Christian the
matter of moment is not his *theory* of sin and suffering, but
4 the way in which he deals with it : **'While daylight lasts, we
must be busy with the work of him that sent me** (' we ' sums
up in one Christ and his own) : **night comes** (the time of rest ;
Ps. 104 : 23 ; with a reference to Jesus' own death and
passing from his earthly labours ; cf. 13 : 30), **when no one
can do any work.'** Note here the same emphasis on the
necessity of work, even on the Sabbath, as in the healing
5 of the paralytic (5 : 17). **'When I am in the world, I am light
for the world '** (8 : 12, etc.) : this is the spiritual truth of which
the miracle is but a symbolical illustration ; Jesus' work, like
6 God's in the beginning, results in the creation of light. **With
these words**—suiting his action to his words, the act being the
direct application of the principle just enunciated—**he spat
on the ground and made clay with the saliva, which he smeared
on the man's eyes.** Note that here, in contrast as usual to the
Synoptic accounts, Jesus takes the initiative without being
petitioned by the sufferer : the light cannot but shine.
Apparently both saliva (Mk. 8 : 23) and clay were considered
efficacious for the treatment of blindness. Tacitus relates
that a blind man begged Vespasian ' ut . . . oculorum orbes
dignaretur respergere oris excremento ' ; and a physician of
the time of Caracalla prescribes ' turgentes oculos vili circum-
line coeno.' Jesus' act was a symbolical one calculated to
inspire faith by suggesting that the cure emanated from the
person of the healer himself. It is suggested that John may
connect the process with that of Gen. 2 : 7, so that for him it
becomes symbolical of a new creation. It is suggestive that
Jesus first seals the eyes which he is about to open (cf. his use of
Parable, Mk. 4 : 11 ff.). ' By adding to the real blindness,
which he alone could cure, that artificial and symbolic blindness which the waters of Siloam were to remove, he declared
in fact : what Siloam effects typically, I accomplish in reality '
(Godet). Jesus, then, completes bis prescription by **saying,**

'Go and wash them in the pool of Siloam' (Siloam meaning 7 'sent'). The pool was in the south-east of Jerusalem in the valley of the Kidron and was fed by the Virgin's Spring (note on 5 : 2 fin.). The meaning of the name in the form we have it seems to be 'sending' rather than 'sent,' i.e. 'the sending forth of the water' (cf. Is. 8 : 6). But the Evangelist interprets it as 'sent' for the sake of the symbolical reference to him who was 'sent' by the Father (6 : 29, 17 : 3, etc.). For the command to wash compare the story of Elisha and Naaman. We have a trace here of the sacramental tendency of the Gospel. The perfection of the new life and light comes only after Christian baptism in the name of him who was 'sent' and who 'came by water, blood, and Spirit' (1 Jn. 5 : 6; and cf. 13 : 8-10). So off he went and washed them, and went home seeing. Whereupon the neighbours and those to whom 8 he had been a familiar sight as a beggar, said, 'Is this not the man who used to sit and beg ? ' The astonishment of the neighbours emphasizes the reality of the miracle. Some said, 9 'It is ' ; others said, 'No, but it is like him ' (or possibly ' it is one like him ') ; He said 'I am the man.' So they asked 10 him, 'How were your eyes opened ? ' Unlike the paralytic (5 : 13), the blind man knows who his healer is : He replied, 11 'The man they call Jesus made some clay and smeared my eyes with it and told me, "Go and wash them in Siloam "; so I went and washed them, and I got my sight.' The mention of the making of clay, which would be an infringement of the Sabbath, prepares the way for the charge at verse 16. 'Where 12 is he ? ' they asked—that he may be arrested for breaking the Sabbath. He answered, 'I do not know.' So being unable to arrest the healer they arrest the man healed : They brought 13 him before the Pharisees, this man who had once been blind. Now it was on the sabbath day that Jesus had made clay and 14 opened his eyes ; this was the ostensible reason for the Pharisees' annoyance, the feature of the miracle which technically gave offence. So the Pharisees asked him again how he 15 had regained his sight, and he told them, 'He smeared some clay on my eyes, and I washed them, and now I can see.' Then 16 some of the Pharisees—seizing on this evidence of a technical violation of the Sabbath—said, ' This man is not from God, for he does not keep the sabbath '; others said, ' How can a sinner perform such Signs ? ' (For the hostility cf. 5 : 16 and for the rejoinder of the minority 3 : 2). They were divided on this (7 : 43), some denying Jesus' divine mission on the ground of the violation of the Sabbath, others implicitly denying the violation of the Sabbath by their assumption that only a man with a divine mission could perform such a miracle. Accordingly they appeal again to the blind man, in the hope perhaps that even he may admit the guilt of his healer :

17 So they asked the blind man once more, ' What have you to say about him, for opening your eyes ? ' But they only got the answer of the Samaritan woman (4: 19) : The man replied, ' I say he is a prophet.' The Jews next try to cast doubt on the reality of the miracle : no real miracle could be reconciled with the breaking of the Sabbath ; they suspect fraudulent

18 collusion : Now the Jews (i.e. the majority of ver. 16) would not believe he had been born blind and had regained his sight, till they summoned the parents of the man who had regained

19 his sight and asked them, ' Is this your son, the son you declare was born blind ? How is it that he can see now ? ' The parents explode the theory of collusion, but are unwilling to compromise themselves by admitting that the man owes his

20 cure to Jesus. His parents answered, ' This is our son, and he

21 was born blind ; we know that. But how he can see to-day, we do not know, nor do we know who opened his eyes. Ask himself ; he is of age—and therefore his parents can no longer

22 be held responsible for him—he can speak for himself.' (His parents said this because they were afraid of the Jews ; for the Jews had already agreed that anyone who confessed him to be

23 Christ should be excommunicated. That was why the man's parents said, ' He is of age, ask himself.') There is no evidence that excommunication from the Jewish synagogue for the profession of Jesus ever took place in our Lord's own day ; but it was certainly enforced at the time the Evangelist wrote. Moreover, in Jesus' day in Palestine only the Sanhedrim had power of excommunication : in Asia Minor the synagogue took the power to itself, authority naturally being decentral-

ized. This chapter throughout reflects the conditions of John's own time and locality (cf. 3 Jn. 10, Jn. 16 : 2).

At this point ' the physical miracle gives place to the spiritual miracle in the mind of the Evangelist, the miracle of personal experience as a testimony to the truth and power of Jesus' (Strachan). The Jews, no longer able to question the fact, try to ' annihilate fact by dogma' (Godet). While compelled to admit the miracle they ' suggest ' to the man that it is due to God alone, not to one whom—begging the question—they ' know' to be a sinner : So the man born blind was summoned a 24 second time and told, ' Now give God the praise (an adjuration to tell the whole truth and confess his error ; cf. Josh. 7 : 19) ; this man, we know quite well, is only a sinner '—because he has violated the Sabbath. To which he replied somewhat ironi- 25 cally that for him experience has more weight than such theoretical ' knowledge': ' I do not know whether he is a sinner ; one thing I do know, that once I was blind and now I can see.' ' What did he do to you ? ' they repeated— 26 trying again to convict Jesus on account of the *means* used on the Sabbath—' How did he open your eyes ? '—in the hope perhaps that the man might involve himself in contradictory statements and so convict himself of fraud. The man loses patience, and cuts them short with an ironical pleasantry. He retorted, ' I have told you that already, and you would not 27 listen to me. Why do you want to hear it over again ? Do you want to be disciples of his ? '—the most biting gibe possible— *you* his disciples ! The Jews in turn lose their temper : Then 28 they stormed at him : ' You are his disciple, we are disciples of Moses ! We know (doctors of the law as we are) God spoke to 29 Moses (on Sinai ; the Greek perfect implies that God's words still stand written ; cf. Heb. 1 : 1), but we do not know where this fellow comes from,' i.e. whether he comes from God or not (contrast 7 : 27 where the point in question is Jesus' earthly origin ; cf. Mk. 11 : 27 ff). The man replied to them (again 30 ironically), ' Well, this is astonishing ! You do not know where he comes from, and yet he has opened my eyes. God, 31 we know, does not listen to sinners ' (16), i.e. it is not at the demand of a sinner that such a miracle as this is performed ;

' He listens to anyone who is devout and obeys His will. It
32 is unheard of, since the world began, that anyone should open
a blind man's eyes.' Perhaps the Evangelist hints at the
impossibility of ever opening the eyes of his own Jewish
33 contemporaries to their folly. ' If this man were not from
God, he could do nothing,' i.e. could not thus heal the blind
34 (cf. Acts 5 : 38 f.). They retorted, 'And so you would teach
us—you, born in utter depravity ! ' His very blindness was
proof of congenital sinfulness, and yet he presumed to instruct
the pure and the wise ! Then they expelled him, not merely
from their presence, but implying excommunication from the
religious community (22).

35   Jesus heard that they had expelled him, and on meeting him
36 he said, ' You believe in the Son of man ? ' The ' meeting '
is regarded as providential (1 : 41, 5 : 14) : Jesus' love, knowing
his straits, has sought him out. The question is intended to
prompt his faith. It is taken for granted that the man would
understand ' Son of man ' to mean Messiah (in the Johannine
sense, 1 : 51), which indeed he does. He admits that such a
one exists, but desires to know who fulfils that rôle. Jesus,
whom he has already hailed as a ' prophet,' should be able to
tell him : ' Who is that, sir ? ' said the man, ' tell me, that I
37 may believe in him.' ' You have seen him,' Jesus said (an
allusion perhaps to his restored sight), ' he is talking to you.'
38 (For the dramatic announcement cf. 4 : 26.) He said, ' I do
believe, Lord '—and he worshipped him, a word regularly
used of the adoration of divine sovereignty (4 : 20, 12 : 20, but
contrast Mt. 18 : 26).

Theme : Christ the Light, the Good Shepherd, the Door
(9 : 39–10 : 42)

The last three verses of the chapter sum up the spiritual
39 significance of the miracle. Then said Jesus, ' It is for
judgment (the result of judging rather than the process)
that I have come into this world, i.e. for the revealing of realities, for exhibiting in its results the true inward state of each
human heart, to make the sightless see—that those who are

in darkness and conscious of it and willing to have light may
be enlightened—**to make the seeing blind,**'—that those who are
stubbornly content with the light they have may lose even
that. At the coming of the Christ ignorant Gentiles are
saved, while 'enlightened' Jews stand self-condemned; those
predestined to salvation welcome him (6: 37, 65), while
the reprobate become still more obdurate. (For the meaning of Christ's 'judgment' see notes on 3: 17–21 and
5: 22.) **On hearing this the Pharisees who were beside** 40
him (' there because the author has need of them' to add point
to the words—Loisy) **asked, 'And are we blind?'** Jesus'
answer is unexpectedly crushing: would to God they *were*
blind! **Jesus replied, 'If you were blind**—like the pagans— 41
you would not be guilty—your ignorance would excuse you
(15: 22, 24)—**but, as it is, you claim to have sight**—to be the
only possessors of truth, while you shut your eyes obstinately
to the light, satisfied with the light you have (cf. 1 Jn. 1: 8)—
and so your sins remains.' The very fact that, as God's
privileged people, they should have known so much better,
is their condemnation (note on 5: 45). They are guilty of
'sin against the Holy Ghost' which for ever 'remains'
unforgivable (8: 21). Note that in the Synoptics (Mk. 3:
22–30) the reference to such an unforgivable sin follows as
here (8: 48) close upon the charge that Jesus is in some way
in league with the devil. (See also notes on 20: 23.)

10.

The Jews were again divided over these words. A number ¹⁹₂₀
of them said, 'He is mad. Why listen to him?' Others 21
said, 'These are not a madman's words. Can a madman
open the eyes of the blind?'

Then came the festival of Dedication at Jerusalem; it was 22
winter, and Jesus used to walk inside the temple, in the 23
portico of Solomon. So the Jews gathered round him and 24
asked, 'How long are you going to keep us in suspense?
If you are the Christ, tell us plainly.' Jesus replied, 25
'I have told you, but you do not believe; the deeds I do
in the name of my Father testify to me, but you do not 26
believe, because you do not belong to my sheep. My 27

28   sheep listen to my voice, and I know them and they follow
me ; and I give them eternal life ; they will never perish,
29   and no one will snatch them out of my hand. **My Father
who gave me them is stronger than all, and no one can
snatch anything out of the Father's hand.'**

At this point we insert 10 : 19–29. In its present context
22–23 are clearly out of place ; some would place them as an
introduction to 8 : 12–20, while Bacon thinks that the two verses
are an editorial addition ' to complete a total of five festal self-
presentations of Jesus' (*Fourth Gospel*, p. 493). But by transposing the whole section 10 : 19–29 to the close of chapter 9
a greatly improved sequence is obtained. 19–21 round off
the chapter, which otherwise closes abruptly ; it is no longer
necessary to delete 22 f. in order to remove the difficulty of
supposing that in 25 ff. Jesus renews to a different audience,
and even at a new feast, the Sheep-discourse of 10 : 1–18,
the whole of which will now be assigned to the Feast of
Dedication ; finally, note that 21 obviously alludes to the
miracle of chapter 9, and that with the removal of 19–29 there
is a perfect sequence from 18 to 30.

19   The account of Jesus' visit to the Feast of Booths concludes
with a note of the varied impressions left : **The Jews were
again divided** (as at 7 : 43, 9 : 16) **over these words. A number**
20 **of them said, ' He is mad!** (7 : 20, 8 : 48) **Why listen to him ? '**
21 **Others said, ' Can a madman open the eyes of the blind ? '**
The argument is similar to that of 9 : 16 ; but there the
question was of ' sin,' here of ' madness.'

22   **Then came the festival of Dedication at Jerusalem.** The
festival (Ezra 6 : 16) began on 25th Chisleu (middle of Dec.)
and lasted eight days in commemoration of the reconsecration
of the temple by Judas Maccabaeus after its profanation by
Antiochus Epiphanes in 168 B.C. Two to three months would
have elapsed since Jesus' teaching at the Feast of Booths
(some suppose that this interval corresponds with the period
covered by the special Lucan section 9 : 51–19 : 28). Yet,
even if the proposed transposition be accepted, the situation
as between Jesus and his opponents is unchanged, and so far

as the discourse is concerned the Evangelist would seem to be
conscious of no interval. **It was winter, and Jesus used to walk** 23
(7 : 1) **inside the temple, in the portico of Solomon**—in order
to get protection from the weather. Some see in ' winter '
a hint of the chilly attitude of the Jews ; surely symbolism
gone mad ! Solomon's portico (Acts 3 : 11, 5 : 12) was a
cloister on the east side of the temple area perhaps built on a
remnant of Solomon's temple. With the following verses
cf. Lk. 22 : 66 ff. So the Jews **gathered round him** (' ringed 24
him round '—as if to prevent his escape) **and asked, ' How
long are you going to keep us in suspense ? If you are the
Christ, tell us plainly '**—' in so many words,' ' without
ambiguity ' (7 : 13, 11 : 14, 16 : 29). The question is outwardly sincere enough, yet nothing argues the will to disbelieve
more clearly than a demand for proof, when full proof has
already been given. Accordingly **Jesus replied, ' I have told** 25
you, but you do not believe.' Though in this Gospel Jesus never
declares his Messiahship in so many words either to his enemies
or to the general public, but only to his disciples and individuals
such as the Samaritan woman (4 : 26) and the man born
blind (9 : 37), yet by the whole of his teaching about his relation
to the Father ' he has told them ' that he is the Christ :
' The deeds I do in the name of my Father (as His representative with His commission) **testify to me** (i.e. that I am Christ,
and what sort of a Christ ; cf. 5 : 36), **but you do not believe.'**
Loisy well notes that Jesus refuses a definite answer ' in order
to mark the sovereign independence of his words as regards men
and all human authority.' The ' self-determination ' of Jesus
(7 : 30 note) extends to his words as well as to his deeds :
he refuses to be pushed to an issue before his ' time ' either in
word or deed. The Jews do not believe **' because you do not** 26
belong to my sheep ' (some MSS. followed by A.V. add ' as I
said unto you '—probably a gloss, referring to 10 : 3–5, added
after the displacement took place). With our transposition
this is the first use of the metaphor, which is developed in
allegory in verses 1–5 and then interpreted in 7 ff. The Jews,
by nature and by predestination (6 : 65), are incapable of
belonging to the flock of Christ. (For the use of the term

233

' Shepherd ' of God in the O.T. cf. Ps. 23, Is. 40 : 11, Jer. 23 :
27 1–4, Zech. 11 : 4 ff.) ' **My sheep listen to my voice, and I know**
28 **them and they follow me ; and I give them eternal life.'** The
thought is developed and explained in the allegory which
follows. Shepherd and sheep have each two reciprocal characteristics : they ' listen ' and he in turn ' knows ' and
acknowledges them (Mt. 10 : 32) ; they ' follow,' and he in
turn gives them the reward of moral obedience which is
' eternal life ' (8 : 12). The final security of Christ's own is
emphasized when he adds, ' **they will never perish, and no one**
will snatch them out of my hand ' (cf. 6 : 39, 17 : 12)—a promise
29 illustrated in verses 12–15. ' **My Father who gave me them is**
stronger than all, and no one can snatch anything out of the
Father's hand.' An alternative reading gives a neuter pronoun
which some prefer on the ground of John's usage in 6 : 39
(where see note for force of the word ' gave '), translating,
' that which my Father hath given me is stronger than everything' (cf. 1 Jn. 5 : 4). But this thought is out of place
when the figure of *sheep* is being used ; and the last clause of
the verse suits better the first reading.

Chapter 10 : 1 ff.

The allegory of the Shepherd, the Sheep, and the Door
awakens echoes of several passages in the Synoptics, e.g.
Mt. 7 : 13–15, 9 : 36, 18 : 12–14, 26 : 31. It provides a good
example of what have been described as *conglomerate*
passages (cf. 4 : 35–38), i.e. passages where several short
sections, existing perhaps independently in an original source,
but dealing with kindred subjects, have been worked up
together into a single paragraph. Thus we have here : *first*
(1–5) a simple allegory descriptive of the ideal shepherd ;
second (7–10) an interpretation of this in which Christ appears
not, as might be expected, as the Shepherd, but as the Door ;
third (11–18), another more natural interpretation in which
Jesus himself is pictured as the ' Good Shepherd.' As a
result it is impossible to trace throughout one sequence of
thought or a consistent use of the similes. One might conjecture that ' the Witness ' has preserved recollections of two
(or three ?) independent allegories, and that the Evangelist

has incorporated them in a single paragraph. Throughout the allegory in relation to the fold (the Church and her Teachers) Christ is the Door, in relation to the flock (individual Christians) he is the Shepherd.

In 1-5 we have a simple allegory descriptive of the ideal Shepherd—an ideal realized no doubt in Christ (at 11 ff.), 'but for the present this personal application lies in the background' (Westcott). Notice the connexion of thought between 29 and 1 in the idea of robbery—another point in favour of our transposition.

'Truly, truly I tell you, he who does not enter the sheepfold 1 by the gate but climbs up somewhere else, he is a thief and a robber': his method of entry shows that he has no right to lead the sheep out. The 'fold' is a walled enclosure without roof, but with a heavy door watched by a 'gate-keeper.' The true shepherd on the other hand may be known both by his mode of entrance, and by the understanding existing between him and the sheep. 'He who enters by the gate is the 2 shepherd of the sheep. The gate-keeper opens the gate for 3 him, and the sheep listen to his voice'—because it is familiar ; 'he calls his sheep by name and leads them out.' The 'gate-keeper' is probably a purely descriptive detail, and is not to be interpreted as, e.g., God, the Holy Ghost, Moses, the Baptist, etc. Eastern shepherds give their sheep names as we would to horses or cows (so also, e.g., in Theocritus). The special name is proof of individual knowledge and love (Is. 43 : 1, Rev. 3 : 5, Jn. 20 : 16). The phrase 'lead out' figures the separation of Christianity from Judaism. The excommunication of the blind man is still in view, and the thought is that Christ's flock is already being led out of the Jewish fold. 'When he has brought all his sheep outside 4 (the very Greek word used of the excommunication of the blind man in 9 : 34), he goes in front of them (the regular eastern custom, to guide them ; Ps. 80 : 1), and the sheep follow him because they know his voice.' Sir G. A. Smith (*Hist. Geog. of Palestine*, p. 312) gives a good illustration : 'Sometimes we enjoyed our noonday rest beside one of these Judaean wells, to which three or four shepherds come down

with their flocks. The flocks mixed with each other, and we wondered how each shepherd would get his own again. But after the watering and the playing were over, the shepherds one by one went up different sides of the valley, and each called out his peculiar call, and the sheep of each drew out of the crowd to their own shepherd, and the flocks passed away
5 as orderly as they came.' **'They will not follow a stranger, they will run from him, because they do not know the voice of strangers.'** Plummer tells the story of a Scottish traveller who changed clothes with a Jerusalem shepherd and tried to lead the sheep ; but the sheep followed the shepherd's voice and not his clothes.

6 **Jesus told them this allegory, but they did not understand what he was saying to them**—the conventional phrase (Lk. 8 : 10) which opens the way for the interpretation. An 'allegory' is a narrative in which truth is expressed by the use of pictorial similes. The word is also used of a brief symbolic saying or 'figure' (16 : 25, 29 ; A.V. 'proverb'). Godet well distinguishes between an 'allegory' and the true 'parable' as we have it in the Synoptics : 'In the parable, the thought is clothed in a form which has meaning apart from its moral application ; in the allegory, the application is directly felt in each feature of the picture—a parable is a picture ; an allegory a transparency.'

There follows (7–10) an interpretation in which the figure 'Door' or 'Gate' is used to illustrate Christ's relation to the true shepherds of his flock, and through them to the flock itself. The true pastor approaches the flock only through and in the name of the Christ who, as the Gate, himself protects the flock from false teachers. The Gospel (21 : 15) has in view 'under-shepherds' as well as the 'good-shepherd' himself, and here John, writing from the standpoint of his own day, insists that only those who act in Christ's name and possess his spirit have a right to assume that office. As this thought of the leaders of the Church being themselves 'shepherds' belongs to the appendix, and verses 7–10 also reflect this idea, it is tempting to conjecture that these verses, which are evidently out of harmony with the rest of the section (where Christ himself is the shepherd), may also be due to the Redactor.

So he said to them again, ' Truly, truly I tell you, I am 7 the *Gate* of the sheep ! ' Doubtless *shepherd*, as is read by Moffatt, might be expected rather than *gate*; but the textual evidence is overwhelmingly against this reading. By Christ alone can the sheep be protected from danger, and through him alone can they come out to pasture. Through Christ alone can the true teachers approach the flock, for by him alone are they commissioned. It is not the Pharisees but Christ who alone can admit to or expel from the true fold of God. ' All who ever came before me have been thieves and 8 robbers.' It must be admitted that the contrast here would seem to be between the robbers and Christ as the ' shepherd ' rather than as the ' gate ' ; there is evidently a certain confusion of thought as the result of the amalgamation of two inconsistent allegories. Probably *before me* should not be stressed in either a temporal or local force, as if Christ were impugning the honesty of, e.g., Moses or the prophets, whom elsewhere he rather calls to witness as his allies (5 : 46, 8 : 56, 12 : 41). The phrase ' before me ' is part of the simile, as if an impostor were pictured presenting himself to the gate-keeper in the early hours of the morning before the true shepherd arrives. Writing from the standpoint of his own day John thus sums up all false teachers who are trying to seduce Christians from the true community of Christ, whether they be false Messiahs, Jewish reactionaries, or Gnostic heretics ; perhaps he has in mind especially the Jewish doctors who from the viewpoint of the outworn creed of bygone days are prejudicing people against Christ. They are *robbers* in intention rather than in fact, not because they have actually done much damage, but because they are unauthorized trespassers. (Cf. Ezek. 34 : 1–19, Jer. 23 : 1–4.) ' But the sheep would not listen to them ' ; the true children of God have ' tested the spirits to see if they come from God ' (1 Jn. 4 : 1) and have found them false. ' I am the Gate ; 9 whoever enters by me will be saved, he will go in and out and find pasture.' (Cf. 14 : 6, and for the thought and phrase-

R   237

ology, Num. 27 : 15–21.) Strictly the reference must still be
to the true leaders of the Church (not the 'sheep,' but the
'under-shepherds,' though, as a result of the confusion of
thought noted above, the content of the allegory as a whole
—as contrasted with its *form* in this particular verse—
demands rather a reference to the 'sheep'; but 'even the
shepherds are sheep also'—Westcott) who must first find
salvation through Christ for themselves before they can act as
guides to the flock (1 Tim. 4: 16, 1 Cor. 3: 5). Only when
commissioned by Christ and endued with his spirit have they
freedom and authority to go about their sacred duty (to *go
in and out* is the common expression used to denote the un-
hindered activity of daily life: Deut. 28: 6, Ps. 121: 8, Jer.
37: 4) of *finding pasture*—i.e. providing spiritual sustenance—for the sheep. While Christ is an open door, the
Pharisees are a door bolted against entrance into the kingdom
(Mt. 23: 13). Finally Christ as the Gate which guards the
sheep and admits only the true teachers is contrasted with
10 the false teachers: 'The thief only comes to steal, to slay and
to destroy: I have come that they may have life and have
it to the full.' The impostor seeks only his own aggran-
disement; he exploits and ruins the community. In Christ,
on the other hand, there is 'life to the full' (Ps. 23: 1,
Jn. 4: 14). Vital contact with Christ enriches a man's whole
personality.

But such a communication of life is possible only by the
sacrifice of Christ's own life first, and in virtue of this sacrifice
he is now pictured as the 'good shepherd.' The simile changes
and a new allegory begins. (For another classic description
of the ideal shepherd, cf. Plato, *Republic*, p. 345.) The love
of the early Church for this figure of Christ comes out in the
frequency with which the emblem of the Good Shepherd
11 occurs on the walls of the Catacombs. 'I am the good
shepherd': the Greek adjective is almost untranslatable,
and combines the ideas of 'beautiful,' 'fit,' 'competent,'
'one who excels at his work'; perhaps the Scots word 'braw'
comes nearest to it. 'A good shepherd lays down his life for
the sheep.' The Logos-Christ strips off his earthly life like a

garment (15, 18, 13 : 4) ; this, rather than the idea of a
pledge or ransom, is the force of the metaphor. That this
was originally a separate allegory appears from the fact
that the false teachers are now symbolized not by bold robbers
but by a timid hired man, the rôle of ' robber ' now being
filled by the ' wolf ' : 'The hired man, who is not the shep- 12
herd and does not own the sheep, deserts them when he sees
the wolf coming ; he runs away, leaving the wolf to tear
and scatter them '—pictorial details not to be stressed, but
summing up all the harmful influences brought to bear on the
Christian community, the seduction of heresy, the threat of
persecution, etc.—' just because he is a hired man, who has 13
no interest in the sheep.' He is working for his own gain
and not for the sheep's protection. On the other hand, the
mutual trust and understanding existing between the true
shepherd and his flock make it impossible for him to desert
them : ' I am the good shepherd, I know my sheep (their 14
marks, names, ways), and my sheep know me (as proved by
their willingness to follow—ver. 4), just as the Father knows 15
me and I know the Father, and (as a result of my insight
alike into the need of the sheep and the will of the Father)
I lay down my life for the sheep.' Know means properly
to ' know by experience,' and even of Christ it may be said
that it was through life's testing experiences that he came
to the perfect knowledge of God's will—though John never
emphasizes this. The relation of mutual understanding
between Christ and the Christian is the same as that between
the Father and Christ (cf. 6 : 57, 15 : 9, 17 : 11 ; 1 Cor. 3 : 23).
This theme is developed at length in the farewell discourse.

This passage well illustrates the place held in John's thought
by the concept of knowledge. In this he shows sympathy
with the ' Gnostic ' point of view, though by deliberately
avoiding the special term ' gnosis ' he would seem to desire
to dissociate himself from current Gnostic doctrine. Moreover, for John ' knowledge ' is not a purely intellectual process,
but includes religious and moral elements by virtue of which
it approaches in content Paul's idea of ' faith.' Just as for
Paul ' the just shall live by faith ' (Rom. 1 : 17), so for John

'eternal life' consists in the 'knowledge' of God (17 : 3).
(For the relation of 'knowing' to 'believing' in our Gospel,
cf. 6 : 69, 10 : 38, 17 : 8, and note on 3 : 14 f.) By use of the
concept of 'knowing' John tries to interpret in terms of
reason the facts of spiritual experience. Hence for him
'knowledge' of God is primarily knowledge of His will and
ethical character rather than initiation into some esoteric
Gnostic discipline. Though in our Gospel, as for Plato and
Philo, the intellectual aspect of religion is always prominent
(4 : 22, 8 : 32, 13 : 17, 14 : 5, 17 : 7), yet for John, as for the
Hebrew psalmists and prophets, to 'know the Lord' is also
to trust him, to serve him, to bend one's being to his will
and purpose (17 : 25, 8 : 19).

It is under the moral compulsion of such a 'knowledge' of
God that the Good Shepherd 'lays down his life for the sheep.'
Now according to John one of the chief results of Christ's
death is to bring about a world-wide extension of his Church
and ensure unity among believers (11 : 52, 17 : 21 ; cf. Eph.
16 2 : 13, 14). Accordingly Jesus proceeds : '**I have other
sheep, too,**—i.e. Gentile believers—**which do not belong to
this fold,**' i.e. to the Jewish community so far as it has already
recognized Christ. Jesus already 'has' these believers
because, though they are not yet gathered in, they are destined
for him by the Father (6 : 37, Acts 2 : 47, 18 : 10). '**I must
bring them also** (Eph. 2 : 11 ff., Mt. 8 : 11), **and they will
listen to my voice ; so it will be one flock, one shepherd '**—
not 'one fold,' as A.V., which Westcott truly calls a 'disas-
trous' mistranslation. The ideas of the fold and the flock
are deliberately contrasted. The bond is not in a common
organization, but in a common relationship to one Lord. There
may be various folds, though but one flock and one shepherd.

17 The Evangelist now answers what may well have been a common objection to Christ's claims : is it possible that a teacher
whose mission ended in the ignominy of a gibbet can have
held a divine commission ? So far, replies John, from Jesus'
death being a sign that God has disowned him, '**this is why
my Father loves me, because I lay down my life.**' Moreover,
Christ's death is not an argument against his divine power

but a proof of it. He gives up his life voluntarily '**to take** 18
**it up again. No one takes it from me, I lay it down of my
own accord.**' Again Jesus' ' self-determination ' is emphasized (note 7 : 30). One cannot help contrasting the touch-
ingly human Jesus of the Synoptic Gethsemane scene with
this Johannine Christ who moves serenely among his enemies,
the proud master of his fate. Our Gospel insists that Jesus'
death was due not to circumstances, not to the strength of
the opposition but to his *own free will*, upon which no outward
constraint can be laid (19 : 11): ' **I have power to lay it down
and also power to take it up again.**' The fact that he has
power to take his life back again at will is proof of the freedom
of the sacrifice. But does it not also rob the sacrifice of
reality ? This is hardly a Christ who is ' made perfect by
suffering,' but rather one raised above suffering by the divine
' power ' within him. Yet in thus determining his own
destiny Christ is not setting his own will against the Father's ;
even in this he ' does nothing of his own accord ' (8 : 28):
'**I have my Father's orders for this.**' Both Cross and Resurrection are part of the Father's commission to the Son. The
Son's freedom consists in spontaneously obeying the Father's
commandment, for (note how admirable is the connexion
resulting from the transposition of 19–29), '**I and my Father** 30
are one—.' (Cf. 17 : 21–23.) The unity here claimed is
ethical rather than metaphysical, a unity of will rather than
of essence and personality, a mystical unity implying two
separate personalities as in 38 below and 1 : 1—' the Logos
was with God.' Christ never claims even in this Gospel to
be one in essence with God (see note on 5 : 18). The unity
with the Father which he does claim is a similar unity of
will and purpose to that which he prays may exist between
Christian and Christian (17 : 11). An indivisible unity of
nature in Father and Son is not implied, as Jesus himself
makes clear when in verse 36 he interprets his present claim
as meaning not ' I am God,' but ' I am God's Son.'

The claim to a special relationship towards God has its
usual sequel (5 : 18): **The Jews again** (as in 8 : 59) **caught** 31
up stones to stone him. Jesus replied—with bitter irony— 32

' I have let you see many a good deed of God ' ; Jesus' acts
are ' God's deeds ' because they are done ' in His name '
(10 : 25), i.e. according to His will and purpose ; ' for which of
33 them do you mean to stone me ? ' The Jews retorted, ' We
mean to stone you, not for a good deed, but for blasphemy,
because you, a mere man, make yourself God.' The charge
of blasphemy (for the law concerning which see Lev. 24 : 10–
16 ; Deut. 18 : 20) made, according to the Synoptists, at the
trial (Mk. 14 : 64), is anticipated here. There is no fresh
charge of blasphemy at the trial, for there Jesus merely refers
his accusers to his previous teaching (18 : 19–21), as if the
claim to be the Son of God, which in the Synoptics appears
to come as a new shock to his judges, had long been known to
34 all the world—the true Johannine standpoint. Jesus answered,
' Is it not written in your Law (' your '—as if disjoining him-
35 self from them), "I said, you are gods "'? If the Law (here
used of the O.T. in general ; cf. 12 : 34, 15 : 25, Rom 3 : 19,
etc.), said they were gods, to whom the word of God came—
36 and scripture cannot be broken—do you mean to tell me,
whom the Father consecrated (i.e. anointed as Christ) and
sent into the world (on a mission of salvation—3 : 16–17),
"You are blaspheming," because I said, " I am God's Son "? '
The quotation is from Ps. 82 : 6, where God says to the judges
of Israel, ' I have said, Ye are gods ; and all of you are
children of the most High.' The people's rulers were regarded
as the representatives of God Himself ; so of the King (Ps.
45 : 6 and cf. Exod. 4 : 16). The argument may be paraphrased thus : If those who were consecrated to their
office by the saying of God which I have quoted (or perhaps
more generally, If those who in the past have been the
organs of the divine word) were actually called ' gods '—
and they must have been so called, for Scripture says so—
surely the consecrated ambassador of the Father may without
blasphemy call himself ' God's Son.' The argument is *a
fortiori* : if human leaders have been called ' gods,' how much
more may one greater than they make a lesser claim—to be
not ' God,' but ' God's Son '! If the organ of the divine
word may be called ' god,' how much more the divine Logos

himself. The argument is admittedly *ad hominem* and indeed is little better than a play on words, for Jesus claims to be the ' Son of God ' in a very different sense from that in which the judges of Israel are ' children of the most High.' But the analogy of the use made of O.T. quotation by Paul and in the Epistle to the Hebrews makes it quite credible that in John's time such arguments may have been used against the Jews to defend the divinity of Christ. ' If I am not 37 doing the deeds of my Father, do not believe me ; but if I 38 am, then believe the deeds, though you will not believe me— if you will not accept my statements, then at least yield to the evidence of my deeds (10 : 25, 5 : 36, 9 : 33)—that you may learn and understand that the Father is in me and I am in the Father.' The Father is in Christ, as in the organ through which He expresses Himself : Christ is in the Father as in the element in which he lives and from which he draws his power. The words are a more detailed statement of the mystical unity claimed in 30. ' Learn and understand ' implies a progressive knowledge—' perceive once for all, and then go on advancing in ever fuller perception ' (Westcott). Note too how the thought passes over almost unconsciously from the idea of ' believing ' to that of ' knowing.' (Cf. note on 6 : 69, 10 : 15, 17 : 7 f.)

Once more they tried to arrest him (as at 7 : 30, 32, 44) 39 but he escaped their hands (cf. 8 : 59 : ' his time had not yet come ') and went across the Jordan, back to the spot 40 where John had baptized at first, i.e. at the time when Jesus first appeared on the earthly stage. This is better than to suppose that the Evangelist is distinguishing between the first (1 : 19 ff.) and the second (3 : 23 ff.) occasions on which John bore evidence to Christ. (For the place see note on 1 : 28.) There he stayed (till 11 : 7) ; and many came to him, saying, 41 ' John did not perform any Sign, but all he ever said about this man was true.' And many believed in him there—the 42 last word is emphatic, the faith of the Pereans, like that of the Samaritans, being contrasted with the unbelief of the Jews. The reference to John seems suggested by the locality with which his name was associated. The mention of him here at

the close of Jesus' public preaching at Jerusalem corresponds
to that by the Synoptists in Mk. 11 : 27–31. In the Synoptics
we have hints (e.g. Mt. 14 : 2) that tradition must have
attributed miracles to the Baptist. But our Evangelist as
usual emphasizes the fore-runner's inferiority and the fact
that his sole mission was to testify to Jesus. Cf. with this
verse 1 : 8—' He was not the Light (' he did not perform any
Sign ') ; it was to bear testimony to the Light that he appeared '
(' all he ever said . . . was true '). Verses 40–42 have been
suspected of being an addition by the Redactor. A number
of grammatical peculiarities have been noted (see *Expository
Times*, xxvii, p. 237), and it is suggested that this may be one
of the links inserted by the Redactor for the sake of preserving
historical sequence—in this case to translate Jesus to the
locality beyond Jordan, where he is when Lazarus dies. The
Synoptic record preserved in Mk. 10 : 1 is thus reaffirmed.
The verses thus present three traits characteristic of ' R '
passages—Synoptic echoes, proximity to textual dislocation,
and a desire to emphasize Christ's superiority to the Baptist.
(See pp. xliv, 368.)

Section III. The Divine Work of the Christ: the Gift of Life and the Awaking of Faith

Illustration : The Raising of Lazarus (11 : 1–57)

1   **Now there was a man ill, Lazarus of Bethany—the village
of Mary and her sister Martha.** ' Lazarus ' is the Greek form
of ' Eleazar,' and means ' God is my help '—a name appropriate to the miracle of which he is the hero. Possibly John
has borrowed the name from Lk. 16 : 19 ff. Bethany, now
called El-Azirieh (from El-Azir, the Arabic for Lazarus), lies
on the south-east slope of Olivet, about two miles from Jerusalem (18), and must be distinguished from the place of the
same name mentioned at 1 : 28. John marks this distinction
by calling it ' the village of Mary and her sister Martha,' a
definition which also serves to connect Lazarus with figures
well known in Synoptic tradition (cf. Lk. 10 : 38–42, where,
however, it is stated neither that they lived at Bethany nor

that they had a brother). Mary is mentioned first as being
the better known on account of the 'anointing' incident,
though Luke implies that Martha was the mistress of the
house. **The Mary whose brother Lazarus was ill was the 2
Mary who anointed the Lord with perfume and wiped his feet
with her hair.** The verse is probably a gloss : the incident is
not recorded till 12 : 1–8, but in John's time Mary would be
particularly remembered for this act. For the whole question of this ' identification' see notes on 12 : 1–8. (Moffatt
at this point inserts verse 5, but see note *in loc.*). **So the 3
sisters sent to him, saying, ' Lord, he whom you love is ill.'**
The bald message veils an unexpressed prayer: ' sufficit ut
noveris ; non enim amas et deseris' (Augustine). **When 4
Jesus heard it, he said, ' This illness is not to end in death—**
there may be death, but that will not be the final issue—
**the end of it is the glory of God, that the Son of God may
be glorified thereby.'** (For the thought cf. 9: 3, where, as here,
we are shown the underlying motive according to John of
all Jesus' miracles.) The words are perhaps intended rather
as a reflection of Jesus than as a reply to the sisters' messenger.
There would seem to be a play on the two senses of the word
' glorify,' for as a result of the miracle Jesus was ' glorified'
in two ways : in the ordinary sense inasmuch as many
believed in his Messiahship ; and in the peculiar Johannine
sense, because the incident was the prelude to the Cross, the
point d'appui for the final assault upon Jesus by his enemies.
(Cf. 7 : 39 note.) The ' glory' of God consists in the ' glorifying' of the Son—and that through the Cross (cf. 13 : 31).
The intention of Jesus' words is not that Lazarus will not
die, but that death will not have the last word. (Cf. Mk. 5 : 39,
which is echoed again in verse 11.)

Now Jesus loved Martha and her sister and Lazarus. This 5
certainly fits in more naturally between verses 2 and 3. Yet
when the verse is left in its present position we may perhaps
find special point in the ' so ' with which the next verse opens.
We have already noticed two occasions (2 : 4, 7 : 6) on which
Jesus deliberately resisted the appeal of affection lest he
should be ' rushed' against his better judgment. The present

6 circumstances are the same : Jesus loved Lazarus, so, when
he heard of the illness, he stayed where he was for two days.
The reminder of Jesus' love also helps to remove the suspicion
that the words just spoken (4) and the subsequent delay
betokened coldness towards the Bethany family. Baur, e.g.,
insists that Jesus deliberately delayed in order that he
might have the ' glory' of raising a putrefying corpse. But
though the delay certainly serves to heighten the miracle,
this is not its primary motive ; nor is it to test the faith of
the sisters, but rather that Jesus himself may be sure of the
Father's will. It is possible, alternatively (indeed, the Greek
particles favour this) to find the consequence implied in ' so,'
not in verse 6 but in 7 : Jesus loved . . . so, when he heard . . . ,
7 he stayed indeed where he was for two days, but then, after
that, he said to the disciples, ' Let us go back to Judaea.'
Jesus says ' to Judaea' not ' to Bethany,' because the
Evangelist wishes to contrast believing Peraea with unbelieving Jerusalem, and also because it was the re-entry into the
province of Judaea which put Jesus' life to the hazard. This
8 at once appears : ' Rabbi,' said the disciples, ' the Jews were
trying to stone you (10 : 31) only the other day (some three
9 months before) ; are you going back there ? ' Jesus replied,
' Are there not twelve hours in the day ? '—every man has
but a definitely limited period within which to work (cf. the
thought of Lk. 13 : 32)—' If one walks during the day he
10 does not stumble, for he sees the light of this world ; but if
one walks during the night he does stumble, for the light is
not in him.' (Cf. 9 : 4, 12 : 35.) Verses 9–10 state a general
truth, but obviously with special reference to Jesus' own
case. While the time definitely allotted to him by the Father
lasted, Jesus could come to no harm, for ' the knowledge of
God's will, which is man's moral light, guides him' (Dods).
When God's time had run out for Jesus ' it was night' (13 : 30).
But when a man prolongs his activity beyond the time
appointed by God, he does stumble, having lost the light of
God's guidance (cf. 1 Jn. 2 : 10–11). Verse 10 has no particular application to Jesus' own case, save to emphasize the
need of haste. Two truths are asserted : first, that no harm

can come to Jesus save in God's own time ; second, that an
important task remains to be accomplished while there is yet
time.   Hence we continue: This he said, then added (others 11
translate ' and after this '—supposing an interval of two days
at this point; but see note on 17), ' Our friend Lazarus has
fallen asleep ; I am going to waken him.'   (For death described
as sleeping cf. Mt. 9 : 24, 27 : 52, Acts 7 : 60, 1 Thess. 4 : 13,
1 Cor. 15 : 6.) With Jesus' earlier words (4) in mind, the
disciples now understand him literally: ' Lord,' said the 12
disciples, ' if he has fallen asleep, he will get better '—for sleep
is the best of all cures : they hint that there is no need to take
the risk of a visit to Judaea.   The misunderstanding serves
as usual to throw into prominence Jesus' real meaning:
Jesus, however, had been speaking of his death ; but as they 13
imagined he meant natural sleep, he then told them plainly 14
(i.e. without ambiguity or figure of speech—10 : 24), ' Lazarus
is dead ; and for your sakes—though grieving for Lazarus 15
and the sisters—I am glad that I was not there—implying
that had he been there Lazarus would not have died (21)—
that you may believe—the motive in a phrase of Johannine
miracle ; in the Synoptics Jesus does miracles out of pity :
in our Gospel even pity is crushed back that miracle may
increase faith—Come now, let us go to him.'   Whereupon 16
Thomas (called ' the Twin ') said to his fellow-disciples, ' Let us
go too, let us die along with him.'   The disciples are not yet
supposed to have grasped the fact that Jesus means to raise
Lazarus, and Thomas speaks ' in no mood of expectant faith,
but in loyal despair' (Strachan) (Cf. Mk. 8 : 34–35, 14 : 31).
His words well express Thomas' character, in which obstinate
incredulity is combined with an equally obstinate loyalty
(14 : 5, 20 : 25, 28). ' Didymus ' (A.V.) is not a surname,
but the Greek translation of the Hebrew for Thomas, which
means ' Twin.'   The nickname is perhaps added here as that
by which Thomas was familiarly known among the Greek
Christians of Asia Minor.

Now when Jesus arrived, he found that Lazarus had been 17
buried for four days.   The burial, as usual in the East, would
take place immediately after death.   If then Lazarus died

about the time when Jesus received the message (3), the four days may be reckoned thus: the first, that on which Jesus received the message; the second and third, the two days during which Jesus delayed (6); the fourth, that on which Jesus made the journey to Bethany. Loisy, who traces throughout the Gospel a chronology based on the number seven, thinks that Lazarus is supposed to have died at the moment when Jesus announced his death (14), that four days are allotted to the journey, and that the whole incident occupies a week (the day of the message, two days waiting, four days' journey), so that Lazarus is raised symbolically on the seventh day. The Jews apparently believed that a soul hovered about the dead body for three days, but on the fourth found it so unrecognizable through decay that it finally forsook it (cf. 39). All life had indubitably departed from Lazarus. (Transpose 18–19 to follow 30; so Moffatt.)

20 **Then Martha, hearing of the arrival of Jesus, went out to meet him, while Mary sat at home**—in the attitude of grief (Ezek. 8 : 14). The contrasted actions of the sisters agree with their characters as painted in Lk. 10 : 38 ff. Martha, in sorrow rather than reproach, puts into words what Jesus himself had

21 implied in 15: **Said Martha to Jesus, 'Had you been here, Lord, my brother would not have died.'** But it is not yet too

22 late: **'But now—well, I know whatever you ask God for, He will grant you'** (9 : 31, 11 : 41–42). 'The reticence of this indirect request is admirable' (Godet). Jesus at once answers

23 Martha's faith with a word of promise: **Jesus said to her, 'Your brother will rise again'**—an assurance capable of being interpreted either in a general sense as referring to the resurrection 'on the last day,' or in a particular sense as promising

24 a special miracle. Martha takes it in a general sense: **'I know,' said Martha, 'he will rise at the resurrection, on the last day.'** (For the idea of a general resurrection, based on such passages as Dan. 12 : 2, etc., see notes on 5 : 28 f., 6 : 39 f., 54.) The hope of reunion at the last day is but poor consolation for Martha, conventional comfort such as she had already

25 had from many condolers. Accordingly Jesus replies that 'the resurrection' and the 'life' which it guarantees, are

not future but present, not doctrines but facts, not events in time but states conditional upon a *personal relationship*: Jesus said to her, ' I am myself resurrection and life : he who believes in me will live—by virtue of the ' eternal life ' which is the reward of faith—even if he dies—in the physical sense—and no one who lives—i.e. who has not yet tasted 26 bodily death—and believes in me will ever die.' The man who through faith identifies himself with the personal life-force of Christ will live in spite of death. If, like Lazarus, he has suffered physical death, it has only been in seeming, for he has carried with him into death that same vital relationship through which he ' lived ' on earth. If he is still alive in the physical sense, then, in virtue of that same relationship, the physical death which one day he must face loses all reality. We may compare Paul's thought of a higher life ' in Christ ' (Gal. 2 : 20 ; Col. 3 : 4) and the last words of Edward the Confessor (quoted by Westcott): ' Weep not, I shall not die, but live ; and as I leave the land of the dying I trust to see the blessings of the Lord in the land of the living.' Jesus crowns his promise with a testing question: **' You believe that ? '** 27 Martha, though still puzzled, is willing to accept the saying for the sake of him who said it ; she welcomes ' truth through personality ' : **' Yes, Lord,'** she said, **' I do believe** (the Greek is an emphatic perfect—a ' complete present ') **you are the Christ, the Son of God, who was to come into the world '** (6 : 14 ; Mt. 11 : 3). **And with these words she went off to** 28 **call her sister Mary, telling her secretly**—in order not to cause excitement and direct the attention of Jesus' enemies to him, and also perhaps to give Mary the chance of a private talk with Jesus—**' The Teacher** (evidently the name by which Jesus was known in the household ; 20 : 16) **is here, and he is calling for you.'** So, **on hearing this, Mary rose hurriedly** 29 **and went to him.** With the same desire for privacy **Jesus** 30 **had not entered the village yet, he was still at the spot where Martha had met him ;** he wished to have only the sisters with him at the tomb, but his desire was thwarted: **now as** 18 **Bethany is not far from Jerusalem, only about two miles** 19 **away, a number of Jews had come to condole with Martha**

and Mary about their brother. The proximity of Bethany
to Jerusalem is mentioned in order to explain the presence of
a crowd from Jerusalem, some of them hostile to Jesus (46).
31 For visits of condolence, cf. the Book of Job. **And when
the Jews who were condoling with her inside the house noticed
her rise hurriedly and go out, they followed her, as they
imagined she was going to wail at the tomb.** The period of
deep mourning lasted for a week (1 Sam. 31 : 13), during
32 which a daily visit would be made to the tomb. **But when
Mary came to where Jesus was and saw him, she dropped at
his feet**—thus expressing the urgency of her prayer (Mk.
5 : 22, Lk. 10 : 39)—**crying, 'Had you been here, Lord,
my brother would not have died.'** Her prayer is the same
as Martha's (21), but Jesus' response is different : the situation
now 'called for the act of power and not for the word of
33 power only' (Westcott). **Now when Jesus saw her wailing
and saw the Jews who accompanied her wailing, he chafed
in spirit and was disquieted.** The word here translated
'chafe' is used with an indirect object in Mt. 9 : 30, Mk.
1 : 43, 14 : 5, and in these passages means 'to charge sternly,'
'to upbraid.' The note of the word is strong feeling, whether
expressed to others, as in the Synoptic passages; or inwardly
felt, as here. Christ's emotion is due to his sympathy with
Mary. It always *cost* him something to do a miracle (Mt.
8 : 17, Lk. 8 : 46, Heb. 5 : 7). The idea of 'indignation'
(R.V. margin), whether with the hypocritical mourners or
with death and its author the devil, is hardly present here,
or, if implied, it is indignation that so many should be weeping
over a dead man in the presence of One who is the Lord of
Life (cf. 38 where the cause of Jesus' emotion is again lack of
faith). The phrase translated 'was disquieted' (for which
cf. 12 : 27, 13 : 21) is in Greek active, 'he disquieted himself,'
as if John wished to hint that not even Jesus' emotions over-
came him involuntarily. 'He took to himself freely those
feelings to which others are subject' (Westcott). Jesus is not
acted upon by the contagion of grief, but enters into it while
34 still retaining perfect self-control. **'Where have you laid
him ? ' he asked**—the only occasion in the Gospel on which

Jesus asks for information—They answered, ' Come and see, sir ' (1 : 46). **Jesus burst into tears.** This particular ex- 35 pression of Jesus' emotion seems to have been isolated and specially emphasized in order the more easily to attach to it the reflections of the Jews which follow. Jesus' tears might have seemed more natural at an earlier point in the narrative, but the truth is that the Evangelist, as already noted, makes Jesus restrain his human grief long enough to show that he is superior to the mere contagion of a wailing crowd. Jesus first chafes at the crowd's lack of faith, and only afterwards —as if spontaneously and under no compulsion of human weakness—he ' bursts into tears.' Yet, however artificial his picture of Jesus' grief, John shows real spiritual insight when he thus teaches that ' it is not with a heart of stone that the dead are raised ' (Hengstenberg). **Whereupon the** 36 **Jews said, ' See how he loved him ! '**—though some of them (still puzzled, if not actually ironical) asked, ' Could he not 37 have prevented him from dying, when he could open a blind man's eyes ? ' Note how the Evangelist deliberately connects the two great miracles of chapters 9 and 11 : they are each symbolical of a great spiritual truth : there (9 : 5) Christ is the ' Light,' here he is the ' Life ' (11 : 25). **This made** 38 **Jesus chafe afresh, so he went to the tomb ; it was a cave with a boulder to close it.** The cave-tomb would be either natural (Gen. 23 : 9) or artificial (Mt. 27 : 60), with a boulder at the entrance to keep out wild animals. This would be placed against an aperture facing the spectator rather than as a lid on the top of a pit (cf. 20 : 1, Mk. 16 : 3). **Jesus said, ' Re-** 39 **move the boulder.'** Christ uses supernatural power only to do that which no other power can do ; the rest he leaves to ourselves (cf. 44). **' Lord,' said Martha, the dead man's sister**—who would therefore shrink from seeing the ravages of death upon one so dear to her—**' he will be stinking by this time ; he has been dead four days.'** Martha's remark means ostensibly that it will be no consolation *now* to look for one last time on Lazarus—which she imagines to be the only reason for the opening of the tomb; but from the Evangelist's point of view the remark serves to heighten the wonder

of the miracle. (For the point of 'four days,' see 17.) It is
evident from 44 that Lazarus was partially embalmed, but
the customary Jewish embalmment would not suffice to arrest
decay. Jesus gently rebukes Martha's incredulity by recalling
his promise, which, however, was made to the disciples (4)
40 rather than to Martha herself (23–26) : **'Did I not tell you,'**
said Jesus, **'if you will only believe, you shall see** (here 'believing is seeing': contrast 20 . 25) **the glory of God ? '** God's
'glory' or majesty will be manifested in Jesus' miraculous
power over death (cf. Rom. 6 : 4), and also in the truth, which
the miracle illustrates, that Christ is the source of all spiritual
resurrection and life (cf. notes on 4). 'The glory of God is
the revelation of the life-giving power which is in God, and
41 which is exercised by Christ ' (Loisy). **Then they removed**
the boulder, and Jesus, lifting his eyes to heaven (17 : 1, Ps.
121 : 1, 123 : 1), **said, 'Father, I thank thee for listening to**
me,'—'simple words of thanksgiving, as if already Lazarus
was restored' (Dods), words uttered in the spirit of true
prayer which is 'the conscious realization of the divine will,
and not a petition for that which is contingent' (Westcott)
(cf. Is. 65 : 24). Miracles are 'just so many answered prayers'
(Godet). Jesus wishes to point the crowd to the true source
of the miracle in God (5 : 19, 30) of whose power he himself
is the instrument ; he prays for the sake of confirming, not his
own faith in his power to raise Lazarus, but the crowd's faith
42 in his divine commission : **'I knew thou wouldst always**
listen to me (9 : 31, 11 : 22), **but I spoke on account of the**
crowd, that they might believe thou hast sent me.' The verse
undoubtedly suggests something theatrical in Jesus' prayer.
Loisy goes so far as to say, 'the Johannine Christ prays in
order to expound the thesis of the Evangelist . . . he prays
for the sake of the gallery, for he prays to the Father only to
provoke faith in his own person.' This is to state a partial
truth with exaggerated emphasis. John's purpose is to
insist that the power Christ exercises is God's power. By
prayer Christ audibly invokes God as his ally ; if then the
miracle fails, let him be acknowledged to be an impostor ; if
43 it succeeds, let him be hailed as God's plenipotentiary. **So**

saying, he exclaimed with a loud cry—expressive of divine
authority (5 : 25)—'Lazarus, come out ! ' Out came the 44
dead man, his feet and hands swathed in bandages, and his
face tied up with a towel. Jesus said, ' Untie him, and let
him move.' Jesus himself was similarly bandaged in the
tomb (19 : 40, 20 : 5, 7), but while it is made clear that Jesus
freed himself without touch of human hand (note on ,20 : 7),
Lazarus has to be freed at the word of Jesus. It is useless to
ask how a man thus trussed up could walk out : that is part
of the miracle. Notice how the Evangelist, having driven
home his lesson, has no further interest in the story, and
leaves it hanging in the air. This is consummate art : ' the
absence of a conclusion invites the reader to raise himself
heavenwards and seek among the celestial verities for that
last word which the story seems to lack ' (Loisy).

The story of the raising of Lazarus presents us with one of
the crucial problems of the Gospel. It is impossible to harmonize the incident with the Synoptic chronology of Jesus'
life ; nor is the attempt to do so necessary. Just as apologetic reasons led John to transpose the incident of the Temple-
cleansing to the beginning of the Gospel, so has a similar
motive led to the insertion of the Lazarus story at this point.
Indeed, once the former incident had been displaced it would
become necessary for John to find some substitute for it as
the event which precipitated the arrest and death of Christ.
The story of Lazarus serves to present the Cross, to which it
was the immediate prelude, not as a disaster, but as a victorious
glorifying of the Son of God (11 : 4). In view of the silence
of the Synoptists it is evidently impossible to accept the
narrative as strictly accurate history. It is inconceivable
that the greatest of all recorded miracles, performed during
the last critical week, and in the presence of crowds of people,
should have been simply omitted by the first three Evangelists.
Accordingly many have concluded that the story is pure
allegory, symbolizing the truth that Christ is the supreme
Life-giver—a method of interpretation which may be carried
to the most fantastic extremes ; e.g., according to Loisy,
' Martha who first meets Jesus symbolizes the first Christian

group of converted Jews, and Mary the believing recruits from among the Gentiles, the two groups, united in Jesus, realizing through him the resurrection of humanity, of the man their brother, who lay dead in the tomb for four days, perhaps the four thousand years which preceded the coming of Christ.' (!)   Others suppose that the story has been built up from hints contained in the Synoptics—the raising of Jairus' daughter and the young man of Nain, the story in Luke of the two sisters Martha and Mary, and above all the parable of the rich man and Lazarus, which ends with the suggestive words, ' they will not be convinced, not even if one rose from the dead ' (Lk. 16 : 31).   Possibly, in the course of preaching, what was originally a parable may have been elaborated into a supposed historical incident.   But in view of the vividness of the narrative and, in spite of much that is artificial, the wealth of the circumstantial detail, it may well be that the story is founded upon a real incident, such as the raising of Jairus' daughter (compare 11 : 11 with Lk. 8 : 52), preserved perhaps by ' the Witness,' and elaborated for didactic purposes by the Evangelist, who exaggerates its effect upon the imagination of the crowd from Jerusalem in order to provide himself with a suitable substitute for the Temple-cleansing as the event which provoked the wrath of Jesus' enemies and precipitated the *dénouement* of his life.   For us, even if it be largely unhistorical, the story is none the less precious, for it testifies to the conviction and experience of the Evangelist, and the Church, in whose name he speaks, of the truth that Christ is himself ' resurrection and life.'

By raising Lazarus from death Jesus has signed his own death warrant, and from this point the narrative moves steadily forward to the Cross.   John as usual (10 : 19–21, etc.) sums up the impression left by the miracle ;   there is a division 45 of opinion :   **Now a number of the Jews who had come to visit Mary** (or perhaps ' come after Mary ' with reference to 31 ; this would explain the omission of Martha's name) **and who** 46 **witnessed what he had done, believed in him.   But some of them** (the presence of ill-wishers was hinted in 37) **went off to the Pharisees** (the Pharisaic members of Sanhedrim) **and** told them what Jesus had done. (For this tale-bearing cf. 5 : 15, where, however, the motive is different.) Whereupon 47 the high-priests and the Pharisees (7 : 32) called a meeting of the Sanhedrin. 'Whatever is to be done ? ' they said. 'The fellow is performing a number of Signs.' 'He is busy at his miracles while we stand by in futile inactivity ! ' 'If we let 48 him alone, like this, everybody will believe in him, and then the Romans will come and suppress our holy Place (the temple, rather than the land ; cf. 2 Macc. 5 : 19) and our nation,'— the people over which *we* at present hold authority. Their outlook is essentially selfish : Jesus, they fear, by drawing the mob around him as Messiah, will provoke the vengeance of the Romans, as indeed happened after the Judaean war, with the result that *they* will be docked of their present pre-rogatives. Note that this fear of revolution fits in better with Jesus' claim (as in the Synoptics) to be ' Messiah ' than with the Johannine claim that he is ' the light of the world,' ' resurrection and life.' But one of them, Caiaphas, who was 49 high-priest that year, said . . . ' Caiaphas ' (Cephas) is a surname added to the original name ' Joseph.' He held office A.D. 18–36, when he was deposed by Vitellius. The remark that Caiaphas was high-priest ' that year ' has been held to imply that the Evangelist imagined the high-priestship to be an annual office : rather does he intend to emphasize the fact that in this year of years, the year of the Cross, Caiaphas was high-priest. The frequent changes of office (Josephus, Ant. 20 : 10, tells us that there were twenty-eight high-priests in 107 years) would alone suffice to justify the language. That this is the Evangelist's meaning seems clear from 51, though the Greek phrase used, in the genitive case, would certainly be more natural were an annual office intended. Could the exact turn of phrase be due to the Redactor's translation into Greek of the original Aramaic (Introduction, p. lxvi f.) ? The Redactor, an Ephesian, may have been misled by the analogy of the Asiarchs, who acted as high-priests in the worship of the Emperor, and held office for one year. If it be the case that the Evangelist held Annas to be high-priest (18 : 13), the clause must be an addition by the Redactor. Caiaphas

50 then thus advises : 'You know nothing about it—you do not understand it is in your own interests that one man should die for the People, instead of the whole nation being destroyed.' 'Have you no wits—searching here and there for a solution which is ready to hand! Put him to death! By so doing you will rid yourselves of an undesirable rival, curry favour with the Romans by ridding Caesar of a rival, and so turn aside a vengeance which otherwise would fall on the whole people!' Caiaphas, the Sadducee, is more emphatic than polite. Of Sadducean manners Josephus remarks (*Bell. Jud.* 2, 8, 14) : 'The Pharisees are friendly to each other— but the manners of the Sadducees are far rougher, both to each other and to their equals, whom they treat as strangers.' John puts his own interpretation on Caiaphas' words (cf.

51 2 : 21, 12 : 33) ; he spoke more truly than he knew : He did not say this simply of his own accord ; he was high-priest that year, and his words were a prophecy that Jesus was to

52 die for the nation, and not merely for the nation but to gather into one the scattered children of God. As the guardian of Urim and Thummim the high-priest was regarded as the mouthpiece of the divine oracle (Exod. 28 : 30, Num. 27 : 21), and though, according to Josephus (*Ant.* 6, 6, 3), this method of divination had long fallen into disuse Caiaphas, in virtue of his priestly quality, is held to be inspired—an interesting touch of sacerdotalism. Caiaphas, with all his cunning malevolence, yet becomes the mouthpiece of a magnificent prophecy that Jesus should die as the Universal Saviour. (For a similar prophecy veiled in a taunt, cf. 7 : 35.) 'In the irony of events Caiaphas used his high-priestly office to lead forward that one sacrifice which was for ever to take away sin and so make all further priestly office superfluous' (Dods). In verse 52 we have another fine example of John's universalism (cf. 10 : 16, 17 : 23). 'Scattered children of God' (cf. 1 : 12) is used proleptically of all who by predestination and inward predisposition are destined one day to be 'sons of God'— whoever they may be by race and country, Jew and Gentile alike. There is irony again in the fact that Caiaphas, as a Sadducee, would not believe in predestination!

As a result of Caiaphas' advice the vague plots against 53 Jesus (5 : 16, 7 : 32, 10 : 39) now come to a head in a definite decree in council : So from that day their plan was to kill him. John anticipates the decision taken according to the Synoptists two days before the feast (Mk. 14 : 1). Accord- 54 ingly Jesus—still unwilling needlessly to precipitate a crisis— no longer appeared in public among the Jews, but withdrew to the country adjoining the desert, to a town called Ephraim ; there he stayed with the disciples. ' The desert ' is the Desert of Judaea stretching northwards of Jerusalem, the wilderness of Bethaven in particular. Ephraim (2 Sam. 13 : 23) lies about fifteen miles north of Jerusalem and some six miles east-north-east of Bethel. In ancient times it was known as Ophrah (2 Chron. 13 : 19), and is now called Et-Taiyibeh. This sojourn in the desert compensates for the omission from our Gospel of the ' Temptation.' Would not Jesus be facing precisely the same problems ?

Now the passover of the Jews (2 : 13, as contrasted with the 55 Christian ' passover,' 1 Cor. 5 : 7) was near, and many people went up from the country to Jerusalem, to purify themselves before the passover, i.e. to perform the expiatory ceremonies and sacrifices necessary in order to put themselves in a state of ritual purity in preparation for the feast (Lev. 7 : 21, Num. 9 : 10 ff., 2 Chron. 30 : 17–18, Jn. 18 : 28, Acts 21 : 24–26). They looked out for Jesus, and as they stood in the temple 56 (where these rites would be performed) they said to one another, ' What do you think ? Do you think he will not come up to the festival ? ' (Cf. the discussion 7 : 10–13.) Will Jesus be true to his habit of coming up to the feast ? They doubt it ; for the high-priests and the Pharisees had given orders (in conse- 57 quence of the decision of 53) that they were to be informed, if anyone found out where he was, so that they might arrest him. It would not have been difficult for the authorities to discover Jesus' place of refuge ; yet they are represented as powerless to do so. Even when Jesus appears at Jerusalem he is left unmolested till one of his own circle betrays him. Not a finger may be laid on him ' till his time is come.'

Theme (i) : The Homage of a Disciple (12 : 1-8)

Chapter 12 serves at once as a conclusion to the story of Lazarus and as a prelude to the Passion. John's version of the anointing at Bethany is a good example alike of his dependence upon the Synoptists, and of his independence in the treatment of detail. In the Synoptics he found two accounts of an anointing of Jesus : according to Mark (14 : 3-9) and Matthew (26 : 6-13) it occurred in Bethany immediately before Jesus' death ; according to Luke (7 : 36-50) it occurred in Galilee a long time before his death. In both cases the master of the house is called Simon, and though in Mark and Matthew he is a leper, and in Luke a Pharisee, the fact that the name was in each case the same seems to have led John to identify the two incidents. Accordingly we find traits drawn from each story (see ver. 3). Moreover, though neither Mark nor Matthew mentions the woman's name, John (possibly through a previous identification of the ' woman who was a sinner ' and ' stood at his feet ' in Lk. 7 : 37-38 with the ' Mary ' who ' sat at Jesus' feet ' in Lk. 10 : 39) is prepared to identify the woman of the anointing incident with Mary of Bethany, the sister of Martha and Lazarus. In point of fact there is no evidence for the popular identification either of Mary of Bethany or of Mary Magdalene with ' the woman that was a sinner.' The close verbal agreements with Mark and Matthew are clear proof of John's dependence.

1 Six days before the festival, Jesus came to Bethany, where Lazarus stayed (whom Jesus had raised from the dead). The Synoptists (Mk. 14 : 1) date the incident two days before the festival, but according to them the triumphal entry had already taken place. John's date is probably intended to have symbolical significance. Schmiedel, reckoning inclusively from Saturday 15th Nisan, the first day of the feast, fixes the date as Monday the 10th, the day on which the sacrificial lamb was consecrated (Exod. 12 : 13) ; on that day the ' Lamb of God ' was consecrated for his sacrificial death (12 : 7, Mk. 14 : 8). Westcott, who gives the date as 8th Nisan (the Saturday, the triumphal entry following on ' Palm Sunday '),

remarks that ' John appears to mark the period as the new
Hexaemeron, a solemn period of six days, the time of the new
Creation. His Gospel begins and closes with a sacred week.'
Loisy, reckoning exclusively from 14th Nisan (the day of the
Passover meal, which he assumes to be for John the beginning
of the feast, the Thursday before this being, according to
13 : 1, the eve of the festival), also fixes on 8th Nisan, the last
Sabbath before the Passion. Schmiedel's date seems more
probable as providing a symbolical motive for John's anticipa-
tion of the Synoptic date, though Loisy's better suits 13 : 1.

**They gave a supper for him there ; Martha waited on him 2
(Lk. 10 : 40), and Lazarus was among those who reclined at
table with him.** The presence of Lazarus is mentioned in
order to emphasize the reality of the miracle. John evidently
supposes the supper to have taken place in the house of Jesus'
three friends ; those who would harmonize John's narrative
with that of the Synoptists hold that the supper was given by
Simon, and that Lazarus was merely present as a guest. **Then 3
Mary, taking a pound of expensive perfume, real nard, anointed
the feet of Jesus and wiped his feet with her hair, till the house
was filled with the scent of the perfume.** The ' pound ' would
be slightly over 11 oz. av. The meaning of the Greek word
(*pistikos*) here translated ' real ' is much disputed. Others
take it to be a place-name (e.g. from Opis, a town in Babylonia)
or a botanic term (Pistacia terebinthus), or translate it as
' drinkable ' (!). The word is taken over from Mark (14 : 3),
and in any case the force is that the perfume was ' expensive '
—also a Synoptic echo (Mt. 26 : 7). Note how John somewhat
artificially combines traits from Mark and Luke. In Mark the
woman anoints Jesus' head, a natural and appropriate action ;
in Luke she weeps over Jesus' feet, dries the tears with her
hair, and finally anoints his feet, again a beautiful act of
homage. Here the tears of a sinful woman do not suit the
case of Mary, and accordingly John makes her wipe the *perfume*
with her hair from Jesus' feet, surely a very unnatural pro-
ceeding. Symbolically, however, there is a certain fitness
in the alteration. Mary, who figures the Church, receives
back to herself at Jesus' feet the perfume of the Gospel which

fills the whole world—an idea (' the house was filled ') which takes the place of another saying about the Gospel in the Synoptics (Mk. 14 : 9).

4 One of his disciples, Judas Iscariot (who was to betray him)
5 (6 : 71), said, ' Why was not this perfume sold for ten pounds (from Mk. 14 : 5 ; ' a day-labourer's wage for a year '—Dods), and the money given to the poor ? ' Matthew (26 : 8) leaves all the disciples under the reproach which John here transfers to Judas alone ; Mark (14 : 4, ' some of those present ') is still more vague ; John loves to particularize (18 : 10, etc.).
6 Judas' motive was not that he cared for the poor ; he said this because he was a thief, and because he carried the money-box (the word literally means the case in which musicians kept the mouthpieces of flutes) and pilfered what was put in. According to the A.V. translation Judas merely ' *bare* what was put in.' But the word means not only ' to carry,' but to ' carry off.' (Compare the Scots ' lift ' in the sense of ' steal '— ' cattle-lifting.') The ' money-box ' would contain either the general funds of the company, or the money set apart for charity, as was the custom in early Christian communities (cf. 13 : 29). This reference to Judas' love of money takes the place in our Gospel of the Synoptic tradition that Judas sold Jesus for money, a feature which John omits, perhaps as inconsistent with his predominant idea that Jesus was complete master of his fate. Then said Jesus, ' Let her alone, let her
7 keep what she has for the day of my burial.' Apparently only a portion of the perfume has been poured out ; the vessel has not been ' broken ' as in Mark, and Jesus bids Mary's critics allow her to keep the remainder for his burial. But this is a strangely prosaic misunderstanding of Mark's much more deep-sighted explanation that this was a prophetic anointing, a tribute rendered in anticipation of Jesus' approaching death. Loisy, accepting the reading translated above, finds a deeper symbolical meaning in the idea that the Gospel truth (perfume) is to be cherished until the time comes when through the death of Jesus it may be released into all the world (cf. 16 : 7, 13) ; but this is far-fetched. One feels that it is unlikely that John, with his love of the symbolical, should have

failed to seize upon Mark's explanation, especially if, as seems likely, he has in view the idea of the consecration of the Paschal lamb. Hence perhaps the T.R. reading and the A.V. translation may be correct : ' Let her alone ! It is in anticipation of my burial that she has kept this '—instead of selling it. The alteration in the text may have been due to the obtuseness of a scribe who could not perceive how this day of anointing could by anticipation be called Jesus' ' day of burial,' nor how the perfume could have been ' kept ' for it. **' You have always 8 the poor beside you, but you have not always me '**—an almost verbal echo of Mark (cf. Deut. 15 : 11). As the occasion is unique and the opportunity a last one, the extravagance is justifiable. Of this incident Strachan well writes : ' Do we appraise at its true value the artistic, mystical, contemplative, symbolic, as a means of communion with God or of understanding the supreme sacrifice of Jesus ? The thoughts that filled his heart at the supper table lay too deep for words or tears, and he himself took refuge in deathless symbols. In Mary he recognizes a kindred and understanding soul ' (*Fourth Gospel*, p. 158).

Theme (ii) : The Homage of the Jews (12 : 9–19)

Now the great mass of the Jews (as distinct from the author- 9 ities) **learned he was there** (11 : 56), **and they came not only on account of Jesus but to see Lazarus whom he had raised from the dead**—' an easily accessible and undoubted sensation ' (Dods). **So the high-priests planned to kill Lazarus as 10 well, since it was owing to him that a number of Jews went 11 away** (not merely from Bethany, but from the Jewish faith to Christianity) **and believed in Jesus.** The high-priests being Sadducees would feel special animosity against Lazarus as a witness to the possibility of life through death (Mk. 12 : 18).

According to the Synoptists the triumphal entry into Jeru- 12 salem took place several days before the anointing. Note that our Gospel, in the Lazarus story, furnishes a motive for the people's enthusiasm, the reason for which is not sufficiently clear in the Synoptics. **Next day** (see ver. 1 ; the Church

commemorates it as ' Palm Sunday ') the great mass of the
people who had come up for the festival (i.e. they were pilgrims,
not Jerusalemites) heard that Jesus was entering Jerusalem
(i.e. that he had left Bethany and was on his way to the city),
13 and taking palm-branches(the symbol of victory and rejoicing—
Rev. 7 : 9) they went out to meet him, shouting, ' Hosanna !
Blessed be he who comes in the Lord's name, the king of Israel ! '
In the Synoptics (Mk. 11 : 9, etc.) Jesus comes from Jericho,
and is hailed not by a crowd coming out of Jerusalem, but by
his disciples and fellow-pilgrims from the north. ' Hosanna '
is Hebrew for ' save now ! ' The people's cry of welcome is
from Ps. 118 : 25–26, the Dedication Psalm of the Second
Temple, to which John, like Luke, adds the acclamation as
' king,' probably with reference to Zech. 9 : 9 (quoted Mt. 21 : 5).
In the original context the words are the welcome addressed
by the priest to the worshippers. (For ' he who comes ' cf.
6 : 14, 11 : 27.) It is not clear whether, as a matter of history,
the people took Jesus to be Messiah himself, or merely one who
would prepare for his coming, e.g. Elijah (1 : 21, Mk. 9 : 11 f.).
John undoubtedly assumes the former alternative ; accordingly he abruptly introduces the ' ass ' of the Synoptists in
order to point to the fulfilment of Zechariah's Messianic
prophecy. Jesus, hailed as king, accepts the homage, at last
allows the enthusiasm of the crowd to have free course, and
adopts the recognized method of entry predicted for the
14 Messiah : And Jesus came across a young ass and seated
15 himself on it ; as it is written, 'Fear not, daughter of
Sion ; here is your king coming, seated on an ass's colt.'
Whatever rôle the crowd understood Jesus to be adopting,
it seems clear that Jesus himself deliberately set out to
fulfil in detail Zechariah's prophecy, thus unmistakably
laying claim to the Messiahship. According to the Synoptists
Jesus had previously obtained the ass with this end in view.
John makes the fulfilment of the prediction seem even more
striking by suggesting that Jesus ' came across ' the ass by
a providential chance (1 : 43, etc.). The whole incident reminds us that the question, how far O.T. prediction and the
naïve desire to represent Jesus as its fulfilment may have

influenced the facts of the Gospel narratives, is one well worth thought. ' Daughter of Sion ' is the city personified. John changes Zechariah's ' rejoice greatly ' into ' fear not,' perhaps echoing Is. 40 : 9. Nor does he quote the Hebrew poetic parallelism which leads Matthew to imagine a foal as well as an ass! The ass, in contrast to the usual war-horse of a victorious leader, is symbolic of lowliness and peace. Jesus comes, not as a military, but as a spiritual Messiah. There follows a com- 16 ment, evidently the reflection of one writing long afterwards, added apparently by the Evangelist in order to emphasize the fact that the Messianic entry was not stage-managed by Jesus and his disciples as might appear from the Synoptic account : His disciples did not understand this at first ; but when Jesus was glorified (i.e. crucified, risen, ascended—7 : 39), then they remembered (14 : 26) this had been written of him and had happened to him—literally ' they had done this to him ' : ' the disciples had themselves assisted in accomplishing a prophecy of which at the time they were not thinking' (Godet).

John's chief interest in the triumphal entry is to relate it on the one hand to the raising of Lazarus as its cause and on the other hand to the Crucifixion as its sequel. This he does in the next three verses. Now the people who were with him when 17 he called Lazarus from the tomb and raised him from the dead, testified to it—i.e. to the fact of the miracle ; and that was why 18 the crowd went out to meet him, because they heard he had performed this Sign. Then said the Pharisees to one another, 19 ' You see, you can do nothing ! ' How ineffective our half-measures! Follow Caiaphas' advice (11 : 49)! ' Look, the world has gone after him.' For the expression cf. *tout-le-monde* : on the Pharisees' lips it would mean ' the common mob,' but in the thought of the Evangelist literally ' all the world ' (11 : 52, 12 : 3).

Theme (iii): The Homage of the Gentile World (12 : 20-36)

The acclamation of Christ's own people is now crowned by the tribute of the Gentile world. In the visit of the Greeks some with unnecessary ingenuity see a reference to the visit of Abgarus of Edessa recorded by Eusebius 1 : 13.

20 **Now there were some Greeks among those who had come up to worship at the festival.** These would be Greek proselytes or semi-proselytes (' god-fearers,' ' adherents' of Judaism) perhaps from Decapolis, not Hellenist Jews, but pure Greeks
21 who practised Jewish rites. **They came to Philip of Bethsaida in Galilee and appealed to him.** (For Bethsaida see 1 : 44.) They would consult Philip perhaps as a Greek speaker—his name at least is Greek—or because they had known him in Galilee; or possibly Philip is selected by the Evangelist simply because his was a well-known name in the district where John wrote (see 1 : 44). They came saying, ' Sir, we want to see Jesus.'
22 Philip, as usual (6 : 7, 14 : 8) is cautious : **Philip went and told Andrew** (his fellow-townsman, 1 : 44, and regularly paired with him, 6 : 7–8, Mk. 3 : 18) ; **Andrew and Philip went and told Jesus.** John hints that it is only by the mediation of Apostolic preaching that the Gentiles can be brought to Christ. Note that we are not even told whether the request for an interview was granted : we pass straight on to Jesus' reflections prompted by the request. John has no interest in the story for its own sake. The Greeks are brought on the stage only as a cue for Jesus' great discourse upon the necessity of his death and the *universal* salvation (32) which will result from it. The reply to the Greeks' appeal is that, though Jesus in the flesh confined himself chiefly to the Jews (Mt. 15 : 24), yet by the power of his Spirit he will draw also the Gentiles to himself. In Jesus' cry of triumph John sees the promise of that Gentile mission in which Christianity was to achieve its permanent success.

23 **And Jesus answered, 'The hour has come for the Son of man to be glorified '**—outwardly in this the homage of even the Gentile world, but also in the profounder sense that the Cross, itself the step to the throne of glory, is at hand (11 : 4). At last his hour (2 : 4, 13 : 1) has come ; he is to be enthroned as the world's Messiah ; yet there is only one way to the
24 throne, the way of death : **' Truly, truly I tell you, unless a grain of wheat falls into the earth and dies**—being broken up in

process of germination—it remains a single grain—because
it is sterile—but if it dies—thus letting loose the hidden life-
force—it bears rich fruit' (Mk. 4 : 8). The allegory is suggested perhaps in part by 1 Cor. 15 : 36–37. We are also
reminded of the image of the ' bread of life,' especially 6 : 51.
The verse states a general truth, but has of course special
reference to Jesus' own death. His earthly life is like a seed,
buried for a time only to reappear in greater fulness. It is
only by Jesus' physical death that his spiritual powers can be
released into the world and multiplied beyond measure (cf.
7 : 39, 16 : 7). ' One chief element in the Johannine theory
of the death is that it was the appointed means of freeing the
work of Christ from its necessary limitations and making it
available for all the world ' (E. F. Scott) (cf. 14 : 12). Note
that the analogy of the decay and rebirth of vegetation, which
was the root idea of the Demeter mysteries, would have a
special appeal to Greek enquirers. The principle is next
extended from Christ, the giver of eternal life, to every seeker
after it : ' He who loves his life (*psyche*, the physical life of 25
the senses) loses it, and he who cares not for his life in this
world will preserve it for eternal life ' (*zōe*, the living state).
The saying is borrowed almost verbally from the Synoptics
(Mk. 8 : 35, etc.), though ' eternal life ' here carries its peculiar
Johannine significance. The man who hoards up life's powers
and opportunities and uses them only for selfish ends stultifies
life's fruitfulness and ' dies ' ; he who lavishes life on others
will find it given back to him with interest in the world of the
spirit. Christ thus passes judgment on Hellenism : ' for what
was Greek civilization but human life cultivated from the
view-point of enjoyment, and withdrawn from the law of
sacrifice ? ' (Godet). ' If anyone serves me, let him follow me, 26
and where I am, there shall my servant be also.' Jesus speaks
as if *already* he were in his ' glory.' The idea of ' following '
also occurs in the parallel Synoptic passages, but there it
precedes the promise of life gained through death. The
word here used for ' servant ' (*diakonos*) is appropriate as
meaning one in close attendance as opposed to a *doulos* who
may serve at a distance and out of sight and mind. The

true pledge of loyalty is obedience even to death (cf. 21 : 19) : its reward is to share the Master's ' glory ' ; for even as the Master is ' glorified,' so shall the servant be ' honoured ' : ' If anyone serves me, my Father will honour him ' (cf. Mt. 10 : 32). It is the holder of the humble office who has the greater honour (Mt. 20 : 27 and the whole thought of 13 : 1–17).

In the following verses we have the Johannine counterpart of the agony in Gethsemane, which the Evangelist omits as inconsistent with his doctrine of Christ's person. On the 27 threshold of the Passion Jesus for a moment trembles : ' My soul is now disquieted ' (Mt. 26 : 38)—his soul (the *psyche*, physical life, of ver. 25), which must be lost in order to be preserved and yet shrinks from the ordeal of death. In 11 : 33 and 13 : 21 it is in ' spirit ' that Jesus is disquieted. ' What am I to say ? (Am I to say) "Father, save me from this hour " ? ' Perish the thought ! John thus tacitly corrects the Synoptic tradition that Jesus was ever subject enough to human weakness to pray ' My Father, if it is possible, let this cup pass me ' (Mt. 26 : 39). ' Nay, it is something else that has brought me to this hour—or perhaps ' it is for this very purpose (to endure this death) that I have come 28 to this hour '—I will say, " Father, glorify thy name." ' In the Synoptics Jesus prays ' thy will be done ! ' John, who teaches that Jesus' will is ever identical with the Father's (8 : 28–29) changes the language while preserving the thought. Similarly he preserves the saying about the cup (18 : 11), but in an exactly opposite sense. ' Glorify thy name ' means ' complete the revelation of thy holy love—even at the price of my agony.' Then came a voice from heaven, ' I have glorified it, and I will glorify it again.' The Father's ' name,' or true character, had already been manifested in Jesus' works (5 : 36, 11 : 40, etc.), and was soon again to be manifested in the Passion and its issue, the triumph of the Resurrection and the victories of the Spirit through the preaching of the Gospel. The idea of ' a voice from heaven ' (the *Bath Qol* or ' daughter-voice') is common in Rabbinical literature. In the Synoptics it is heard at the Baptism (Mk. 1 : 11) and at the Transfiguration (Mk. 9 : 7), which in Mark, as here, follows a foreboding of the Passion. John figuratively conveys the thought that Jesus' prayer is 'heard' and 'answered.' The voice takes the place of the consoling angel in Luke (22 : 43), and is so interpreted : When they heard the 29 sound, the people standing by said it had thundered ; others said, 'An angel spoke to him.' A divine voice can be heard only by those who have the spiritual capacity for hearing ; those without moral and spiritual insight put a materialistic interpretation even upon the self-revelation of God.

> The angels keep their ancient places ;
> Turn but a stone and start a wing ;
> 'Tis ye, 'tis your estrangèd faces,
> That miss the many-splendoured thing.

Compare the various accounts of Paul's conversion (Acts 9 : 7, 22 : 9, 26 : 14). Jesus answered, 'This voice did not 30 come for my sake—he had no need of reassurance—but for yours '—in order that all the world might learn the relation between the Cross and the Glory. 'Now is this world to be 31 judged ; now the Prince of this world (i.e. Satan—Rev. 12 : 7 ff., Eph. 2 : 2, 2 Cor. 4 : 4) will be expelled (Lk. 10 : 17 ff.). But I, when I am lifted up from the earth, will draw (6 : 44, 32 Hos. 11 : 4) all men to myself.' Soon Jesus is to be tried before his people ; yet it is not so much he as they who are on trial : by their attitude to Christ the moral condition of all men is to be judged (3 : 18, 5 : 27, Lk. 2 : 34). Satan too, by prompting the betrayal (13 : 27), thought to destroy Jesus ; but in truth he was but bringing judgment on himself. (16 : 11), for the Cross would destroy the power of sin and become the mighty magnet whereby Christ would draw the world to himself. As is clear from the comment which follows—by this he 33 indicated the kind of death he was to die (probably a gloss ; cf. 18 : 32, 21 : 19)—the primary reference in 'lifted up' (cf. 3 : 14, 8 : 28 : the Aramaic word would mean both 'lift' and 'crucify') is to the elevation on the Cross. But the word is deliberately chosen to make possible the *double-entente* whereby the Cross is again shown to be the step to the Throne, and the Passion, wherein the Spirit broke through the limitations of Jesus' physical life and became communicable to ' all men,' is hailed as the climax of Jesus' exaltation to glory (Phil. 2 : 8 f., Col. 2 : 14 f.).

(For the rearrangement of the text suggested at this point see note on p. 77 f.) We propose after 12 : 32 (12 : 33 being treated as a gloss) to insert 3 : 14-15, then to read 12 : 34 followed by 3 : 16-21, the whole paragraph finding an appropriate climax in 12 : 35-36. For commentary on verses from chapter 3 see notes *in loco*).

' Indeed the Son of man must be lifted on high, just as Moses lifted up the serpent in the desert, that everyone who believes 34 in him may have eternal life ' (3 : 14-15). So the people answered, ' We have learned from the Law that the Christ is to remain for ever ; what do you mean by saying that the Son of man must be lifted up ? Who is this Son of man ? ' The Cross is ' to the Jews an offence ' (1 Cor. 1 : 23), for, according to their programme, the Messiah was to be the perpetual vicegerent in a new theocratic state. That he was to ' remain for ever ' would be deduced from such passages as Ps. 110 : 4, Is. 9 : 7, Ezek. 37 : 25, Dan. 7 : 14 ; cf. Lk. 1 : 32 f. How is this consistent with the hint that ' this Son of man ' (an expression which presupposes the use of the title by Jesus in the previous verse ; this is obtained by our insertion) must die ? Clearly the ' Son of man ' cannot be identical with the Christ (note on 1 : 51). Who then is he ? Jesus' answer, we suggest, is contained in 3 : 16-21, which we insert at this point : **Then Jesus said to them ' God loved the world so dearly . . .'** (See notes *in loco*.)

35 As the text stands Jesus, as at 8 : 54, etc., refuses to give a direct answer, but rather meets his questioners' difficulties by ' charging them to use the opportunities which they still had for fuller knowledge ' (Westcott). But verses 35-36 have very much more point when they are read as the climax of 3 : 16-21, thus : ' And this is the sentence of condemnation, that the Light has entered the world and yet men have preferred darkness to light. . . . Anyone whose life is true comes out into the light, to make it plain that his actions have been

divinely prompted (3 : 19–21). 'The Light will shine among
you for a little longer yet (7 : 33, 13 : 33, 14 : 19, 16 : 16 ff.) ;
walk while you have the Light, that the darkness may not overtake you. He who walks in the dark does not know where he is
going.' (For the imagery cf. 8 : 12, 11 : 9 f., Jer. 13 : 16.
'Overtake' is the same word as 'master' in 1 : 5 ; cf. 1 Thess.
5 : 4.) The general truth expressed in the last sentence is now
applied to the special case of those who find their 'Light' in
Christ : 'While you have the Light, believe in the Light, that 36
you may be sons of the Light.' '*Sons* of the Light' (Lk. 16 : 8,
1 Thess. 5 : 5, Eph. 5 : 8) is the common Hebraism expressive
of close relationship. (Mt. 8 : 12, 9 : 15, Mk. 3 : 17, etc.)
'Sons of Light' are those who find the source of their life in the
Light (8 : 12) and live by the ideals which that Light reveals.

Conclusion : The Struggle of Faith with Unbelief (12 : 36–50)

Verses 44–50 should be transposed to this point. In its
usual position Jesus' renewal of his address at 44 is awkward
after his withdrawal at 36 *b* and 'the cry does not suit the
secrecy' (Moffatt). With the proposed transposition the idea
of 'light' is carried on without interruption, 44–50 supplies
the climax of Jesus' speech, at 36 *b* Jesus withdraws (the verse
according to Bacon is 'a carefully elaborated ending of the
public ministry'), and finally in verses 37–43 the Evangelist
gives us his customary summing up. Bacon (*Fourth Gospel*,
p. 506) argues that this order is confirmed by Tatian.

And Jesus cried aloud—as if uttering a momentous oracle 44
(1 : 15, 7 : 28, 37)—'He who believes in me believes not in me
but in Him who sent me,—for it is as God's ambassador that
Christ comes (5 : 36 f., 7 : 16, 8 : 19, 42 ; 13 : 20)—and he who 45
beholds me beholds Him who sent me (14 : 9). (For the connexion of 'believing' and 'seeing' in the Gospel cf. 3 : 15, 6 : 40.)
I have come as light into the world (1 : 4 f., 3 : 19, 9 : 5), that 46
no one who believes in me may remain in the dark (8 : 12,
9 : 39–41, 1 Jn. 2 : 9 ff.). If anyone hears my words and does 47
not keep them, it is not I who judge him ; for I have not come
to judge the world but to save the world. (See notes on 3 : 17,

T

48 5 : 24, 8 : 15.)   He who rejects me (1 : 11, Lk. 10 : 16, 1 Thess. 4 : 8) and will not receive my words has indeed a judge : the word I have spoken will judge him on the last day.'   For the ' sifting ' power of Jesus' teaching see notes on 3 : 18 and 5 : 28 f., and for the significance given to Jesus' *words* see 6 : 63, 68. Christ will confine himself to applying to each life the rule of his word ; each man will be judged by his response to the light which he has received, the spiritual opportunities which he has enjoyed ; nor will any personal bias enter into Christ's judgment ; indeed, his words have this power to ' judge ' simply because he is but the mouthpiece of God (5 : 30, 8 : 16) :

49 ' for I have not spoken of my own accord (7 : 16-18)—the Father who sent me, He it is who ordered me what to say and what to speak—i.e. the doctrine and the words in which it is clothed, the content and the form of the teaching (cf. 8 : 43).

50 And I know His orders mean eternal life.   Therefore when I speak, I speak as the Father has told me.'   Jesus means not merely ' my commission is one to preach the message of eternal life,' but ' my commission is one which issues in eternal life.'   The words spoken by Jesus in obedience to the Father's orders have themselves the power to bestow life (6 : 63, 68). Note how these concluding verses set forth at the close of Jesus' public teaching the leading ideas concerning faith, light, judgment, life, which have run through the whole Gospel, and summarize the issue both for those who believe and those who do not.   Jesus' public ministry is now over ; he withdraws from the world which has rejected him

36 into the bosom of his own friends : **With these words Jesus went away and hid from them.**

The Evangelist now sums up the result of the public ministry :

37 **Now for all the Signs he had performed before them, they did not believe in him.**   John assumes more miracles than the seven which he narrates as types (7 : 31, 11 : 47, 21 : 25). That the Jews of all people should have rejected the Christ, and this in spite of so many signs conspicuously performed, would, John feels, require explanation : the reason was

38 that the word spoken by the prophet Isaiah might be fulfilled : ' Lord, who has believed what they heard from us ?   And

to whom has the arm of the Lord been revealed ? ' John
expresses himself as if it were not the coming event which
prompted the prediction but the prediction which determined
the event—not improbably a true explanation of some of the
details recorded in the Gospels (note on 12 : 14). The quotation is from Is. 53 : 1 ff., the famous passage dealing with ' the
Servant of the Lord,' in whom, though not originally a
Messianic figure, Christian tradition, based probably on our
Lord's own teaching, recognized Jesus. The words translated
' what they heard from us ' may mean either ' the message
which came from us ' or ' the message which concerns us.'
In the original the reference is to ' the message received from
God by the prophet '—which none would believe. Paul
(Rom. 10 : 16) applies it to ' the message which they heard from
us,' i.e. the Apostolic testimony. John sees in it an allusion
to Christ's teaching, just as in ' the arm of the Lord ' he sees
an allusion to the divine power manifested in his miracles.
This was why they could not believe : the words refer both back 39
to one prophecy and forward to another about to be quoted.
Verse 40 indeed gives ' a reason for the reason ' (Loisy) :
' This was why they could not believe ; **for Isaiah again said,** 40
**' He has blinded their eyes and made their hearts insensible, to
prevent them seeing with their eyes and understanding with
their hearts and turning for me to cure them.'** The quotation
is from Is. 6 : 9–10. In the original the words are a command
addressed by God to the prophet. The Synoptists (Mt.
13 : 14 f., Mk. 4 : 12, Lk. 8 : 10 ; cf. Acts 28 : 25 ff.), following
the LXX, give the imperatives a less personal form, and use the
passage to explain the reason for Jesus' parabolic teaching
and the failure of his Galilean ministry. John suggests that
God Himself is responsible for the blinding. ' By abuse of
light nature produces callousness ; and what nature does, God
does ' (Dods). ' For me to cure ' is here understood of Jesus,
in whose name Isaiah is supposed to speak. John also adds
a comment—**Isaiah said this because he saw his glory and spoke** 41
of him—whereby he identifies the divine Being seen by Isaiah
(6 : 1) with that Christ who is ' the likeness of the unseen
God ' (Col. 1 : 15) ' stamped with God's own character '

271

(Heb. 1 : 3).   The Targum renders Isaiah's words here ' I saw the Lord's glory.'

Yet to this general unbelief there were exceptions even in those quarters where least they might have been expected :
42 Still, a number even of the authorities (7 : 26, 48 ; i.e. the members of the Sanhedrim) believed in him, though they would not confess it on account of the Pharisees, in case of being
43 excommunicated (9 : 22) ; they preferred the approval of men to the approval of God (5 : 44).   Of these Westcott says : ' This complete intellectual faith (so to speak) is really the climax of unbelief.   The conviction found no expression in life ' (cf. Rom. 10 : 10).   Godet would rather call them ' Erasmuses ' who welcomed the new truth but clung to the old system.   We have examples in Nicodemus who ' came one night to Jesus ' (3 : 2), and in Joseph of Arimathea who is described as ' a secret disciple—for fear of the Jews ' (19 : 38).

ACT III.   THE ENJOYMENT OF THE NEW GOSPEL : CHRIST'S COMMUNION WITH HIS OWN

Illustration (i) : The Washing of the Disciples' Feet (13 : 1–38)

Jesus having withdrawn from the world devotes himself to the instruction of ' his own.'   The din of polemics is hushed, and in the following chapters, as the mystic Tauler puts it, ' how sweetly and how gladly has Christ opened the Door into the Father's heart, into the treasure-chamber of God, and there within he unfolds to us the hidden riches, the nearness and the sweetness of companionship with himself.'

The incident of the washing of the disciples' feet takes in our Gospel the place occupied in the Synoptics by the institution of the Lord's Supper.   Why John, with his intense love of the symbolical, should have chosen to omit the Institution of the Sacrament from his narrative of the Last Supper has been partly discussed in connexion with chapter 6, where see notes on verses 11, 20, 53, 59, 63.   It is held by some that the Evangelist is a mystic who puts no value on Sacraments (cf. 4 : 2), surely a strange misreading of the mind of the man who could write

3 : 5 and 6 : 52–58. Rather may we explain the omission by John's desire to detach his sacramental teaching from any historical occasion and attach it to the eternal realities of the Spirit. In particular John wishes to connect the Sacrament less with Christ's death and more with his life-giving power. Hence in chapter 6 the institution is associated with the life-giving miracle of the feeding of the multitude, while the place held in the Synoptics by the institution is here filled by the feet-washing, which symbolizes not Christ's death but his spirit of lowly service. This suggests that once again John wishes to counteract superstitious sacramentalism : just as in 6 : 63 he insists that ' what gives life is the Spirit,' so in 13 : 8, 15, does he insist that the Sacrament can be effective only when the Spirit of the Master possesses the disciples. The bequest which Jesus left his disciples in the Sacrament was not a ritual ordinance but a spirit of love and service which would unite them in fellowship one with another and with himself and would be the badge of their discipleship (13 : 34 f.). John here emphasizes the ethical aspect of the Lord's Supper, the neglect of which renders impossible the appropriation of that dying love of Jesus which in the Sacrament we symbolize : ' Unless I wash you,' says Jesus, ' you will not share my lot ' (13 : 8).

Now before—(or ' on the eve of ')—**the passover festival 1 Jesus knew the time had come for him to pass from this world to the Father** ; his ' hour ' which had tarried at 2 : 4, 7 : 6, etc., which he had hailed at 12 : 23, is now upon him. According to the Johannine chronology the evening will be that of Thursday 13th Nisan, and the supper in question will not be the Passover meal, but an ordinary meal taken on the previous evening. For according to John Jesus was crucified before the Feast proper (i.e. the 15th), the execution taking place before six o'clock on the evening of the 14th—Christ's death thus coinciding with the evening Passover meal at which the Paschal lamb was killed. (On the question of the date of the Crucifixion see Introduction, p. xiii.)

He had loved his own (cf. 1 : 11 ; but here the phrase seems restricted to the inmost circle of his peculiar friends) **in this**

world—the place which he had stooped to and is about to abandon, leaving his friends to represent him—**and he loved them to the end**—not merely ' to the end of his life ' nor ' to the utmost degree,' but ' to the utmost limits of love.' ' Love . . . bears it out even to the edge of doom ' (Shak. Sonnets, 116).

2 **So at supper** (not ' when supper was over,' which is contradicted by 21 ff.), **knowing that though the devil had**
3 **suggested to Judas Iscariot, Simon's son, to betray him, the Father had put everything into his hands,** i.e. ' had remitted to him the whole work of salvation and the means of accomplishing it ' (Loisy) (cf. 3 : 35). The remark about the devil's suggestion to Judas might seem to anticipate 27, and to avoid this some MSS. read ' the devil having formed the idea in his own heart that Judas should betray him.' But the suggestion here instilled may be supposed not to take possession of Judas' mind till 27 : ' The idea had been entertained if we cannot say that the purpose had been already formed ' (Dods). Jesus, then, **knowing that he had come from God and was going to God**—conscious of his divine mission and his divine destiny (thus is the supreme condescension of his act
4 emphasized)—**rose from the table, laid aside his robe, and tied**
5 **a towel round him, then poured water into a basin, and began to wash the feet of the disciples, wiping them with the towel he had tied round him.** It seems strange that the feet-washing did not precede supper ; but Jesus may well have postponed the act to make it more impressive. A host was expected to provide water to wash his guests' feet heated with the dust of the road (Lk. 7 : 44). When Jesus and his companions were fending for themselves the office would be performed by one of the disciples. But according to Lk. 22 : 21–30 (where the announcement of the betrayal immediately precedes the quarrel about precedence in the kingdom and Jesus' rejoinder about the nobility of service), the disciples were at the moment standing on their dignity, and none would be willing to stoop to the menial office. So Jesus does it himself ; he will ' set them an example ' ; the washing of one another's feet, like the breaking of bread in the Synoptics, the place of which it here takes, is to be the

memorial tribute of the disciples to one who gave himself in
service to them (14; Mk. 10 : 45). The 'laying aside' of his
robe is symbolic of the 'laying down' of his life (10 : 17–18;
the Greek word is the same). Common folk wore a tunic
and over it a cloak, and the latter, sometimes even the former,
would be removed for work. Jesus thus waited upon his
disciples in the garb of a slave. What a contrast to the
Emperor Caligula who, Suetonius tells us, required his senators
to attend him at table.' succinctos linteo,' like waiters ! Note
that by making the idea of ' washing,' which cannot but be
symbolical of Baptism, the central feature of the incident which
for John takes the place of the institution of the Lord's Supper,
the Evangelist emphasizes, as in 19 : 34, the intimate connexion between the two sacraments.

He came to Simon Peter—apparently having washed the feet 6
of others without protest—' Lord,' said he, ' you to wash my
feet ! ' Jesus answered him, ' You do not understand just now 7
what I am doing, but you will understand it later on.' Peter
would take this as a promise that Jesus will explain in a
moment the import of his action, as indeed he does in part in
12 ff. ; but Jesus' deeper meaning is that his act has a symbolic
and mystical significance which will appear only in the light
of his approaching death and resurrection. The coming of the
Spirit will bring a more perfect understanding (16 : 13, 15, 25).
Said Peter, ' You will never wash my feet, never ! ' No 8
promised explanation can justify *this* ! The service Jesus is
offering under these symbols is his death for the sanctification
of ' his own ' ; hence Peter's protest is parallel to that of
Mt. 16 : 22. Peter is humble enough to see the incongruity
of Christ's action, yet proud enough to dictate to his Master.
' Unless I wash you,' Jesus replied, ' you will not share my lot.'
Again the words might be superficially understood in the sense
that only if washed could Peter sit at table with Jesus ;
but the deeper meaning is that only through the possession of
Jesus' *spirit* is vital union with him possible, only through
the baptism of the Spirit, ministered symbolically in the
sacraments of Baptism and the Eucharist, can the believer
have communion with Christ and share in the benefits of his

death (cf. 7 : 37–39). (For a similar insistence upon the necessity of the spiritual *experience* which is merely typified 9 in the sacraments, cf. 3 : 5, 6 : 53, 63.) 'Lord,' said Simon Peter, 'then wash not only my feet but my hands and head.' ' A moment ago he told his master he was doing too much : 10 now he tells him he is doing too little ' (Dods). Jesus said, ' He who has bathed only needs to have his feet washed ; he is clean all over.' On the surface the meaning is : the guest who comes to table having first bathed in his own home needs only to have the dust of the road removed from his feet. But again the words have a deeper sense : for those who are true and loyal disciples the experience of regeneration typified in their initial baptism (here symbolized by the washing of the whole body) has no need to be repeated ; what does need to be repeated is the ' washing of the feet,' the removal of life's travel-stains by fellowship with Jesus, the doing for the sake of others what Christ has first done for us (14–15). Baptismal regeneration remains effective only if the Spirit of Jesus is perpetuated. Some MSS. read simply, ' he who has bathed does not need to be washed,' omitting all reference to a washing of the feet ; this would limit the sense to a statement of the finality of an initial baptismal regeneration. Note that, so far as there is any allusion here to the sacraments, Baptism is typified rather in the washing of the whole body than in the feet-washing, which, taking the place of the institution of the Eucharist, symbolizes all that is implied in the second great sacrament—the giving of the Lord himself in service to humanity. In the practice of the Church Baptism is not repeated, but the Eucharist, the washing of the feet, is. For a similar expression of the benefits of Christ's death (usually symbolized in the Eucharist) under the symbolism of ' washing,' which belongs more fittingly to Baptism, cf. 1 Jn. 1 : 7, Rom. 6 : 3. Both sacraments are, according to John, but empty ritual unless accompanied by the Spirit which renders life holy and ' clean.' Thus Jesus adds, 'And you are clean— but not all of you '—they became regenerate when they professed Christ's discipleship, and to that discipleship they are 11 loyal—all save the traitor—(he knew the traitor (6 : 64, 70 f.) ;

that was why he said, ' You are not all clean.') Judas' treachery did not take Jesus unawares : his death was wholly self-determined. Judas' feet had been washed as clean as Peter's ; but he did not bring to the supper that regenerate spirit apart from which it is but an empty form. We all come to the Sacrament, all partake of the same elements, but how many go forth ' clean ' ?

Then, after washing their feet and putting on his robe, he 12 lay down again. ' Do you know,' he said to them, ' what I have been doing to you ? ' It is when Jesus ' puts on his robe,' takes up his life again (10 : 17 f.) in the power of the Spirit, that he will make all things plain (7). The question implies that what has gone before is symbolical and has a deeper meaning than might appear. ' You call me Teacher and Lord— 13 *Rabbi*, master of teaching, and *Mar*, master of life—and you are right : that is what I am (Mt. 23 : 8). Well, if I have 14 washed your feet, I who am your Lord and Teacher, you are bound to wash one another's feet.' (Cf. Mk. 10 : 44 f.) Jesus with an argument *a fortiori* sums up the inward significance of the whole incident. When he bids the disciples ' wash one another's feet ' he is enjoining them to perpetuate ' not the act itself but its moral essence ' (Meyer), though the act itself came to be regarded as typical of all charity (1 Tim. 5 : 10), and is still literally practised by the Pope on Maundy Thursday. The service of our fellows in the Spirit of Christ is the truest of all sacraments, ' for I have been setting you an 15 example, that you should do what I have done to you '—words which recall the form of institution in 1 Cor. 11 : 24, ' do this in memory of me.' (Cf. Phil. 2 : 3 ff.) The Christian disciple may well condescend to do for others what his Master has first done for him, for ' Truly, truly I tell you, a servant is not 16 greater than his master, nor is a messenger (literally ' apostle ') greater than he who sent him ' (Mt. 10 : 24, Lk. 6 : 40, 22 : 27). This is the only place in the Gospel or First Epistle in which the word ' apostle ' occurs : it is never used specifically of the Twelve. The disciple is ' sent ' by Jesus, as was Jesus by the Father, and is to represent Jesus in spirit and character, as Jesus represents God (17 : 18, 20 : 21). ' If you know all this, 17 blessed are you if you really do it'—not merely repeat the symbolic act, but practise the whole Christian life—the loving of others as Christ has loved us—which it typifies. There is a Jewish saying : ' If a man knows the Law but does not do thereafter, it had been better for him that he had not come into the world.'

Verses 18–19 may possibly be an addition by the Redactor, as they break the thread of thought which is picked up again
18 at 20. 'When I say "you," I do not mean you all (10–11). I know the men of my choice,' that is, the worth of the eleven and the treachery of the twelfth. The reference here is to the call of the disciples (6 : 70) ; there is no thought of ' election to salvation.' (For the insight implied in ' I know ' cf. 1 : 48, 2 : 24 f.) ' I made my choice that this scripture might be fulfilled, "he who eats my bread has lifted up his heel against me." ' John again insists that Jesus was not deceived in his choice ; he selected Judas with his eyes open ; even the betrayal was self-determined ; Jesus anticipated it ' from the very first ' (6 : 64, 70 f.) ; indeed, it was foreordained by prophecy (note on 12 : 38) ; and at the end he gives himself up voluntarily (18 : 4 f.). The citation is from Ps. 41 : 9, in which the speaker is, according to the title, David (perhaps speaking of Ahithophel), according to some critics, Jeremiah. To ' eat one's bread ' is a pledge of friendship ; to ' lift one's heel ' (originally of a horse—to kick) is to show violence or contempt.
19 ' I am telling you this now, before it occurs (14 : 29, 16 : 4), so that when it has occurred you may believe who I am ' (8 : 24, 28) —by noting how my case fits the Messianic prophecy. The betrayal should confirm rather than upset their faith.
20 The following verse has no clear reference to nor logical connexion with the preceding allusion to the betrayal, unless it be that Jesus intends to confirm the disciples' confidence in their apostolate, which might have been shaken by this hint of disloyalty. On the other hand, the verse connects perfectly with 16–17, the idea of ' Sender ' and ' Sent ' being carried on, while here as above the disciple is the representative of Christ, as Christ is of God. The verse is modelled on Mt. 10 : 40, Lk. 10 : 16, where, however, the context is

different. We must either bracket 18–19 as an interpolation by the Redactor, added to exclude Judas from the promise of blessedness, or more probably transpose 20 to follow 16. ' Truly, truly I tell you, he who receives anyone I send receives me, and he who receives me receives Him who sent me.' He who acts towards his fellows in the spirit of the feet-washing is really doing the kindness to Christ (Mt. 25 : 45) and through him to God Himself, and is therefore indeed ' blessed ' (Mt. 25 : 34) according to the promise of 17. It is worthy of note that the word used for ' receiving ' is not *dechesthai*, as in Matthew, but *lambanein*—the word used of receiving the Eucharistic elements (Mk. 14 : 22, Jn. 6 : 7)—in tone with the sacramental colouring of the whole section.

Before delivering his intimate farewell discourse Jesus unmasks the traitor and secures his withdrawal. **On saying 21 this** (presumably 18–19, 20 being transposed), **Jesus was disquieted in spirit** (11 : 33, 12 : 27) : **he testified and said,** ' Truly, truly I tell you, one of you will betray me.' ' Testified ' is always used of a momentous declaration (4 : 39, 44, etc.), and here perhaps hints that Jesus is about to reveal a secret supposed to be known only to the devil and Judas. The hint of 10 and 18 is now made explicit in the exact words of the Synoptists (Mk. 14 : 18). **The disciples looked 22 at each other, at a loss to know which of them he meant**—but they do not, as in the Synoptic account, search their own consciences. For the sake of vividness John as usual (cf. 12 : 4) puts into the mouth of one disciple the general question which in the Synoptics is asked by all in turn. **As one of his 23 disciples was reclining on his breast—he was the favourite of Jesus** (the ' disciple whom Jesus loved ')—**Peter nodded to 24 him, saying, ' Tell us who he means,'** implying that Peter thought Jesus had already whispered the traitor's name to the Beloved Disciple. The latter is here introduced as such for the first time (see Introduction, p. xlvi). It has been suggested that his presence at the supper in a place of honour may have been the occasion of the disciples' quarrel about precedence (Lk. 22 : 24–30). **The disciple just leant back on the 25 breast of Jesus and said, ' Lord, who is it ? '** The guests lay

on a divan propped on their left elbows, so that the Beloved
Disciple's head as he lay next to Jesus would reach to the
height of his Master's girdle ; in order to address him he
26 would lean back on his breast and look up. **Jesus answered,
'The man I am going to give this piece of bread to, when I
dip it in the dish.' Then he took the piece of bread, dipped it,
and gave it to Judas, the son of Simon Iscariot.** In contrast
to the Synoptic story the details show that Christ wished to
avoid a public denunciation. The question is whispered and
the answer is conveyed symbolically in a way which would
reveal the truth to Jesus' confidential friend, but screen it
from the rest. Indeed, suspicion would be turned from Judas,
for the offer of a 'tit-bit' by the host would be a sign of
special favour ; possibly Jesus hoped thus to make a last
appeal to Judas' better feeling. Some suppose that by the
'piece of bread' is meant the slice of unleavened bread dipped
in bitter sauce which was handed round by the head of the
house at the Passover meal, and that John therefore conceives
this to be the actual Paschal supper. But it may be that he
has merely borrowed the detail from the Synoptists, who
suppose themselves to be dealing with that meal. The
'Beloved Disciple,' whoever he be historically, is certainly
used as a type of the true disciple who 'leans on Jesus' breast,'
the fountain whence springs all spiritual blessing (7 : 38,
19 : 34) ; he is on Christ's breast as Christ is on God's (1 : 18).
Note too that Peter and the Beloved Disciple are constantly
mentioned together (20 : 4, 8, and perhaps 18 : 16), as if to
hint that the Petrine and Johannine traditions are comple-
mentary. Here it is the two undoubtedly loyal disciples who
seek to unmask the traitor.

27 The devilish suggestion already instilled into Judas' mind
(2) now becomes crystallized into a devilish decision : **and
when Judas took the bread, at that moment Satan entered into
him** (Lk. 22 : 3). (For the thought that in the very act of
receiving the bread Judas surrendered his soul to the devil,
cf. 1 Cor. 11 : 29.) The sacramental meal became for Judas
the means of communion not with Christ but with the devil.
John pictures Judas as not merely dipping his hand in the

dish along with Jesus (Mk. 14 : 20), but as receiving the morsel direct from Jesus, as if to suggest that the Master himself gave him his choice of allegiance, and when he proved obdurate handed him over to the devil (1 Cor. 5 : 5, 1 Tim. 1 : 20). Then Jesus told him, 'Be quick with what you have to do '— an enigmatic order, again intended to screen Judas. Jesus himself determines the hour of his betrayal. None of those 28 at table (not even Peter and the Beloved Disciple ?) understood why he said this to him ; some of them thought that as Judas 29 kept the money-box (12 : 6), Jesus told him to buy what they needed for the festival (a hint that the feast was still in the future) or to give something to the poor. So Judas went out 30 immediately after taking the bread. And it was night. It is useless at this point to discuss the psychology of Judas : according to John, the devil formed the resolution in Judas' heart, Jesus himself gave it free play because his hour had come, and therefore Judas 'went out.' 'This theological mechanism has nothing in common with psychology' (Loisy). The statement that ' it was night ' (9 : 4, 11 : 10) is symbolical (cf. Lk. 22 : 53, 1 Thess. 5 : 5, Rev. 21 : 25, 22 : 5), and is intensely dramatic : ' We see the door open, and in contrast to the light within, the outside is darkness ' (Strachan).

It will be convenient at this point to note suggestions for the rearrangement of the order of the text. The climax of the farewell discourse is reached at 14 : 31, ' Rise, let us be going,' and it seems strange that just after the address is thus broken off there should follow chapters 15 and 16, in which the same topics are renewed, especially in view of 14 : 30, ' I will no longer talk much with you.' If the canonical arrangement be accepted, we must suppose either that 15 and 16 were spoken *en route* for Gethsemane, which seems unlikely in the case of words so solemn and intimate, or that the party lingered in the doorway throughout the discourse of 15 and 16 and the prayer of 17, an explanation which may be accepted as regards 17 but hardly as regards 15 and 16. Accordingly it is generally agreed that 15 and 16 have been displaced from an original position before 14. But exactly at what point should they be inserted ? There are three main suggestions :

(*a*) After 13 : 31*a* immediately following the words ' when he had gone out Jesus said ' (Spitta, Moffatt). But this destroys the characteristic Johannine idea that Christ's glory is directly contingent upon the betrayal and the Cross in which it issues (note on 13 : 32), and also the postponement of 31*b* ff. to a position at the end of chapter 16 interrupts the very apt transition from 16 : 33 (' courage ! I have conquered the world ') to 14 : 1 (' let not your hearts be disquieted '). (*b*) After 32 (Warburton Lewis), an arrangement which obviates the first objection to Moffatt's order but not the second ; moreover, 13 : 34 (where the commandment to love is called ' new ') should surely come before 15 : 12, 17. (*c*) After 13 : 35 (Wendt, F. J. Paul), an arrangement which we adopt. Immediately after the announcement of the ' new commandment ' there follows the parable of the Vine and the discourse of chapter 15, in which that commandment is illustrated and enforced. Moreover, as 13 : 36–38 is almost certainly a later addition by the Redactor (see notes *in loco*), the transition from 16 : 33 to 14 : 1 is not now interrupted. Again 13 : 33, with its reference back to 7 : 34, 8 : 21, is retained in the more natural position before 16 : 16. Nevertheless, any rearrangement still leaves its difficulties. For example, Thomas' question in 14 : 5 seems unnatural after Jesus' words in 16 : 5 ff., and the disciples' assurance in 16 : 30 ; also of the two allusions to the ' Helper ' in 14 : 16 f. and 15 : 26 the former quite clearly seems to be the first and indeed is presupposed in the second (see notes *in loco*). These difficulties, together with the fact that in 14 there are so many almost needless repetitions of 15 and 16, suggest that the two sections may possibly be independent redactions of the same original material which have been set side by side but could not be arranged in a perfectly self-consistent manner. It may be noted that certain subtle differences in doctrinal point of view may be traced in 15 and 16 as compared with 14. In the latter the Spirit appears to mediate Christ's spiritual presence : in the former he more definitely takes Christ's place (compare 14 : 15–26 with 15 : 26, 16 : 7 ff.) ; consequently the personal return of Christ himself as distinct from the indwelling of his Spirit is more

clearly indicated in the one section than in the other (compare
14 : 2–7 with 16 : 16–33).

When he had gone out Jesus said, ' Now at last the Son of 31
man is glorified, and in him God is glorified.' The ' glorifying '
of Jesus through his death (7 : 39, 11 : 4, etc.) is at hand,
nay has already taken place, for the traitor has ' as it were
already completed his deed ' (Winer). Remember that John
writes and his readers read from the point of view of those
for whom communion with the glorified Christ is an accomplished fact. Note the characteristic use of the title ' Son
of man ' : it was by the very humiliation of the betrayal
that Jesus obtained his glory (note on 1 : 51). Moreover,
' in him God is glorified,' because by his giving of himself
to death Christ reveals God's true nature (12 : 28, 17 : 4),
just as in turn the Spirit ' glorifies ' Christ by disclosing
Christ's true nature (16 : 14). Indeed, so truly is the ' glory '
of the Son and the Father one ' glory ' that Jesus can add :
' if God is glorified in him (a clause probably to be omitted with 32
the best authorities) God will glorify him in Himself and
glorify him at once ' ; in glorifying God Christ himself becomes
partaker of the divine glory (17 : 4 f., Acts 7 : 55). ' These
two verses sound like a shout of triumph from the heart of
Jesus at seeing the traitor depart in the darkness ' (Godet).
It is with the hope of this *immediate* ' glory ' (' at once ' ;
cf. 12 : 23, 17 : 1), that Jesus continues : ' My dear children, 33
I am only to be with you a little longer—the entrance to
glory must be by way of separation—then you will look for
me, and, as I told the Jews I tell you now, where I go you
cannot come ' (7 : 33 ff., 8 : 21). The argument is a little
unnatural, for in the case of the Jews the application is quite
different, and in 14 : 2–3 Jesus seems to contradict his words
here ; note, however, that Jesus does not say, as he did to
the Jews, ' you will not find me.' Here then is the Master's
farewell injunction : ' I give you a new command, to love one 34
another—as I have loved you, you are to love one another.'
The command is old in the letter (Lev. 19 : 18) ; how then is
it ' new ' ? Because here it is a question not of loving one's
' neighbour,' but of a special love of Christian to Christian,

of *philadelphia* in distinction to universal *agape* (Holtz-mann). 'Because the love of Christ's friends for Christ's sake was a new thing in the world' (Dods). There is to be a new love-circle, the Christian Church, dependent upon a new love-centre, Christ. 'As I have loved' indicates the *kind* of love rather than the *degree*, which was defined in 13 : 1. (Cf. 1 Jn. 2 : 8–10, 3 : 23, 2 Jn. 5.) Probably the giving of the 'new commandment' takes for John the place of the actual institution of the Eucharist. Just as in 13 : 14–15, so here he emphasizes the moral side of the sacrament—the spirit of love without which the mere *opus operatum* is valueless. The 'new commandment' is parallel to the 'new covenant ratified by my blood' (1 Cor. 11 : 25) and the 'new covenant-blood' (Mt. 26 : 28). It is not merely a common ritual, but the spirit of mutual love which gives

35 the right to the title of a Christian disciple : '**By this everyone will recognize that you are my disciples, if you have love one for another.**' 'The heathen are wont to exclaim with wonder, See how these Christians love one another ! ' (Tertullian) (cf. 1 Jn. 3 : 10, Acts 4 : 32).

36 Apparently picking up Jesus' words in 33, '**Lord,**' said Simon Peter, '**where are you going ?** ' The Vulgate here has ' Domine, quo vadis ? '—the words which Peter in the legend addresses to Jesus, when in his flight from Rome he met the Master entering the city. Rather than speak plainly of his death Jesus replies with a riddle, for the solution of which see 21 : 19 : '**I am going where you cannot follow me at present ; later on you will follow.**' Peter, imagining that Jesus is about to undertake some perilous adventure, feels this to be a slight

37 upon his love and courage : '**Lord,**' said Peter, '**why cannot I follow you just now ? I will lay down my life for you !** '—the boast of all the disciples in the Synoptics (Mk. 14 : 31, etc.). ' In the zeal of love he mistakes the measure of his moral

38 strength ' (Meyer). **Jesus replied, ' Lay down your life for me ? Truly, truly I tell you, before the cock crows, you will have disowned me thrice over.**' The ' cock-crowing ' was a recognized interval of the night, say between 2 and 4 a.m. (Mk. 13 : 35). By his repetition of Peter's words Jesus seems

to admit that one day the boast will be made good—but after how many failures !

Chapter 20, which it is agreed is the conclusion of the Gospel in its original form, contains no hint of any shame on Peter's part in consequence of his denial, which suggests that there was no reference to the denial in the body of the Gospel. Verses 36–38 interrupt the connexion between the ' new commandment ' (35) and the allegory in which it is enforced (15 : 1 ff.) and make the opening of the latter very abrupt. On the other hand, the relation of this incident to the reinstatement passage in the Appendix (cf. the use of ' follow ' in each passage ; 21 : 19) suggests that both may be due to the Redactor. Possibly the verses were originally inserted by the Redactor to follow 16 : 33 (a position to which they are restored by many critics ; see note following 13 : 30) ; 16 : 31–32 (' you will be scattered to your homes every one of you ') is the Johannine counterpart of Jesus' Synoptic prediction, ' I will strike at the shepherd and the sheep will be scattered ' (Mk. 14 : 27). Indeed, Jn. 16 : 31–32 *plus* 13 : 36–38 is an exact parallel to Mk. 14 : 27–31. Moreover, the Redactor could hardly have introduced Peter's question (36) *before* Jesus' complaint in 16 : 5. But placed at the end of chapter 16 the section would interrupt the very clear transition from 16 : 33 to 14 : 1. It may be that a later copyist had sense enough to recognize this, and as he searched for an alternative context the present position may have been suggested to him by the *apparent* connexion of 13 : 36 with Jesus' words in 13 : 33. (For examples of similar ' engineered ' connexions cf. that between 8 : 14 and 8 : 21, between 7 : 14 and 7 : 15, and between 3 : 30 and 3 : 31, though in each case the connected verses belong in fact to quite distinct sections.) We may even find an explanation here of the notorious displacement of chapter 14, which originally followed 15 and 16, to a position before them. In the process of copying, 13 : 36–38 (originally inserted by the Redactor immediately before chapter 14) may have been transposed to its present position before chapter 15 and may have carried chapter 14 with it. We have here an excellent example of the intimate connexion between the interpolation of Synoptic material and the dislocation of the text : wherever these two phenomena are seen in conjunction it is probable that the Redactor is responsible (see Introduction, p. lxvi).

Illustration (ii): The Allegory of the Vine (15 : 1–17)

The ' new commandment ' (13 : 34), obedience to which gives the right to the title of a Christian disciple, is illustrated in the allegory of the Vine. Such a spirit of mutual Christian love can have its source only in life-union and love-union with Christ himself. The allegory is probably suggested (if indeed any suggestion need be sought for so natural an illustration) by the wine at the table, rather than by, e.g., a vine trailing over the window of the Upper Room or by the view of the vines on the slopes of Olivet. The whole section, with its thought of the *agape* or ' love-feast ' between Christ and the disciple and between one disciple and another, has close affinities with the eucharistic ideas of chapter 13 and frequently echoes its thought. (Cf. 15 : 2–3 with 13 : 10–11, 15 : 16 with 13 : 18, 15 : 20 with 13 : 16.)

1 ' I am the real Vine '—the genuine fulfilment of those qualities which a vine illustrates (cf. 6 : 32) : ' real,' perhaps in contrast to Israel which was regularly spoken of by the prophets as God's vine (Is. 5 : 1, Jer. 2 : 21, Ezek. 15 : 6, 19 : 10–14, Ps. 80 : 8 ff.). In the *Didaché* Christ is called the ' Vine of David.' He is the divine prototype of all that was implied in the prophet's typology. ' And my Father is the vine-dresser,' who planted the Vine here on earth in the person of Christ and tends the Christ-life expressed now in his Church. The Evangelist throughout writes from the point of view of his own time : ' Jesus, before he closes his life-work, throws his mind into the future, and shadows out the history of his Church ' (E. F. Scott). Just as Judas has already been eliminated from the
2 Christian Society, so ' He cuts away any branch on me which is not bearing fruit—as the chapter proceeds we see that this fruit is love—and cleans every branch which does bear fruit, to make it bear richer fruit,'—prunes away the useless shoots

which would rob the vine of its strength.   John thus explains
the problem of apostasy, which must have perplexed his
contemporaries : it is God pruning the Vine, purging the
Body of Christ.   The word ' cleans ' is used in view of the
next verse, which itself points directly back to 13 : 10 : **'You 3
are already clean, by the word I have spoken to you '** ; Judas
being gone there is now no exception.   But ' clean,' which in
13 : 10 meant ' cleansed of sin,' is now given a more active
sense and virtually means ' capable of bearing fruit.'   The
cleansing instrument has been Christ's *word*—his whole
message and revelation—which has shown up their faults and
pruned them of those failings which make them unfruitful.
(For the power of Jesus' words cf. notes on 6 : 63, 12 : 48.)
And yet it is not enough simply to hear the word : its effect
must be maintained (5 : 38, 8 : 31) by constant union with him
who spoke it, by the co-operation of the hearers' wills with his :
**' Remain in me, as I remain in you : just as a branch cannot 4
bear fruit by itself without remaining on the vine, neither can
you, unless you remain in me.'**   This is one of the passages
in which the gift of ' life ' seems to have for the Evangelist
an almost semi-physical character, an energy transmitted
directly from its main source (see Introduction, p. **xxxix**).
But, though the Evangelist may employ the thought-forms
of the semi-physical mysticism of his day, union with Christ
is for him ' more a matter of will and moral effort than of
feeling. . . .   To be " in Christ " (in this Gospel) is just to
accustom oneself to breathe the atmosphere of the moral standard Jesus has set—to develop within us a set of Christian
instincts ' (Strachan).   **'I am the vine, you are the branches**— 5
the main stem and the branches making together one tree with
one common life (cf. Paul's comparison of the body and its
members, 1 Cor. 12 : 12, Rom. 12 : 4 f., Eph. 4 : 4)—**he who
remains in me, as I in him**—for the effort to maintain fellowship is not ours alone (cf. 16 and Phil. 2 : 12 f.)—**bears rich
fruit**—and conversely when separated from Christ bears no
fruit at all—**because apart from me you can do nothing'**: not
that a non-Christian life can never have any moral worth
but apart from union with Christ there can, in the Johannine

6 sense, be no 'harvest for eternal life' (4 : 36). 'If anyone does not remain in me, he is thrown aside like a branch and he withers up'—he is deprived of eternal life, as the severed branch is of the sap, and in consequence loses his natural capacity for fruit-bearing. The unworthy Christian is 'thrown aside,' excommunicated (the word is the same as in 9 : 34), and that 'not as a future consequence but as an inevitable accompaniment of the separation' from Christ (Westcott). He has proved himself to be in no true sense one of Jesus' 'own' (cf. 1 Jn. 2 : 19), and therefore is excluded from the guarantee that none of Jesus' own shall be lost (6 : 39, 10 : 28 f.) : 'then the branches are gathered and thrown into 7 the fire to be burned (Mt. 13 : 30, 40, etc.). If you remain in me and my words remain in you, then ask whatever you like and you shall have it.' Note that just as in verse 4 the thought of Christ himself is substituted for that of his word (ver. 3), so here we revert from Christ to his 'words' : 'It was in his words that these men experienced the power of his personality. So with us, who have not seen him' (Strachan). When Christ's 'words' 'remain in' a disciple the latter's prayers become but echoes of those words and must needs be answered (14 : 13, 15 : 16 ; cf. Mt. 18 : 19 f.). The prayers are prompted by the indwelling Spirit of Christ, and 'a prayer thus inspired is a child of heaven : it is God's promise transformed into petition' (Godet). Such prayer is indeed 'fruit-bearing,' part of the natural function of the Christian (cf. 16) ; hence 8 Jesus continues : 'As you bear rich fruit and prove yourselves my disciples, my Father is glorified' (13 : 31), just as the fruitfulness of the vine redounds to the credit of the husbandman. 'The Father is glorified in everything which demonstrates that through Christ his grace reaches and governs men' (Dods). And what an incentive to true discipleship should they find in the assurance that Christ's love for them is no less than the Father's love for the Son! (3 : 35, 5 : 20, 10 : 17, 9 17 : 24). 'As the Father has loved me, so have I loved you ; remain within my love'—for to retain that precious possession you must conform to the spirit of it. Love, so to say, is the atmosphere in which they are to continue to dwell. More-

over, as Christ's love for his disciples is paralleled only by the
Father's love for Christ, so is the condition of ' remaining in it '
the same—obedience, in this case conformity to the ' new
commandment ' to love one another (12 and 1 Jn. *passim*) :
'If you keep my commands you will remain within my 10
love, just as I have kept my Father's commands and remain
within His love.' The Farewell Discourses abound in passages
where the relationship between Jesus and the Christian is
compared with that between the Father and himself (cf. 14 : 10,
12, 20 ; 17 : 11, 18, 21–23 ; 20 : 21).

' I have told you this—invited you to remain in my love and 11
assured you that through obedience you can do so—that my
joy may be within you and your joy complete ' (16 : 24, 17 : 13,
1 Jn. 1 : 4, 2 Jn. 12)—in the knowledge that Christ loves them
as the Father loves Christ and that they stand to Christ in the
same relation as he does to God. ' My joy '—the joy possessed
by Jesus himself through his communion with God—is a joy
which may be the disciples' through a like communion with
Christ on the same condition of obedience ; and 'this is my 12
command : you are to love one another as I have loved you '
(13 : 34) : Jesus' love is to be at once the source and the
measure of theirs ; and that is the greatest possible measure,
for ' self-sacrifice is the high-water mark of love ' (Dods) :
'to lay life down (10 : 11) for his friends, man has no greater 13
love than that ' (1 Jn. 3 : 16). Paul finds a proof of love
greater still in giving life for one's enemies (Rom. 5 : 8–10).
Christians are here called Christ's ' friends ' possibly with a
reference to the official Roman title ' friend of the Emperor,'
a position roughly corresponding to Privy Councillor. Abraham is called ' God's friend ' (Jas. 2 : 23), as also are the
prophets (Wis. 7 : 27). The use of the word ' friend '
instead of the Synoptic ' neighbour ' (Mk. 12 : 31) does not
necessarily narrow the love-circle for whom Christ is thought
to die : rather does it emphasize the intimacy of the love.
Yet it must be remembered that Christ's command is ' new '
just because it enjoins not only universal love of man to man,
but the duty of special love of Christian to Christian. (See note
on 13 : 34.) So here the Evangelist stresses the peculiar love

of Jesus to 'his own,' but not at all to the exclusion of 'the world' from his love. Indeed, 'his love to the world has assumed a new meaning for all time, because John was able to realize so intimately his love for his own ' (E. F. Scott).

14 'You are my friends—if you do what I command you '—for such is the condition of the love of which we are speaking (9–10). Yet this is no servile obedience (8 : 35, 12 : 26, Ps. 119 : 45) :

15 'I call you servants no longer—as e.g. at 13 : 16—because a servant does not know what his master is doing ' ; he renders a mere unintelligent obedience and has no sympathy with or interest in his master's purpose ; 'his not to reason why ' : 'I call you friends (Lk. 12 : 4), because I have imparted to you all that I have learned from my Father ' (5 : 19, 8 : 28). The last words so far as they are addressed merely to the Eleven contradict 16 : 12, but they are true when referred to the believers of all ages as progressively enlightened by the holy Spirit (14 : 26). Such will obey Christ, not mechanically like a slave, but as being united to him by an inward harmony of will and a perfect understanding of his motives and purposes.

In the life of divine communion the initiative is always taken by God (1 : 38, 1 Jn. 4 : 19, Eph. 2 : 8, Gal. 4 : 9) :

16 'You have not chosen me, it is I who have chosen you.' The reference in 'chosen ' is primarily, as in 6 : 70 and 13 : 18, to the call to the Apostolate, but may be extended to include not only the Eleven but all Christian disciples. The link of love was forged not by them but by Christ ; he will keep it strong ; it is not for them to seek to break it, but rather to go forth on love's service. For, says John, putting on Christ's lips a message to the missionary Church of his own day, Christ chose you 'appointing you to go and bear fruit—fruit that lasts, so that the Father may grant you whatever you ask in my name.' In the word ' appointing ' (for which cf. Acts 20 : 28, 1 Cor. 12 : 28) the primary reference is again to the Eleven and their Apostolic mission (Mt. 28 : 19, etc.), but includes also the duty of every Christian to engage in fruitful activity which may have permanent results ; and again, as in verse 7, inter-cession which wins its end is regarded as a typical example of such fruitful activity. The word for ' go ' is the same as that

used in Jesus' words (14 : 28) ' I am going away and coming
back to you,' and implies the launching forth from the inner
circle of love to the needy world without ; as Godet says,
it brings out ' the kind of independence to which Jesus had
gradually raised them.' To ask ' in Christ's name ' means to
pray in such a way that the petition is in complete harmony
with the whole nature of Christ ; the phrase is a summary of
the truth expressed in verse 7. The allegory of the Vine now
closes with a final repetition of the ' new commandment '
(13 : 34, 15 : 12) which it has served so suggestively to illustrate : 'This is what I command you, to love one another.'   17

Theme (i): The Time of Separation (15 : 18–16 : 33)

In the following verses the Evangelist is evidently trying to
allay the surprise which must have been felt by the early
Christian Church at the world's animosity against the Gospel of
Jesus. The world being what it is, such an antipathy is inevitable (7 : 7, 1 Jn. 3 : 13, 1 Pet. 4 : 12 ff.). A certain dualism,
characteristic of the Evangelist, appears in the fact that, while
the universality of the Gospel is more fully recognized than in
any other N.T. book (e.g. 3 : 16, 10 : 16), yet a distinction is
everywhere presupposed between ' Christ's own ' and that
' world ' in which they dwell and which represents the sum-
total of the forces opposed to Christ (note on 1 : 10 f.). ' The
farewell discourses are based throughout on the conception of
a chosen community which has broken with the life around it
and is complete within itself ' (E. F. Scott).

'If the world hates you, remember it hated me first'— 18
before you, in point of time and also of degree. The words
are obviously spoken from the point of view of the Evangelist's
own day, the indicative in the conditional clause expressing
not a future contingency, but a present fact. ' If you belonged 19
to the world—if you were morally identified with it—the world
would love what it owned (1 Jn. 4, 5) ; it is because you do not
belong to the world, because I have chosen you from the world,
that the world hates you '—the word ' chosen ' here conveying
the idea of ' election ' to faith rather than of the ' call ' to the
Apostleship (16). The verse is the exact converse of 7 : 7.

The Jews the world cannot hate : the Christians it cannot but hate. Such hatred should be regarded not as a calamity, but rather as a guarantee that they are of the number of Christ's ' own ' and will share his glory (Rom. 8 : 17, cf. Lk. 6 : 26). Meantime the sincerity of their communion with their Master may be measured by the extent to which they are called upon to 20 share his lot : ' Remember what I told you (13 : 16), " A servant is not greater than his master." ' The principle is illustrated in 2 Tim. 2 : 11 ff., 1 Pet. 4 : 13 ff. ' If they persecuted me—as indeed they did—they will persecute you. If they hold to my word (8 : 51)—as they do *not*—they will hold to yours.' The man who is identified with Christ will find his experience identical 21 also. ' They will do all this on account of my name, because they know not Him who sent me ' : ' all this ' persecution, to which John's contemporaries are subject, is the result of antipathy to Christ—to ' his name,' to all for which he stands— and of ignorance of God ; or rather not so much ignorance of God (8 : 54 f.) as failure to understand that ' He who sent ' Jesus *is* God (5 : 38, 7 : 28). On the other hand, true knowledge of God would have carried with it a better appreciation of Christ (8 : 42, 1 Jn. 5 : 1). (For what Dods calls ' the efficacy of this consolation ' cf. Acts 5 : 41, Phil. 1 : 29 f.)

The sin of the world in rejecting Christ and persecuting ' his own ' is the more deadly in that it is committed in the presence 22 of light ; it is the ' sin against the Holy Ghost ' : ' they would not be guilty (a Johannine phrase for which see 19 : 11, 1 Jn. 1 : 8) if I had not come and spoken to them ; but, as it is, they have no excuse for their sin.' (For the thought see note on 9 : 41.) Moreover, just as knowledge of God Himself is involved in the knowledge of His representative (8 : 19), so does hatred of 23 the representative involve hatred of God : ' he who hates me hates my Father also ' (5 : 42). Sin for John appears sometimes to be not so much a positive principle as a deprivation of moral ' light.' Its moral culpability is minimized and, where a sincere plea of ignorance is advanced, disappears. Yet according to Jesus even the sin of ignorance requires some measure of forgiveness (Lk. 23 : 34, 12 : 48), and Paul, though he pleads ignorance, yet admits that he stood in need of mercy (1 Tim.

1 : 13). How much more heinous the guilt when there can be
no plea of ignorance : ' They would not be guilty, if I had not 24
done deeds among them such as no one has ever done (3 : 2,
7 : 31, 9 : 32) ; but, as it is, they have seen—and they have
hated—both me and my Father.' In Christ's acts (5 : 17,
19, 20) no less than in his Person (1 : 18, 14 : 9) the Father
had been clearly revealed ; yet they had rejected him, and
in him the Father also. Note that the sin consists not in
rejecting Jesus as a dogmatic proposition, but as one who has
been manifested as an active force for good in the world.
' Have we any moral right to be ignorant of Jesus, when all
history rings and echoes with his deeds ? ' (Strachan). Yet
such obdurate blindness was predestined by prophecy (cf.
12 : 37 f.) : ' It is that the word written in their Law may be 25
fulfilled : "they hated me for no cause." There is no exact
parallel in the O.T., the nearest being Ps. 35 : 19, 69 : 4.

The logical continuation would seem to be at 16 : 1, and
verses 26–27 are a parenthesis anticipating the section on the
Helper which begins at 16 : 7. The theme of persecution
suggests this idea of the Spirit which will uphold Christians
and with them bear witness to Christ. But 26–27 here seem
out of place and should probably be transposed after 16 : 3,
where the connexion is perfectly apt (' they have not known '—
but—' the Spirit . . . will bear witness ').

' When the Helper comes, whom I will send to you from 26
the Father, even the Spirit of truth which issues from the
Father, he will bear witness to me.' The idea of ' the Helper '
is introduced as if already familiar, and when we compare this
verse with 14 : 16 the latter certainly leaves the impression of
being the first allusion (see note on rearrangement after
13 : 30). The word translated ' Helper ' (Greek, *Paraklētos*)
is properly a passive form meaning ' one called in to help,'
as either plaintiff or defendant might call in a friend to aid
him in a lawsuit. Properly it is a legal term (Latin, *advoca-
tus* ; so translated in 1 Jn. 2 : 1). The Spirit is one who will
champion the Church in her suit against the world and appear
as a decisive ' witness ' for the defence (cf. Mk. 13 : 11, etc.).
He is one who pleads a cause, whether it be the Church's

cause with the world as here, or Christ's cause with the believer
as in 14 : 26. It has been thought that John borrows the term
directly from Philo, who writes (*Vita Mos.*, iii. 14) : ' For
it was necessary that the man consecrated to the Father of the
world should employ as *advocate* His son, most perfect in virtue,
to ensure forgiveness of sins and a supply of richest blessings.'
But the ' son ' in this passage evidently refers not to the Logos,
but to the whole universe as the perfect Creation or ' son ' of
God, so that the ' Helper ' of the Gospel shares with that of
Philo only the name and the idea of pleading implied in it.
The Helper is ' the Spirit of truth ' (cf. 14 : 16), i.e. the Spirit
which is truth and which reveals it—' truth ' being ' God
revealed in His essential nature' (Godet ; cf. 14 : 6). Jesus
is himself ' the truth ' ; the Helper who takes his place and
continues his work is ' the Spirit of truth,' who ' makes divine
truth enter the soul, gives it entire reality within us, and makes
it *the truth* to us' (Godet). Note that in 14 : 16 the Father
gives the Helper, while here Christ sends him ' from the
Father,' a thought which is further emphasized by the clause
' which issues from the Father.' Loisy well notes that John
has in view here not the eternal relation of Father, Son, and
Spirit—the much-debated question of the ' procession ' of
the Spirit from Father, or Son, or both—but their respective
contributions to the work of salvation. The words ' issues
from the Father ' refer not so much to the nature of the Spirit
as to his mission. Hence the emphasis laid on his function of
' witnessing,' which as in the Synoptics (Mt. 10 : 20) is closely
related to the persecution of the Church. The witness of the
Spirit is given by the interpretation of the inward meaning of
Jesus' words and life through the personal experience of his
followers. It also appears in the victorious power in which
they surmount persecution. The witness of the Spirit must
always be expressed through the witness of disciples ; hence
27 it is added, ' and you too are witnesses, for you have been with
me from the very beginning ' (Mk. 3 : 14, Acts 1 : 21 f.), from
the commencement of the Messiah's public work, and therefore are able to bear evidence to the historical facts (Acts
13 : 31), even as the Spirit bears witness to their true meaning.

The Spirit is similarly related to the Apostolic witness in Acts
1 : 8, 5 : 32. Here John seems to distinguish those to whom
Christ is actually speaking, whose evidence is that of eye-
witnesses, from those through whom the Spirit witnessed in
his own day. The Evangelist's own ' Spiritual Gospel '
is itself the best of all commentaries on the profound truths
of verses 26–27. (See Introduction, p. xxvi.)

Chapter XVI

' I have told you all this—i.e. the certainty both of persecution 1
and of support in it—to keep you from being repelled '—
literally, ' scandalized,' ' tripped up,' ' staggered ' (6 : 61),
and therefore tempted to turn from Christ under the pressure
of opposition and disappointment (Mt. 11 : 6). The words
seem to connect with 15 : 25. ' Forewarned is forearmed.'
' They will excommunicate you ' (9 : 22, 12 : 42)—again a type 2
of persecution to which John's contemporaries in Asia rather
than Jesus' personal followers in Palestine would be exposed.
' Indeed the time is coming when anyone who kills you will
imagine he is performing a service to God '—just as did Saul of
Tarsus himself (Acts 26 : 9). The word used for ' service '
(*latreia*) means usually ' sacrificial worship ' (Rom. 9 : 4) ;
in Exod. 12 : 25 it is used of the Passover ; later it meant more
generally ' a work well pleasing to God ' (Theophylact ; cf.
Rom. 12 : 1). Meyer quotes a Jewish maxim : ' Omnis
effundens sanguinem improborum aequalis est illi qui
sacrificium facit.' It is needless to trace an allusion to any
particular massacre of Christians, e.g. at the time of Bar
Cochba's rising. ' This they will do to you, because they have 3
not known the Father nor me ' : a repetition of the thought of
15 : 21.

At this point we have suggested the insertion of 15 : 26–27 :
' They have not known the Father nor me. When the Helper
comes . . . he will bear witness to me. . . .' Jesus then
continues : ' I have told you all this, so that when the time for 4
it arrives, you may remember what I said to you,' that being
forewarned you may be forearmed, and that your faith may
be strengthened rather than undermined—practically a

repetition of verse 1 (cf. 13 : 19, 14 : 29), to which is added a reason for Christ's silence hitherto concerning the inevitability of persecution. Though Mt. 10 : 17–23 records just such a warning spoken by Christ at an earlier date, the statement holds good of this Gospel, where there has been no previous reference to persecution: **'I did not tell you this at the beginning, because I was with you then '**—and they were not likely in his companionship to fall victims to foreboding nor to feel the need of such a ' Helper' as has just been promised (cf. Mt.

5 9 : 15). **'But now I am going to Him who sent me,'** returning with my commission fulfilled ; and bearing the brunt of hostility alone you will need such comfort as I now give you. **' And yet not one of you asks, " Where are you going ? " '** (13 : 36 and note after 13 : 38). The disciples are so distressed about Christ's departure that they forget the compensating factor of *where* he is going and the blessings which his departure will bring in the gifts of the Spirit. ' The exclusive interest, which we often find to-day in the historical Jesus, as distinct from the risen Jesus of personal experience, is an example of the refusal to ask the question, " Whither goest thou ? " '

6 (Strachan). **' No, your heart is full of sorrow at what I have told you**—about my departure and your coming troubles—a sorrow

7 due to wounded affection and baffled hopes—yet—**I am telling you the truth** (however strange it seems to you !)—**my going is for your good. If I do not depart, the Helper will not come to you ; whereas if I go, I will send him to you '** : Jesus will be able to do so, for he himself will now be living in the Spirit in the presence of that Father who is the source of the Spirit's mission (15 : 26). The withdrawal of Jesus from bodily fellowship with his intimate circle is the necessary condition of his spiritual fellowship with the Church universal. The Helper is to take in the future experience of the Church the place held by Jesus himself in the lives of those who were his friends in the days of his flesh. His departure is a great gain. The limitations imposed by a life in the flesh will be broken down, and Christ will be able as spirit with spirit to hold with his people everywhere a communion as close as once he did with his immediate disciples (cf. 14 : 16).

(For the style and language of the following verses, cf. 1 Jn. 5:6–8.) 'And when he (the Helper) comes, he will 8 convict the world, convincing men of sin, of righteousness, and of judgment: of sin, because they do not believe in 9 me; of righteousness, because I go to the Father and you see me no more; of judgment, because the Prince of this world has been judged.' The Spirit expressing him- 10 self in men's hearts and lives and through the verdict of 11 history and experience will reverse the world's present judgments and triumphantly vindicate Christ's claims (cf. Paul's thought in 1 Cor. 14:24–25). As that Spirit enlightens men's minds the world which now condemns the Christian, and takes credit to itself for so doing (16:2), will itself be on trial with the Spirit as accuser; the result will be ' conviction '—that is, the demonstration of the truth in so clear a light that it must be acknowledged as the truth, and the consequent condemnation of those who in spite of light reject that truth. Thus ' conviction ' is used in a double sense: the world reaches the ' conviction ' that Christ is the truth, and it is ' convicted ' of the crime of rejecting the truth. In that verdict there will be three counts: (a) On the question of ' sin ' the verdict will be that the guilt was not on the part of Christ, but on the part of those who in spite of light refused to believe (15:22, 24; 3:18, 19, 36). (b) On the question of ' righteousness '—in the widest sense of the word—the verdict will be that this is on Christ's side, as proved by his triumphant exaltation to the Father—a return which is itself demonstrated by the fact that an invisible ministry of the Spirit has taken the place of Christ's earthly ministry (' you see me no more ': ' the invisibility was the evidence of his victory '—Dods). (c) On the question of ' judgment '—in the sense of 7:24—the summing up of the issue as between Christ and the world, the verdict here too will be in favour of Christ, for, as a result of the Cross and its influence upon men's thought as interpreted by the holy Spirit, ' the Prince of this world has been judged '; that is, the anti-Christian point of view, the principles which govern the actions of worldly men, have been once and for all discredited and

condemned (12 : 31 f., 1 Cor. 2 : 8, Col. 2 : 15). The work of
the Spirit manifested in the history of Christianity verifies
the judgment that by Christ's death evil has been condemned
utterly : the Devil is fighting a losing battle.

The true function of the Spirit appears only when it is
understood that the revelation of truth and the understanding
of it are alike progressive and can be bestowed through the
Spirit only in proportion to the receptivity of the learner :
12 '**I have still much to say to you** (note on 15 : 15), **but you cannot
bear it just now** ' (Lk. 11 : 46, Acts 15 : 10). There are problems
for the understanding of which their minds must be prepared
by the defining power of Christian living. Epictetus is
recorded to have thus cautioned a would-be philosopher :
' Sir, consider if you can bear it ! ' ' 'Tis the taught already
that profit by teaching.' (Compare the thought of 1 Cor. 3 : 1,
13 Heb. 5 : 11–14.) '**However, when the Spirit of truth comes, he
will lead you into all the truth** '—a form of words implying not so
much a revelation of entirely new truth as a deeper understanding of the truths already revealed by Jesus, and of Jesus
himself who *is* the Truth (14 : 6). To bestow such an understanding is essentially the work of the Spirit in the Church
to-day (14 : 26). There is an interesting parallel in Philo :
' The mind (of Moses) would not have gone thus straight to the
mark unless there had been a divine Spirit which guided
it to the truth ' (*Vit. Mos.*, iii. 36). Our Gospel registers an
eternal protest against all fixity of dogma : ' The Spirit, as
John conceives it, is a principle of inner development by which
the traditional forms of belief may from time to time be
broken up, in order to reveal more perfectly their essential
content ' (E. F. Scott).

As the representative of Jesus the Spirit will follow the
rule laid down by Jesus himself (5 : 30, 7 : 16, 14 : 10) : '**for he
will not speak of his own accord, he will say whatever he is
told**—by the Father from whom he comes and by the Son who
sends him (15 : 26)—**and he will disclose to you what is to
come** '—explain the significance of the seeming tragedy which
confronts Jesus and proclaim a message of hope and victory
for the future destiny of the Church. The phrase ' what is to

come' (*erchomena*) means, properly, 'things that are on the way.' It is a question not of foretelling the future, but of interpreting tendencies: 'Through all history the prophets who have tried to detail future history have failed ; but the great ones among them, who have seen into the heart of things and declared in what direction they were moving, have succeeded. The truth of prophecy is not truth to fact, but truth to idea' (Percy Gardner, *Ephesian Gospel*, p. 263). The function of the Spirit is not to disclose what lies ahead, but to light up the difficulties of the road as we progressively meet them and to give the assurance that the road along which we follow Christ leads at last to victory. Thus, says Jesus, '**He will** **glorify me**': the Spirit will make Christ known in his full majesty, and this he will do by revealing in the experience of the Christian Church Jesus as he now is in his risen spiritual power ; for the 'glory' of Jesus is all that is implied in his death, resurrection and ascension, and to reveal him as he now is, having passed through these, is to 'glorify' him. And this the Spirit does, '**for he will draw upon what is mine**—from Christ's own treasure of truth—**and disclose it to you.**' Though the Spirit is the perennial source of new truth, yet this truth is nothing more than the interpretation, under new forms and in larger measure, of the truth taught by Jesus himself (cf. 14: 26). And indeed there is no richer store upon which the Spirit could possibly draw, for '**all that the Father has is mine** (13: 3, 17: 10 ; cf. 1 Cor. 15: 24–28, Heb. 2: 8) ; **that is why I say, "he will draw upon what is mine and disclose it to you."**' It is noticeable that John allows to the Spirit little independent action or influence. His function is to represent Christ and to ensure that *his* influence shall continue, even as Christ's function is to represent God. Like every N.T. writer, John presents us not with any formulated doctrine of the Trinity, but only with those facts of Christian experience upon which such a doctrine must be based.

'**In a little while**—after Jesus' death on the following day— **you shall behold me no longer** ; then, **after a little**—when the experience typified in Pentecost begins—**you shall see me.**' Up to this point Jesus has been speaking of the coming of the

Spirit as a *substitute* for himself : he now promises his own return ' after a little.' Is this a contradiction ? Rather is it John's method of meeting the disappointments and doubts of his own day by thus identifying Christ's expected ' Parousia,' or ' second coming,' not with an apocalyptic manifestation, but with the same coming of the holy Spirit which the Church had already experienced at Pentecost and was daily experiencing. We have already noted (6: 62) that for the Evangelist the Resurrection, Ascension and Parousia are almost telescoped into one experience. In the words, ' after a little you shall see me,' while the immediate reference, as addressed to the Eleven, may be to the post-resurrection appearances, the analogy of 14: 19 suggests that the larger reference is rather to the realization of the *spiritual* presence of Christ in his Church as exemplified in Pentecost. Christ has indeed returned, hints the Evangelist, and if the Church still feels disappointment and perplexity, it is only because she has mistaken the nature of his coming. The following verse vividly reflects such questioning on the part of contemporary

17 Christians : So some of his disciples said to one another, ' What does he mean by telling us, " In a little while, you shall behold me no longer ; then, after a little, you shall see me " ? and, " I go to the Father " ? ' The last phrase is an allusion back to 16: 10, the meaning of which they have not yet grasped.

18 They said, ' What is the meaning of " In a little " ? We do not understand what he is saying.' Note the tentative nature of the question : they do not presume to ask Jesus directly ; they are still muttering among themselves. As usual (cf. 14: 5 ff.) the perplexed question prepares the way for a fuller

19 explanation by Jesus : Jesus knew they wanted to ask him— by supernatural intuition (2: 25, 6: 61, etc.) as well as from their obvious embarrassment ; so he said to them, ' Is this what you are discussing together, why I said, " In a little while, you will not see me : then, after a little, you shall see me " ? ' Jesus shows that he knows what is puzzling his disciples ; without giving a definite answer to their question he reveals

20 how sorrow is to be changed to joy : ' Truly, truly I tell you, you will be wailing and lamenting—as those who mourn their

dead—while the world is rejoicing—in its triumph over its enemy; we see the prediction fulfilled in Mk. 16: 10—you will be sorrowful, but then your sorrow will be changed into joy'—as indeed happens at 20: 20. Jesus then adds a typical illustration of joy born out of dread: 'When a woman is in 21 labour she is sorry, for her time has come; but when the child is born she remembers her anguish no longer, for joy that a human being has been born into the world.' (For the figure, cf. Ps. 48: 6, Jer. 4: 31, 6: 24, Is. 26: 17, etc.) The mother's 'time' which 'has come' recalls Jesus' 'time' which has also 'come' (12 : 23), while her 'anguish' hints at the coming 'persecution' of the Church (Gk. *thlipsis*; cf. Rev. 7: 14). Though the chief point of the illustration is simply the changing of sorrow into joy, the analogy of Is. 66: 7–9, Hos. 13: 13 f., Mic. 4: 9–10, 5: 2, suggests that John intends us to understand that the N.T. Church is actually born at the Resurrection out of the travail of the Cross. (See also the imagery of Rev. 12.) Here then is the point of the illustration: 'So with you. Just 22 now you are in sorrow, but I shall see you again and your heart will rejoice—with a joy no one can take from you.' Again (cf. ver. 16) the promise is literally fulfilled in Jesus' appearance after his resurrection (20: 19 ff.), but more perfectly still in the mystic communion of the Church through all the ages with the Spiritual Christ; for it is in this sense that joy will be *permanent*.

'And on that day you will not ask me any questions' (Gk. 23 *erōtan*), for 'you will understand on that day' (14: 20), and all mysteries will have been solved (25). But there is another kind of 'asking,' the asking of prayer: and, adds Jesus, 'truly, truly I tell you, whatever you ask (Gk. *aitein*) the Father, He will give you in my name' (15 : 16). Up to this point they have indeed asked questions enough, but 'hitherto 24 you have asked nothing in my name '; that is, they have not turned to account the truth that those who in their petitions enter fully into the mind and purpose of Jesus cannot fail of an answer (note on 15 : 7). It is also hinted that only after Jesus' exaltation as Paraclete and Intercessor is prayer 'in his name' possible (but see 26): 'Prayer must have been rather

w

hindered by the visible presence of a sufficient helper ' (Dods).
Let them then make good their lost opportunities : ' **Ask and
you will receive** (Mt. 7 : 7 f.), **that your joy may be full** ' (15 : 11,
17 : 13). The joy will consist not merely in the fact that
prayer is answered, but in the results that follow answered
prayer—success in their mission and the glorifying of God in
Christ (14 : 12–14).

25 ' **I have told you this**—not merely the immediately foregoing
utterance, but with reference to the reserve which has marked
much of the discourse (12, 16 ff., etc.)—**in figures, but the
time is coming when I shall speak to you in figures no longer ;
I shall let you know plainly about the Father** '—the chief
theme of Jesus' teaching in this Gospel. ' Figure ' (*paroimia*)
is the word used both for a ' parable ' or ' allegory ' (10 : 6),
such as the ' Good Shepherd ' or the ' Real Vine,' and also
for a ' dark saying ' or riddle such as verse 16. Such utterances are contrasted with those spoken ' plainly,' ' without
reserve,' and therefore intelligibly (cf. 1 Cor. 13 : 12). The
verse perhaps hints the reason why John has omitted from his
Gospel all the Synoptic ' parables.' He evidently supposed
that they were intended to obscure Jesus' true teaching,
whereas his own Gospel purposed to disclose the ' truth.' The
promised ' plain ' revelation ' about the Father ' will be
through the agency of the Spirit : Christian experience will
define what now seems dark in Jesus' words (16 : 12–15).
' All teaching in words is but a parable until the Spirit explains
it ' (Godet). It is this thought which is the justification of the
Fourth Gospel. The Evangelist who, it may be, never saw
Christ in the flesh can yet rightly claim to interpret the
' inwardness ' of his teaching more truly than those who were
his personal friends.

26 ' **On that day**—after Christ's spiritual communion with his
Church is established—**you will ask in my name** (24), **and I
do not say to you I will ask the Father on your behalf.**' Whereas
the writer to the Hebrews represents Christ as ' interceding '
(7 : 25), and Paul speaks not only of Christ (Rom. 8 : 34) but
also of the Spirit (Rom. 8 : 26 ; for Paul the Spirit *is* Christ,
2 Cor. 3 : 17) ' pleading for us,' John so closely identifies

Christ with the Father, and the believer with Christ, that he regards no such separate intercession on the part of the Risen Christ as necessary. Prayer ' in Christ's name ' is equivalent to Christ's own prayer as Intercessor. When men ' remain in ' Christ (15 : 7), their wills are in fact wholly one with the Father's will : when they pray ' in Christ's name,' they are in direct touch with God ; those whose fellowship with Christ is real will cease to think of him merely as an intermediary, for ' having seen him they have seen the Father ' ; therefore, apart from any special intercession by Christ, prayer will be answered : ' **for the Father**—without any such pleading on my 27 part—**loves you Himself.**' Yet Jesus does not deny the fact of his Intercession, which indeed seems implied in 14 : 13 ff., 1 Jn. 2 : 1, and in the very term ' Paraclete ' : he only denies its necessity. The certainty of answer to prayer depends not solely on such intercession, but primarily on the Father's love, and this love is bestowed in return for our love for Christ— which has first been prompted by his love to us (1 Jn. 4 : 19) —and our faith in his divine mission : ' **because you have loved me and believed that I came forth from God. From the Father** 28 **I came**—owing to Him my divine origin—**and I entered the world ;**—charged with a divine commission—again—my mission fulfilled—**I leave the world and I go to the Father.**'

The disciples, forgetting that only the progressive revelation of the Spirit can ' lead them into all truth ' (16 : 13), think that the hour promised in verse 25 has already come and express themselves satisfied : ' **Now**—in contrast to the past 29 when Jesus spoke in riddles—**you are talking plainly at last, not speaking in figures. Now we are sure you know every-** 30 **thing, and need no one to put questions to you. This makes us believe you have come forth from God.**' In verses 17–18 the disciples had hinted that Jesus was perhaps veiling his own bewilderment behind a cloud of obscurity : they are now satisfied that he sees his way clear, that he has perfect know-ledge, and is willing and able to communicate it without being questioned ; consequently their faith is confirmed that he is God's ambassador (3 : 2). Jesus replied, ' **You believe it at** 31 **last ?**—it may be truly enough for the time (17 : 8) ; but

32 how evanescent will their faith be—**Behold, the time is coming, it has come already**—so imminent is it in Jesus' thought —**when you will be scattered** (10 : 12) **to your homes, every one of you, leaving me alone.'** The words are an echo of Mk. 14 : 27, Mt. 26 : 31 (quoted from Zech. 13 : 7), all the more remarkable here because according to John's narrative the disciples did not immediately scatter, but remained at Jerusalem, where they were all found together on the Resurrection day. Jesus then adds, as if the Evangelist intended to correct the impression of Mk. 15 : 34 : '**But I am not alone, for the Father is with me.'** ' When ye have shut the door and made darkness within,' says Epictetus (*Diss*. i. 13, 14), ' remember never to say that ye are alone ; for ye are not, but God is

33 within and is your spirit.' '**I have said all this to you that in me you may have peace ; in the world you have trouble, but courage ! I have conquered the world**' (cf. 14 : 27). At one and the same time the Christian lives in two contrasted environments—' in me,' ' in the world ' (cf. Col. 1 : 2 : ' in Christ . . . at Colosse '). Those who maintain communion with Christ may have peace even in the midst of the storm (cf. 17 : 15). Note that for Jesus ' peace ' means not a negative thing— freedom from anxiety and striving, mere stagnation of soul— but the possession of a soul in harmony with the victorious Christ in the midst of conflict. As Jesus has conquered the world and its prince (12 : 31), so may his disciples (1 Jn. 5 : 4, Rom. 8 : 37).

Theme (ii) : The Promised Communion (14 : 1–31)

1 The triumphant note of 16 : 33 is continued : ' **Let not your hearts be disquieted** (13 : 21, 12 : 27) **; you believe—believe in God and also in me**' ; or perhaps better, taking both the verbs as imperatives, ' Believe in God, and (if that is too hard, then) believe in me ' (whom you have seen ; cf. ver. 9).

2 '**In my Father's house there are many abodes**' : according to later Jewish thought each individual had a heavenly ' abode ' assigned to him according to his worth ; there is room for each and all with Christ in the Father's dwelling-place. The Vulgate translation *mansiones* (from which comes the A.V.

' mansions ') is used especially of resting-places on a road ;
perhaps the thought here too is of a resting-place on life's
eternal pilgrimage : ' The contrasted notions of repose and
progress are combined in this vision of the future ' (Westcott).
' Father's house,' used in 2 : 16 of the Temple, here means
God's immediate presence, to which Jesus, as Son, has right
of access (8 : 35). The translation of the following words is
much disputed ; at first sight Moffatt's rendering seems best :
**' were it not so, would I have told you I was going to prepare
a place for you ? '** But it seems a fatal objection that nowhere
in the Gospel has Jesus said that he is ' going to prepare a
place.' Hence the usual translation should perhaps be retained :
' Were it not so, I would have told you ; for (I have been
speaking of my departure to the Father, and the purpose of
that departure is that) I am going to prepare a place for you
(and I could not have thus misled you into thinking that a
place awaits you, were it not the case).' **' And when I go 3
and prepare a place for you, I will come back and take you
to be with me '**—one of those peculiar ' concessions ' (cf.
21 : 22, 1 Jn. 2 : 28) to the more materialistic Synoptic and
Pauline view of an eschatological ' Parousia ' of Christ in
person, which however is at once offset by a return to the
more mystical Johannine thought—**' so that you may be where
I am '** (cf. 2 Cor. 5 : 8, Phil. 1 : 23, 1 Thess. 4 : 17). The ' abode '
is really Christ himself (15 : 4) : ' It is not in heaven that we
are to find God, but in God that we are to find heaven ' (Godet).
' What is heaven to a reasonable soul ? Naught else but Jesus '
(Luther). **' And you know the way to where I am going.'** 4
This would be better taken as a question : ' And do you know
the way to the place where I am going ? ' Jesus' destination
(the Father) has been clearly indicated in 16 : 28 ; they are
now to learn the route by which they are to reach that destination. **' Lord,' said Thomas** (the materialistic, matter-of-fact 5
man, rather lacking in vision, as appears from 11 : 16, 20 : 24 f.),
**' we do not know where you are going, and how are we to know
the way ? '** If Thomas' professed ignorance of Jesus' destination seems strange after 16 : 28, we must remember that his
question is in fact a leading one, the usual artifice of the

Evangelist to prepare the way for the momentous declaration
which follows (cf. the dialogue with Martha, 11 : 21–27),
in which Jesus claims not only to point out the way, but
6 to *be* it : Jesus said to him, 'I am the real and living way.'
(For the thought of Christ as ' the way ' into God's presence, cf.
Heb. 9 : 8, 10 : 20, Eph. 2 : 18, Acts 9 : 2.) The literal translation is, ' I am the way, and the truth, and the life '—the
last two substantives serving to define the first. Jesus is the
' real ' (15 : 1) way and the ' living' (6 : 35, etc.) way, that is,
the way which leads to all real knowledge of God and consequently alone leads to ' life ' (cf. 17 : 3). For if ' truth ' is
' God revealed in his essential nature,' then ' life ' is ' God
communicated to the soul' (Godet). Hence Jesus can add :
' no man comes to the Father except by means of me '—not by
accepting my teaching, or believing in my claims, but only by
way of mystical communion with *myself*. The mention of the
Father answers Thomas' doubt about Jesus' destination.
Possibly the Evangelist here glances at the Gnostics : he who
has fellowship with Jesus has no need of any other ' gnosis.'
Jesus' next words give us the key-thought of the whole
7 Gospel : ' If you knew me, you would know my Father too '
(8 : 19, 1 : 18). In the knowledge of Jesus the disciples have
been unconsciously acquiring knowledge of the Father ; as
a result of Jesus' present ' plain ' speaking (16 : 29) that knowledge is now to become *conscious* : ' You know Him now and
you have seen Him.' But Philip, no mystic but the practical
man (6 : 7), for whom, like Thomas (20 : 25), ' seeing is believing,' wishes a sensible proof of the reality of ' the Father' :
8 ' Lord,' said Philip, ' let us see the Father ; that is all we want.'
(For the request cf. Exod. 33 : 18.) At this Jesus expresses
pained surprise : the disciples' long companionship with himself
9 should have given to them a deeper insight. Jesus said to
him, 'Philip, have I been with you all this time, and yet you do
not understand me ? He who has seen me has seen the Father.
What do you mean by saying, "Let us see the Father"?'
—for one who, like Philip, has seen the Son has no reason to
make such a request. In this verse we reach the culminating
point of the Gospel's teaching. For John Christ's revelation

of God consists not, as for the Synoptists, in his teaching about
God's fatherly love, nor, as for Paul, in his supreme act of
self-sacrifice on the Cross, but rather in the vision of his own
Person which Christ manifests to the world, in which mankind
may ' see the Father.' In the contemporary pagan Mystery
Religions the climax of the initiation ceremony was the vision
of the god, through which the worshipper was ' reborn into
eternity.' Christianity is the perfect Mystery, and in the
vision of the Father in Christ is the sure guarantee of eternal
life. Note that there is a play here on the word ' see ' :
Thomas wishes to ' see ' the Father in a material sense ; but
to ' see ' Christ in that sense, as even his enemies had seen him,
would not be to ' see ' the Father ; for in Jesus' meaning ' see '
here signifies to grasp with spiritual vision. In fact, to ' see '
includes a moral factor and practically means to ' believe '
(see note on 3 : 14 f.), a fact which clearly distinguishes John's
point of view from that of the Mysteries. Hence it is added :
' **Do you not** *believe* **I am in the Father**—reading His will and 10
mind—**and the Father is in me** '—communicating to me His
knowledge and power ? The result of this intimate union
of Father and Son appears both in Jesus' teaching (7 : 16)
and in his deeds (5 : 19) : ' **The words I speak to you all I do not
speak of my own accord ; it is the Father who remains ever in
me, who is performing His own deeds.**' Whatever Jesus says
and does is indeed the Father's saying and doing. What Paul
can say of Christ (Gal. 2 : 20, ' It is no longer I who live, Christ
lives in me '), Christ himself can say of the Father: ' **Believe** 11
me, I am in the Father and the Father is in me '—let them take
Christ's word for that truth ! or, if they are still incredulous,
surely his deeds are proof enough ! (cf. 10 : 38)—**or else,
believe because of the deeds themselves.**' It is worth noting that
in this Gospel as contrasted with the Synoptics (Mt. 13 : 58)
faith is the result not the necessary condition of miracle. Yet
just as in Mk. 11 : 22 ff. the summons to faith is at once
followed by a promise of the miraculous power of faith, so
here there follows the assurance that Christ's great deeds may
through faith be perpetuated in the disciples' own persons :
' **Truly, truly I tell you, he who believes in me will do the very** 12

deeds I do'—just as Christ by 'remaining in the Father' does deeds which are in truth God's deeds. The work of the Church is but 'a continuation, under larger conditions, of the work of Christ himself' (E. F. Scott). So G. L. Brace gives to his account of the beneficial results of Christianity upon civilization the title *Gesta Christi*—the Deeds of Christ. In this sense 21: 25 is no hyperbole. 'And,' adds Jesus, they will perform 'still greater deeds than these,' than Christ's own—because with Christ's departure the full power of the holy Spirit will be liberated into the world (note on 16: 7). These 'greater deeds' (cf. 1: 50, 5: 20) include all the missionary triumphs of the Church which will be achieved in the power of the Spirit of the departed Christ (cf. Lk. 24: 49, Acts 1: 8, Eph. 4: 8 ff., Phil. 4: 13). This comes out in the next clause: 'For I am going to the Father' ; and, as in 16: 23 f., the power of prayer is made contingent upon the diffusion of the Spirit following upon that return to
13 the Father: 'and I will do whatever you ask in my name, that the Father may be glorified in the Son' (13: 31)—that through the deeds of Christ's disciples, achieved in answer to prayer, God's purpose in sending the Son into the world may be accomplished and Himself 'glorified.' The promise is con-
14 firmed and emphasized by being repeated: 'I will do whatever you ask (me) in my name.' Probably 'me' should be omitted with many ancient authorities ; it seems redundant with 'in my name,' and moreover, the only prayer of which this Gospel speaks is prayer to the Father in the name and spirit of Christ, not prayer to Christ direct.

Yet another promise is about to be given ; but it is conditional upon moral obedience, which is the practical expression
15 of love to the Master: 'If you love me you will keep my commands'—especially the injunction to mutual love (13: 34). Cf. 15: 10, 1 Jn. 5: 3 ; we have the converse proposition in 14: 21 and the reverse in 14: 24. Let such obedience be
16 present, 'and I will ask (notwithstanding 16: 26 where see note) the Father to give you another Helper,' one who will replace Jesus himself in that rôle, and whose mission it will be, unlike the Incarnate Christ who had but a temporary commission,

'to be with you for ever.' (For the 'Helper' see note on 15 : 26.) In relation to Christ the Spirit is 'another Helper,' in all respects Christ's own *alter ego*. Just as Christ is one with the Father and yet distinct from Him, so is the Spirit one with Christ and yet distinct (cf. 2 Cor. 3 : 17). Hence for John the coming of the Spirit and the future Parousia of Christ are in fact interchangeable ideas (16 : 16 note), though sometimes, apparently with the desire to conserve traditional belief, he appears to discriminate between them (cf. 14 : 3 note). Christ himself being 'the Truth' (14 : 6), the 'Helper' who is to take his place and continue his work is here called 'even the Spirit of truth' (15 : 26 note). But, as sympathy is the necessary condition for understanding, 'the world cannot receive him' : the spiritual can be apprehended not by worldly men, but only by those whose souls are attuned to the spiritual realm. It has been noted that a distinction is indicated here between the Spirit, which is held to manifest itself only within the Church of Christ, and the Logos, which is universally present as the 'light which enlightens every man' (1 : 9). Moreover, in this Gospel the action of the Spirit is frequently connected with the sacraments (3 : 5–8, 6 : 63, 1 Jn. 5 : 6–8), in which the outside world can have no part. To the Spirit then the world is unresponsive 'because it neither sees nor knows him'—it neither has the spiritual vision nor the mystical experience which alone can make the action of the Spirit intelligible. There is an exact parallel in 1 Cor. 2 : 14 f. How different the case of the disciples : 'but you know him'—they have that first-hand experimental knowledge through their knowledge of Christ ; for the Spirit was present in Christ for his contemporaries just as for us Christ is present in his Spirit ; thus they may 'know' that Spirit 'because he remains with you—in the person of Jesus meanwhile—and will be within you'—when the promised Helper takes Jesus' place. As addressed to the Eleven the words must be understood thus ; but they become natural only when we realize that John has in view not Jesus' hearers but his own readers, whose only experience of Christ is such a spiritual experience as is here in question. The point of view, as usual, is that of the later Church.

Bequeathing to his disciples the permanent fellowship of
18 his own *alter ego*, Jesus is able truly to say, ' I will not leave
you forlorn,' as children bereft of a father (13 : 33), for Christ
himself will be present in the Spirit even as the Father is present
in Christ ; thus his apparent departure is really a more intimate
19 approach, and he can add, ' I am coming to you. A little while
longer—till the close of his earthly life and his return as a
spiritual presence—and the world will see me no more—
' because it neither sees nor knows him ' (17)—but you will see
me, because I am living and you will be living too.' The last
words can be rightly understood only as addressed to the
Church of all ages ; Jesus, as an abiding spiritual presence,
and his disciples, as perpetuated in the Church, will so to
speak always be contemporaries who can ' see ' and ' know '
each other. Nay more, the best proof of Christ's continual
spiritual presence will be found just in the sustained ' life '
of his disciples. As in 16 : 16 the primary reference in ' you
will see me ' may be to the Resurrection appearances, but the
deeper intention is to point to that spiritual communion with
Christ as an abiding presence which is the normal experience
of the Christian and one more to be coveted than the enjoyment of special appearances granted, it may be, to confirm
20 an unstable faith (20: 29). ' You will understand, on that day—
the allusion again being firstly to the day of Resurrection or of
Pentecost, but also in a more profound sense to the new era,
inaugurated by those days, during which the Spiritual Christ
shall rule and by his sustained communion with Christians will
convince them, as Jesus puts it—that I am in my Father—
drawing life from its supreme source (14: 10)—and you are
in me—in your turn receiving that divine life (15: 4)—
and I am in you '—continually renewing the supplies of that life
and expressing my will and purpose in and through you.

This mystic communion of Father, Son, and Believer is now
stated in terms of *love*: the condition of it is that moral obedience which is the best expression and proof of love (14: 15).
21 ' He who possesses my commands (literally ' has ' them, ' holds
them in mind ') and obeys them is he who loves me, and he who
loves me will be loved by my Father, and I will love him and

appear to him '—' manifest myself to him,' the very word used
by Moses in Exod. 33 : 18 ; in the spiritual presence of Christ
is the clearest possible revelation of God. To this Judas—
probably to be identified with Thaddaeus or Lebbaeus, the
brother of James (Mt. 10 : 3, Lk. 6 : 16)—replies by hinting
that an outward manifestation, by which the disciples' faith
might be vindicated in the eyes of an unbelieving world,
would be more effective (cf. 1 Jn. 5 : 4 f.) : ' Lord,' said Judas 22
(not Judas Iscariot), ' why is it that you are to appear to us, and
not to the world ? '—or better, ' What has happened that you
are to appear to us and not to the world ? '—as if something
had occurred to change the expected programme. (For the
question cf. Acts 1 : 6.) It is likely that critics of the Church
would lay stress upon the small number of those who could
witness to the Resurrection, as indeed Celsus actually does.
John meets this sort of objection, as well as the complaints of
impatient Christians at the delay of the Parousia, by arguing
that the power of apprehending such a revelation depends upon
obedience resting on love, and that the best evidence of the
continued spiritual life of Christ is the divine life of every
individual Christian : **Jesus answered, ' If anyone loves me 23
he will obey my word, and my Father will love him, and we will
come to him and take up our abode with him '**—Father and
Son alike : ' The whole power of the Godhead is manifested
in the individual believer ' (Strachan). The word ' abode '
recalls the O.T. idea of God dwelling among His people
(Exod. 25 : 8, 29 : 45 ; cf. Mt. 18 : 20, 28 : 20). The verse is
a repetition of 21, save that ' take up our abode ' replaces
' appear,' implying that better than any dramatic manifestation is the abiding inward presence. Jesus now states the
reverse truth : **' He who does not love me does not obey my 24
word ; and**—this is disobedience to God Himself, for what
you hear me say is not my word but the word of the Father
who sent me '** (14 : 10, 7 : 16, 12 : 49). As in verse 21 Jesus
associates the Father with himself in the closest possible union :
through disobedience to Jesus, which is in fact disobedience
to God, will be forfeited that love of the Father which is
promised with Jesus' own love and also the capacity for

apprehending his ' appearing.'   For the phrase ' he who does
not love ' defines what in verse 22 Thomas calls ' the world '
and explains why no spiritual manifestation is possible to it.

25   'I have told you all this,' continues Jesus, ' while I am still
with you ' (contrast 16 : 4*b*)—implying that his personal
ministry in the flesh is about to end ; but it will be continued
26 by his *alter ego* : ' but the Helper, the holy Spirit (this full
title occurs only here in the Gospel) whom the Father will send
in my name—to take my place, represent my interests, fulfil
my purpose—will teach you everything '—which may still
have been left unsaid (16 : 12) ; yet he will be but cultivating
the seeds of truth already sown by Jesus ; he will illuminate
' and recall to you everything I have said.'   The Spirit's
teaching is but the development and complement of Jesus'
(cf. 16 : 13–15 notes).   Echoes will be reawakened and a fuller
meaning given to old truths.   The verse is another (cf. 16 : 25)
admirable commentary on the character of the Fourth Gospel,
which is the result of an indissoluble mingling of Jesus' own
teaching, daring reinterpretations of that teaching under the
guidance of the Spirit, and the recollections of the Evangelist
and his associates also enriched by long years of spiritual
experience.

As if making his last will before death, Jesus now leaves
to his disciples his most precious possession—Peace.   It is
the ordinary word of farewell, but Christ so speaks it that what
upon other men's lips is a mere conventional wish, on his
27 becomes a divine bequest (cf. 20 : 19) : 'Peace I leave to you—
yet this is no ordinary peace : it is my peace I give to you '—
the peace to which Jesus himself had attained, peace in the
midst of storm, ' the inward serenity based upon reconcilia-
tion with God ' (Godet).   (Cf. 16 : 33, Phil. 4 : 7, Col. 1 : 20,
3 : 15, Rom. 5 : 1 ; contrast Mt. 10 : 34.)   'I give it not as the
world gives its " Peace ! " ' '—not by way of a mere polite
greeting, but such peace as is peace in very truth, a real defence
against disquiet ; thus Jesus adds, echoing verse 1, ' Let not
your hearts be disquieted or timid '—not without a hint of
reproach, as if with such protection it were cowardly to be
afraid (cf. Rev. 21 : 8).   Besides, this farewell is but *au*

revoir; 'You heard me tell you I was going away (16:28, 28 14:2) and coming back to you (14:3); if you loved me—a half-playful reproach, ' if you thought of me and the fulfilment of my purposes as well as of yourselves '—you would rejoice (16:20-22), both for my sake, that I am going to the Father, and for your own sakes—for the Father is greater than I am '—and therefore the apparent end of Jesus' life was in truth its absorption into a great Divine Life whereby he would have the greater power to fulfil his purposes and to protect his own (10:29). Though the Father and the Son are ' one ' (10:30), yet the Father is ' greater ' than Jesus (cf. 13:16); and yet, ' God alone can compare Himself with God ' (Godet).

' I tell you this now, before it occurs, so that, when it does 29 occur, you may believe ' (cf. 13:19, 16:4), that being forewarned, and matching the event with the promise, you may find your faith actually confirmed when the storm breaks upon you. ' I will no longer talk much with you '—a saying which 30 could hardly occur here if the whole of chapters 15 and 16 were still to follow; ' Time presses,' says Jesus, ' I must be done! '—' for the Prince of this world is coming '—to meet me in the conflict of which the Cross is the symbol and in which he is to be overthrown (12:31 f.). Possibly the idea is that at this very moment Satan, in the person of Judas whom he has possessed (13:27), is preparing for the betrayal. But ' he has no hold on me ': literally the translation is ' he has nothing in me '; the meaning apparently is, firstly, that Satan has a hold on no element in Christ's nature which will yield to him—a reference to our Lord's moral supremacy; secondly, that Satan has no authority in virtue of which he can retain his hold on Christ—a reference once again to the purely spontaneous quality of Jesus' self-sacrifice. Even as against Satan it is true that ' no one takes his life from Christ ' (10:18), but that ' he lays down his life of his own accord ' because ' he has his Father's orders for this '—a saying on which the next verse is a commentary: ' His (Satan's) coming (as 31 symbolized in the crime of the Betrayal) will only serve to let the world see (not that Satan has power over me, but) that

I love the Father and (following my own rule, 14 : 15) that I am acting as the Father ordered '—the Father's order being that he should die (10 : 18). ' Rise, let us be going ' (Mk. 14 : 42 Mt. 26 : 46). Christ goes forth to face the conflict.

Theme (iii) : The Prayer of Consecration (17 : 1–26)

Before leaving the Upper Chamber, or possibly in the courtyard below before setting out for Gethsemane, Jesus prays for ' his own ' whom he is about to leave ' in the world ' ; his ' teaching is crowned by prayer' (Westcott). This sacramental prayer, offered by the Master before he sacrificed himself for mankind, the eternal intercession of the Great High-priest (Heb. 7 : 25, Rom. 8 : 26, 27, 34), gave form to the Eucharistic liturgies of the early Church : cf. e.g. the prayers in the *Didaché* (IX–X). The prayer falls naturally into three divisions : (*a*) Jesus' prayer for himself (1–5) ; (*b*) his prayer for his immediate disciples (6–19) ; (*c*) his prayer for the Church Universal in all ages (20–26). Most of the ideas spring directly from the teaching of chapters 14–16 and will therefore require the less exposition.

1 So Jesus spoke ; then, lifting his eyes to heaven, he said (the language (cf. Ps. 121 : 1, 123 : 1) suggests that Jesus is standing in the open air ; but this is not necessary, for, as Meyer puts it, ' the eye of one who prays is on all occasions raised towards heaven') : ' Father (Rom. 8 : 15, Gal. 4 : 6), the time has now come ' : the ' hour,' which had ' not yet come ' in 2 : 4, 7 : 6, 8, 30 ; 8 : 20, which was imminent in 12 : 23, 27, has now struck—the hour in which Christ is to be ' glorified ' in his death and the victory which followed it (see note on 12 : 23) ; therefore Jesus prays, ' glorify thy Son that thy Son may glorify thee.' The Father's ' glory,' which consists in the revelation of Himself for the salvation of the world, is involved in the ' glory ' of the Son (see 13 : 31 f. note), i.e. in that victorious death which is the condition whereby alone Christ's spiritual power can transcend all limitations and perfect that revelation which is God's ' glory.' ' Grant me the Ascension,' Jesus prays, ' that I may execute the work of

Pentecost' (Godet). This mutual 'glorification' of Father
and Son is essential to the fulfilment of the divine purpose:
'**since thou** (the Father) **hast granted him** (the Son) **power 2
(13 : 3) over all flesh to give eternal life to all whom thou hast
given to him,**' and only by means of this 'glorification' can
this gift be bestowed (7 : 39, etc.). The phrase 'all flesh'
(Gen. 6 : 12, Is. 40 : 6, etc.) signifies the human race as possessed of physical life apart from the gift of 'eternal life' which
is now thus defined: '**And this is eternal life, that they know 3
thee, the only real God, and him whom thou hast sent, even
Jesus Christ**' (cf. 1 Jn. 5 : 20). 'Eternal life' (3 : 15 note)
results from the 'knowledge' of the 'only' (Is. 37 : 20) 'true'
(Exod. 34 : 6, Jer. 10 : 10, 1 Cor. 8 : 5 f.) or 'real' God; for
such knowledge is the only possible basis of the life-giving
love-fellowship on which Jesus has been dwelling. But to
such knowledge of God must be added knowledge of God's
ambassador: the Christian idea of God and that Christian
communion with God, wherein eternal life consists, can be
obtained only through the knowledge of and communion with
Jesus Christ himself (cf. 1 : 18, 14 : 6). The verse, with its
reference to Christ in the third person, though the words are
ostensibly spoken by Jesus himself, reads like a fragment of a
liturgical hymn of praise (cf. such verses as 1 Jn. 4 : 2, 1 Tim.
3 : 16, 6 : 13, 2 Tim. 2 : 8). (For the emphasis on the necessity
of 'knowledge' see note on 10 : 15.)

'**I have glorified thee on earth by accomplishing the work 4
thou gavest me to do**' (13 : 31) ; it was by making the Father
'known' through the teaching and miracles which marked his
earthly ministry that Jesus 'glorified' God. Note that, while
for Paul Jesus' earthly life had meaning only as a necessary stage
towards the Cross, John can speak of Jesus' work as 'accomplished' even before the Crucifixion. The revelation of God
is in Christ's life (cf. 14 : 9 note), and his death but puts the
final seal upon that revelation. Christ can therefore pray—
not as if seeking reward, but rather, his earthly mission being
complete, in order that he may pass on to the next stage,
first to the Cross and then to the heavenly exaltation:
'**Now, Father, glorify me** (through the Cross and the resulting 5
315

glory) in thy presence with the glory which I enjoyed in thy presence before the world began '—an eternal glory, laid aside for a season, and now to be restored. We have here (cf. 1: 1–5, 6: 62, 8: 52 ff.) a clear assertion of Jesus' divine pre-existence. 'There is consequently . . . a continuity of the consciousness of the historical Christ with the Logos' (Tholuck). John, like Paul (Phil. 2: 5–11), represents Christ as recovering, through the accomplishment of his mission, a glory which he had enjoyed from eternity, but had for a time voluntarily relinquished in order to undertake that mission; 6 his earthly life is an interlude between two eternities. 'I have made thy Name (i.e. God Himself in His divine nature and purpose) known to the men whom thou hast given to me from the world ' : according to our Evangelist the sphere of Christ's mission is limited; the manifestation of God has been made only to the elect, a minority which has been separated 'from the world' by the bestowal upon them of a spirit responsive to Christ's call (see 6: 37–44 notes). 'Thine they were, and thou gavest them to me ' : they were godly men even before they attached themselves to Jesus (e.g. Nathanael 1: 47) ; God first 'elected' them to salvation, and then accomplished that salvation by 'giving them to Christ'; 'and they have held to thy word ' : in contrast to the Jews of 5: 38 they have remained loyal to God's earlier revelation by recognizing its completion in the revelation of Jesus; they have accepted Jesus' word as being but a faithful reproduction of God's : 7 'they know now (as a result of obedience, 7: 17) that whatever thou hast given me comes from thee'—that my words 8 and works alike are those of God Himself (14: 10)—'for I have given them the words thou gavest me, and they have received them '—and, again as the result of this moral obedience (7: 17)—'they are now sure that I came from thee and believe that thou didst send me ' : they are persuaded that Christ's origin and mission are alike divine (16: 30). Note once again how for John the immediate condition of belief is knowledge, 'being sure' (cf. notes on 6: 69, 10: 15, 10: 38). 'Knowledge' completes itself and becomes effectual in 'belief.' 'Faith as described in the Synoptic teaching is simply the opening of the heart to God, and the humble and child-like are the most capable of it. The Johannine " belief " is the result of " knowledge." It presupposes a mind fully enlightened, and equal to high speculations on the Person and nature of Christ ' (E. F. Scott, *The Fourth Gospel*, p. 275).

' I pray for them—not for the world but for those whom thou 9 hast given me (6) do I pray ; for they are thine '—and therefore prayer for them must have peculiar power of appeal— ' all mine is thine (because from God he received it ; ver. 7) 10 and thine is mine (by the gift of the Father ; 3 : 35, 13 : 3) ; and I am glorified in them '—i.e. in the ' life ' communicated to the disciples through faith in Christ. ' The Church itself is the best proof that Jesus is alive or " glorified " ' (R. H. Strachan) (cf. 14 : 12-13). The pronouns ' mine ' and ' thine ' are neuters, as if to hint that ' the community of property and therefore of interest is unlimited, absolute ' (Dods). ' Any man may say, " What is mine is Thine," but only the Son can say, " What is Thine is mine " ' (Luther). The line of separation between the Christian community and the ' world ' (i.e. the section of society deliberately hostile to the Church) could not be more strongly stressed than by putting on our Lord's own lips the words, ' I pray not for the world.' One cannot but contrast the answer which in the Synoptics Jesus gives to the question, ' Who is my neighbour ? ' (Lk. 10 : 29 ff.). We have already noted how the Evangelist, who at one moment voices a splendid universalism (e.g. 3 : 16), at another limits the scope of the Gospel to a narrow circle so that the ' Saviour of the world ' (4 : 42) becomes in effect the Saviour of the Church. (Yet see note on 15 : 13.) Let it be remembered that for the Evangelist and his contemporaries the barrier between the Church and the world was in fact a very solid one. And indeed in all ages ' a real brotherhood must in some way be separate ; its principles have a definite meaning ; and they are or are not accepted. Life is full of occasions when a man must be for something or against it, and perhaps his worst choice, in God's eyes, is that which on a famous occasion adopted the formula of " neutrality even in thought " ' (Lord Charnwood, *According to St. John*, p. 116).

11   'I am to be in the world no longer—so imminent is the Cross that Jesus speaks as if it were already past—but they are to be in the world ; I come to thee—leaving them in the world ; and therefore I pray—**Holy Father, keep them by the power of** (literally ' in,' as if in a fortress) **thy name which thou hast given me**—for it was ' in God's name ' that Christ came (5 : 43)—**that they may be one**—for in the unity of love alone (15 : 2) will the strength of their discipleship consist (15 : 8)—**as we are one** ' (15 : 9–10). Some MSS. have ' keep those, whom thou hast given me, in thy name,' which seems an obvious correction, unless indeed, as may well be the case, the original reading was the neuter pronoun as in verse 2 and also in verse 24 (where the same variant occurs), which would give the same translation. ' By the power of thy name ' means by the power of God's own nature and personality, here almost ' by the power of thy *holiness*,' for in that quality the whole divine nature is expressed (e.g. to ' swear by God's holiness ' in Amos 4 : 2 is equivalent to ' swearing by Himself ' in Amos 6 : 8). Thus Jesus invokes God as ' Holy Father.' The original idea in ' holiness ' is that of ' separateness ' or ' distance.' Thus the attribute is particularly fitting when used here of the Father, who is to ' keep ' those who are ' separated ' from the world—isolated in it—as His own. The ' Holy Father ' will ' keep ' His own ' holy ' in the midst of the world's sin.

12   Christ prays the Father to grant a protection which he himself once afforded, but can do so no longer : ' **When I was with them, I kept them by the power of thy Name which thou hast given me**—the tense once again reflecting the time-point not of Jesus but of the Evangelist, as if the departure had already taken place—**I guarded them, and not one of them perished** (6 : 39, 10 : 28 f., and see the allusion to this verse in 18 : 9)—**only the son of perdition, that the scripture might be fulfilled** ' (Ps. 41 : 9, cf. 13 : 18). Notice the play on the words ' perished,' ' perdition.' ' Son of perdition ' is a Hebraism and means ' one closely identified with perdition ' (cf. Is. 57 : 4, Mt. 23 : 15 and 12 : 36, ' sons of the Light '). The reference is of course to Judas.

'But now I come to thee'—again Jesus sees beyond the 13
Cross ; ' I speak thus in the world—before leaving it, my task
triumphantly complete—that they may have my joy complete
within them '—this joy of victory born in the sense of a completed task. (See notes on 15 : 11, 16 : 24.) Jesus implies
that this prayer would be granted by the Father even without
the Son's asking (16 : 26), but the utterance of it (' I speak
thus ') will confirm the faith and complete the joy of those
who hear it (cf. 11 : 42). The guardianship of the Father
is the more necessary because ' I have given them thy 14
word—the revelation which the Father has commissioned the
Son to declare—and—in consequence—the world has hated
them ' (15 : 18-20) ; the acceptance of Jesus' teaching has
set them in opposition to the world which hates them,
' because—as ' children of God ' (1 : 18)—they do not belong
to the world (15 : 19 note) any more than I belong to the
world. I pray not that thou wilt take them out of the world ' 15
—which might appear the surest and quickest deliverance ;
but they have still a part to play in the world ; an ascetic
or puritan renunciation of the world is often easier than
Christianity, which is a way of life *in* the world ; therefore
Jesus prays not for an easy escape, ' but that thou wilt
keep them from the evil one '—Satan (1 Jn. 2 : 13 f., 3 : 12,
5 : 18 f.), who is the ' Prince of this world ' (12 : 31, 14 : 30)
in which the disciples must remain and the author of their
persecution and temptation. (For the petition cf. Mt. 6 : 13.)
' They do not belong to the world any more than I belong to 16
the world '—a repetition of 14 : as citizens of another kingdom
it is not to be imagined that Satan should have any more
hold on the disciples than upon the Master himself (14 : 30).
That they may in very truth be thus exempted from Satan's
authority Jesus prays : ' Consecrate them by thy truth '—or 17
perhaps ' by the power of thy truth ' (cf. ver. 11). ' Consecrate ' is the verb corresponding to ' holy ' (Heb. 9 : 13) :
Jesus is praying the Father to make the disciples His own
separate possession, cut off from the world and its power.
This God will perform ' by the power of His truth ' (for
' truth ' see 14 : 17, 16 : 13)—words which recall the thought

of verse 3 that the Father is ' the only *real* God,' and that
consequently His ' word,' as spoken by Jesus and revealed
in *the* Word (Logos), is also ' reality ': **' Thy word is truth.'**
The purpose of this ' consecration ' is that the disciples may
be fitted to carry on Christ's work, even as Christ himself had
first been ' consecrated ' to fulfil God's work (10 : 36) ; accord-
18 ingly the prayer continues : **' As thou hast sent me into the
world, so have I sent them into the world '** (cf. 20 : 21) ;
thus is explained Christ's purpose in refraining from with-
drawing his own from the world (15) ; they are to continue
there as Christ's representatives, even as Christ had come
there as the representative of God : ' John accepts in a yet
fuller and more literal sense the idea of Ephesians, that
the Church is the body of Christ—the vesture of flesh which
the eternal Word is always renewing in order to abide with
men for ever. . . . The community of the disciples, as the
germinal Church, is to replace Christ after he is gone, and
to manifest him as still present ' (E. F. Scott). The following
words again stress this intimate connexion between the
19 consecration to service of Christ and of his disciples : **' and
for their sake I consecrate myself that they may be consecrated by the truth '**—or rather ' *in reality* ' : the omission of
the definite article distinguishes the phrase from that used
in verse 17 ; the meaning is not merely that the disciples
are to be ' truly ' consecrated, but that what was formerly,
by O.T. ritual, etc., done in symbol is now to be done ' in
reality ' (cf. 4 : 23, note). Christ is the ' truth,' the reality,
of the old symbolical sacrifices, and his death therefore ensures
a true ' consecration ' for those ' for whose sake ' he died.
For Christ's ' consecration,' though covering the whole of his
life, was supremely illustrated in the Cross (so Calvin). Christ
himself was ' consecrated ' both as the priest whose life is
devoted to a ' holy ' service (Exod. 28 : 41), and also as the
victim devoted in sacrifice to God (Exod. 13 : 2), the offering
of which (cf. Heb. 9 : 14) in turn ' consecrates ' or renders
' holy ' (Heb. 9 : 13) those on whose behalf it is offered. By
thus consecrating himself in death to God Christ achieves
' in reality ' for his followers that consecration to holy service

which the old ritual merely symbolized (Heb. 10 : 10). The approximation of John's thought here to that of Hebrews is most noticeable. The passage also undoubtedly has a sacramental interest, and should be compared with 13 : 14, where the Christian's obligation to service under constraint of the Master's example is similarly emphasized.

The thought of the consecration to service of the inner circle suggests the larger circle of believers which will be the fruit of that missionary service ; for them too Christ prays : ' Nor 20 do I pray for them (the inner circle) alone, but for all who believe in me by their spoken word ' ; and, as the extension of the Church may well endanger its unity, he prays specially : ' May they all be one ! ' (Acts 4 : 32, Eph. 4 : 3). This unity 21 of believers is to find alike its principle and its ideal in the unity of the Father and the Son : it is to be not a co-ordina- tion of organizations, but a personal relationship of mutual love (15 : 9 f.) ; Christians are to be ' one ' because they draw their life from the Father and the Son who are themselves ' one ': ' As thou, Father, art in me—the source of my life— and I in thee—drawing life from thee—so may they be in us—drawing a common life from both—that the world (here regarded not as hostile but as the object of God's purpose of salvation ; 3 : 16) may believe thou hast sent me ' (7 f.) —the simplest possible ' creed ' and ' basis of union.' Just as the Church's lack of unity is the greatest of stumbling- blocks to non-Christians, so will her unity be the chief argu- ment for the divine character of Christ's mission (cf. 23). Moreover, that the unity of believers may fulfil the ideal set forth in the unity of Father and Son, it is necessary that they shall share even the ' glory ' of Christ—a glory defined in 5 and again in 24. Sharers of his mission (18) and of his suffer- ings (15 : 18), they shall finally share his ' glory ' (Rom. 8 : 17) : ' Yea, I have given them the glory thou gavest me, that they 22 may be one as we are one.' Notice the perfect tense, as if the promise were already fulfilled. The glory to be thus bestowed upon believers ' is the filial dignity, the state of '' adoption,'' whereby they have *become* (1 : 18) what the Son eternally *is* (17 : 5), children of God, and objects of His

perfect love ' (Godet). Thus will this triple union of believers,
23 Christ, and God—' I in them and thou in me '—grow until
it becomes ' perfect,' a word with a mystic colouring : they
will at length be fully ' initiated '—' that they may be made
perfectly one,' and may thereby witness progressively to the
divine origin of Christ's mission and to the love of the
Father towards the Church—' so that the world may recognize
that thou hast sent me and hast loved them as thou hast
loved me.' ' The Fourth Gospel may be said to culminate
in this magnificent conception of God Himself eternally
present in the believer, through Christ who unites us with
himself as he is united with God ' (E. F. Scott).

There follows an explanation of what is implied by ' sharing
Christ's glory ' : it is ' to be beside him '—' the consummation of Christian blessedness ' (Dods). Notice that for John
the supreme hope is not the ' second coming ' of Christ, but
the believer's union with Christ in God, a union which may
24 already be enjoyed : ' Father, it is my will—sufficient
prayer for one whose will is one with God's ; Jesus speaks as
if making his last will and testament—that these, thy gift
to me (this translation well brings out the force of the Greek
neuter pronoun) may be beside me where I am—from first
(Mk. 3 : 14) to last Jesus can desire nothing better for his disciples—to behold (and, it is implied, to share ; 22, Rom. 8 : 17,
2 Tim. 2 : 12, Rev. 3 : 21) my glory which thou hast given
me, because thou lovedst me before the foundation of the
world.' Christ's ' glory ' is again defined as being from all
eternity (cf. 5). The verse also suggests ' the road by which
we must seek the solution of the Trinitarian relations ; love
is the key of this mystery ' (Godet).

The prayer ends with an appeal to God's justice not to
suffer believers to share in the retribution rightly meted out
to an unbelieving world. Though the world may deserve
rejection through its misunderstanding of God, the Church
by accepting Christ's revelation of God has shown itself
25 worthy of His love : ' O just Father, though the world has
not known thee (15 : 21. 16 : 3 ; 1 Cor. 1 : 21), I have known
thee, and they have known that thou hast sent me '—the one

necessary credal test (21). Christ 'knows' God directly, believers through accepting Christ as God's commissioned revealer. ' So have I declared, so will I declare, thy Name to 26 them ' : the end and crown of all Christ's revelation of God's nature and purpose is to make men worthy to be loved even as the Father loved the Son—'that the love with which thou hast loved me may be in them (cf. 1 Jn. 3: 1)—and worthy to be Christ's own habitation—and I in them.' ' The love of God in lighting on believers will not attach itself to aught that is defiled. For it will in truth light only on Jesus himself, on Jesus living in them, and upon them as identified with him and reflecting his holy image ' (Godet).

FINALE

I. The Arrest and Trial (18: 1–19: 16)

Chapter XVIII

It is noteworthy that at this point the Evangelist omits all mention of the Agony in Gethsemane and passes at once to an account of the arrest. Such an omission would be strange indeed were John the Apostle, who is expressly stated by the Synoptists to have been present at the Agony, the author of the Gospel ; but it is more understandable on the hypothesis that ' the Witness ' was other than the son of Zebedee. The omission is perhaps due to the fear of unduly emphasizing what might appear to be a moment of weakness on the part of Jesus. Yet there is an echo of Mark's account in 18: 11, as previously in 12: 27.

Having said this, Jesus went out with his disciples across 1 the Kidron ravine—like David (2 Sam. 15: 23), who also passed out of his city over Kidron to return again a victor. The Kidron ' ravine ' (literally ' winter-torrent ' dry for the greater part of the year) separates the Mount of Olives from the Temple Mount. According to some authorities the Greek reads ' ravine of the Cedars.' But there are no cedars in the district, and moreover this reading ' would not correctly represent the Hebrew name (" Kedron," meaning " dark "). But it may have been adopted even by Jews as more euphonious in

Greek, when they were writing for Greeks' (Stanton).
Crossing Kidron Jesus came to an orchard, which he entered in
the company of his disciples. The 'orchard' is the Gethsemane of the Synoptists (Mk. 14: 32), and may well have
belonged to a friend, open or secret, of Jesus. There is no
proof of its exact position, though the traditional site, which
dates from the time of Constantine, when 'the faithful were
eager to offer their prayers there' (Eusebius), may be the true
2 one. Judas the traitor also knew the spot, for Jesus and his
disciples often met there (cf. Lk. 21: 37). The Evangelist
suggests that Jesus made no attempt to hide, thus answering
such taunts as that of Celsus that Jesus 'was taken while
trying to hide himself and to escape in the most disgraceful
way'; on the contrary, Jesus' surrender is entirely voluntary.
3 So after procuring troops (Roman soldiers) and some attendants
(the temple-police, 7: 32) belonging to the high-priests and
the Pharisees (John's description of the Sanhedrim, 7: 32),
Judas went there with lanterns and torches and weapons. The
'lanterns' were part of the regular equipment of the Roman
army and also of the temple-police. Even with the light
of the Passover full-moon they might be necessary for searching the dark corners of the olive-grove. The word 'troops'
means strictly the cohort of six hundred men, under a
chiliarchos or 'military tribune' (12), which garrisoned the
Tower Antonia; but possibly only a detachment of these
is thought of as being present. The Synoptists make no
mention of Roman soldiers on this occasion. It has been held
that this Gospel proves that there had been negotiations
about Jesus' arrest between the Jewish authorities and Pilate.
That Pilate was informed beforehand of the Sanhedrim's
intentions is possible enough. But if Roman soldiers had
effected the arrest Jesus would almost certainly have been led
direct to Pilate. John probably adds the feature of the
Roman soldiers for dramatic and symbolical reasons. The
presence of a strong body of Roman troops among those who
'fell back and dropped to the ground' (6) before Jesus
emphasizes his power and sovereign liberty and the voluntariness of his surrender, while his arrest at the hands of Romans

becomes typical of the persecution of the Church in after-years
and a comfort to later martyrs who are but suffering as did
their Lord before them (15 : 20).

Then Jesus, who knew everything that was to happen to him, 4
came forward—out of the shadows where he was lingering with
his disciples. Again the voluntariness of Jesus' surrender is
strongly emphasized (10 : 18, etc.). He ' knew ' what lay
ahead ; he went to meet his fate with his eyes open, not as the
victim of *force majeure* ; he was not dragged out of some
hiding-place, but freely came forward **and asked them, ' Who
are you looking for ? '** ' Jesus the Nazarene,' they replied— 5
that is, ' the man of Nazareth ' (1 : 46, Acts 24 : 5). Jesus said,
' I am he.' And Judas the traitor was standing beside them.
According to John, it is not necessary for Jesus to be pointed
out by Judas, who merely stands by as a spectator while Jesus
spontaneously gives himself up. Judas, like the Roman
soldiers with whom he is grouped, is powerless to force the
issue ; Satan, in the person of Judas (13 : 27), ' has no hold
on ' the Christ (14 : 30). The temple-police are supposed not
to know Jesus by sight in spite of previous encounters with
him (e.g. 7 : 32). Jesus is pictured as in complete command
of the situation, and now the powerlessness of the whole band
of his assailants before his divine majesty is still further brought
out : **When he said, ' I am he,' they fell back and dropped to** 6
the ground. This would be regarded as a fulfilment of Ps.
27 : 2. Jesus admits that he is the wanted man ; but for
John the words ' I am he ' signify much more than a mere
statement of identity (see notes on 8 : 24, 28 ; 13 : 19).

So he asked them once more, **' Who are you looking for ? '** 7
And when they replied, ' Jesus the Nazarene,' he answered, 8
**' I told you that I am he ; if it is me you are looking for, let
these men get away.'** Jesus repeats his question, and on the
same reply being given reminds the soldiers that on their own
showing their sole duty is to arrest himself ; for the apprehen-
sion of his companions they have no warrant. By his free
surrender of himself Jesus ' lays down his life for his friends '
(15 : 13 ; and again note the analogy with David, 2 Sam.
24 : 17). ' The power of the army is held in check until the

last moment, until Jesus has guaranteed the safety of his own' (Loisy). So voluntary is his surrender that he makes it only on his own conditions—the release of his comrades. In the view of the Evangelist (or possibly of the Redactor, for the comment shows an obvious lack of spiritual discernment as to the true intention of Jesus' promise ; see Introduction, p. xliv) Jesus thereby makes good his guarantee given in

9 17 : 12 : **This was to fulfil his own word : ' I did not lose a single one of those whom thou didst give me '**—a saying of Jesus intended certainly in a spiritual sense which here finds its symbol in the bodily escape of the disciples. The allegorical teaching of 10 : 11–15 also receives practical illustration. The idea that Christian disciples were subject to arrest merely on the charge of being disciples agrees with the conditions of a later age. Note too that the statement of the Synoptists that the disciples ' all forsook him and fled ' (Mk. 14 : 50), from which might be argued their Master's powerlessness to hold them, gives place to an assertion of the Master's power to secure their unimpeded escape.

10   **Then Simon Peter, who had a sword** (Lk. 22 : 36 ; to carry a weapon on the feast-day was forbidden), **drew it and struck the high-priest's servant, cutting off his right ear**—in an attempt, no doubt, to cleave his head—**(the servant's name was Malchus).** The incident is borrowed from the Synoptics, perhaps by the Redactor (like other ' Peter ' incidents ; cf. notes on pp. 165, 285), for it is out of harmony with the spirit of the rest of the narrative, which is one of triumphant non-resistance. Peter does not wish safety at his Master's expense, and gives a practical exhibition of the spirit expressed in 13 : 37. The fondness of the Gospel for detail appears in the statement that ' Peter ' was the aggressor, that the ' right ' ear was wounded, and that the name of the servant (a personal slave to be distinguished from the ' attendants ') was ' Malchus ' —apparently a common enough name (Neh. 10 : 4). From this appearance of inside information it might be argued that the verses rest on the authority of ' the Witness ' himself, who may have been acquainted with the High-priest's household (18 : 16). Jesus reproves the misplaced zeal of his impetuous

disciple and asserts the necessity of a voluntary submission
to the death which is the Father's purpose for him (10 : 18).
**Whereupon Jesus said to Peter, ' Sheathe your sword. Am I 11
not to drink the cup which the Father has handed me ? '**
The words are an echo of the Agony (Mk. 14 : 36). (For the
figure of the ' cup ' cf. Ps. 75 : 8, Ezek. 23 : 31–34, Is. 51 : 17,
22 ; Mt. 20 : 22.)

Our Gospel's version of Jesus' trial shows marked divergence
from that of the Synoptists. According to Mark (14 : 53), Jesus
was first led ' to the High-priest,' and during the night, at a
preliminary trial or *anakrisis* held for the purpose of
preparing evidence and examining witnesses, he was tried and
condemned by a quorum of the Sanhedrim, which early the
next morning (Mk. 15 : 1) met in the temple-chamber Gazith
(Mt. 27 : 5) for a second trial, possibly, as Luke implies
(22 : 66 ff.), to register their sentence more formally, and in
any case to convey Jesus to Pilate in a body. John omits all
reference to this second early-morning gathering (unless ver.
24 contains a hint of it), while he alone alludes to an appearance before Annas. The section 18 : 12–27 is in its present
order full of difficulties. These seem to be due to the Redactor's
desire to bring the account into line with the Synoptics and to
his insertion of the denial story as a sequel to 13 : 36–38,
verses which we have already suspected to be the work of
the same hand. The difficulties are as follows : Jesus is
first led to Annas (13). In the same verse and again in 24
Caiaphas is distinctly named as the High-priest, a statement of
course historically correct. Yet in 15, 19, 22, the official at
whose house and before whom Jesus is being tried—presumably Annas, for it is not till 24 that Jesus is sent to
Caiaphas—is also called ' High-priest.' This difficulty can
only be overcome either by omitting 24 (or transposing it to a
position before 15) and assuming that from the first it is Caiaphas before whom the trial is being conducted, and that it
is he all through who is named ' High-priest.' ; or else we may
make the same assumption possible by arbitrarily translating
the pure aorist ' sent ' in 24 as a pluperfect ' had sent,' which
the A.V. translators, perceiving the difficulty, have actually

done. The second difficulty is that at 24 the scene of the trial is changed (unless indeed we are prepared to accept the somewhat naive suggestion that ' Annas and Caiaphas occupied different portions of a range of buildings round a common court-yard '; Stanton), and yet 25 represents Peter standing and warming himself in exactly the same position as in verse 18 before the change of scene takes place. In the original Gospel the scene of the trial probably remained unchanged until at 28 Jesus is led to the Praetorium. But the Redactor by prematurely changing the scene has reduced Peter's position to absurdity. As Prof. Bacon has shown (op. cit., p. 485), the confusion is explained once we realize that the Redactor has, as usual, interpolated Synoptic material and thereby dislocated the text. Note the close parallel with Mk. 14 : 53 ff. Jn. 18 : 15–18 is equivalent to Mk. 14 : 54. In Mark the story of the denial is at this point interrupted by verses 55–65 ; then in verse 67 occurs the second reference to Peter standing and warming himself. The Redactor, closely following the source from which he is interpolating, at 25*a* also inserts a second reference to the ' warming ' in spite of the change of scene at 24. The Evangelist's own conception of what happened was probably either (*a*) that Jesus was tried before Annas whom John mistakenly imagined to be High-priest (cf. Acts 4 : 6). The confusion is then caused by the Redactor, who, as usual following the Synoptists, has introduced the allusions to Caiaphas before whom he assumed that Jesus must afterwards have been tried. (Cf. 11 : 49, where the emphasis on ' that year ' may simply be due to a similar anxiety on the part of the Redactor to correct the Evangelist's idea that the High-priest of the day was Annas.) Alternatively (*b*) the Evangelist may have meant that Jesus was taken to the house of Annas (possibly the ' bazaars,' for which see note on 13), but tried there by Caiaphas the High-priest ; there he was detained till 28 ; but the Redactor, assuming that in 19–23 the Evangelist is recording a trial by Annas and wishing to harmonize the story with that of the Synoptists, according to whom the trial was before Caiaphas, has interpolated the references to Caiaphas and caused the consequent confusion.

A tolerably satisfactory sequence may of course be reached by rearranging the order of the text: (*a*) as Moffatt, 12–14, 19–24, 15–18, 25 ff.; (*b*) as Spitta, 12–13, 19–23, 24, 14, 15–18, 25 ff.; (*c*) as the order is actually found in the Sinaitic Syriac MS., 12–13, 24, 14–15, 19–23, 16–18, 25. The last rearrangement, possessing as it does MS. authority, is particularly attractive, though the evidence of *Sin. Syr.* probably proves no more than that the confusion of the present text was early recognized and that there were skilled textual critics before Spitta ! The true solution would probably be to render all such ingenious transpositions superfluous by regarding 13*b*–18, 24–27 as interpolations by the Redactor. Yet the order of *Sin. Syr.* deals best with the text as it stands and may be adopted for purposes of exposition. According to this rearrangement, Jesus is first taken to Annas (possibly at the 'bazaars,' which would be near the place of arrest), who at once sends him on for trial to the legal High-priest Caiaphas.

So the troops and their commander and the Jewish attendants 12 (18 : 3) **seized Jesus, bound him**—shackled his hands behind his back, a detail not mentioned at this point by the Synoptists—**and led him first of all to Annas.** ' First ' has reference to the 13 subsequent proceedings at 24, 28, and reads like a correction of the Synoptists. Annas (or Hanan, Ananias) was High-priest himself from A.D. 6 till 15, when he was deposed by Valerius Gratus, and after him his five sons held the office at intervals. He would thus on account of his rank and family connexions still be a person of commanding influence : **for Annas was the father-in-law of Caiaphas, who was high-priest that year** (11 : 49). The verse explains both how it was that the prisoner was led to Annas—he was a close relative of the ruling High-priest—and also how it happened that Caiaphas, who held office till 37, was High-priest in the midst of a succession of the sons of Annas. Possibly the meaning is that Jesus was taken to the famous ' bazaars of the sons of Hanan,' to which the Sanhedrim is said to have been in the habit of retiring when it left the chamber ' Gazith.' There is some evidence that these ' bazaars ' were on the Mount of Olives, close to the place of arrest, and they may well have been a

rendezvous where members of the Sanhedrim favourable
to the hierarchical oligarchy might meet at night. But here
24 Jesus was not long detained : **then Annas had him bound and
sent him to Caiaphas the high-priest.** The fact that there is no
account in the Gospel as it stands of the interrogation before
Caiaphas, which according to the Synoptists was the chief
Jewish trial, suggests the possibility that verse 24 should be
transposed to this position, so that 19–23 are made to refer to
Caiaphas' examination. Note that while John records the
passing of no formal verdict of conviction against Jesus by
the Jews, whose part is little more than to denounce him to the
Roman power, and therein reflects the procedure followed in the
prosecution of Christians in his own day rather than gives a
strictly accurate account of Jesus' own trial, yet he emphasizes
throughout the bitter hostility of the Jews, and insists that
upon them lies the guilty responsibility for the death of the
Christ, rather than upon the weak Roman whom they use
14 as the instrument of their crime (19 : 11). **Now Caiaphas was
the man who had advised the Jews that it was for their interests
that one man should die for the people :** we are reminded of the
incident of 11 : 50, and get a hint as to what Caiaphas' treatment of Jesus is likely to be.

15 **Simon Peter followed Jesus along with another disciple ;
and as this disciple was an acquaintance of the high-priest, he
passed into the courtyard of the high-priest with Jesus, while
Peter stood outside at the door.** Having transposed 24 we
may now assume that the High-priest in question is Caiaphas.
The 'courtyard' would be not the interior where the interrogation was conducted, but the quadrangle round which the
house was built, where Peter later conversed with the servants,
and which in Mk. 14 : 66 is 'downstairs' and in Mt. 26 : 69
is 'outside' in relation to the judgment-hall. The 'other
disciple' is generally supposed to be the Beloved Disciple,
which is rather improbable if the latter is indeed John the son
of Zebedee, for it is hardly likely that a Galilean fisherman
would have access to the High-priest's house. But if the
Beloved Disciple and Witness of our Gospel is, as we suppose,
a Jerusalemite disciple, he may well have moved in priestly

circles. This conjecture is strengthened if we may suppose that it is to him that Eusebius refers when he quotes the testimony of Polycrates that ' John too who leaned on the Lord's breast, who had *been a priest and worn the high-priest's mitre,* both witness and teacher—he sleeps in Ephesus.' (See Introduction, pp. xlviii and lxiv, for the still more attractive suggestion that the ' other disciple ' here in question is not the ' Beloved Disciple-Witness,' but the ' Evangelist ' himself.)

Note that according to John there is no formal trial, no citation of witnesses as in the Synoptics, but rather an attempt to gather damning evidence to lay before Pilate. **Then the high-** 19 **priest questioned Jesus about his disciples and about his teaching,** in order to discover whether he made converts as a simple Rabbi or as one who claimed to be Messiah. But there is nothing to be learned beyond what Jesus has already publicly proclaimed: **Jesus answered, 'I have spoken openly** 20 **to the world ; I have always taught in the synagogues** (6 : 59) **and in the temple, where all Jews gather ; I have said nothing in secret. Why ask me ? Ask my hearers what I have said** 21 **to them ; they know what I said.'** (For ' openly,' ' in secret,' cf. 7 : 4.) We are reminded of Socrates' protest to his judges (Plato, *Apol.*, 33) : ' If any one says that he has ever learned or heard anything from me in private which the world has not heard, be assured he says what is not true.' Perhaps the Evangelist is rebutting the objection frequently brought against Christianity (cf. Origen, *Celsus*, ii. 70), that its founder had preached only in an obscure corner of Galilee and made disciples but of a few country folk. Rather was Jesus a conspicuous public figure at the headquarters of his national religion ! ' All Jews,' not merely a clique, have sat at his feet.

As he said this, one of the attendants who stood by gave 22 **him a blow** (literally a ' blow with a rod,' but used in later Greek of the open hand), **saying, ' Is that how you answer the high-priest ? '**—is this the correct demeanour of an accused man before his judge ? Of all the mocking, spitting, and buffeting recorded by the Synoptists, John mentions only this single blow, thus perhaps seeking to preserve the majesty

23 of the Christ. (For a similar incident cf. Acts 23 : 2.) ' If I have said anything wrong,' replied Jesus, ' prove it ; if I said what was true, why strike me ? ' In Jesus' answer, so restrained and reasonable, the blow recoils upon the head of the striker.

The ' other disciple' now returns to report to Peter the progress of the examination and gets permission for him to 16 enter: **Then this other disciple, who was an acquaintance of the high-priest, came out and spoke to the woman at the door, and brought Peter inside.** The porter is said to be a woman apparently because in the Synoptics it is a maidservant who first provokes the denial. Each of the four evangelists records three denials by Peter, but with interesting divergence in details : all agree, however, that the first to accost Peter was a 17 woman : **The maidservant at the door then said to Peter, ' Are you not one of this fellow's disciples ? '** This she would deduce from the fact that Peter had been introduced by one who 18 entered in Jesus' company. At once Peter denies : **He said, ' No ! ' Now the servants and the attendants**—who had assisted at Jesus' arrest—**were standing and warming themselves at a charcoal fire which they had lit (for it was cold), and Peter also stood beside them and warmed himself.** In the text as usually arranged the last sentence is repeated at the beginning of 25 in order to pick up the thread of the denial story broken at 18. The fire is not mentioned by Matthew ; in Mark the first only of the denials takes place beside it, in Luke all three. It was not yet dawn and Jerusalem at 2,500 feet is cold at that 25 hour in spring. **They asked him, ' Are you not one of his** 26 **disciples ? ' He denied it, saying, ' No ! '** Said one of the high-priest's servants, a kinsman of the man whose ear had been cut off by Peter—who therefore would particularly note the assailant and eagerly denounce him—**' Did I not see you with** 27 **him in the orchard ? ' Again Peter denied it.** The dawn was now at hand, and at that very moment the cock crowed, the prophecy of 13 : 38 thus being fulfilled—one of John's intensely dramatic sentences, even more so than if, as in the Synoptics, the warning had been recalled and the effect of remembrance on Peter noted. John neither emphasizes the vehemence of the third denial (Mk. 14: 71) nor the agony of repentance that followed ; for him it is enough that Jesus' prediction has been fulfilled.

Our Evangelist gives a fuller account than the Synoptists of the scene before Pilate and enlarges upon Jesus' personal conversation with the Roman governor ; but he makes no allusion to Luke's story of a reference to Herod.   **Then from the house 28 of Caiaphas they** (apparently the Jewish authorities) **took Jesus to the praetorium.**   Probably the Evangelist means that Jesus was led to Pilate direct from the place where the enquiry just recorded had taken place.   The Synoptists make it clear that a second and more formal meeting of the Sanhedrim was held at dawn to ratify the verdict of condemnation already passed. This in any case would be held at Caiaphas' official residence. But it is doubtful whether even this second meeting was legally in order, for no regular meeting of the Sanhedrim might be held sooner than 6 a.m. and John adds that still **it was early morning,** a Greek term apparently used technically of ' the fourth watch ' (Mk. 13 : 35), i.e. 3 till 6 a.m.   Jesus was never legally tried before the Jewish authorities, the whole proceedings being carried through with indecent haste in order that the execution might be over and the body removed (19 : 31) before the beginning of the Passover day at 6 p.m. The ' praetorium ' was the residence of the Roman governor, according to the traditional view Pilate's quarters in Antonia, but more probably the former palace of Herod the Great in the western part of the upper city.   Herod's son Archelaus had been expelled in A.D. 6 and a Roman procurator installed in his place.

Jesus is taken inside the palace to be interrogated, while Pilate in concession to their scruples converses with his accusers in the portico outside, for **they would not enter the praetorium themselves, in case of being ceremonially defiled—** by entrance into a pagan house—**for they wanted to eat the passover.**   John is at pains to emphasize the fact that this, the day of Jesus' death, is also the day of the Paschal feast, which, according to this Gospel, takes place the same evening, not, as in the Synoptics, the evening before.   **So Pilate came 29**

Y   333

outside to them and asked, ' What charge do you bring against this man ? ' Pilate is mentioned without introduction as if well known. He was appointed by Tiberius in A.D. 26 procurator of Judaea, which comprised the former kingdom of Archelaus. His severity in quelling a rising in Samaria led to his recall in A.D. 36. Though a weak man, John pictures him as endeavouring to uphold Roman ideals of justice. He desires from the Jews a definite charge against Jesus. What this was is hinted in 33. The Sanhedrim had condemned Jesus as a false Messiah who had threatened to destroy the Temple (Mk. 14: 58, Jn. 2: 19), a charge which would carry no weight with Pilate. Accordingly when asked to state their case Jesus' accusers reply evasively that they are here ' not to have their judgment revised, but to have their decision con-

30 firmed and the punishment executed ' (Dods) : **They retorted, ' If he had not been a criminal, we would not have handed him**
31 **over to you.'** Then said Pilate, ' Take him yourselves, and sentence him according to your own Law '—an apt retort with which cf. Gallio's in Acts 18 : 14 f. ' If you have already come to a verdict,' says Pilate, ' then pass sentence yourselves according to your own law and within the limits of your own competency '—an attempt to save Jesus' life, for the power still left to the Jewish court did not extend to the death penalty, which would require to be ratified by the Roman procurator. Accordingly, and hereby showing their real intentions towards Jesus, **the Jews said, ' We have no right to put anyone to**
32 **death.'** Their reply, John adds, took this form **that the word of Jesus might be fulfilled, by which he had indicated the kind of death he was to die.** The prophecy noted in 12 : 32 f. (cf. 3 : 14, 8 : 28) was to be fulfilled, for if put to death by Romans Jesus would be *crucified*, a form of execution never employed by the Jews even when they had the power. According to John, Jesus *must* die upon a cross because he had so foretold ; the very manner of his death was self-determined ; hence again and again he had escaped stoning. Such a conception of cause and effect seems of course strange to us ; yet ' the reality of the principal fact which gave point to John's words, namely the contrivance of the Jews that the

Romans should put Jesus to death, cannot be challenged'
(Stanton). It was not enough that Pilate should merely
ratify the Jewish sentence and hand over Jesus to a Jewish
execution ; Jesus must be sentenced by Roman authority, and
so put to death *upon a cross*. Hence the subtle conversion
of the charge into one of ' high treason,' on which Pilate now
questions Jesus in private.

So Pilate went back inside the praetorium and called Jesus, 33
saying, ' Then *you* are king of the Jews ? '—with emphasis on
the pronoun. In Pilate's question pity is mingled with
contempt. With ' king of the Jews ' contrast ' king of Israel '
(1 : 49 note). It is assumed that Pilate knows the charge
brought against Jesus (Lk. 23 : 2). According to the Synoptists (Mk. 15 : 5), Jesus having admitted his kingship refuses
further to answer Pilate. John, by staging this scene in
private, avoids too glaring a discrepancy with the Synoptists,
and makes it possible to put in Jesus' mouth the great declaration of 36 f., which in view of the emphasis of the Synoptists
on Jesus' silence John could hardly claim to have been made
in public. It must be confessed that the evidence of the
Synoptists and Roman usage, which required that a prisoner
should be examined in the presence both of his accuser and
witnesses, make it doubtful whether this private interrogation
can actually have taken place. But none will deny that
John's drama sets forth in a clearer light even than does the
exact history of the Synoptists the spiritual significance of
the hour when Christ confronted Rome. Jesus replied, ' Are 34
you saying this of your own accord, or did other people tell you
about me ? ' The responsibility for Jesus' condemnation is
cast on the Jews—a characteristic of this Gospel ; Pilate is a
mere tool. But the words perhaps have a deeper meaning ;
as Godet well puts it, ' In the political sense which a Roman
naturally gave to the term " king of the Jews " Jesus could
repudiate the title ; but in the religious sense given to it by
every believing Jew Jesus must accept it. . . . Everything thus
depended on the question whether the charge proceeded from
Jewish or Gentile lips.' But such a distinction would be
unintelligible to Pilate, who replies, ' Am I a Jew ?—what 35

interest have I in your theocratic subtleties ?—**Your own
nation and the high-priests**—who might have been expected
to support their ' King '—**have handed you over to me.
What have you done ? '** Pilate is impatient to get to the
practical point ; he is convinced that this is a mere matter
of religious quibbling, and that there is nothing in the treason-
charge. Jesus' reply confirms this conclusion, and also
36 explains the reason for his own people's antagonism : **Jesus
replied, ' My realm does not belong to this world '** (8 : 23,
15 : 19, 17 : 14, 16). The answer ignores Pilate's outburst
in 35 and picks up the question of 33. According to the
Synoptists, Jesus simply allowed Pilate to understand the
term ' king of the Jews ' as a Roman naturally would, and
as the accusers intended that he should—as a rival to Caesar :
according to John, Jesus enlightens him. His kingdom is
neither of a worldly nature, nor is it defended by worldly
power : **' If my realm did belong to this world, my men**
—the retinue which had he been a king he would presumably
have had at his disposal (the word is the same as that translated ' attendants ' in vers. 3, 18)—**would have fought to
prevent me being handed over to the Jews.** But as it is—
as may be deduced from the fact that Jesus did not rely on
armed resistance—**my realm lies elsewhere '**—in the region
of the spirit, though this is not explicitly stated. The words
read like an appeal to the political authorities of the Evangelist's own day to recognize the Church for what it is, not a
37 treasonable society but a spiritual community. **' So you are
a king ? ' said Pilate, ' you ! '** The Greek particle is used in
questions ' mostly in irony ' (L. and S.). Pilate means : ' So,
notwithstanding your reservations, you still claim to be a
king ? ' **' Certainly,' said Jesus, ' I am a king '**—literally, ' thou
sayest that . . . ,' the emphatic Jewish formula of affirmation
as in Mk. 15 : 2, etc. Dods would translate, ' Certainly, for
a king I am ! ' Moreover, Jesus is king not merely of one
small nation, but of the most universal of all realms—truth :
' This is why I was born (1 : 14), **this is why I came into the
world** (1 : 9, 16 : 28), **to bear testimony to the truth** (1 : 17,
3 : 11, 32 f.). **Everyone who belongs to the truth**—by moral

affinity (cf. 'belongs to God,' 8 : 47)—listens to my voice'
—and obeys it, as the Greek word implies. The meaning is
that those who are morally sincere instinctively yield to
Christ's will and become subjects of his kingdom. ' Truth,
absolute reality, is the realm of Christ ; and every one who has
a vital connexion with the Truth recognizes his sway '
(Westcott).

'Truth!' said Pilate, 'what is truth!'—not a sincere 38
request for light, but a contemptuous and sceptical ejacula-
tion. Is this then all that the case amounts to ?—a mere
philosopher's argument about the meaning of ' truth '! This
is no king threatening insurrection, but one who is nothing
more than ' un grand mystagogue!' (Loisy). Accordingly
Pilate goes out with the intention of releasing Jesus forthwith
as a harmless visionary. Note that at this point the remitting
of Jesus to Herod (Lk. 23 : 6 ff.) is omitted. With these
words he went outside to the Jews again and told them, ' I
cannot find anything wrong about him.' By ' the Jews ' is
meant the mob that had gathered rather than Jesus' actual
accusers ; Pilate perhaps hoped to enlist the support of the
former against the latter. But he also saw the chance of
conciliating the mob by making an act of bare justice appear
to be an act of grace ; he therefore adds : ' But it is your 39
custom that I should release a prisoner for you at the passover.
Is it your will that I release you the king of the Jews ? ' The
' custom ' would provide an excuse for setting aside the
sentence of the Sanhedrim, while at the same time enhancing
Pilate's own reputation for clemency. We have no evidence
elsewhere that this was a regular custom, though Josephus
(*Ant.*, xx., 9, 3,) says that at one Passover Albinus released
some robbers. If Pilate really wished to conciliate the mob
and save Jesus, it is hardly likely that he would risk still
further exacerbating them by the use of the title ' king of the
Jews.' But from the Evangelist's point of view the title
throws into stronger relief the Jews' blindness in preferring
a robber to their king. Note too that in this Gospel it is
not Pilate who mentions Barabbas as an alternative ; the
Jews themselves deliberately choose him : **Again they yelled,** 40

' No, not him ! Bar-Abbas ! ' The Evangelist emphasizes the tragedy of their choice in the dramatic words, **Now Bar-Abbas was a robber.** According to Mk. 15 : 7 he was a murderer and a *rebel*, and as such, by a strange irony, guilty of the very crime for which Jesus was innocently condemned (Lk. 23 : 5). John makes him a mere insignificant ' robber,' the better to use him as a foil to the rejected king. Origen sees a mystery in the fact that the name of both prisoners is ' the Son of the Father,' that being the meaning of Bar-Abbas. John writes ' *again* they yelled,' though this is the first outcry mentioned in this Gospel ; but there had been several in the Synoptic account (Mk. 15 : 8, 13, 14) which the Evangelist evidently has in mind. Indeed, on the ground that the indignities heaped on Jesus prior to the crucifixion are elsewhere in this Gospel omitted, and that 19 : 5 f. appears to be an anticipation of 19 : 13 ff., it has been held that the whole section 18 : 39–19 : 6 is a redactional insertion added chiefly for the sake of the Barabbas incident in order to bring the account into line with the Synoptic tradition. According to the Synoptics (Mk. 15 : 16 ff.) the mockery by the soldiers took place only after Jesus had been handed over for execution, which in view of Pilate's favourable attitude to Jesus is much more likely than John's version.

Chapter XIX

1 **Then Pilate took Jesus and had him scourged.** According to Mark and Matthew the scourging took place only after the crucifixion had been decreed. Here Pilate first has Jesus scourged, evidently in the hope that the Jews will be satisfied with something short of the death penalty (Lk. 23 : 22). But such punishment before sentence would be contrary to Roman judicial procedure, and perhaps we should assume that at this point Pilate pronounced sentence of death, and that the scourging was the usual legal preliminary to crucifixion. The victim was bound in a stooping attitude to a low column and lashed with thongs weighted with lead or bone. Then, according to John, followed the mockery which Luke (23 : 11) ascribes to the soldiers not of Pilate but of

Herod. John here follows Mark and Matthew very closely. And the soldiers twisted some thorns into a crown and put it 2 on his head—thus ridiculing his kingship—and arrayed him in a purple robe—probably a red military cloak as worn by Roman officers—marching up to him and shouting, 'Hail, 3 king of the Jews ! '—a parody of the customary salute, ' Ave, Caesar ! '—and striking him. According to Matthew (27 : 31) this mockery took place *after* Jesus had been handed over for crucifixion. If Pilate really permitted it at an earlier stage in the proceedings, his motive was probably to save Jesus' life by having the charge laughed out of court : again Pilate 4 went out and said to them, ' Look, I am bringing him out to you. Understand, I cannot find anything wrong about him.' But in the Evangelist's own perspective it is not the mockery that is conspicuous, but those symbols of royalty wherein Jesus' enemies seem unconsciously to prophesy his true kingship : So out came Jesus, wearing the crown of thorns 5 and the purple robe (Is. 63 : 1 ff., Rev. 19 : 13)—bearing even in his humiliation the insignia of empire—and Pilate said, ' Here the man is ! ' The substantive is one of contempt— almost ' the creature ! ' How can such a pitiable object be accused of treason ! But the definite article lends it dignity and suggests that Pilate's words are an unconscious prophecy (cf. 11 : 50 f.) of Jesus' uniqueness : ' Here is *the* Man '—the Son of Man, the Man *par excellence* foretold by the prophets.

At this point John again emphasizes how it was the priests who stampeded the mob into demanding Jesus' death : Now when the high-priests and their attendants saw him, 6 they yelled, ' Crucify him, crucify him ! ' Pilate said, ' Take him and crucify him yourselves ! I find nothing wrong about him.' Pilate does not yet wash his hands of the matter ; he does not do so till verse 16. Rather in a fit of exasperation does he dare the Jews to exceed their powers and take the crucifixion into their own hands. He says in fact, ' Crucify him if you dare ! If die he must, then yours must be the responsibility ! ' That the Jews will *not* dare, and that they know it themselves, is implied in their reply : The Jews 7 retorted (' we have no right to put to death '), ' But we

have a Law, and by [our] Law he is bound to die, because he
has made himself out to be God's Son ' ; though innocent of
treason in Roman eyes he is guilty of blasphemy in Jewish
eyes and therefore must die (Lev. 24 : 16). Off their guard
with excitement, Jesus' accusers reveal the true nature of the
charge. As Pilate had suspected, it is not political but
religious. Jesus, as is recorded in Mark's account (14 : 61 f.)
of the trial before the Sanhedrim, had professed to be the
' Son of God,' i.e. Messiah. The charge against Jesus as a
pretender to the Messiahship on its political side (' king of
the Jews ') having failed to move Pilate, the religious side of
the claim (' Son of God ') is now stressed as a capital offence
against Jewish law, which Pilate is bound to respect. But
the title ' Son of God ' carries even here its full Johannine
significance (1 : 34, 5 : 18) as implying something far more
than a national ' Messiah.' Pilate himself is supposed to read
a deeper meaning into the title ; hence the hint that he is
now seized with that superstitious fear which so often haunts
8 the sceptic : **Now when Pilate heard that, he was still more
afraid.** Pilate begins to feel awe in the presence of his
captive. Perhaps too he once again scents treason and fears
lest his clemency may be misconstrued in high quarters ;
for was not the Emperor himself a *divi filius*, son of God ?
9 Accordingly **he went inside the praetorium again and asked
Jesus, ' Where do you come from ? '**—what is the meaning
of this claim to a divine origin (cf. 8 : 14, etc.) ? **Jesus made
no reply** (Is. 53 : 7). Pilate has virtually admitted his
innocence ; why then argue more ? ' Jesus always assumed
10 and did not assert his claims ' (Strachan). **Then Pilate said,
' You will not speak to *me* ? '** The last word is emphatic.
Pilate feels slighted by Jesus' silence, and therefore asserts
his authority. Silence before the Jews might be intelligible,
but hardly before the man who has power of life and death :
**' Do you not know it is in my power to release you or to
crucify you ? '** That Pilate speaks not of justice but of power
11 implies that he considers Jesus innocent. **Jesus answered,
' You would have no power over me, unless it had been
granted you from above.'** Once again Jesus insists that his

340

death is brought about by no outside compulsion, but by the
will of God which he himself does (10 : 17 f.). His death is
self-determined. Pilate is but the tool of the Jews to whose
guilty machinations Jesus willingly surrendered himself.
' So you are less guilty,' says Jesus, ' than he who betrayed
me to you.' As Calvin well puts it, ' He who delivered me
unto thee is the more guilty of the two, because he *criminally*
makes use of thy *lawful* powers '—powers that have been
' granted you from above.' Alternatively we may paraphrase :
' Because your power is not your own but God's, therefore my
betrayer is more guilty than he would otherwise have been,
for in persuading you to put me to death he is turning against
me a power which is in fact delegated from God.' The holier
the power the more blameworthy the misuse of it. But the
comparison is evidently between Pilate's guilt and the Jews',
rather than between the Jews' present guilt and their hypothetical guilt under other circumstances. Our translation is
truer to the thought of the Gospel : it was decreed that Jesus
should die, and upon a Cross ; Pilate is but the instrument
of the Jew's animosity and ultimately of the divine will, and
therefore his guilt is the less. As already noted, John habitually enlarges upon the Jewish as over against the Roman guilt
for Jesus' death. By ' he who betrayed me ' is evidently
meant Caiaphas, though the phrase is regularly used of
Judas (but in 18 : 30, 35 the verb is used of the Jews). Perhaps we should rather translate ' *he who handed me over to
you.*' Loisy supposes that the reference is to Judas, or rather
to Satan working through Judas (13 : 2, 27). (For the idea
that the Roman power is divinely sanctioned, though this
is not directly in view here, cf. Paul's words in Rom. 13 : 1 ff).

This made Pilate anxious to release him (Acts 3 : 13). Why ? 12
Probably because Jesus' reference to things spiritual
(' granted you from above ') confirms Pilate's conviction that
the prisoner is not a revolutionary but a visionary. But—
as if to counteract this impression—the Jews yelled, ' If you
release him, you are no friend of Caesar's ! Anyone who
makes himself a king is against Caesar.' To compromise
with a pretender like Jesus is to conspire against the Emperor.

Dropping the religious charge Jesus' accusers once again press the political one, with an appeal to Pilate's own interests and fears. The charge of high treason, they hint, may recoil on Pilate's own head—the more so that Tiberius was the most suspicious of despots, while Pilate's conduct had on a previous occasion been brought under review (Lk. 13 : 1).

13 On hearing this, Pilate brought Jesus out and seated him on the tribunal—the raised platform from which justice was administered—at a spot called the 'mosaic pavement '—the 14 Hebrew name is Gabbatha (it was the day of Preparation for the passover, about noon). 'There is your king ! ' he said to the Jews. Undoubtedly the meaning is that Pilate set Jesus upon the tribunal, rather than that he took his own seat in order to pronounce final judgment in presence of the crowd. The passage is so understood by Justin Martyr (*Apol. I*, 35), and in the *Gospel according to Peter*. This interpretation makes the scene much more dramatic and alone suits the words ' There is your king ! ' In the details of John's account historical probability should be considered less than symbolical fitness. Dramatically the Jews are shown rejecting their king. Pilate makes one final attempt to have the case laughed out of court ; but John thinks not of the ridicule but of the unconscious prophecy : it is really Jesus who is King and Judge. Such an incident no doubt seems historically improbable, but the very fact that the Evangelist so carefully marks place and hour shows that he attached great importance to the event, which in his view must have been something *extraordinary*. By the ' mosaic pavement ' is apparently meant a paved space in front of the praetorium ; there is no other reference to it, no attempted identification of the spot is satisfactory, and it may be that the Evangelist simply assumed its existence from custom. Suetonius says (*Vit. Div. Jul.*, 46) that Julius Caesar carried about with him when with his army a tesselated pavement which was laid down to mark the spot where his judicial decisions were given. But the Hebrew name ' Gabbatha ' suggests that a definite spot is in view. The word is not a translation of the Greek for ' pavement,' but a name given

to the place from its being 'raised,' and would seem to apply to the tribunal rather than to the pavement. The derivation is perhaps *Gab-baitha*, meaning 'ridge of the house.' The allusion may be to a paved portico outside the palace upon which stood the tribunal under some kind of cupola. ' Day of Preparation ' is the usual name for Friday, the day before the weekly Sabbath. But in this case, though the day was in fact a Friday, its relation not to the Sabbath but to the Passover feast is emphasized. In Mk. 15 : 42 the Passion day is similarly called the ' day of Preparation,' but there merely with reference to the Sabbath—on account of the difference in chronology (Introduction, p. xiii). There is some difficulty about the hour, which John states to have been ' about the sixth,' i.e. about noon ; Mark, on the other hand, puts the crucifixion at ' the third hour,' i.e. 9 a.m. The apparent discrepancy may be partly explained by the fact that the day was divided into four parts of three hours each. The second quarter would begin at ' the third hour ' (9 a.m.), and end at ' the sixth hour ' (noon). As mention is scarcely ever made in the N.T. of any hours except the third, sixth and ninth (cf. Mt. 20 : 1-5), most statements of time being qualified with the word ' about,' an event taking place say midway between 9 a.m. and noon might well be referred by one narrator to the former hour and by another to the latter. But this is only a partial solution, for allowance must be made for the elapse of time between Pilate's sentence and the actual execution. Mark's apportionment of the Passion day seems to be the more probable, and possibly some symbolical motive may underlie John's preference for ' the sixth hour ' (cf. 4 : 6).

Then they yelled, ' Off with him ! Off with him ! (possibly 15 meaning, ' take him off the tribunal ! ') Crucify him ! ' ' Crucify your King ? ' said Pilate—a flash of irritable sarcasm which so stings the Jews that in hatred of Jesus they actually renounce the theocracy and make abdication of the Messianic hope : The high-priests retorted, ' We have no king but Caesar ! '—a declaration which is ' the crowning apostasy of Judaism ' and ' the utterance of a nation turned traitor

to its noblest traditions' (Strachan). Compare the cry in
16 Mt. 27 : 25. **Then Pilate handed him over to them to be
crucified.** Again the Evangelist insists that Pilate took no
active part in Jesus' death, but merely gave the necessary
authorization. Accordingly, while Mark makes it plain that
Roman soldiers carried through the execution, John implies
that it was the Jews who hurried Jesus off, and were responsible for the crucifixion (17–18), though at verse 23 the
Roman soldiers reappear.

II. THE CRUCIFIXION OF CHRIST (19 : 17–42)

The details in the crucifixion story peculiar to this Gospel
are : the Jews' objection to the inscription (20–22) ; Jesus'
last bequest (25–27) ; the two sayings, ' I am thirsty ' and
' It is finished ' (28–30) ; the wounding of Jesus' side (31–37) ;
17 the last ministry of Nicodemus (39 f.). **So they** (i.e. the Jews)
took Jesus, and he went away—outside the city where it was
customary to execute criminals (cf. Heb. 13 : 12 f.)—**carrying
the cross by himself** : this, too, was customary (cf. Mt. 16 : 24).
The words read like a correction of Mk. 15 : 21, according to
which Simon the Cyrenian was forced to carry the cross,
but they may merely imply that Jesus set out with the
cross on his shoulders though he was afterwards relieved of it.
The fact that Jesus carried his own cross again suggests in
symbol the voluntary nature of his sacrifice, while the parallel
is also noted with Isaac (Gen. 22 : 6), who in Jewish-Christian
thought was used as a type of Christ (Tertullian, *Adv. Jud.*,
10). Certain Gnostics (e.g. Basilides) taught that Simon was
crucified instead of Jesus ; but the evidence seems too late
to permit the supposition that John is here combating this
heresy (see Irenaeus, *Haer.*, i. 24, 4). **Thus then they came
to the spot called ' the place of the skull '—the Hebrew name
is Golgotha.** The exact site cannot be located with certainty
because of doubt about the line of the northern wall of the
city at this time. ' Golgotha ' lay probably just beyond this
wall and close to the road (Mk. 15 : 29) leading out through
a gate near to the praetorium. The traditional site, where

the Church of the Holy Sepulchre now stands, seems too far within the walls of the city. The name ' place of the skull ' would be due to the hillock's bare top and skull-like contour rather than to its grim associations. **There they crucified** 18 **him, along with two others, one on each side and Jesus in the middle** : thus ' he was classed among criminals ' (Lk. 22 : 37). Matthew and Mark call his fellow-sufferers ' robbers.'

Pilate had written an inscription to be put on the cross— 19 probably a white board nailed to the gibbet and inscribed with the name and offence of the victim. **What he wrote was,** JESUS THE NAZARENE, THE KING OF THE JEWS—an insult directed by Pilate in his chagrin against the Jews rather than against Jesus, as appears from 22. **Now many of the Jews** 20 **read this inscription, for the place where Jesus had been crucified was close to the city ; besides, the inscription was in Hebrew, Latin, and Greek,** and so would be intelligible to all. That the inscription was in three languages is recorded by John alone, for the clause in Lk. 23 : 38 is an interpolation ; again we have an unwitting prophecy of Christ's universal kingship. **So the Jewish high-priests**—piqued by the inscrip- 21 tion, as they were meant to be, as though Jesus' claim had been officially admitted—**said to Pilate, ' Do not write,** THE KING OF THE JEWS ; **write,** HE SAID I AM THE KING OF THE JEWS.' **Pilate replied, 'What I have written, I have written.'** 22 This, hints the Evangelist, is a true prophecy. The Greek perfects imply that what is written stands, and that the matter is closed. The incident well reveals the temperament of Pilate, who, according to Philo (ii. 589), was ' by nature obstinate and stubborn.'

Now when the soldiers crucified Jesus they took his clothes 23 —the usual perquisite of the executioner—**and divided them into four parts, one for each soldier.** Four soldiers was the customary detachment for such purposes (a ' quaternion ' ; Acts 12 : 4). The ' four parts ' would perhaps consist of head-dress, shoes, outer-garment and girdle ; there would remain the undergarment or tunic : **But as the tunic was seamless, woven right down in a single piece, they said to** 24 **themselves, ' Don't let us tear it. Let us draw lots to see who**

gets it.' John alone records that the tunic was 'seamless,' for he sees in the fact a symbolical meaning. The full-dress of the High-priest (Exod. 28 : 31 ff.), so Josephus tells us (*Ant.*, xi, 7, 4), was similarly seamless. Christ on the Cross is the world's High-priest (Heb. 3 : 1 and *passim*). Philo uses the High-priest's seamless robe as a symbol of the Logos, the eternal Principle of the Universe, and Cyprian uses it as a symbol of the undivided Church. The incident, John suggests, took place that the scripture might be fulfilled, 'they distributed my clothes among them, and drew lots for my raiment.' The reference to the prophecy in Mt. 27 : 35 is interpolated from our Gospel. Ps. 22 : 18 is exactly quoted from the LXX. John would seem to apply the first member of the verse to the 'clothes' and the second to the 'tunic,' whereas in the original the repetition is simply the Hebrew poetic parallelism, and is so understood by the Synoptists, who do not distinguish the tunic. (For a similar misconception cf. Mt. 21 : 2, 5, of the ass of Zech. 9 : 9.) This was what the Roman soldiers did : thus even the rudest and blindest agents became an instrument for the fulfilment of prophecy.

25 Now beside the cross of Jesus (contrast Mk. 15 : 40, Mt. 27 : 55) stood his mother and his mother's sister, Mary the wife of Clopas, and Mary of Magdala. It is not clear whether three or four women are mentioned, for ' Mary the wife of Clopas ' may be in apposition to ' his mother's sister ' and refer to the same person. But probably the two are distinct, for it is unlikely that both the Virgin and her sister would be called ' Mary.' (To obviate this difficulty some have supposed that Clopas is a brother of Joseph, mention of whom by Hegesippus is recorded by Eusebius, in which case the two women would be sisters-in-law.) According to Mt. 27 : 56 and Mk. 15 : 40 the group included Mary of Magdala, Mary the mother of James and Joses, and Salome the mother of the sons of Zebedee, whence it has been assumed that ' his mother's sister ' is Salome (in which case Jesus and John the Apostle would be cousins, an attractive hypothesis, for those who identify the Beloved Disciple with the Apostle, in view of 26 f.), while ' Mary the wife of Clopas ' would be Mary

the mother of James and Joses, in which case ' Clopas ' might
be identified with ' Alphaeus ' (Mt. 10 : 3). But there is no
evidence for the first identification (indeed Lk. 24 : 10 mentions ' Joanna ' as the third woman), while the argument that
' Clopas ' and ' Alphaeus ' are derived from a common Aramaic
original has not been satisfactorily established. The alternative identification of Clopas with the ' Cleopas ' of Lk. 24 : 18
is purely conjectural and is denied by Deissmann (*Bible
Studies*, p. 315) on the ground that the former name is Semitic
and the latter Greek. No certain conclusion can be reached
as to these identifications. ' Mary of Magdala ' is first mentioned in Lk. 8 : 2 as one of a company of women who accompanied Jesus on his second mission through Galilee. Magdala
(now Mejdel, a decayed village) was a place of some importance,
three miles from Capharnahum, on the Lake of Galilee.
According to the Talmud, it had an evil reputation for harlotry,
from which, together with Luke's remark (8 : 2 : ' out of
whom seven devils had been driven '), it has been generally
assumed, on slender enough evidence, that Mary was a re-
formed courtesan.

So when Jesus saw his mother and his favourite disciple 26
standing near, he said to his mother, 'Woman, there is your
son ! '—one who will take my place as your protector. In the
word ' Woman ' there is no such harshness as the English
suggests ; rather have we ' a very tender application of the
wider thought of 17 : 11 ' (Strachan). (Cf. 2 : 4 with which
the present incident closely connects itself.) Jesus' ' time '
is now indeed come. Then he said to the disciple, ' Son, there 27
is your mother ! ' Jesus' true brother is the ideal Christian
(Mk. 3 : 31-35). In Lucian's *Toxaris* Eudamidas makes a
similar bequest : ' I leave to Aretaeus the care of nourishing
and providing for my mother in her old age.' The trust is
at once assumed : and from that hour the disciple took her
to his home—which most naturally, but not necessarily,
implies that the Beloved Disciple had a home at Jerusalem ;
if so, it supports the idea that he was a Jerusalemite rather
than John the son of Zebedee. Symbolically the incident is
interpreted as meaning that Jesus commends his mother, the

Jewish Church (2 : 3 note)—the spiritual heritage of the race from which Jesus sprang, the ancient faith which had given birth to Christianity—into the keeping of the perfect Christian believer. Such a believer is to be regarded as the legitimate ' son ' of the O.T. faith. But the mother goes to the son's house, not the son to the mother's ; the old faith must accommodate itself to the new, not the new to the old. ' What was valuable and permanent in Judaism has now passed over to Christianity : the " mother of Jesus " dwells in the house of his disciple ' (E. F. Scott). All this may possibly be legitimate interpretation ; but again we must remind ourselves that the fact that an incident is capable of being allegorized is no proof that it is not historically true (2 : 1 note).

28 **After that, as Jesus knew that everything was now finished and fulfilled** (i.e. brought to its purposed end : Christ's mission is now complete), **he said** (to fulfil the scripture), ' " I am thirsty." ' The Evangelist writes as if Jesus deliberately set himself to fulfil prophecy ; his request prompted the fulfilment of Ps. 69 : 21 (cf. also Ps. 22 : 16) in the offer of the vinegar. (See notes on 12 : 14, 38.) The Greek word used here for ' might be fulfilled ' is unusual, and suggests that ' the subject in question is *the finishing* of the fulfilment of the Scriptures as a whole, and not the fulfilment of this particular prophecy ' (Godet) (cf. Acts 13 : 29). John alone records the word from the Cross ' I thirst '—possibly with an apologetic purpose directed against Docetic doctrine. The Jesus on the Cross was as truly real and human as he who thirsted 29 at Jacob's well (4 : 7). **A jug full of vinegar was lying there ; so they put a sponge full of vinegar on a spear and held it to his lips.** The word translated ' spear ' is literally ' hyssop,' from a branch of which the ' spear ' may have been made ; an improbable alternative is that by ' hyssop ' is meant some substance that was mingled with the vinegar. Matthew and Mark state that the sponge was put on the end of a ' reed ' or ' stick.' Probably some symbolical intention underlies John's alteration, for ' hyssop ' was used for ceremonial purposes in connexion with the Paschal lamb (Exod. 12 : 22).

Another allusion to the Paschal ritual follows in 36. The vinegar or sour wine was the ordinary drink of the soldiers, and would be offered out of compassion. It is probably to be distinguished from the drugged wine, which was regularly given to criminals before execution and which Jesus had already refused (Mt. 27 : 34, 48), though possibly the mention of two separate offers of wine is again due to the poetic parallelism in the prophecy fulfilled (Ps. 69 : 21). **And when 30 Jesus took the vinegar, he said, ' It is finished,' bowed his head, and gave up his spirit.** Jesus' last words are a declaration that his commission is fulfilled (17 : 4, 19 : 28) and that his ' time ' having now fully come he may voluntarily lay down his life (10 : 17–18). Every clause in this verse stresses the voluntariness of his sacrifice, while we also find emphasized John's characteristic idea that at Jesus' death his spirit was set free from the limitations of the body that it might be bestowed upon the Church (7 : 39, 20 : 22). Matthew and Mark simply say that Jesus ' expired.'

Now, as it was the day of Preparation, in order to prevent 31 the bodies remaining on the cross during the sabbath (for that sabbath-day was a great day), the Jews asked Pilate to have the legs broken and the bodies removed. The ' day of Preparation ' means ' the eve of the Sabbath ' (14)—a Sabbath which in this case was a ' great day ' or ' high day ' because, according to John's reckoning, it would be not only the weekly Sabbath but also Nisan 15th, the first day of the feast of unleavened bread, which was celebrated by a ' holy convocation ' (Lev. 23 : 7) ; it was therefore a double-sabbath. The Roman custom was to abandon corpses of criminals to dogs and vultures, but Jewish law forbade the leaving of a body on the gibbet overnight. In this case the law would be the more stringently enforced as the next day, beginning at 6 p.m. the same evening, was a ' great day.' The Evangelist again stresses the fact that Jesus died at the very time when in every Jewish home the Paschal lamb would be slain. The breaking of the legs or *crurifragium* was a customary means of hastening death. Jesus' companions in misery are thus despatched : **So the soldiers went and broke the legs of the 32**

first man and of the other man who had been crucified with him ;—but it is emphasized that Jesus had already died 33 *spontaneously*—but when they came to Jesus and saw he was 34 dead already, they did not break his legs ; only, one of the soldiers pricked his side with a lance—perhaps to test whether he was really dead—and out came blood and water in a moment. It is said that the soldier ' pricked ' rather than ' pierced ' Jesus' side : the word is not so strong as that used in verse 37, though 20 : 25 suggests that the wound was large, as would be made by a full thrust by the Roman *hasta*, which had a broad head.   Endless controversy has raged around the words ' blood and water.'   It has been argued, though the medical evidence is extremely doubtful, that if the immediate cause of death had been rupture of the heart, a spear thrust in the pericardium may have been followed by a flow of blood and watery lymph.   It is just possible that ' the Witness ' may have actually noticed some such physical phenomenon and that the Evangelist, with an apologetic purpose directed against Docetic doctrine, emphasizes it as a proof that Christ really died upon the Cross.   But it is necessary for us, as Sanday well remarks (*Criticism of the Fourth Gospel*, p. 181), ' to distinguish between the fact itself . . . and the train of speculation to which it gave rise.'   It is the latter, the symbolical meaning of what may or may not be a natural phenomenon, which has importance for the Evangelist.   The shedding of ' blood ' and of ' water ' almost certainly typifies the bestowal of the benefits of Jesus' death and of the gift of the Spirit in the two Christian sacraments of the Eucharist and Baptism.   The thought of Christ's death being immediately before us, the ' blood ' is mentioned first, for the Eucharist is the sacrament of Christ's death.   In 1 Jn. 5 : 6 Baptism, according to the logical order of the sacraments, is alluded to first.   (See also note on 7 : 38.)

The historicity of the incident just recorded is now vouched 35 for in the most emphatic manner possible : **He who saw it has borne witness (his witness is true ; God knows** [literally, ' he knows '] **he is telling the truth), that you may believe**— the aim of the whole Gospel (20 : 31).   Taking into account

the peculiar Johannine force of the words translated ' true '
(Gk. *alēthinē*, ' conformé à la réalité mystique de son
objet,' Loisy) and ' truth ' (Gk. *alēthē*, the ' real ' as
opposed to the symbolical), the words may mean not only
that the incident is historically ' true,' but also that the
account just given adequately represents the spiritual reality
of the outward facts. But who is the witness to whom the
verse appeals ? If we owe it to the Evangelist himself, is he
' by these words objectifying, and as it were looking back
upon himself, or is he pointing to some third person unnamed
in the background ? ' (Sanday). Is he himself claiming to be a
witness, or is he appealing to another whose evidence he
guarantees ? *Pace* the defenders of the traditional theory
of authorship, the former alternative is surely impossible.
Quite apart from the difficulty of the use of the Greek pronoun
ekeinos by the writer as referring to himself, ' whoever
heard of a writer employing such ambiguities to make the
simple statement, " I myself saw this " ? ' (Bacon, *Fourth
Gospel*, etc., p. 192). It is more probable that the Evangelist
is appealing to the authority of ' the Witness ' whose memoirs
he has before him (this would be the force of the present tense
' he is telling '). In this case the word *ekeinos*, unless, as
is natural enough, it merely picks up the subject of the previous clause, may conceivably refer to Christ, as several times
in the First Epistle (1 Jn. 3 : 3, 5). The phrase would then
be ' just a formula of strong asseveration like " God knows ! " '
(Sanday), and this translation we have adopted above. That
the appeal is to the testimony of a third party is suggested
by 5 : 31, 8 : 13. But on the whole the most likely solution is
that the verse is a comment interjected by the Redactor. It
rudely interrupts the connexion between 33 f. and 36, and
seems to be one of the verses in which the point of view of
the Appendix is thrown back into the body of the Gospel in
order to suggest that the Witness-Evangelist (according to
the Redactor they are one person) is to be identified with the
Beloved Disciple (see Introduction, p. xlix f.). The verse should
be considered in close connexion with 21 : 24. ' The man who
saw this,' says the Redactor, ' has set down his evidence, and

here in his Gospel we have, God knows ! a true account.'
A further tentative suggestion may be made. Is it possible
that the Redactor is here making a subtle distinction between
'the Witness' and the Evangelist? The former has seen and
borne witness, while the latter (*ekeinos*), that 'Elder'
known to all, by his writings corroborates its truth : e.g. in
I Jn. 5 : 7 he testifies to this very same phenomenon of
blood and water in the words, 'The Spirit is the witness to
this, for the Spirit is truth.'

The following two verses connect with 34, verse 35 being
a parenthesis. Again the Evangelist notes the fulfilment of
36 prophecy : **For this took place that the scripture might be
fulfilled, 'Not a bone of him will be broken.'** The words are
an echo of Exod. 12 : 46, Num. 9 : 12, passages referring to
the Paschal lamb, with which Jesus is identified (cf. Ps.
37 34 : 20). **And another scripture also says, 'They shall look
on him whom they have impaled '**—a quotation from Zech.
12 : 10 describing the martyrdom of an unknown hero, who
may be regarded as a ' good ' shepherd, in contrast to the
' foolish shepherd ' of Zech. 11 : 15, and so as a type of Christ.
Our Gospel gives a more accurate translation of the original
Hebrew than that of the LXX. See also Rev. 1 : 7, where
the passage is alluded to in the sense that one day the crucified
will triumph over his executioners—an idea which is doubtless
present in the Evangelist's mind also. The whole incident
of the spear-thrust is peculiar to John, who at 20 : 20 again
alludes to ' his side,' while Luke has ' his hands and feet '
(24 : 40).

Had the Jews' request to ' have the body removed ' (31)
been granted, the body would have been dealt with as in e.g.
Josh. 8 : 29. But at the very moment of Jesus' deepest
humiliation two members of the Jewish aristocracy who had
hitherto shrunk from making open profession of faith have the
courage to save the Master from this last dishonour : Christ
on the Cross has a power greater even than Jesus the Rabbi
38 to ' draw men to himself ' (12 : 32). **After this, Joseph of
Arimathaea, a disciple of Jesus but a secret disciple**—for fear
of the Jews—**asked Pilate** for permission to remove the body

of Jesus—though from 31 we would gather that Pilate had
already ordered the bodies to be removed. **And Pilate allowed
him**—in accordance with Roman custom except in extreme
cases (cf. also Mt. 14 : 12, Acts 8 : 2). Joseph was evidently
a rich man (Mt. 27 : 57) and a member of the Sanhedrim
(Mk. 15 : 43). Arimathaea is not certainly identified, but is
probably the same place as Ramathaim (1 Sam. 1 : 1 ; 1 Macc.
11 : 34), now Beit-Rima, thirteen miles east-north-east of
Lydda. Like Nicodemus, with whom he is now associated,
Joseph had not yet ' shown his colours ' ; hence Mark's statement that he '*ventured* to go to Pilate.' **So he went and 39
removed the body, accompanied by Nicodemus (he who had first
come to Jesus by night)**—his nervousness then setting off his
boldness now—**who brought a mixture of myrrh and aloes,
about a hundred pounds of it.** The spices were a compound
made of the gum of the myrrh tree and powdered aloe wood
(Ps. 45 : 8) and according to our scale would amount to about
70 lb.—a vast amount and the expression of a rich man's
homage. The embalmment was on a kingly scale (cf. 2 Chron.
16 : 14). ' Judas had been scandalized at the use of one
pound of perfume for the living Jesus (12 : 3-5), and here
are one hundred pounds brought to his corpse ! ' (Loisy).
**They took and wrapped up the body of Jesus in the spices and 40
in bandages (11 : 44), according to the Jewish custom of burial**
—evidently an explanation intended for Hellenistic readers
and contrasting, not Jewish methods of embalmment with
e.g. Egyptian, but the custom of embalming with that of e.g.
burning. The elaborate embalmment at this point seems
out of keeping with the need for a quick disposal of the body
in view of the approaching Sabbath and with the hint of Mark
(16 : 1) and Luke (23 : 56, 24 : 1) that the women prepared
spices over the Sabbath and brought them to the tomb on
the Sunday morning.

**Now at the spot where he had been crucified there was an 41
orchard, and in the orchard a new tomb where no one had yet
been laid.** The orchard, according to Mt. 27 : 60, contained
Joseph's own new tomb and was presumably his property.
That the tomb was new is a fact ' which belongs to the glory

of Jesus. When a king is received, the objects devoted to his service are such as have never yet been used ' (Godet) (cf. Lk. 42 19 : 30). So they put Jesus there, since it was the Jewish day of Preparation (14 note), seeing that the tomb was close by— to the place of crucifixion. The position of the ' orchard ' as of Golgotha is uncertain. The near-by tomb was utilized because the near approach of the Sabbath, which began the same evening at 6 p.m., left no time to remove the body else-where.

3. THE RESURRECTION OF CHRIST (20 : 1–31)

It is impossible completely to harmonize the various Gospel accounts of Christ's resurrection appearances. The chief variation of Mark and Matthew from John (though in this feature Luke agrees with our Gospel) lies in the statement that the women, after finding the tomb empty, were commissioned by an angel to bid the disciples go to Galilee, where they would see the Risen Lord. The fulfilment of this promise is recorded by Matthew (28 : 16 ff.), and must also have been mentioned in the original conclusion of Mark which has been lost and replaced by 16 : 9–20. In Luke and John (excluding the Appendix) all the appearances of the Risen Lord take place in or near Jerusalem. Even advanced critics have found much in this chapter to suggest that it is based on the memories of an eye-witness. ' The story is told so simply, and so cir-cumstantially, that it is hard to accept any view in regard to its origin except that it came to the Evangelist on the authority of one of the Apostles. . . . It is no doubt very difficult ever to judge from the naturalness and vividness of a story that it is really historic. But it is very hard for any reader not to think that we have here a simple piece of testi-mony, an uncoloured narrative of fact ' (Percy Gardner, *Ephesian Gospel*, p. 288). Verses 2–10 have been widely held to be an interpolation by the Redactor on the grounds (*a*) that they interrupt the story of Mary's meeting with her Master which is broken off at the end of verse 1 and resumed, as if there had been no interruption, at verse 11, where Mary is still standing where the narrative of verse 1 had left her ; (*b*) that the passage emphasizes, as the Evangelist himself does not, the fact of the empty tomb and the absence of the *material* body, the supposition being that the Redactor is strongly anti-docetic and is here counteracting a tendency to give a docetic interpretation to the original Gospel. But (*a*) the first argument is ' an example of that pedantic kind of criticism which demands that every detail, however easily the reader can imagine it, shall be stated in so many words ' (Stanton, op. cit., p. 56) ; and (*b*) the point of the evidence described (esp. 6 f.) seems to be that Christ's body had ' evanesced ' from a physical to a non-physical and spiritual entity, while on the other hand the Evangelist is just as anxious as the Redactor to safeguard the human reality of the crucified Jesus (cf. 19 : 28, 34).

On the first day of the week Mary of Magdala went early to the 1 tomb, when it was still dark—so that she could not see what the disciples afterwards saw. The hour would be the dark before the dawn, some time between 3 and 6 a.m. (cf. 18 : 28). Mk. 16 : 2 says it was ' after sunrise ' that Mary, accompanied by two other women, visited the tomb. John, with his love of individualizing, mentions but one woman, but, as is hinted in the next verse (' we '), there may have been others with her. But as she saw the boulder (11 : 38) had been removed from the tomb—and would fear that the tomb had been violated— she ran off to Simon Peter and to the other disciple, the favourite 2 of Jesus, telling them, ' They (i.e. the authorities, for some purpose of their own) have taken the master out of the tomb, and we do not know where they have put him ! ' In the following verses it is hard to doubt that we have the evidence of ' the Witness ': So Peter and the other disciple set out 3 for the tomb ; they both started to run, but the other disciple 4 ran ahead, faster than Peter, and got to the tomb first. The Beloved Disciple was the younger and more active man, while Peter perhaps would hang back ' ob conscientiam culpae ' (Lampe). The race between the two disciples has often been interpreted allegorically—surely a fantastic example of the misuse of a method of interpretation for which the Gospel gives ample scope. ' A common reader sees in this

the charming reminiscence of an old man recalling his emotion
of that morning, and therewith (as such things live in memory
endeared) the little fact that once he could run fast, and the
thrill with which he did so then. No, says a certain critic,
this would have been " vanity unbecoming to an Apostle."
With this monumental commencement he proceeds to his own
more becoming exposition. This little touch in the Gospel
exhibits, he tells us, the jealousy between the Johannine and
the Petrine school ! ' (Lord Charnwood).

5   The Disciple, then, reached the tomb first ; he glanced in—
this rather than the idea of ' stooping ' (A.V.) seems to be the
sense—and saw the bandages lying on the ground, but he did
not go inside—through reverence and delicacy of feeling and
possibly also through fear of ceremonial pollution. But Peter,
6 as usual, is more impetuous and has fewer scruples : Then
Simon Peter came after him, and went inside the tomb ; he
noticed—the word implying a more careful scrutiny than
John's ' glance '—not only that the bandages were lying on the
7 ground, but that the napkin which had been round his head was
folded up by itself, instead of lying beside the other bandages.
Had the tomb been rifled everything would have been in dis-
array ; had the disciples removed the body—a Jewish libel
current in John's own day—the wrappings would have been
taken with it. John insists that all the evidence pointed to a
deliberate act of resurrection. The word used of the napkin,
' folded up,' means properly ' twirled ' turban-like, just as it
had been wound around the head. The napkin too, John
notes, is ' by itself,' a little apart from the body-wrappings.
The whole language seems to have been carefully chosen to
suggest that Jesus' physical body had passed into a spiritual
and ' glorified ' Risen Body without disturbing the grave-
clothes, which had simply settled down on the ledge within the
8 tomb in their original positions. Upon this the other disciple,
who had reached the tomb first, went inside too, and when he
saw for himself he was convinced—that Jesus had indeed risen
from the dead. In the words ' saw ' and ' convinced ' ' we
have in short fact and the discerning interpretation of fact,
both of which were held to be of such immense importance

by the writer of the Gospel' (Stanton). But conviction had been reached only as the result of the evidence of the disciples' own eyes, **for as yet they did not understand the Scripture 9 that he must rise from the dead**—a *moral* necessity for which cf. 7 : 7 and Lk. 24 : 26, Acts 2 : 24. The implication is that, if the disciples had already possessed true insight into Scripture, no such proof as that just afforded would have been necessary (cf. 20 : 29). But such insight, because in this Gospel Jesus' predictions of his resurrection have been ' in riddles ' (2 : 19, 10 : 18, 12 : 24), the disciples did not possess 'as yet'; later, in John's phraseology, they would ' remember ' (2 : 17, 22 ; 12 : 16). The ' Scripture ' is Ps. 16 : 10 ; cf. Acts 13 : 35, Lk. 24 : 21, 25 ff., 44 ff. Generally speaking, the Evangelist lays more stress upon the evidence of prophecy and of experience than upon that afforded to the senses by the fact of the empty tomb. But he may also imply here that the Beloved Disciple's faith was due not to presuppositions based on scripture, but to the strength of the visible evidence.

Then the disciples returned home—convinced that a further 10 search for the body was useless ; **but Mary** (who had presum- 11 ably followed the disciples back to the tomb) **stood sobbing outside the tomb.** Sometimes the tears of sorrow quicken spiritual vision : **As she sobbed, she glanced inside the tomb**— as if refusing to believe that Jesus was indeed gone—**and 12 noticed two angels in white, sitting where the body of Jesus had lain, one at the head and one at the feet.** The mention of the ' angels ' appears to be an echo of Lk. 24 : 4 ff. and a relic of the Synoptic tradition according to which the women are commissioned by an angel to bid the disciples go to Galilee to meet the Risen Lord. Dods, quoting Lücke, well says that ' neither the believing nor the critical enquirer can lift the veil that hangs over the appearance of angels.' Perhaps for the Evangelist they are symbolic of the cherubim on the mercy-seat (Exod. 25 : 22). **' Woman,' they said to her, ' why are you 13 sobbing ? '** (For the mode of address, the same as that used by Jesus to his mother, cf. 2 : 4, 19 : 26.) It is interesting to note that, according to Ephrem, the words of 17 are addressed not to Mary of Magdala but to the Mother of Jesus, and that in Tatian's *Diatessaron* the whole incident seems to be narrated of the Virgin. **Mary said, 'Because they have taken away my master, and I do not know where they have put him!'** 14 **With these words she turned round and noticed Jesus standing— though she did not know it was Jesus.** Why Mary failed to recognize Jesus it is out of place to speculate; certainly not because of any abnormal change in Jesus' glorified body (though cf. Mk. 16:12 'in another form'; Lk. 24:16), for in that case Mary would hardly have mistaken him for a gardener; the Evangelist probably supposes it still to be 15 dark. **'Woman,' said Jesus, 'why are you sobbing? Who are you looking for?'** Supposing he was the gardener— the first person that would occur to her as likely to be abroad at so early an hour and to question her thus—she said, **'Oh, sir, if you carried him away, tell me where you put him, and I will remove him.'** Mary does not mention her master by name; One alone fills her thoughts and she assumes that the 'gardener' will know whom she means by 'him.' The word translated 'carried away' implies the bearing of a heavy weight (19:17) and makes all the more touching the weak woman's offer to 'remove him' and give him seemly burial. There follows the greatest recognition scene in all literature—and one told in 16 two words! **'Mary!' said Jesus. She started round and said, 'Rabboni!' (a Hebrew word meaning 'teacher').** Mary has been talking listlessly turned half towards the 'gardener' and half towards the tomb. The speaking of her own name and the very tone of its utterance by Jesus calls up memories and awakens recognition; in a flash she turns and faces her Master. 'She is beginning to *experience* the risen Lord; only then does she *recognize* him' (Strachan). *Rabboni* (Mk. 10:51), which is Aramaic rather than 'Hebrew,' is a more respectful title than Rabbi; it means literally '*my* teacher,' but the pronominal suffix had lost its force as in *monsieur*. Even in the hour of his glory Mary addresses Jesus as the 'teacher' of the old familiar days. In this wonderful recognition scene John dramatically illustrates the truth of 10:4—'the sheep follow him, because they know his voice.'

In the first flush of her joy Mary starts forward to embrace her Master : Jesus said, ' **Cease clinging to me** (the word 17 means not merely to ' touch ' but to hold on to an object with the desire to retain possession of it). **I have not ascended yet to the Father ; but go to my brothers**—not his blood-relatives of 7 : 3, but his disciples, brothers of the Spirit (Mt. 12 : 50)— **and tell them, I am ascending to my Father and yours, to my God and yours.'** Is this a Johannine counterpart of the commission to tell the disciples to meet the risen Christ in Galilee (Mt. 28 : 10) ? Note that John always distinguishes the sense in which Christ and men are ' sons ' of God—even using different words (1 : 12 note) ; hence he speaks of ' my ' Father and ' yours ' rather than of ' our ' Father. It is by Christ's ascension to the common Father that an abiding tie will be knit up between himself and the ' brothers ' he leaves behind. It is in this thought that we are to find the reason for Jesus' refusal meantime to allow Mary to ' cling to him.' Quite apart from the fact that, according to our Evangelist, Christ's risen body is a purely spiritual one which passes out of grave-clothes and through closed doors and therefore cannot be ' clung to,' it is one of his central doctrines that the abiding possession of Christ, for which Mary yearns, may be enjoyed only after his ' ascension to the Father.' It is only ' after a little while '—when men's spiritual experience of the ' ascended ' Christ begins—that they shall truly ' see ' him. (See note on 16 : 16 and cf. 14 : 18 f.) For Mary this ' little while ' is not yet passed and the time for lasting fellowship with the Risen Lord is not yet. Our Evangelist teaches that the true proof of the Resurrection and the true possession of the Risen Christ (a desire for both of which is expressed in Mary's gesture) is not to be looked for in any ' resurrection appearance ' nor verified by any physical contact, but is to be realized in the normal spiritual experience of the believer. And such an experience can be enjoyed only after the ' ascension,' which John regards as the final moment in one process of ' glorification ' (7 : 39, 12 : 16). This ' ascension ' is apparently assumed to take place between the events of verses 11–18 and 19 ff., and accordingly the appearances which follow

are subtly distinguished from that to Mary : e.g. at verse 27
Thomas is encouraged to test the reality of Christ's presence—
this ' post-ascension ' appearance being symbolical of the
abiding spiritual presence, for proof of which, it is nevertheless
added (29), no sensuous evidence should be necessary. It is
difficult to estimate the place of an ' ascension ' in John's
thought. As has been several times noted, Christ's Death,
Resurrection, Ascension, and Parousia appear often as but
four moments in one process of ' glorification,' the three last
being practically merged in one another. The ' Resurrection '
is realized in a ' return to the Father ' which marks the commencement of that larger spiritual activity in which Christ
manifests himself again to his disciples. Yet there are
occasional hints, such as we have in the present passage, of the
survival of the point of view of the Synoptists, who regard
Resurrection, Ascension, Parousia, as three events distinct in
space and time. John clothes in more spiritual form the more
realistic conceptions of primitive thought ; yet consciously or
unconsciously he makes 'concessions' to the older point of view.
' The Parousia is separated from the Resurrection by a scarcely
perceptible interval, and even this is bridged over by the
meeting in which he is seen and heard by Mary, although
he withdraws himself from her touch. We can scarcely be
wrong in perceiving here one of John's concessions to the
primitive tradition, which he sought to conserve in form,
even while in substance he broke with it ' (E. F. Scott, op. cit.,
p. 308).

The scene ends with Mary hurrying off to fulfil her commission to the disciples as in Mk. 16 : 10, Mt. 28 : 8, Lk. 24 : 10 :
18 **Away went Mary of Magdala to the disciples with the news,
' I have seen the Lord ! '**—telling them what he had said to her.

There follows an account of the first appearance to the
19 assembled disciples : **On the evening of that same day, the
first day of the week**—the date is emphasized as being the first
Christian Sunday—**though the disciples had gathered within
closed doors for fear of the Jews, Jesus entered and stood among
them, saying, ' Peace be with you ! '** Thus is the promise of
14 : 18 f.. 16 : 16 fulfilled, for the ' little while ' is now past.

The fact that the doors were shut is mentioned as significant of the nature of Christ's risen body, which could pass where it would ; for it is evidently implied that Christ passed through the doors rather than that he miraculously unlocked them (cf. also note on 6 : 19). Many a band of Christians skulking behind locked doors in days of persecution must have plucked up courage as they recalled this incident and realized the same experience of the Risen Christ in the midst (Mt. 18 : 20). Jesus' salutation is the conventional greeting of every day. But ' a great soul can redeem his words from triviality. He takes the most conventional expressions, the small change of ordinary courtesy, which on the lips of other men mean nothing, and in his mouth they have such heart and substance that you go on, cheered and bettered by his greeting ' (W. M. Macgregor, *Jesus Christ the Son of God*, p. 165). ' Peace ' had been almost Jesus' last word before he led his companions to Gethsemane (14 : 27) ; and now the Risen Lord picks up the broken thread. Then, as if to remind his disciples of the victory won in the interval, as if to prove the identity of this divine figure with the human Jesus who had suffered for them, **so saying he showed them his hands and his side** (Lk. 24 : 39 f.). John, who alone narrates the incident of the spear-thrust, is also the only evangelist who represents Jesus as calling attention to the wound in his side. While John emphasizes throughout the spiritual nature of Jesus' resurrection body, he is so concerned to combat Docetism and to stress the identity of the Risen Christ with that Jesus who was the Logos made flesh that the spiritual body is represented, as in the Synoptists, as actually bearing the marks of the wounds, which are unaffected by the change wrought by ' resurrection ' and ' ascension.' **And when the disciples saw the Lord they rejoiced**—according to the promise of 14 : 28, 16 : 22.

An attractive suggestion is made by Strachan (*The Fourth Evangelist*, p. 312) that verses 21–23 should be transferred to follow 29. The doubt of Thomas is then immediately contrasted with the joyful faith of his comrades, while the original Gospel fittingly concludes with the gift of the holy Spirit, from which Thomas is no longer excluded, as appears to be the case if the present order of the text be retained. The repetition of the greeting 'Peace be with you' also becomes more natural : Jesus takes final farewell of his disciples in the same words with which he saluted them when first he appeared as Victor over death. We pass therefore to 24.

24 **Now Thomas, one of the twelve, who was called ' the Twin '** (11 : 16), **was not with them when Jesus came**—why, it is useless
25 to speculate—**and when the rest of the disciples told him, 'We have seen the Lord,' he said, ' Unless I see his hands with the mark of the nails, and put my finger where the nails were** (reading *topon*, ' place,' instead of *tupon*, ' mark,' at the second occurrence of the word, and apparently implying that the wounds were healed), **and put my hand into his side, I refuse to believe it.'** Thomas appears here as the type of those who base their faith upon ocular miracles. He is a ' realist ' and represents the materialist attitude towards the resurrection body of Christ which appears e.g. in Luke (esp. 24 : 39–43), and to which our Evangelist is opposed. Yet Thomas is not so much an intellectual sceptic as one who, being by disposition a pessimist (11 : 16, 14 : 5), finds it difficult to replace his own mood of despair, born of the spectacle of the Crucifixion which is still printed indelibly in all its details upon his imagination, by his companions' mood of newly-awakened joy and faith. First he must have a vision of triumph as vivid as the former vision of defeat ; he must be sure that this risen figure, which his fellows claim to have seen, is the same *crucified* Jesus bearing upon his body the very marks of his execution.

According to Luke, all the appearances of the Risen Christ, and indeed the Ascension, took place on the first Easter Day. John here probably intends us to understand that on the following Sunday Jesus again appeared : as the Church meets on the Lord's day week by week for praise and sacra-
26 ment the Risen Master is ever present. **Eight days afterwards his disciples were together again, and Thomas with them. Though the doors were closed, Jesus entered and stood**
27 **among them, saying, ' Peace be with you ! '** Then he said

to Thomas, ' Look at my hands, put your finger here ; and put your hand here into my side ; cease your unbelief and believe.' Christ repeats Thomas' own words ; he knows the very words in which we express our doubts. John hints that even while Thomas was voicing his incredulity Jesus was present though unseen. Verse 27 has commonly been assigned to the Redactor on the ground that it emphasizes, as the Evangelist himself does not, the corporeality of the resurrection body. If the verse be omitted we are left to understand that in Thomas' case also, as previously in the case of the other disciples, the experience of Christ's ' peace ' (19) and the spiritual contemplation of his wounds (20) were sufficient evidence of the Resurrection ; verse 27, on the contrary, represents Jesus as yielding to Thomas' demand for sensuous evidence. The suspicion that 27 is an addition is strengthened by the fact that Thomas does not accept the invitation, but immediately makes his adoring confession. On the other hand, if the verse be genuine, we may suppose that the Evangelist again intends to show the sufficiency of spiritual proof by hinting that the test offered by Jesus was one which was at once seen to be incongruous and therefore refused. ' Put your hand into my side,' says Jesus, ' *if you still think such a test needful !* ' Whereupon **Thomas answered** 28 **him, ' My Lord**—the familiar title given to the Master in the days of his flesh—**and my God !** ' Thomas means, ' It *is* Jesus himself and now I recognize him as Divine ' (Burkitt). Pliny in his letter to Trajan (A.D. 112) states that the Christians ' sing hymns to Christ *as God.*' In Thomas' confession —and it is specially significant as coming from one who had at first wavered—the gradual victory of faith over unbelief, which is one of the leading motives in the Gospel-drama, reaches its climax. The equality of Christ with God, which has hitherto been claimed only by implication in such words as 14 : 9 and is seemingly disavowed by Jesus himself in 5 : 18 f., 14 : 28 (cf. Phil. 2 : 6) is now explicitly asserted. The keynote with which the Gospel opened (1 : 1) is struck again at its close : to the Christian believer Christ is none other than *God Himself.*

Thomas' failure to avail himself of the test offered by
Jesus has thus thrown into prominence the incongruity of
demanding sensuous evidence of spiritual truth ; this funda-
29 mental principle of the Gospel is now driven home : **Jesus
said to him, ' You believe because you have seen me ?—a**
question with an affirmative implication—**Blessed be those
who believe though they have never seen me.'** True faith
in the Resurrection and in the abiding power and presence of
Christ is based not on the evidence of the senses or on miracles,
but on an individual experience of the power of the risen
life—an experience corroborated by the living testimony of
the Church of all ages. The Evangelist has in view those
of his own generation and of all following generations to
whom no ocular vision of the Risen Christ could be vouchsafed. Let them not, like Thomas, reject the testimony of
those who have had an experience denied to themselves ;
but relying on that testimony let them make the experiment
of faith, which in turn will become an experience. Men
' can only become Christians when they lay hold of the inner
life of Jesus in that report which has come down to us in the
Christian brotherhood.' But ' the man who feels the strength
of Jesus' love, and sees that confidence of victory which welled
from his peace of soul, and who is startled and humbled by
these—that man will no longer see a historical problem in
Jesus, but a Reality before whom he bows ' (Hermann, *Communion with God*, p. 154).

21 **Jesus then repeated, ' Peace be with you ! '** But it is not
such peace as the world conceives of (14 : 27), but the *active*
peace of service ; for, adds Jesus, ' **as the Father sent me
forth, I am sending you forth** ' (cf. 17 : 18)—words that recall
the great commission of Mt. 28 : 19 f. Two distinct words are
used here to express the idea of sending (*apostello, pempo*) :
Jesus is God's ' apostle ' or ambassador, the disciples are
Jesus' envoys. Having given a commission, Jesus now
22 confers the power to fulfil it (Lk. 24 : 49, Acts 1 : 8) : **And
with these words he breathed on them, and added, ' Receive
the holy Spirit ! '** The phrase ' holy Spirit ' is without the
article, but the omission (*pace* Westcott) has no significance,

as if the meaning were that the disciples are now to receive
'a gift of the holy Spirit in preparation for Pentecost' when
the holy Spirit would be given. Similarly Godet : 'What
Jesus gives . . . is not the fulness of the Spirit ; it is an
earnest . . . This communication is to the Resurrection
what Pentecost will be to the Ascension.' But this scene
is for John almost certainly the counterpart of Pentecost ; for,
as we have seen (ver. 17 above), he 'telescopes' Resurrection,
Ascension, and Pentecost into one event of 'glorification.'
With the breathing of the Spirit is consummated in its fulness
the promise of 14 : 16, 16 : 7. Note, firstly, that for John, as
for Paul, the Spirit is not a fitful and 'miraculous' gift,
an ecstatic and non-ethical experience, but rather an abiding
endowment—the principle of spiritual living. Just as in
Gen. 2 : 7 'God breathed into man's nostrils the breath
of life' and thus communicated the *divine* life of man as
opposed to the life-principle of other animals, so does Christ
here impart his own divine life-spirit, wherein lies the secret
of 'eternal life.' Jesus (the Logos) is the author of a new
spiritual creation (1 : 3 f.). Note, secondly, that by the words
'*receive* the holy Spirit' it is implied that the recipient is not
merely passive but must become a partaker of life by an *act*
of faith. The whole scene symbolizes the truth that the
Spirit is the gift of the same Jesus who, as a man in history,
lived and suffered for his own, and is not to be 'sublimated into
a merely ecstatic experience' (Strachan).

Having thus bestowed the holy Spirit Jesus adds : '**If you 23
remit the sins of any, they are remitted : if you retain them,
they are retained** '—one of the cruces of the Gospel. The
most satisfactory interpretation seems to be as follows : By
the inbreathing of the Spirit Christ himself becomes incarnate
in the community of the disciples, i.e. the Church. Accordingly there is a sense in which the world (separate from that
Church, 17 : 6, 14) will be judged by its attitude towards the
Christian community and its message. Just as to accept
Jesus as Son of God means forgiveness of sin and to reject
him means the 'retaining' of sin (8 : 24, 9 : 41), and in this
sense Christ is said to 'judge' men (3 : 17 f.), so may the

Church be said to 'judge' men—to forgive or retain their sin—when, as a result of either accepting or spurning the Church's message, men deliberately choose either life or death (2 Cor. 2 : 16, Is. 6 : 9 f.). The verse means that to 'every member of the Christian community who abides in closest communion with his Lord, is given the last and final word on the sins of frail humanity ; the last and decisive word in removing the wrongs of our tangled world ; the last and decisive power of judgment on the distinction between right and wrong' (Strachan). Westcott well remarks that in the verse 'the pronouns in this case are unemphatic' ; i.e. the Apostles are not singled out (indeed others may have been present with the Eleven ; Lk. 24 : 33), in virtue of special ordination, to be the possessors of an inherent power to absolve from sin. Rather is the Church, as a society organized for teaching, fellowship, and discipline, confirmed in an authority derived directly from its Founder Jesus to declare the promise and the conditions of forgiveness. (Cf. Mt. 16 : 19, 18 : 18.) Just as in Matthew the life and authority of the Church are to be founded on faith exemplified in Peter, so here are they derived from the gift of the Spirit bestowed on the gathered disciples. There is an echo also of the commission as given by Luke (24 : 47) 'that repentance and the remission of sins must be preached in his name to all nations.' One cannot but remark the frequent echoes of Lk. 24 in this chapter. Can the generally held view be justified that our Evangelist was not acquainted with Luke's Gospel ? (Cf. 4 : 47, 6 : 3, chap. 21 *passim*, and Introduction, p. x f.)

Verses 30 f., which are obviously intended to be the conclusion of the original Gospel, define its method and sum up
30 its purpose : **Many another Sign did Jesus perform in presence of his disciples, which is not recorded in this book :** thus does John guard his work against comparison with the Synoptics. The additional 'Signs' alluded to are not only resurrection appearances but miracles in general, and are stated to have been performed ' in presence of his disciples ' because miracles are regarded as an incentive to faith and the disciples are the predestined witnesses to future generations. The Evangelist

has selected particular miracles on account of their value for his didactic purpose. Apart from the Resurrection there are *seven*, all of which are ' transparencies through which was manifested the " glory " of Jesus ' (Strachan). Accordingly John concludes : **But these Signs are recorded so that you—** 31 in the first case the circle of Christian disciples in Ephesus, but the words extend to all of us—**may believe Jesus is the Christ, the Son of God, and believing may have life through his Name** (1 : 12). Thus is defined the guiding purpose of the whole Gospel which is to confirm faith in a dogma and to transmit to future generations a divine gift. The phrase ' Christ, the Son of God ' is full of significance (cf. 1 : 14, 34, 49). ' The Messianic title of Jesus is here co-ordinated with a higher title, or rather is superseded by it ; and this use of the double title may be regarded as an index to the nature of the Gospel as a whole. It is a work of transition, in which primitive Christianity is carried over into a different world of thought ' (E. F. Scott). To ' have life in his name ' is to accept Christ for what he claims to be and really is, and thereby to come into that living relationship with him which John calls ' remaining in ' him (15 : 4), wherein consists ' eternal life.'

EPILOGUE. THE APPENDIX (21 : 1–25)

It is now generally agreed that the Gospel as originally planned by the Evangelist must have ended with 20 : 31. The linguistic evidence alone is strongly against the authenticity of chapter 21 (for a good summary see Stanton, op. cit., p. 28 ff.). There is no question at least that 21 : 24–25 are an addition. But these verses seem closely connected with the rest of the chapter, and if we amputate 24 f. not only do we leave the chapter without any suitable ending, but we deprive it of its whole *raison d'être*. For, as Bacon well remarks (op. cit., p. 193), *marturia*, ' testimony,' ' confession,' or ' white and red martyrdom '—to use a phrase felicitously chosen to express the double sense of the Greek (cf. ver. 22)— is the theme of the whole paragraph 15–24, and is illustrated in the respective fates of Peter and the Beloved Disciple. Even

Zahn, who is hailed as ' the Prince of Conservative Scholars,'
agrees that not only 24 f. but the whole of chapter 21 is due
to a hand other than the author of the Gospel : ' the inference
from this that the entire Appendix was attached by the
friends of John who come distinctly to the front in verse 24
must be admitted.' Even those who contend that chapter 21
is by the same hand as the Gospel admit that ' the 21st chapter
is an afterthought ' (Lightfoot). But it is difficult to understand why it should have occurred to the Evangelist to narrate
these incidents only after he had brought his work to the
impressive and carefully planned conclusion of 20 : 30–31.
With the possible exception of the allusion to the future
of the ' Beloved Disciple ' there is nothing in chapter 21 which,
on the supposition that it is the work of the Evangelist, would
not more naturally have been included in the body of the
Gospel, had the Evangelist desired to record it at all. We
can only conclude that the author of chapter 21 had a motive
for recording these incidents which the Evangelist had not.
We may therefore assign the Appendix to the Redactor, whose
motive we suggest was twofold : (a) To emphasize the identity
of the Evangelist with the anonymous disciple and by implication with John the son of Zebedee, and thus secure Apostolic
authority for the Gospel (20–24). (b) To bring the Gospel
more into line with the dominant Synoptic tradition, and in
particular to restore to Peter the position of supremacy
among the Twelve which he occupies in the Synoptics. In
verses 1–14 the Redactor reverts to the Galilean form of the
tradition, whereby the Risen Jesus appears to the disciples not
only at Jerusalem, as in our Gospel and Luke (cf. note at beginning of chap. 20), but also in Galilee (Mk. 14 : 28). This
readjustment would be felt to be specially needful on account
of the Evangelist's concentration of interest upon Jerusalem.
Moreover, the Redactor reintroduces this tradition in a way
which also reasserts the leadership of Peter. The story of
the draught of fishes, which in Lk. 5 : 4–11 is narrated in
connexion with Peter's first call, is here transferred to post-
resurrection days in order to add colour to the new commission
now given to Peter. (It may be noted that a similar fishing

scene occurs in the concluding verses of the fragment of the
' Gospel of Peter,' and is thought by some to be derived from
the lost ending of Mark.) It is important to note the close
affinities of the Redactor's addition to the Synoptic material
from which he borrows. The resemblance both in thought
and language to Lk. 5 : 4–11 can hardly be accidental. (Compare Lk. 5 : 5 and ver. 3 ; Lk. 5 : 6 and ver. 11 ; Lk. 5 : 8
and ver. 7 ; Lk. 5 : 10 and the commission in vers. 15–17.)
Chapter 21, though an addition, must be very early, for no
trace exists in any MS. of a version of the Gospel without it.
This would well agree with the suggestion that it was appended
when the Gospel was first translated and published by the
Redactor (see Introduction, p. lxvi f.).

After that, Jesus disclosed (the same word as that used in 1
7 : 4, 17 : 6) himself once more to the disciples at the sea of
Tiberias (6 : 1 note). It was in this way. Simon Peter, 2
Thomas (who was called ' the Twin '), Nathanael from Cana
in Galilee, the two sons of Zebedee, and two other disciples of
his, were all together. For Nathanael see 1 : 45. His connexion with Cana is mentioned perhaps to emphasize that,
though his home was not by the Lake, he was still with the
other disciples ' all together.' ' The two sons of Zebedee,'
James and John, are here mentioned for the first time ; the
Redactor's motive for thus mentioning them, in face of the
silence of the rest of the Gospel, seems clear. As the chapter
proceeds it becomes *almost* inevitable for the reader, by a
process of elimination, to identify the ' favourite disciple ' of
7 and 20, and ' the disciple who bears testimony to these facts
and who wrote them down ' of 24 with the survivor of the sons
of Zebedee. The Redactor thus secures the identification
of the Beloved Disciple-Witness-Evangelist with John the
Apostle. True, the mention of ' two other disciples ' saves
the identification from being *quite* inevitable. If we choose to
harmonize with the Gospel of Peter these two might be
Andrew and Levi. But possibly the Redactor has added the
two anonymous disciples to the other five, partly because
of his interest in the symbolic number seven, and partly also
on account of a certain timidity in suggesting an identification

concerning which he himself may be of two minds : a ' penumbra of indefiniteness,' to use Bacon's phrase, is secured by the mention of ' two other disciples.' The ' Beloved Disciple ' is thus ' identified with the Apostle John, not explicitly, but by a process of elimination subtly suggested to the reader, who thus assumes the responsibility the Redactor seems loath himself to undertake ' (Bacon, op. cit., p. 194). So also Dr. A. E. Garvie (*The Beloved Disciple*, p. 32) : ' The writer of the Appendix evidently intends to identify " the disciple whom Jesus loved " with one of the brothers ; and yet there seems to be some doubt in his mind, and he leaves himself a door of escape from mistake by adding " two other of his disciples ". without mentioning their names.'

The exquisite story which follows is no doubt intended to symbolize the work of the Apostolic Church ; Jesus' promise in Lk. 5 : 10 receives an allegorical illustration. Note that the disciples are presumed to have gone back to their original calling as fishermen—naturally enough if this was the first appearance of the Risen Christ, but rather inconsistently with the commission given in 20 : 21 ff. The circumstances suit better the setting of Luke, who places the incident *before* 3 the call. Simon Peter said to them, ' I am going to fish.' They said, ' We are coming with you too.' Off they went and embarked in the boat (Peter's ; Lk. 5 : 3), but that night they caught nothing. They have failed during the best hours for fishing ; now comes sunrise when the time for fishing is past. 4 Now at break of day—symbolical perhaps of the dawn of new hope when it is least expected—Jesus was standing on the beach, though the disciples did not know it was Jesus—because of the darkness and distance and their preoccupation with 5 work. ' Lads,' said Jesus, ' have you got anything ? ' ' Lads ' (*paidia*) is the ordinary term of address used to men at work, and is to be distinguished from the characteristic Johannine use of the word (1 Jn. 2 : 14, 18). The question does not necessarily mean ' have you anything *to eat* ? ' (so A.V.). The word (*prosphagion*) is used of anything which might be served in addition to a plain meal of bread and, according to Plutarch, commonly meant ' fish.' Jesus

simply asks ' Have you *caught* anything ? '—a correct technical
use of the Greek word. The disciples confess failure : **' No,'
they answered. So he told them, ' Throw your net on the right** 6
side of the boat, and you will have a take.' Perhaps Jesus had
seen a shoal of fish on that side of the boat, but the *right* side
often has symbolical significance as the side of good omen
(Ezek. 47 : 1 f., Mt. 25 : 33, Lk. 1 : 11). **At this they threw
the net, and now they could not haul it in for the mass of fish.
So the disciple who was Jesus' favourite said to Peter, ' It is** 7
the Lord ! ' We are intended to recognize in the ' favourite '
the second of Zebedee's sons, John. As usual the ' Beloved
Disciple ' has the quickest intuition and recognizes the worker
of the miracle. ' John had a keener insight ; Peter the
greater ardour ' (Euthymius). The latter's usual impetuosity
now shows itself : **Hearing it was the Lord, Simon Peter
threw on his blouse (he was stripped for work) and jumped into
the water, while the rest of the disciples came ashore in the** 8
**punt (they were not far from the land, only about a hundred
yards), dragging their netful of fish.** With instinctive reverence for Christ's presence Peter slips on his ' blouse '—not
the outer robe or *tallith*, but a fisherman's jacket which
would be thrown on over the loin-cloth in which alone Peter
was working. The ' punt ' may be either a more exact description of the ' boat ' (ver. 3), or may mean a smaller craft
attached to it. Curiously nothing more is said about Peter
at this point. Has the Evangelist in mind the incident of
Peter walking on the water (Mt. 14 : 28 ff.), or may we supple-
ment the story from Lk. 5 : 8 ? In Luke the commission to
Peter to ' catch men ' more naturally follows immediately
upon his act of worship ; here that to ' feed my lambs ' is
delayed till after the meal.

When they got to land, they saw a charcoal fire burning, 9
with fish cooking on it, and some bread. Jesus said to them, 10
' Bring some of the fish you have just caught.' As Stanton
remarks (op. cit., p. 20), one cannot but feel ' a lack of self-
consistency and life-likeness and " convincingness " ' in this
part of the narrative. The Redactor seems to waver between
two traditions—that Jesus himself miraculously had the meal

already prepared and that the disciples supplied it from their catch. Perhaps the suggestion is that both Lord and disciples are to make their contribution to the common resources (cf.

11 Paul's thought in Phil. 2 : 12 f.). **So Peter went aboard—** presumably to unfasten the net from the boat—**and hauled the net ashore full of large fish, a hundred and fifty three of them.** The number is undoubtedly symbolical. According to Jerome, ancient naturalists distinguished 153 varieties of fish. The Gospel net is to embrace every conceivable variety of man (Lk. 5 : 10, Mt. 13 : 47). (For a large number of alternative explanations see Westcott *in loco*.) The next sentence also has a symbolical intention : **but for all their number the net was not torn.** (Cf. the seamless robe 19 : 23, and contrast Lk. 5 : 6.) 'The Church's resources with the *risen* Christ in its midst are never overstrained' (Strachan).

The invitation that follows fits in best with the idea that

12 Jesus already had a meal prepared : **Jesus said, ' Come and breakfast.'** The meal is the counterpart of that described in Lk. 24 : 36-43 ; but here it is not actually stated that Jesus himself ate, though probably this is implied in order to emphasize the real corporeality of Jesus' body. Possibly the thought is of a second eucharistic meal at which the Risen Christ presides. Overcome by awe and reverence, the disciples refrain from all inquisitive questioning : **Not one of the disciples dared to ask him who he was ; they knew it was the Lord.** As Luke puts it, they recognized him ' in the breaking of the bread ' :

13 **Jesus went and took the bread and gave it to them, and the fish too.** The very language recalls the first eucharistic meal (cf. 6 : 11), which is here renewed. Though the preceding paragraph appears to be an amalgam of several Synoptic incidents, from the point of view of this Gospel it may be said that

14 **this was the third time now that Jesus appeared to the disciples after rising from the dead**—two previous appearances having been recorded at 20 : 19 and 20 : 26. (For this concluding note cf. that on the miracles 2 : 11, 4 : 54.)

15 **Then after breakfast Jesus said to Simon Peter, ' Simon, son of John . . .'** The use of the full name marks the solemnity of the occasion (cf. Mt. 16 : 17). As one of the motives

of the Appendix appears to be to safeguard the Synoptic tradition by reinstating Peter in his primacy over the other disciples, not excepting the Beloved Disciple, Jesus' question to Peter should probably be understood: '**Do you love me more than the others do ?** '—recalling 13 : 37 and with a recollection of Mk. 14: 29, Lk. 22: 33, where Peter had claimed to be supremely devoted. Some commentators, on the ground that such a question in the presence of the other disciples would show lack of tact and delicacy on Jesus' part, would translate : ' Do you love me more than you love these things ? '— all the accompaniments of your ordinary life (your boat, fishing-gear, etc.), which you are willing to abandon for my sake. A distinction has been thought to be intended between Jesus' question, ' Do you love ? ' (Gk. *agapān*, ' like '), and Peter's answer, ' You know I *love* . . .' (Gk. *philein*), as if the former word implied the esteem existing between benefactor and recipient, and the latter word the personal affection existing between members of the same family. Peter is thought deliberately to change the colder word into the warmer : ' To love Jesus as a benefactor and to love him for himself are lower and higher stages of love ' (Strachan). But in this Gospel the two words are evidently interchangeable (cf. 13: 23 with 20: 2 and see also 11 : 3, 5, 36) and such subtlety is hardly justifiable ; indeed, Westcott and Godet, while also drawing a distinction, consider *agapān* to be the nobler word. The words are interchanged simply for euphony, just as ' feed ' is changed to ' shepherd ' below (16) and ' lambs ' to ' sheep.' It is not concern about the quality of his love that is apparent in Peter's answer, but surprise that the question should be asked at all : '**Why, Lord,**' he said, ' **you know I love you.**' With the memory of his failure Peter cannot appeal to his own record, but he can to his Master's understanding. ' **Then feed my lambs,** ' said Jesus—implying that he answers Peter's love with trust, while Peter must prove his love to Christ by love and service towards his fellows (1 Jn. 4: 20 f.). Peter is constituted chief Shepherd of the Christian flock and bidden to put into practice Jesus' teaching of 10: 1–16. Cf. Mt. 18: 12–14 and Peter's own words (are

they a recollection of Jesus' words to himself?) in 1 Pet.
5 : 1-4. Let Peter make good his boast recorded in Mk.
14 : 27-29. Note that not only is Peter rehabilitated after
his denial but, in accordance with the Synoptic tradition
(Mt. 16 : 18 f., Lk. 22 : 32), his leadership among the disciples
is emphasized.

Jesus repeats his question, but this time without comparing
Peter's love with that of the others, the emphasis thus falling
16 upon the sincerity and reality of the love : **Again he asked him,
for the second time, ' Simon, son of John, do you love me ? '**—
' Are you sure that love and nothing but love is the bond between you and me ? ' Peter replies as before and again the
trust is committed to him : **' Why, Lord,' he said, ' you know
I love you.' ' Then be a shepherd to my sheep,' said Jesus.**
' The lambs require to be fed ; the sheep require to be guided '
(Westcott). Having three times denied his Master, Peter
is asked three times to make profession of his love and
17 three times he is commissioned. **For the third time he asked
him, ' Simon, son of John, do you love me ? ' Now Peter was
vexed at being asked a third time ' Do you love me ? '** Peter
is annoyed that Jesus should seem to doubt him, perhaps all
the more because he feels that he has given cause for doubt ;
he therefore asseverates the more earnestly : **So he replied,
' Lord, you know everything** (16 : 30)—and taking everything into account, even my failure—**you can see I love you ! '**
Experience (' you see ' contrasted with ' you know ' above,
which implies intuitive knowledge) has surely proved Peter's
love to Jesus. **Jesus said, ' Then feed my sheep.'**

Jesus now warns Peter that the impetuous devotion of his
18 prime will be sorely tested in later days : **' Truly, truly I tell
you, you put on your own girdle and went wherever you wanted,
when you were young.'** The meaning is that *now* Peter has
the power to choose his own line of service and vigorously to
equip himself for it ; but the use of past tenses shows that
the words are framed from the point of view of a later age.
In the words ' put on your girdle ' there is doubtless a reference
to the impulsive act of verse 7. **' But when you grow old,
you will stretch out your hands for someone to gird you, and**

you will be taken where you have no wish to go.' The language
suggests the feebleness of an old man who must be tended by
another and have the whole of life ordered for him irrespective
of his own desires. But in the words ' stretch out your hands '
there is a deeper reference to the stretching out of the victim's
arms as the executioner straps him to the cross. If Peter's
love is real, then he will indeed have to make good his boast
(13 : 37) and be faithful unto death. In this sense the Redactor himself interprets Jesus' words : **He said this to** 19
indicate the kind of death by which Peter would glorify God
(12 : 23, 28). ' The phrase " to glorify God," to signify martyrdom, became a technical term in later ecclesiastical writings.
Here we find it still in its original freshness ' (Godet). Peter's
martyrdom is generally placed in A.D. 64, at Rome, and is
attested by Tertullian (*Scorp.*, 15), while Origen states that
at his own request he was crucified with his head downwards.

Jesus had thus hinted at Peter's future martyrdom ;
then he added, ' Follow me ! ' Superficially the words imply
that Jesus led Peter aside from the rest ; but undoubtedly
there is a latent reference to 13 : 36 f. Soon Jesus' promise
that ' later on you will follow me ' will be fulfilled, and Peter
will have the chance to make good his boast by ' following '
Jesus to the death of the Cross (cf. 1 : 43 note).

The following verses prove that at the time the Appendix
was written the Beloved Disciple (whom the Redactor, be it
remembered, identified with John the Apostle) was dead,
though there existed a tradition (perhaps due to the misinterpretation of such sayings as Mk. 9 : 1, 13 : 30, Lk. 9 : 27)
that Jesus had promised that he would be alive at his coming.
The Redactor endeavours subtly to reconcile this contradiction by stressing the conditional nature of Jesus' promise.
Peter turned round and saw that the favourite disciple of Jesus 20
was following, the disciple who had leant on his breast at
supper and put the question, ' Lord, who is to betray you ? '
Again the surface meaning is that the favourite disciple went
after Jesus and Peter as they retired apart from the rest, but
with the deeper implication that John too had ' followed '
Jesus to death. The elaborate description of the Beloved

Disciple is meant to explain that it was by right of peculiar intimacy that he presumed to follow, and also to prepare the way for his subsequent identification, in verse 24, with the 21 Witness-Evangelist. **So, on catching sight of him, Peter said to Jesus, 'And what about him, Lord?'** Peter's question exactly expresses the perplexity of the Redactor's contemporaries about the death of John. Witness the fanciful tradition, actually mentioned by Augustine ' on the authority of grave men,' that John was still sleeping in his grave at Ephesus, where the moving earth testified to his breathing! 22 Jesus replied, **' If I choose that he should survive till I come back, what does that matter to you? Follow me yourself.'** ' The ambiguity of the answer which Jesus returns is deliberately designed to cover both forms of the tradition ' (Bacon, op. cit., p. 134), i.e. (*a*) that John was, like Peter, executed—a ' red martyrdom '; (*b*) that he lived to a great old age to ' witness ' (the same Greek word as ' martyr '; cf. 24) to Christ— a ' white martyrdom.' (See note at beginning of chapter.) There were two kinds of ' witness ' which John might have borne, ' the testimony of blood by martyrdom, and that of speech by a Johannine and priestly activity ' (Godet). The stress laid upon the Parousia or ' coming back ' of Christ as a definite personal event distinguishes the Redactor from the Evangelist (cf. 16 : 16, etc.). Dods well compares with these words of Jesus the thoughts of Thomas à Kempis on the man who ' neglects his duty, musing on all that other men are bound to do ' (*Im. Christi*, ii. 3). ' Follow me yourself,' says Jesus. ' Don't let your doubts and perplexities about others hinder your own service.' But there is also a hint that Peter at least is to die before the Parousia, to ' follow ' Jesus to the Cross.

Having recorded this ambiguous answer of Jesus the Redactor now endeavours to reconcile the contradiction involved by the death of the Beloved Disciple. While allowing that 23 this (answer of Jesus) **started the report among the brotherhood** (a name for the Christian community common in Acts but here only in the Gospels) **that the said disciple was not to die,** he insists that Jesus however did not say he was not to die ;

what he said was, ' If I choose that he should survive till I come back, what does that matter to you ? ' In other words the traditional promise of Jesus, which has apparently been falsified, that John should not die till after the Parousia, is contingent first upon Christ's own *will*, which it is not for us to scrutinize, and secondly upon the interpretation which is to be put upon his ' coming back.' To explain the latter has been the purpose of the last half of the Gospel. In the Johannine sense at least Christ *had* come back (in the Spirit) before the Beloved Disciple's death.

The Gospel closes with a certificate of authenticity parallel so that of 19 : 35. The Beloved Disciple, who has already by implication been identified with the Apostle John, is now guaranteed to be not only an eye-witness of the events recorded but also the actual writer of the Gospel : **This was the 24 disciple who bears testimony** (the ' Witness ') **to these facts**— not merely the preceding incidents but the contents of the Gospel as a whole—**and who wrote them down** (the ' Evangelist ') ; **his testimony we know** (i.e. the Redactor and his school speaking for the Church of his day) **is true.** The Beloved Disciple is one who still ' bears testimony ' ; whether or no his ' martyrdom ' was ' red,' certain it is that it is ' white.' Yet the use of the present tense does not necessarily imply that the Beloved Disciple is regarded as still alive. His ' witness ' may continue after death just as does that of Moses and the prophets (5 : 39). The Redactor thus identifies not only the ' Witness ' but also the ' Evangelist ' with the Beloved Disciple. Yet it is upon the testimony rather than upon the writing that he lays emphasis. ' The words " and wrote these things " seem to be added to " beareth witness concerning these things " as a kind of afterthought. Most prominence at all events is given to his having borne witness. From the position and form of this reference to writing, it is not unfair to infer that there may have been some uncertainty in the mind of the framer of the statement as to the extent to which it was to be attributed to the same disciple ' (Stanton, op. cit., p. 134). The Redactor is sure that the Beloved Disciple is ' the Witness ' ; he is not quite so sure that he is the actual author of the Gospel.

Finally, the Redactor picks up the thought of the true conclusion of the Gospel in 20 : 30 f., and adds a hyperbolical 25 description of the scope of Jesus' activities : **Now there is much else that Jesus did—so much, that if it were written down in detail, I do not suppose the world itself could hold the written records.** There is no reason to suppose that the verse is by a hand other than that which wrote the whole of the Appendix. The hyperbole amply explains its excision from the Sinaitic MS. And yet can we justly call it hyperbole when we consider the mighty ' Gesta Christi ' through nineteen hundred years ? (Cf. 14 : 12.)